"In this timely book, Juliana Martínez and Zachary Kahn have assembled a profoundly diverse group of voices in an astonishingly coherent fashion, examining how people of every stripe manage the transition into adulthood. Each essay boasts its own insights, but it is, ironically, their multitude of juxtapositions that reveal their commonalities. In responding to recent social experiences and movements—from COVID-19 to Black Lives Matter—these invaluable pages offer a guide that could transform the work of therapists and parents alike. Its theories and ideas plead to be applied in the real world."

–**Andrew Solomon, PhD,** Professor of Clinical Psychology, Columbia University, Lecturer in Psychiatry, Yale University, National Book Award-winning author of *The Noonday Demon* and *Far from the Tree*

"The topic of this book is not only timely and critically important, but it is approached with both clinical sophistication and a noteworthy attention to the currents of race, class, and gender that so often are given only secondary and superficial consideration. I am very familiar with the work of many of the authors, and they are a stellar group with precisely the expertise needed to carry this off most effectively. An indispensable resource."

–**Paul Wachtel, PhD,** CUNY Distinguished Professor, Doctoral Program in Clinical Psychology, City College of CUNY

"Rarely does one find a psychology text that is so timely and relevant for both therapists and patients alike. Engaging with the uncertainty and excitement of the current moment as gender, race, identity, and subjectivity itself are reconfiguring and transforming, this endlessly compelling anthology offers a vibrant mix of research, theory, clinical insight, and personal narrative that illuminates and struggles with the challenges that emerging adults and the clinicians who work with them encounter today."

–**Robert Grossmark, PhD,** ABPP, New York University Postdoctoral Program in Psychoanalysis and Psychotherapy, author of *The Unobtrusive Relational Analyst: Explorations in Psychoanalytic Companioning*

"This book's most remarkable contribution is its expanding of the reader's compassion and understanding about the ways in which our emerging adults' intersectional identities, and sociopolitical and cultural realities, impact their development and needs. This is an essential read if we as a field are dedicated to uplifting this next generation with curiosity and mindful attention to the unique landscape we find ourselves in."

–**Gillian Scott, PhD,** Clinical Psychologist, Private Practice, BodySoulPsych, Director/Producer of *Back to Natural: A Documentary*

"This book on emerging adulthood, edited by Zachary Kahn and Juliana Martínez, is a terrific addition to the literature about a stage of development that is currently garnering more and more attention. It is remarkable in a number of different ways. First, its focus is broad and covers theory, research, and especially practice innovations, which are highlighted in clinical vignettes. Second, while the volume includes an exploration of emerging adulthood as a construct, it does so without overgeneralizing: several chapters discuss diversity, ethnic, and racial differences with subtlety and sophistication. Third, the editors should be congratulated for taking the lead in acknowledging and reflecting on the implications of the pandemic on emerging adulthood. Although human life has been dramatically affected at every stage of life, there are compelling reasons to consider emerging adulthood as one of the most affected stages, given that for many people, it is a time of transition from home and school into the world. This book will be of great interest to emerging adults and their families as well as to educators and mental health professionals at every level of training."

–**Elliot Jurist, PhD,** Professor of Psychology and Philosophy, GC, and CCNY, CUNY

EMERGING ADULTS IN THERAPY

EMERGING ADULTS in THERAPY

A Contemporary Anthology of Theoretical, Sociocultural, and Clinical Essays

Zachary Kahn
and
Juliana Martínez

Foreword by Jeffrey Jensen Arnett

W. W. NORTON & COMPANY
Independent Publishers Since 1923

We dedicate this book to our patients, who entrust us with their inner worlds and inspire us to grow with them.

Contents

Section I

ADULTING 101: DEVELOPMENTAL FRAMEWORKS FOR EMERGING ADULTHOOD

Section II

BECOMING AN ADULT IN TODAY'S WORLD

Section III

YOUNG ADULTS IN TREATMENT

Foreword

Going Off Track and Finding Your Way in Emerging Adulthood

JEFFREY JENSEN ARNETT

When I first proposed the theory of emerging adulthood in 2000, my main goal was to draw people's attention to how much the age period from 18 to 29 had changed over the past 50 years (Arnett, 2000). I gave it a new name to help distinguish it from the adolescent period that precedes it or the more established adulthood that follows. Prior to that time, the late teens and early twenties had often been called "late adolescence," because many people that age had not yet taken on the traditional responsibilities associated with adult life and long regarded as defining the transition to adulthood: stable work, marriage, and parenthood. But "late adolescence" never worked very well, because adolescence has long been bounded by the physical changes of puberty, and for most people these changes are over by age 18 or 19 and far behind by the mid-twenties. Plus, once I began interviewing people in their twenties, I quickly found that they fiercely rejected the label "late adolescents," and I think it's a good general rule for developmental psychologists that we should avoid labeling developmental stages with terms that are detested by the people being described.

"Young adulthood" did not, and still does not, work much better as a developmental term for persons ages 18 to 29. The problem with "young adulthood" is that its meaning is too elastic; it has been applied to people as young as 8 or 9 (see any "young adult" book section) and as old as 35 or 40 (next comes "middle age," and no one longs to be middle-aged before age 40).

Any life stage term that can be applied to 8-year-olds as well as 39-year-olds is not going to be very useful.

So I proposed "emerging adulthood" to enhance recognition that traditional adult transitions are coming later than ever, and in their place from age 18 to 29 is a new life stage that is unprecedented: a period of a decade or more when people are no longer children or adolescents, but not yet adults; when they are freer from parental constraints than when they were younger but have not yet taken on the new constraints that accompany adult roles like marriage and parenthood; when their main challenge is to try to make their way gradually toward a more or less stable and satisfying adult life, often with some bumps and wrong turns along the way. I interviewed 300 American 18-to-29-year-olds in the course of the 1990s and concluded that there were five features that seemed to make this period developmentally distinctive: identity explorations; instability; self-focus; feeling in-between adolescence and adulthood; and an optimistic sense that anything is possible, that they can build for themselves the kind of future they envision (Arnett, 2007, 2015).

Emerging adulthood turned out to be an idea that many people were waiting for. Many had observed, as I had, that ages 18 to 29 had changed vastly from what they had been decades before and were hungry for a new concept and a new term that would fit their intuitive sense that this is a distinct new life stage. Calling it "emerging adulthood" resonated with their personal experiences and observations and gave them a new way of thinking about it. My original emerging adulthood article (Arnett, 2000) quickly became widely read, and by now it has been cited nearly 20,000 times, making it one of the most-cited articles in psychology in the past 20 years. With many brilliant and energetic colleagues, I developed the Society for the Study of Emerging Adulthood (SSEA) into a thriving international organization (see www.ssea.org). Emerging adulthood also received broad public attention thanks to a cover story in the *New York Times* Sunday magazine in 2010 (https://www.nytimes.com/2010/08/22/magazine/22Adulthood-t.html). It was the most-read article in the magazine that year.

As part of the spread of the idea and the new theory, the concept of emerging adulthood has been fruitfully applied to mental health issues by many therapists and researchers (e.g., Maynard, Salas-Wright, & Vaughn, 2015; Schwartz & Petrova, 2019; Tanner et al., 2007). Jesse Viner's *Yellowbrick* program in suburban Chicago was perhaps the first residential program for emerging adults with serious mental health problems, constructed using the principles of emerging adulthood theory (https://yellowbrickprogram.com/). Darrell Fraize and his colleagues in Portland, Maine developed the Onward Transitions program with a similarly well-informed developmental focus on emerging adults (https://www.onwardtransitions.com/). Although I am a developmental psychologist, not a therapist, I have sought to contribute to these efforts to apply the developmental insights of emerging adulthood to mental health problems, issues, and challenges (Arnett, Žukauskienė, & Sugimura, 2014). The second edition of my book on emerging adulthood (Arnett, 2015) includes a chapter on mental health issues, and the advice book for parents of emerging adults that I wrote with Elizabeth Fishel (Arnett & Fishel, 2014) also contains substantial material on mental health.

The present book goes much farther than any previous work in exploring and clarifying the clinical and developmental issues that often coincide with and collide in emerging adulthood. The editors and authors have done a wonderful job integrating the clinical and developmental perspectives. The authors cover a wide range of forms and issues that may arise in therapy with emerging adults, from substance abuse to gender identity to internet dating. This book will be an invaluable resource for therapists working with a broad and diverse clientele of emerging adults.

A key part of the value of integrating clinical and developmental perspectives is that it enables us to recognize when a presenting problem is unusual and when it is a typical part of development for a person that age. For example, today it is common for young people to stay in their parents' household into their twenties or move back in at least once after moving out. Fifty years ago, this may have been viewed as a "failure to launch," but today it is common enough to warrant multiple possible interpretations. It could indicate that these emerging adults are struggling with mental health problems, yes, but it could simply be that they are between jobs, or between the ending of their education and the beginning of a job, or that they have just moved out of a cohabiting situation, or that the family's cultural background includes a value on young people remaining in their parents' household until marriage. What was once abnormal is now often normal and may not be a cause for concern.

The chapters are well-informed and research-based, which is welcome and gratifying. There are many unfortunate stereotypes about this generation of emerging adults: that they are lazy, that they seek to avoid adult responsibilities as long as possible, and that they are "narcissists" who care only for themselves. Thirty years of studying this age group have taught me that these stereotypes are both false and destructive (Arnett, 2013). No one ever benefitted from being called a lazy narcissist and related aspersions. I have repeatedly found that virtually every person in their twenties earnestly wants to make a good life for themselves and realizes this is a crucial decade for setting that foundation. For young people who are languishing, it may be an indicator not that they are lazy or don't want to grow up, but that they feel disempowered, depressed, or anxious.

The chapters in this book help dispel destructive stereotypes and instead provide many insights into why many emerging adults are struggling to make their way in life and are in need of mental health treatment. Many of the chapters in the book provide case studies from therapy. As a person who has long valued qualitative methods in my research, I especially enjoyed and learned from these case studies. I am certain other readers will learn a great deal from them and will be moved by them.

The case studies demonstrate that identity struggles are often what drives emerging adults to seek psychotherapy. Identity struggles are a theme that carries across almost all chapters, varying in focus from ethnicity to gender to sexuality to love and work, and even including the roles of social media and internet dating. This resonates well with what I have found in decades of research with emerging adults, but it may be a surprise for some readers. Identity formation is a concept that has long been associated mainly with adolescence, going back to Erik Erikson's (1950) theory in the mid-twentieth century. Yet in interviewing emerging adults, their identity issues come out all the time. What should I do with my life? What kind of person do I want to be? How am I like my parents and other family members, and how am I different? What do I value most, and what values do I choose as the guideposts for living my adult life? What kind of work would I most like to do—and is that path available to me? What are the qualities I most want to find in a potential life partner? These are questions that all emerging adults confront, and sometimes an inability to answer them effectively brings emerging adults into the therapeutic setting. They may be depressed or falling into substance abuse or suffering from debilitating anxiety, but for some, they are simply wrestling with normative developmental issues and are in need of gentle guidance from a knowledgeable and sympathetic therapist.

One of the features that surprised and moved me most in my early interviews with emerging adults was that nearly all of them spoke optimistically about their futures, even when they were confused and unhappy in the present, as many of them were. Nearly all of them believed the future was full of possibilities and that they would eventually get what they wanted out of life (Arnett, 2015). This optimism dismayed me at first, because it seemed so out of touch with the reality of their current lives. However, eventually I came to see it as a psychological resource. How will you ever summon the motivation to rise above adversity, frustration, and disappointment—all commonly experienced during the emerging adult years—unless you believe that a bright and happy future is out there for you somewhere? They may not attain everything they dream of, but for nearly all, there is the possibility of a satisfying and enjoyable adult life.

When emerging adults seek out therapy, it is sometimes because the light of those possibilities has gone cold. Even the best therapists can't relight it for their emerging adult clients; that is something emerging adults can only do themselves. But therapists can assist emerging adults in making sense of the problems and challenges confronting them and in offering them a setting where they can generate the confidence to create their own solutions. This book provides a lot of material that will help therapists help emerging adults to reignite the flame of their hopes so that they burn bright again.

REFERENCES

Arnett, J. J. (2000). Emerging adulthood: A theory of development from the late teens through the twenties. *American Psychologist, 55,* 469–480.

Arnett, J. J. (2007). Emerging adulthood: What is it, and what is it good for? *Child Development Perspectives, 1,* 68–73.

Arnett, J. J. (2013). The evidence for Generation We and against Generation Me. *Emerging Adulthood, 1,* 5–10.

Arnett, J. J. (2014). The emergence of emerging adulthood: A personal history. *Emerging Adulthood, 2,* 155–162.

Arnett, J. J., & Fishel, E. (2014). *Getting to 30: A parent's guide to the twentysomething years.* New York: Workman.

Arnett, J. J., Žukauskienė, R., & Sugimura, K. (2014). The new life stage of emerging adulthood: Implications for mental health. *The Lancet: Psychiatry, 1,* 569–576.

Arnett, J. J. (2015). *Emerging adulthood: The winding road from the late teens through thetwenties (2nd ed.).* New York: Oxford University Press.

Erikson, E. H. (1950). *Childhood and society.* New York: Norton.

Maynard, B. R., Salas-Wright, C. P., & Vaughn, M. G. (2015). High school dropouts in emerging adulthood: Substance use, mental health problems, and crime. *Community mental health journal, 51*(3), 289–299.

Schwartz, S. J., & Petrova, M. (2019). Prevention science in emerging adulthood: A field coming of age. *Prevention Science, 20*(3), 305–309.

Tanner, J. L., Reinherz, H. Z., Beardslee, W. R., Fitzmaurice, G. M., Leis, J. A., & Berger, S. R. (2007). Change in prevalence of psychiatric disorders from ages 21 to 30 in a community sample. *The Journal of Nervous and Mental Disease, 195*(4), 298–306.

Acknowledgments

This book was truly a team effort. The contributors—people who have been our mentors, friends, and colleagues, as well as those we met because of their expertise on the psychology of young adults—brought great thoughtfulness, energy, clinical acumen, and care to this project. We are so grateful to each of the contributors. We are also immensely appreciative of the young adults we have seen in therapy—for the time spent together, for trusting us with their inner worlds, and for allowing us to be a part of their journeys. Having trained together in the City College Clinical Psychology PhD Program, we recognize how much this place has shaped the people we are today. We are grateful to our professors, our supervisors, and the friends we made at City. We want to recognize how special it is to have had our graduate school advisors, Steve Tuber and Denise Hien, be a part of this project. We would also like to thank Deborah Malmud and her team at Norton for their guidance, their vision, and for believing in us.

Coediting this anthology was an expedition into uncharted waters for both of us. Though working collaboratively on a big project with a dear friend can be complicated, as a team, we built on each other's strengths, playfully called out each other's weak spots, and figured out a way to make this process creative, fun, and deeply enriching. We couldn't have done it without each other.

The coeditors also could not have done this without the love and support of their families. While this project didn't officially have an agent, Jody Kahn was our advocate and unofficial editor, and has been Zach's rock, love, and partner throughout his young—and now getting toward middle—adulthood. Zach would like to acknowledge his parents, Asher Kahn and Sheri Katz, who were more than good enough, and whose support and belief are "beyond beyond"; his brilliant sister Alexandra Kahn, who is an inspiration as a human being and a scientist; and last but not least his son, Lev Kahn, for filling his heart with joy. Juliana would not have been able to participate in this project without the constant and unwavering love and support of her husband, Jorge Rivera-Schreiber, who always believes in her. She would also like to express her utmost gratitude to her parents, Yvette Piovanetti and José Luis Martínez, for being the example always guiding her path; to her brothers Fernando and Alfonso; and to her friends who are like family, Alexia Dellner and Dan Palmer in particular, who encouraged her to take on this challenge and supported her along the way. Juliana would like to dedicate this book to her daughter, Amelia, and soon-to-be-born son, Gabriel, who inspire her daily.

A Preface by Juliana Martínez

When my daughter was a baby, I learned about infant mental leaps, loosely defined as sudden periods of neurological and physical growth accompanied by extra fussiness, increased nursing, difficulty sleeping, and clinginess. Tracking these leaps became a bit of an obsession.

I found an app called the Wonder Weeks with a calendar that showed when to expect these growth spurts to appear. As promised by the app, after a challenging few days or so, at the end of each leap, something wonderful happened: my daughter would suddenly be back to her happy self, proudly exhibiting all her newly acquired tricks (smiling, rolling, pointing, babbling, etc.). Witnessing this process in my daughter helped me better understand the pains we—and on many occasions those closest to us—experience as we are transitioning into new psychic terrain, as well as the beauty of what awaits on the other side.

Becoming an adult, for the most part, is a gradual and elusive process (there is no app or calendar for this transition). Aside from a few socially normative external milestones that are increasingly less applicable to all (i.e., moving out of the family home, graduating college, starting a career, getting partnered, becoming a parent, etc.), the parameters of this process are largely undefined. Emerging adulthood is, rather, another transitional period in the series of transitions that make up our developmental life span. The term emerging adulthood (EA) was coined by Dr. Jeffrey Arnett to describe a distinct developmental period between adolescence and adulthood, typically spanning ages 18 to 29. According to Arnett, EA tends to be characterized by "obtaining a broad range of life experiences before taking on enduring—and limiting—adult experiences" (2000, p. 474).*

Major life transitions can be psychologically challenging because they conjure up uncertainty and loss; and we are, by nature, skeptical of what we do not know and apprehensive in letting go of what is familiar, known, or safe. At the same time, transitions (like mental leaps) provide powerful opportunities for growth and revitalization.

My appreciation for overcoming transitional periods is why I thoroughly enjoy working with young adults in therapy. It is a stage that can be both playful and poignant given that many 20-something-year-olds are trying out new identities to see what ultimately fits. A lot of my emerging adult patients are college or graduate students attempting to define themselves in a professional role, experiencing first serious romantic love and/or painful heartbreak, experimenting and understanding their sexuality, and coming to grips with various sorts of traumas (including but not limited to familial, interpersonal, sexual, social oppression, and racial discrimination) for the first time. Of course, a lot of this work begins in adolescence, but my practice has shown me that it is really in one's 20s (perhaps due to pubertal hormones settling in and neurological development stabilizing as well as increased independence) when people are truly ready to examine the interaction of their inner and outer lives. This examination or therapeutic endeavor can be at times chaotic and destabilizing, but more often than not leads to identity consolidation as well as the opportunity for young people to discover their authentic selves.

Below is an account written by Carmen, a Latina, cisgender female who started therapy in her mid-20s:

G oing to therapy has allowed me to identify the triggers and negative repetitive actions that cause me to feel unhappy or stuck. Before therapy, I never asked myself what makes me happy. I always

---

* Arnett, however, does not view EA as merely a transition into adulthood. For him, it is a distinct developmental period. Many of the chapters in this book review Arnett's theory in more depth.

associated happiness to achieving a goal, whether it was sports or an academic achievement or getting my first job out of college. I focused on achieving something and moved on to the next.

I started going to therapy because I was unhappy. Unhappy with my job, my relationships, and myself. I wanted desperately to vent to someone in hopes that they had this formula to fix me somehow. I wanted to deal with my underlying childhood trauma instead of running away from my past by endlessly filling up my time with unfulfilling goals.

My first attempt at finding a therapist didn't go very well. We didn't click. It seemed like she was trying to do her job, but there was no connection. I felt as if she was cold and culturally missing any insights to how I felt. I stopped going after a few sessions. I took the win of at least attempting to go as enough and started repeating the same bad habits.

A few years later I wanted to really face my fears. I was able to get a new job, which was a big factor in my unhappiness with my career. But I still felt really bad about myself, so I decided that talking to someone again was worth it. So this time I wanted a Hispanic woman. I figured maybe someone that was of similar background would be more empathetic and make me feel more at ease. I've encountered sexual trauma so for me a male therapist was out of the question. After a month of searching, I found a therapist who looked promising. I was very apprehensive at first but things worked out and I've been going consistently for almost three years. I've found therapy to be a form of self-reflection. Like many other things, you get as much out of it as you put in. Meaning that you have to be honest with the therapist and yourself. Being vulnerable and listening to the patterns they notice and adding a label to negative or triggering behavior to allow me to identify them and hopefully self-correct in the future has been a real journey. It's not a formula to happiness but a sort of mirror of the present and how the past impacts me today.

I'm happier than the day I started. I've learned that being happy is not this linear path. It's filled with ups and downs and that's OK. Giving myself permission to be OK with the journey and change the self-deprecating habits into positive substitutes is hard. I would never have had the courage to face my past fears without these sessions and for that I'm very grateful.

Although this is only one person's therapy experience and clearly not representative of everyone, Carmen brings up a few common themes that I have observed repeatedly in my work with young adults, irrespective of their specific *DSM-5* diagnosis.*

First is this idea of achievements as a means to happiness. Starting early in childhood, we seem to be rewarded mostly for our concrete accomplishments above and beyond any other aspect of our lives. Naturally, it can be very satisfying to see positive results after putting in hard work, and this can certainly lead to a sense of fulfillment. However, oftentimes we are blindly chasing goals that are prescriptive rather than inherently connected to our values or interests. Particularly for young adults who have just finished traditional schooling and are used to working for a grade to gain admission to exclusive clubs or institutions, the idea that happiness is not tied solely to material success can be difficult to grasp. As Carmen points out, one can be high achieving and unhappy if other parts of the self—such as traumatized parts that require healing—remain neglected.

Second, the right fit between a therapist and patient is crucial for a positive therapeutic experience. Numerous research studies support the notion that the therapeutic alliance is a significant variable in predicting therapy outcomes (Horvath et al., 2011). Given time and financial constraints, it is unrealistic for everyone to test out or shop around for the right therapist; however, I am a big proponent of listening to one's gut, and if after a couple of sessions one does not feel like they can begin to open up and trust the therapist, then I would advise that the search for a better match continue. For many BIPOC (Black, indigenous, and people of color) young adults, like Carmen, this is especially true. A lot of my patients seek me out expressly because I identify as Latina. Even though in many cases our backgrounds are not exactly aligned, there is a cultural shorthand that seems to provide a swifter sense of safety and comfort.†

Last, as Carmen explains, "You get as much out of it [therapy] as you put in" and "it's not a formula to happiness." A lot of young adults—and many people of any age, for that matter—enter the therapy space with an idea or

---

* There are many more common themes I could address here, but I chose to focus on the points highlighted by the patient account above.

† This has become even more evident for me in the psychotherapy process group I run specifically for Latina-identified patients.

perhaps wish that the therapists will fix them or tell them what to do, with similar expectations as when one consults a traditional Western medical doctor. The reality is that many therapists act more like guides, creating a judgment-free zone for the mind to wonder and explore. One of my young adult patients described the role of therapist as a lighthouse aiding in the navigation process. There are, of course, variations on how this happens, depending on the therapeutic school of thought or style, but there is never a one-size-fits-all formula to this process. The more open, uncensored, and vulnerable you can be in your therapy, the more you will feel seen enough to effect change or acceptance, depending on what's at stake.

Countless important themes and variations come up in the work with emerging adults, many having to do with identity and companionship.* In this anthology we do not cover every topic pertinent to this unique developmental period. Instead, we offer a selection of interesting and original ideas that are specifically related to emerging adults and not often talked about in the existing literature. The authors, many of whom are on the younger side and emerging into their professional careers, are all mental health experts (psychologists or psychiatrists) with diverse personal and professional backgrounds. We, the editors, hope this book will be a useful resource for training and practicing clinicians working with young people, as well as for young adults and their parents who are interested in both the psychological challenges facing young people in today's world, and the therapeutic practices that can help them navigate those challenges.

---

* Erik Erikson famously called the stages of adolescence and young adulthood Identity versus Role Confusion and Intimacy versus Isolation respectively; in Chapter 2 of this book, Tuber and Tocatly plant an argument of why these stages should be merged, given today's cultural vicissitudes.

A Preface by Zachary Kahn

The editors of this book, Drs. Juliana Martínez and Zachary Kahn, met in graduate school. This was 2010, and we were in the same cohort of 12 young people beginning to learn how to be psychologists at the City College Clinical Psychology PhD Program in Harlem, New York. At the time, Juliana was 24 and I (Zach) was 26 years old. Being at City, as the program is colloquially called, was revelatory. I remember the feelings of that time well: a giddy excitement at being surrounded by bright, curious people; a palpable sense of nerves; but mostly a feeling of sweet relief. It felt like I'd found my people. Looking back, I am so grateful for both having been able to figure out a way to work that engaged my mind and my spirit, and for having many privileges that afforded my ability to pursue this work.

Since I first began seeing patients, I've worked with young adults. I've also worked with children, adolescents, veterans (of all ages), and people old enough to be my grandparents. But seeing young adults in therapy continues to be a real passion of mine. Part of what has drawn me to this clinical work is the dichotomy it often represents. Young adulthood is ripe with endless possibilities for all the ways that life can be lived, but at the same time, young adults can feel so overwhelmed by the pressure of making big life choices, leading to stuckness, brittleness, and downfall. Here we have life—when one's identity around work, relationships, art, race, and gender begins to gel and bloom—clashing with the potential for death: too many young folk feel isolated, incapable of seeing beyond their current station, and prone to making impulsive choices, too often resulting in psychological turmoil, suicide, or even murder.

Working with young adults has given me many opportunities to reflect upon that time in my own life. While I didn't realize it then, looking back upon that time now, I can recognize that I was struggling at 19. Back then, I could pass for fine or even better than that; I had good friends, was doing well enough academically, and had had a winning season as a college athlete. At the same time, I had gained much more than the "freshman 15," and after a friend from college took his own life in the winter of my sophomore year, I sank into what I can now recognize as depression. Unfortunately, Jake is not the only young person I've known who's committed suicide. He was the first, though. Jake was a wonderful young man—kind, funny, very likable; I can still picture his goofy smile. I don't know why he did what he did. Whatever his motive, I imagine that Jake felt trapped (for whatever reason), and did not have hope that things could be different, let alone better.

It was just a few months after Jake's death that I had the opportunity to spend a semester studying abroad. Melbourne, Australia, seemed about as far away as I could go from my liberal arts college in upstate New York. Going away to that place, on my own, at that time in my life, changed everything. The world as I knew it opened up. Being far away from my college, my family, and my childhood friends gave me a freedom to try out new parts of my identity, to make new kinds of friendships, to flirt, and to feel attractive in a way that I hadn't before. I grew my hair long, started running, and came back with a new belief in myself and in the future.

Now, almost 20 years after that time abroad, I am a clinical psychologist, and I have a 22-year-old patient who has been processing what's been lost developmentally because of COVID-19. In January 2020, David began a study abroad program in Europe. "While it might not sound like such a big deal," he told me, "it was the first time I've really ever cooked my own meals." For David, being abroad was a big deal. He was making new friends, outside of any preexisting social circles; he enjoyed his classes; and he was exploring a new city in a new country, excited about what was beginning and what lay ahead. As we all now know, with COVID-19 came an immediate disruption of the world as we knew it. David was and is privileged: he is a young, healthy, white American male who comes from a family that can afford to pay for both his education and his therapy. His family was also able to provide David with a place to go when he left the study abroad program in March 2020 in haste and in fear—like many of his peers and like many young (and older) adults looking for a safe haven from the virus, David returned to his childhood home.

Going abroad was an opportunity for David to do something genuinely new, independent of the safety nets and familiar social and familial environments in which he had spent his first 22 years. The psychic whiplash of being jettisoned from this newfound agency and independence to his childhood bedroom was jarring. For David, like countless other young adults in the early dark days of the pandemic, returning to his childhood home provided a semblance of safety amid grave danger and fear, but was also a regression of sorts; here was a young man beginning to learn how to take care of himself on his own, to make new friends, and find secure footing out there on his own, who, because of circumstances far beyond his control, was now living at home for the longest stretch since high school.

Though traveling halfway across the world to find yourself at age 20 is a real privilege that most young people don't have, every young person has their own individual process of finding themselves. In this book, our contributors explore some of the many critical psychological hurdles of emerging adulthood. To navigate such hurdles, young adults must have the psychic space to experiment with different areas of study, different types of work, and to play with their conceptualizations of racial identity, of gender identity, and of the kind of partner (or not) they want to be. Such exploration is tied to one's capacity for play, in a Winnicottian sense.* The editors hope that this anthology will allow readers to play with some of the many ways young adults come into their own.

---

* Donald Woods Winnicott was a British pediatrician and psychoanalyst who, thanks to Steve Tuber, has had a great influence on the editors' conceptualization of psychotherapy and what it means to be a person. Winnicott came up with critically important psychological ideas such as the transitional object, the good-enough mother, the true and false self, the holding environment, and the importance of (the capacity to) play. To learn more about Winnicott, the editors recommend Steve Tuber's book, *Attachment, Play, and Authenticity: Winnicott in a Clinical Context*, and *Are You My Mother* by Alison Bechdel.

REFERENCES

Arnett, J. J. (2000). Emerging adulthood: A theory of development from the late teens through the twenties. *American Psychologist, 55*(5), 469–480.

Horvath, A. O., Del Re, A., Fluckiger, C., & Symonds, D. B. (2011). Alliance in individual psychotherapy. *Psychotherapy, 48*(1), 9–16.

An Anthology of Theoretical, Sociocultural, and Clinical Essays on the Psychology of Today's Emerging Adults

ZACHARY KAHN AND JULIANA MARTÍNEZ

While the concept for this anthology emerged before we, the editors, had any knowledge of the COVID-19 pandemic, the production of the book happened entirely during this time of global crisis. We knew from the start that in order to write a book on the psychology of emerging adults, it was essential to highlight the contemporary issues facing young adults today and how that sets them apart from previous generations—but we had no idea of the tumult that lay ahead of us. As we entered lockdown in March 2020 and the stark reality of the pandemic set in, the concept of the book evolved to match the crisis we were all facing. For us, and for many of our contributors, it did not make sense to write about emerging adults today without referencing the pandemic and the social justice uprising that characterized this year. In the spring of 2020, the world was rapidly changing, and it became imperative that we also evolve in how we approached our work humanly, clinically, and physically. This necessitated acknowledging the life-and-death stakes of the virus and of racism, and how we were all—therapists and patients alike—impacted by these events. Interventions became more direct and concrete than before, often focusing on self-care and survival. This also meant leaving our offices, which had become safe spaces for many, and moving into the virtual realm in which we could see each other's personal and often vulnerable spaces (cars, closets, bathrooms, our own crying children in the background—you name it!). We have, therefore, dedicated the second and largest section of the book to addressing special topics directly related to the psychological implications of the COVID-19 pandemic and the country's reckoning with its legacy of racism and white supremacy for young adults.

We begin with "Adulting 101: Developmental Frameworks for Emerging Adulthood" as a way of providing a theoretical and clinical foundation to ground the reader in this developmental period. In the opening chapter, "Emerging Adulthood: A Review of Developmental Perspectives," we initiate our journey of understanding what it is like to be a young adult. Frank Bartolomeo, Anna-Lee Stafford, and Andrew Gerber, colleagues at Silver Hill Hospital, define Arnett's theory on emerging adulthood and review the literature from a psychodynamic perspective. Next, Steve Tuber, director of the Clinical Psychology PhD Program at the City College of New York, and Karen Tocatly, a doctoral student in the program, creatively revise Erik Erikson's classic theory on developmental stages and provide some vital and culturally relevant updates to the stages pertaining to emerging adults in Chapter 2, titled "Intimacy Versus Isolation Revisited: Some New Ways to Think About Early Adulthood in the Light of Cultural and Technological Change." In Chapter 3, "Substance Use and Young Adults: The Good, the Bad, and the Not So Ugly," Chantel T. Ebrahimi, Alexandria G. Bauer, and Denise Hien, colleagues at Rutgers University Center of Alcohol & Substance Use Studies, discuss the role of substance and alcohol use in this age group, including how experimentation can potentially be a healthy and normative part of identity development. Rounding out this section with a somber but critical topic, Lillian Polanco-Roman and Marjorine Henriquez-Castillo bring attention to suicide in emerging adults as a major public health concern, highlighting the disproportionate burden of suicide-related risk on racial and ethnic minority youth. The authors, who met over a decade ago doing research in the New York State Psychiatric Institute's Boricua Youth Study, titled this eye-opening fourth chapter "Widening the Cultural Lens of Suicide-Related Risk Among Racial/Ethnic Minority Emerging Adults With Acculturation Frameworks."

Section II, "Becoming an Adult in Today's World," which we fondly think of as the heart of the book, is subdivided into two parts. The first part, "Not All Young Adults Are the Same," features six chapters (Chapters 5–10), each dedicated to particular types of identity development.

Chapter 5, "Protect Your Energy: A Clinical Psychologist and Her Clients' Racial Identity Development During the Pandemic and the Black Lives Matter Movement," is a beautiful personal essay by Kathleen Isaac, a psychologist at NYU's School of Medicine. Dr. Isaac explores how the pandemic, racial injustice, and the difficult experiences she and her young adult clients faced in 2020 paved the way for a deeper understanding of both personal and professional identity.

In Chapter 6, "Asians Emerging in America," Elisa Lee thoughtfully examines the historical factors as well as current events, including the discrimination, violence, and racist anti–Asian and Pacific Islander political sentiments enhanced by the COVID-19 pandemic, that have influenced emerging Asian American adults. Through clinical vignettes, Dr. Lee demonstrates how psychotherapy provides a space to acknowledge and voice these important and too-often-overlooked issues.

Chapter 7, "Exploring White Supremacy With Emerging Adults in Psychodynamic Psychotherapy," is another powerful personal essay in which the author, Carolina Franco, utilizes her story as well as her work with young adult patients to illustrate how exploring the impact of systemic discrimination and white supremacy can shed light on core conflicts, support identity development, and promote growth. At the center of this inspiring chapter, Dr. Franco makes the argument that in order to successfully establish oneself as a psychologically healthy young adult, one must reconcile with one's personal and familial conceptualization of racial and ethnic identity in a society that has placed whiteness at the top of the racial caste system.

Next, in Chapter 8, "Veterans and Emerging Adulthood: Contemporary Veteran Identity and Clinical Concerns," Annelisa Pedersen and Peter Lemons partner to write (and yes, they're married) about the psychology of young veterans based on their professional experience as psychologists at the Veterans Administration. Although existing literature on emerging adulthood in the veteran population is limited, Drs. Pedersen and Lemons consider the role of military service, while exploring how research and clinical findings on veteran identity may shed light on the challenges of emerging adulthood in this population.

In Chapter 9, "Gender Identity Development: Case Presentations of Clinical Work with Transgender Emerging Adults," Elizabeth F. Baumann and Zoë Berko review contemporary theory on gender identity and bring the theory to life with two moving and clinically rich psychotherapy cases. Dr. Baumann, clinical director of the Gender and Sexuality Clinic and Consultation Service in the Department of Child Psychiatry at Cambridge Health Alliance/Harvard

Medical School, and Dr. Berko, a psychologist at the New York State Office of Child and Family Services, highlight the importance of being truly seen by ourselves and others, especially for young adults who may be questioning, exploring, or transitioning.

It is impossible to "become an adult in today's world" without navigating the complexities of social media. Chapter 10 provides an insightful and creative approach into the psychological impact of growing up with (and surrounded by) an online presence. Written by Leora Trub and Vendela Parker, lead professor and student, respectively, at Pace University's Digital Media and Psychology Lab, this chapter is titled, "Like Me: Constructing Identity in the Age of Social Media."

The second part of Section II features three chapters (11–13) focused on what Freud called the "cornerstones of our humanness," love and work, in today's pandemic-era young adults. As for love, Chapter 11, "The Wooing Web: Double Binds of Internet Dating," by Leora Trub, playfully examines the world in which so many young adults find (and/or lose) romantic connection: online dating. Moving on to work, in Chapter 12, "Graduating Into a Pandemic: New Grads Navigating Work Life in 2020," Zachary Geller uses clinical vignettes to explore how the COVID-19 pandemic rerouted many emerging adults' traditional paths of going out into the world to establish a professional identity. Closing Section II, in Chapter 13, "Treating Frontline Workers Analytically, Pandemic and All," Danielle La Rocco describes her personal experience as an analyst in training, working with young adult medical professionals directly facing the horrors of the coronavirus during the peak of the pandemic in New York City.

While the entire book is dedicated to treating young adults in therapy, we end our book with Section III, "Young Adults in Treatment," which zooms in on three (of many possible) examples, showcasing different psychotherapeutic treatment modalities that are tailored for the unique challenges of this developmental period.

Chapter 14, "DBT-YA: DBT Adapted for Emerging Adults and Their Families," features Colleen M. Cowperthwait and Kristin P. Wyatt, dialectical behavior therapy (DBT) practitioners with a passion for treating young adults. They saw the need to adapt this well-established treatment for high-risk patients for a young adult population, and created the DBT-YA clinic at Duke University's medical center. Next, in Chapter 15, "Queer Enough or Too Queer? The Effectiveness of Group Therapy in the Facilitation of Queer Young

Adult Identity Formation," Kateri Berasi thoughtfully considers gender and sexual identity development in young adulthood from a historical lens, contemplating the roles of language, time, and place on young people's gender identity formulation. Dr. Berasi integrates conceptualizations of history and culture with her work in the consulting room, focusing on the role of group therapy as a particularly useful treatment modality for this age group. Last, in Chapter 16, "The College Counseling Center: A Developmental Playground for Emerging Adults," Sherina Persaud, a psychologist in Columbia University's Counseling and Psychological Services, contemplates some of the psychological challenges facing college and university students today. Dr. Persaud provides clinical examples to illustrate how college counseling can serve as a safe space for students to explore their forming identities.

There is no one way to capture the emerging adulthood experience. In that vein, this anthology displays a range of voices: some are grounded in theory and research while others take on a more personal and experiential tone. We are aware of the many important topics that were not included in this anthology; that said, we hope that this book sets the stage in valuing a deeper understanding of this developmental period and of the importance of psychotherapy for young people. As our society continues to progress, and new opportunities and challenges arise, there will be an ongoing need to study and understand (so we can continue to provide the best treatments) how young adults adapt to the world around them.

For the editors, the process of assembling this collection was an exciting challenge that pushed us out of our comfort zones and required us to expand our preexisting knowledge and professional networks. It was truly inspiring to see how our contributors engaged with the material with an energy that felt alive and passionate, despite doing it in such a complicated time. We felt how deeply committed the writers are to their work with young adults, and we believe that spirit and care will come through in these pages.

EMERGING ADULTS IN THERAPY

ADULTING 101: DEVELOPMENTAL FRAMEWORKS FOR EMERGING ADULTHOOD

CHAPTER 1

Emerging Adulthood

A Review of Developmental Perspectives

FRANCIS BARTOLOMEO, ANNA-LEE STAFFORD,
AND ANDREW GERBER

O ver 20 years ago, Arnett (2000) proposed the term *emerging adulthood* to describe a new stage of development from the late teens through the 20s (ages 18–29). Driven by social, economic, and cultural shifts in the United States and other industrialized countries, emerging adulthood was conceived as a unique preparatory stage for a knowledge-based economy. Based on Arnett's phenomenological investigations, emerging adulthood is a period of time that is subjectively experienced as intermediary, neither teenager nor adult. Confusingly, Arnett sometimes uses the age range 18–25 and other times 18–29. This difference in age range, he explains, is due to the variations in the subjective or felt sense of being an adult, and when people assume adult roles (e.g., stable work, marriage, and parenthood). Arnett (2016) concludes that either age range can be used depending on the research question at hand.

Since the theory's inception, interest, scholarship, research, and professional concentration related to emerging adulthood have burgeoned. There is now a professional organization, the Society for the Study of Emerging Adulthood (SSEA), the journal *Emerging Adulthood*, and a yearly SSEA conference.

Notwithstanding the increased knowledge and professional specialization in the study of emerging adults, the authors' experience is that many clinicians and therapists remain unfamiliar with Arnett's model and subsequent scholarship about emerging adulthood. Indeed, Arnett, Žukauskienė, and Kazumi, (2014) assert that most mental health systems of care seldom recognize the developmental differences between emerging adults and people in later adult stages.

Unfortunately, lack of knowledge can result in the pejorative labeling of normative (though not universal) pathways to adulthood. Indeed, a cottage industry of young adult therapeutic programs, both outpatient and residential, has arisen in recent years to address the needs of "failure-to-launch young adults." We contend that only through the lens of a multidisciplinary theory of development grounded in the awareness of demographic and sociological trends can practitioners accurately discern the extent and degree to which an individual is psychologically and socially divergent.

This chapter begins with a brief overview of how emerging adulthood is conceptualized, including the difficulties associated with defining this developmental stage, as well as how both language and culture impact our conceptualizations. Subsequently, we discuss the developmental tasks unique to this period, followed by a cursory review of psychodynamic and life span development perspectives, particularly the psychoanalytic concept of separation-individuation. Last, we discuss the current state of the neuroscience of emerging adulthood and its rather limited clinical utility.

Interspersed throughout this chapter is a critique meant to counter current cultural narratives of emerging adults that have negative undertones (e.g., as faulty or conspicuously underdeveloped). Moreover, we include two case vignettes to illustrate the application of the developmental theory in clinical practice.

CONCEPTUALIZING EMERGING ADULTHOOD

The categorization of emerging adulthood has historically been an ambiguous one, primarily influenced by how its boundaries (i.e., adolescence and adulthood) have themselves been delineated. Some early developmental psychologists posited that adolescence ended at age 25, while others considered adulthood to begin promptly at age 17 (Arnstein, 1984). For others still, young adulthood was believed to span an entire generation (ages 20 to 40; Colarusso, 1995), a theory consistent with Erik Erikson's sixth stage of psychosocial development taking place between the ages of 18 and 40 (Erikson, 1950, 1968). However, the consensus in the psychoanalytic literature is that emerging adulthood is distinct from both adolescence and adulthood and spans ages 18 to 25, potentially extending to age 30 (Miller, 2017).

The concept of adolescence itself has shifted tremendously across generations. It now spans a much more extended period due to the earlier onset of puberty on the front end and delayed economic and social independence on the back end (Steinberg, 2014). Emerging adults are transitioning into careers, marriages, and financial independence (i.e., adulthood) at a much later age, resulting in a distinct extension period between adolescence and adulthood. This in-between period only emerged toward the end of the 20th century, when people in many industrialized societies began marrying and entering the workforce after age 20, as opposed to the middle of the 20th century when teens "settled into long-term adult roles" at a much younger age (Arnett, 2007). This paradigm shift also resulted from a so-called new normal of increased postsecondary education pursuits, more frequent job changes, changing career paths, and increased social acceptance of premarital sex, cohabitation, and delayed age of marriage (Arnett, 2007).

The start of puberty is the widely accepted biological marker of the start of adolescence. However, no biological marker seems adequate to encapsulate the end of this stage (Steinberg, 2014). Neuroscience research confirms that while increases in the neuroplasticity and malleability of the brain are a primary characteristic of adolescence, the end of this phenomenon is not definitive. On the contrary, and as is discussed below, the duration of heightened malleability may itself be dependent on environmental factors such as social experiences and opportunities (Steinberg, 2014). Social indicators (e.g., moving into one's own home, starting a full-time job) rather than biological markers are accepted as a more accurate representation of the end of adolescence and emerging adulthood. However, this makes it much more susceptible to individual and cultural influences (Steinberg, 2014).

While the socially influenced entrance into adulthood results in increased flexibility, it also comes with greater social judgment as to why one has delayed adulthood. Steinberg (2014) discusses four different perspectives attributed to those who have delayed adulthood. One perspective is that emerging adults are selfish slackers (Arnett, 2007), which is a far too typical example of the negative connotations associated with emerging adulthood. Rather, it can be a deliberate choice to forgo financial and familial responsibilities in favor of unstructured and more independent lifestyles (albeit in reality more financially dependent on others). In this chapter, we hope to elucidate how these pejorative connotations are overblown and do not accurately represent this potentially fruitful period of the life span.

While establishing an age range for emerging adulthood helps us better identify the population we seek to observe and understand, this task remains futile. Neurodevelopment during this period is much subtler than in early childhood and adolescence, which contributes to the difficulty in identifying clear-cut age boundaries for this stage of life. Additionally, defining features of emerging adulthood lie in individual, cultural, and environmental factors. Some of these include educational pursuits, work, financial independence, and the formation of enduring romantic relationships, the attainment of which varies widely across populations and individuals.

These fluctuations and the lack of hard-set developmental milestones (such as those widely accepted during childhood) result in a period that is inherently ambiguous, socially constructed, and vulnerable to subjective scrutiny. The markers habitually used by society to gauge whether or not an individual has successfully reached adulthood reflect generational and cultural expectations more than the accomplishment and mastery of the developmental demands unique to this period.

NOMENCLATURE MATTERS

Emerging adults have frequently been characterized as narcissistic, self-focused, and floundering (Arnett, 2000; Nelson & Padilla-Walker, 2013). Terms such as *delayed adolescence* or *late adolescence* used to describe emerging adulthood can themselves be problematic in perpetuating these derogatory views of a normative developmental process. Many psychoanalytic and psychodynamic authors have pushed for the reframing of young adulthood from a period of an impediment to a period of transition. Hauser and Greene (1991) nicely captured the more favorable future-oriented definition of the young adult transitional period as one characterized by reflection and self-evaluation, as well as potential upheaval, since the primary tasks of this period include reassessing values and goals and exploring options for growth within the self and within the world. From this perspective, the emerging adult is doing just that, emerging. Through a process of exploration, introspection, and modification, the young adult can develop and establish an enduring identity.

The language used to describe this developmental stage plays a crucial role in the assumptions, attitudes, and expectations we hold for individuals within this group. Language emphasizing movement, transition, and change most appropriately encompasses the reorganization and renegotiations that occur during this period, both within the self and between the self and others. This is not to say that the process or the outcome of emerging adulthood is always positive. In fact, as Pollock (1998) described, development is not always synonymous with growth "and can include progression, regression, new constructions, remodeling, and in some ways, decline." Another popular denotation for this developmental stage is the "extension of adolescence" or the "elongation of adolescence" (Steinberg, 2014). While these phrases accurately describe the cultural changes and the postponed attainment of adulthood, they do not do justice to distinguish this stage from adolescence.

TASKS SPECIFIC TO EMERGING ADULTHOOD

Emerging adulthood theory is grounded in observing dramatic demographic changes in the typical age of marriage, parenthood, and established careers in industrialized societies. These life events were traditional markers of what it means to be an adult. Since 1960, the age of marriage and first childbirth has risen significantly in the United States and other industrialized countries. According to U.S. Census data in 1970, the median age for marriage was 23.2 years for men and 21.8 for women, whereas in 2020, the median age for marriage was 30.5 for men and 28.1 for women. The period between the end of adolescence and the assumption of the traditional roles associated with adulthood is no longer a brief transition, but is now, Arnett proposes, a separate developmental stage that he calls emerging adulthood. Arnett's concept of emerging adulthood is complex in that it incorporates the psychological, sociological, and cultural features that influence the emerging adult experience.

According to Arnett (2007), emerging adulthood is neither an extension of adolescence nor merely a transition into adulthood. It is a separate and unique period of the life course distinct from both adolescence and adulthood, though some overlap exists on both ends. Arnett highlights five interrelated features of emerging adulthood: (1) identity exploration, (2) instability, (3) self-focus, (4) feeling in-between, and (5) increased possibilities. Arnett distinguishes the adolescent developmental search for identity from the more specific identity explorations associated with emerging adulthood. Blos (1967) postulated that whereas adolescence involves identity explorations, identity consolidation occurs during what he called postadolescence. For Arnett, the emerging adult is exploring who he or she is (identity) in the context of love and work. Regarding romantic relationships, the emerging adult is attempting to discern the kind or type of person with whom to share his or her life. This identity exploration is more akin to the concept of self-in-relation to others: That is, who am I (identity) with this particular person?

This discernment process may result in serial monogamy and a reluctance to commit to marriage or a long-term partnership. It can also lead to promiscuity and less than responsible sexual practices among emerging adults, as attested by the high rates of sexually transmitted diseases such as human papillomavirus.

Arnett posits that the women's movement of the 1960s and 1970s is one of the cultural factors that contributed to forming this new period of development. In 1960, women experienced less independence; had fewer opportunities to attend college, enter into the workforce, and have a career; and were often limited to adult roles of wife and mother. What are the implications of marrying at older ages when education, careers, and finances are more established and of finding a mate more compatible with one's professional and personal aspirations? According to an analysis conducted by University of Maryland sociology professor Philip Cohen (2019), the result is a US divorce rate that dropped 18% from 2008 to 2016.

As for identity exploration with love and long-term connection, today's emerging adults are likely to try different types of employment and relocate more frequently. Though geographical and occupational nomadism may appear (especially to parents) as frivolously hopping from job to job or an inability to commit to a career path, the emerging adult is working through a process of defining and refining the sense of self in the context of work, in a manner that was neither socially acceptable nor financially possible for prior generations. Similarly, perhaps unlike the pragmatism born of the necessity of prior generations, today's emerging adults, across social classes, report that finding work that is enjoyable, meaningful, and beneficial to the common good is more important than a focus on money, which reflects the idealism of emerging adults.

Emerging adulthood is an inherently uncertain time because it is the most variable period of the life course and the least structured, especially as the former pathways and identifiers of adulthood are no longer so fixed. Though exaggerated, emerging adults' instability and uncertainty have popularly been called the quarter-life crisis and are fraught with existential anxiety. Freed from the constrictions of previous generations and faced with increased possibilities, the emerging adult must still make choices for which he or she is ultimately responsible. Having numerous options heightens the sense of needing to choose the right one, leading to anxiety-ridden, decisional paralysis.

The emerging adult must also confront the existential reality that making one choice may rule out others. These dilemmas are being explored with one of the author's psychotherapy patients.

Justin is a 22-year-old white male who graduated from an elite college with a degree in computer science. Nine months after obtaining his degree, he had yet to find employment of any type and returned to live in his family home. He sought psychotherapy at the urging of his parents, concerned about his apparent lack of motivation to "move forward with his life." His parents incurred the cost of the psychotherapy. Justin reported feeling "stuck" and was doubting his choice of college major: why had he chosen that field of study? Did he even enjoy computer science and want a career in that profession? The author understood these questions and doubts in the light of identity exploration concerning work. Was he the same "he" that declared his college major while still in high school, and what parental or other external factors influenced his decision? This question of "who wanted what" (he or his parent) represented continued individuation from his parents' aspirations and dreams versus his own. As we worked through those questions, Justin found short-term work as a barista. He eventually began sending resumes to IT firms and was asked to interview for a position. The interview prospect significantly increased Justin's anxiety, and he began questioning if he even wanted to follow through. What emerged was heightened anxiety, not that he would be rejected, but that he might be offered a position. Should he be offered a position, he would need to choose, and he expressed fear about being locked into a position that would interfere with his more immediate desire to live in another country.

During this age of possibilities, for a young man like Justin, the number of personal growth and development options can be so great for those with higher socioeconomic status that it can become overwhelming and potentially paralyzing. Because these options cannot be engaged simultaneously, anxiety about the right choice increases. Reconciling potentialities and actualities is a process that involves loss, as the emerging adult confronts the reality that the choice of any path, or even refusal to choose, may exclude other paths. For Justin, it was accepting that taking a position at a highly respected mechanical engineering firm would preclude him, in the short term, from relocating to another country. His compromise was that in the future, but not for at least two years according to his company's standard practices, he could request a transfer to one of its European offices. Justin also needed to wrestle with anxiety that more conventional choices might lead to a mediocre and mundane life. Moreover, his concerns were realistic.

Justin could easily be labeled a failure-to-launch emerging adult: He was unemployed, living with his parents, and seemingly unmotivated to find a job. Justin, like many emerging adults, had feelings of ambivalence about adulthood. The prospect of living independently and being financially self-sufficient was attractive to him, but he also appreciated that adulthood's responsibilities could be both tedious and burdensome. Justin was wrestling with the reality that becoming an adult, for all its possible advantages, also meant that possibilities would become limited and spontaneity significantly constrained.

For individuals less fortunate than Justin, emerging adulthood is an opportunity for those who have lived in difficult family conditions such as poverty, parental/familial dysfunction, or abuse to leave home and have more autonomy to steer their lives in a different direction. Before emerging adulthood, children and adolescents are essentially trapped in their family circumstances. Being exposed to different experiences, perhaps during college or in the armed services, provides an emerging adult more opportunities to transform his or her life. At no other time period do the relations between the individual and the family shift as they do at the beginning of emerging adulthood.

Within Arnett's (2007) conceptual framework of emerging adulthood, there are two remaining descriptors to address: self-focused age and the age of feeling in-between. Arnett points out that by postponing marriage, children, home ownership, and other long-term obligations, the emerging adult is permitted to be self-focused with the greatest autonomy in his or her own life. Arnett (2007) clearly distinguishes self-focus from the self-centeredness or egocentricity so common among adolescents. A maturation of social cognition occurs between adolescence and emerging adulthood so that emerging

adults are more capable of empathy and perspective taking (Lapsley & Woodbury, 2016; Taber-Thomas & Perez-Edgar, 2016). This growing social cognitive
maturity enables emerging adults to understand themselves and others better
than adolescents. This shift can especially be seen in the relationship between
the emerging adult and his or her parents. The emerging adult is more capable
of perceiving his or her parents as actual people, not merely parents, and can
have greater empathy for them.

Unlike adolescence, when one still resides at home under the structure
and rules of parents, emerging adulthood can be the most empowering and
enjoyable period of one's life. However, within this independence and freedom
is the construct of acquiring the self-sufficiency needed to be an adult. The
downside of this freedom from social and familial obligations is the potential
to experience loneliness and isolation. According to Arnett (2007), across the
life span, emerging adults spend more leisure time alone than the elderly and
more time in work or graduate studies than any age group under 40.

In his research interviews with emerging adults, Arnett (2000) continually heard about the subjective experience of feeling in between being an
adolescent and an adult. Indeed, this experience was largely the rationale for
the conceptualization of an intermediate stage of development that became
the theory of emerging adulthood. Though no longer adolescents living at
home with their parents, attending secondary school, and going through the
biological changes of puberty, the 18- to 29-year-olds that Arnett studied did
not see themselves as adults. Most responded, "in some ways, yes, and some
ways no." Arnett postulates that there is remarkable consistency in the popular standards for what it means to be an adult in the United States and other
industrialized countries and among various ethnic groups. These standards
include accepting responsibility for oneself, making independent decisions,
and becoming financially independent.

While there is general consistency on what it means to be an adult, there
are, within the emerging adult framework, variations in the age when both
the subjective and objective criteria for adulthood are achieved. According to
Arnett (2007), while most people in their late 20s and early 30s feel that they
have reached adulthood, a substantial number still feel in-between; it is not
until the age of 35 that most people feel unambiguously adult.

CRITIQUE

Arnett's proposal for a new stage of development in the life span immediately elicited numerous challenges and criticisms (Syed, 2016). Critics contend that the concept of emerging adulthood is merely the product of socioeconomic cultural conditions in industrialized countries, is nonuniversal, and thus should not be considered a true life stage. Another debate is that the theory of emerging adulthood does not even meet the criteria of a theory because it is descriptive rather than explanatory. It is beyond the scope of this chapter to examine the various debates. Instead, we limit our discussion to the most frequent criticism: that Arnett's theory of emerging adulthood applies primarily to white, upper-middle-class to affluent college-educated individuals who have the privilege and luxury of affording the cost of higher education and the financial support to postpone the responsibilities associated with adulthood. Therefore, according to the proponents of this view, Arnett's theory is not generalizable beyond high-income, industrialized countries, nor even within a particular society like the United States. In brief, critics have argued that the theory of emerging adulthood is limited by social class.

Arnett has challenged these criticisms as inaccurate by pointing out that his original research was based on a sample of 300 18- to 29-year-olds drawn from a diverse range of ethnicities, geographic regions, and socioeconomic statuses. Also, Arnett asserted that he never claimed that his five features of emerging adulthood would be shown to be universal and predicted there would be variations depending on cultural context and economic circumstances.

In 2016, Arnett more directly addressed the question of whether or not the theory of emerging adulthood applied across social classes when he presented data from a national sample of 710 persons aged 18–25 that was demographically similar to the US population. Analyses of this national data indicate that in terms of the five features postulated in the theory of emerging adulthood, there were more similarities than differences across social classes among 18- to 25-year-olds in the United States. The differences occur where one might expect: emerging adults from lower social classes experience their emotional lives less positively, are less likely to report their lives as pleasing and dynamic, and are more likely to report feeling depressed and unfulfilled. Likewise, concerning school and work, emerging adults in the lowest social class were more likely than those in the highest social class to agree that they had not been able to find sufficient financial support to obtain the education they desired.

Even with these disadvantages, most of the emerging adults from lower social classes in the study were surprisingly optimistic about their lives and experiences. These positive findings should not detract from the inequitable access to higher education between social classes, mainly in the United States. Structural inequalities, such as poverty and racism, have adverse consequences on the poorest emerging adults. Nearly half of the poorest emerging adults in Arnett's 2016 national survey did not have the financial resources for tertiary education, which is an egregious loss of human potential and a barrier to upward mobility for many. The United States has stark social class differences and a significant degree of income inequality. The enormous rise in the cost of higher education, if unaddressed, will perpetuate the class divide. The United States is falling behind in the proportion of college graduates because most other developed countries provide free or highly affordable access to higher education.

PSYCHOLOGICAL DEVELOPMENT DURING EMERGING ADULTHOOD

Elizabeth is a 27-year-old third-generation Mexican American female, who entered therapy due to persistent and growing conflict with her mother, with whom she had enjoyed a close relationship. Elizabeth obtained a master's degree in social work and is a rising star at the mental health agency where she is employed. Her employer has recognized and rewarded her skills by promoting her to positions of increasing responsibility and organizational influence, which has enhanced her personal and professional confidence and her sense of competence. During a weekend visit to her family's home in a neighboring state, a disagreement arose in which her mother accused her of being arrogant. Elizabeth found this adjective deeply wounding because it was inconsistent with her self-perceptions and her values. She had long appreciated and respected her mother's opinions and counsel, so it pained her that her mother viewed her in this way. In her therapy session after this exchange, Elizabeth was not only tearful

but also anxiously doubtful about her self-perception and wondered if
her mother's negative appraisal might be accurate. Further arguments
transpired between Elizabeth and her mother over her boyfriend's educational level and occupational prospects. Her mother's assessment of
her boyfriend was blunt; he was not good enough for Elizabeth.

This clinical vignette is rich with illustrations of the complex interplay
between the salient psychological, familial, gender, ethnocultural, and social
factors that impact the development of the emerging adult (which speaks to
Arnett's assertion of the variability of pathways to adulthood). Our discussion
is limited to the intrapsychic and relational restructuring characteristic of the
separation-individuation process.

As the vignette highlights, emerging adulthood can be stressful because
of the realignments occurring in a person's internal and external worlds. The
conflict between Elizabeth and her mother is best examined using the framework of separation-individuation (Colarusso, 2000; Koepke & Denissen, 2012).
This is a fundamental psychoanalytic construct and organizing principle of
human development first described by Mahler as a series of phases resulting
in "psychological birth" during the first three years of life (Mahler et al., 1975).

Arnett was by no means the first scholar to propose an intervening phase
between the end of adolescence and adulthood proper. From a psychoanalytic
perspective, Blos (1967) postulated that adolescence was the second separation-
individuation phase in human development. Separation-individuation is an
intrapsychic process that refers to establishing a sense of self, separate from
other primary love objects (i.e., parent/caregiver), and the acquisition of one's
distinctive individuality. During the second separation-individuation phase,
the adolescent must now separate from the internalized representations of
caregivers formed in early childhood and establish a sense of self that is distinct and individuated. Individuation refers to a process "by which a person
becomes increasingly differentiated from a past or present relational context"
(Karpel, 1976, p. 66). It is generally agreed that separation-individuation has
crucial implications for adaptive functioning and psychopathology across
the life span; there is a continuous relational tension between balancing and
maintaining an autonomous sense of self while remaining attached to significant others.

At the start of her psychotherapy, Elizabeth was externally focused on
convincing her mother that she was not arrogant and that her boyfriend was

more than suitable for her. This wish led to frustration and tears of futility, and we subsequently shifted to explore her deep need for her mother's approval. Concomitantly, Elizabeth benefited from therapeutic support and validation to help her tolerate the growing rift between her and her mother. As most psychodynamic psychotherapists appreciate, growth often entails loss. Mourning the loss of her heretofore unconscious childhood identification was necessary to reduce Elizabeth's psychological dependence on her parental introjects for approval, self-esteem, and a sense of ethical standards. Throughout treatment, Elizabeth acquired a greater capacity to regulate her self-esteem and self-definition apart from her mother's judgments.

As Elizabeth made progress individuating and defining herself, she became less emotionally reactive to her mother's disapproval and provocations. We began to incorporate a mentalization-based treatment approach (Allen & Fonagy, 2006) by playfully wondering what might be happening in her mother's mind rather than merely focusing on her mother's behavior. Elizabeth and her therapist coconstructed the story that her mother was threatened by Elizabeth's growing confidence and self-assertion because it reduced her mother's sense of control, which protected her from grief related to losing "her baby girl." Her mother's accusation of arrogance was an attempt to "rightsize" her daughter, who was "getting too big for her britches."

We speculated that her mother's negative perception of Elizabeth's boyfriend reflected anxiety that Elizabeth would not be sufficiently "taken care of" (also a reflection of her mother's traditional gender role stereotypes). Elizabeth also wondered whether her mother's disappointment with, and resentment (occasionally explicit) about, her husband's role of provider unconsciously contributed to her diminution of Elizabeth's boyfriend.

For the emerging adult, emancipating from one's family of origin is not limited to intrapsychic individuation but also involves a confrontation with reality because power dynamics within the family need to be renegotiated. Tanner (2006) refers to this process as "recentering," representing a shift in power, responsibility, and dependency between emerging adults and their parents. Parental regulation is replaced by self-regulation. At the heart of this relational restructuring is the question as to the appropriate time for emerging adults to make their own decisions based on their values, beliefs, and standards of conduct. Elizabeth will perhaps marry a man who does not meet her mother's standards, but that man's kindness and character may be of more value than college degrees.

NEUROSCIENCE OF EMERGING ADULTHOOD

Over the last two decades it has become the norm in all the social sciences (psychology, economics, sociology, ethics, etc.) to look for neuroscience-based evidence to support current or past theories of human behavior and development. Though we have indeed learned much about brain functioning through new and improved technologies, such as magnetic resonance imaging and electroencephalograms as well as enhanced analytic methods that make use of increased computing power, almost all of these advances have been at the micro level (i.e., cellular networks and biochemical responses). The contributions asserted to have been made by neuroscience toward understanding complex behaviors, including psychopathology and human personality development, are almost or perhaps entirely explanatory (often referred to as "post hoc" or "just-so stories") rather than predictive or clinically useful (Gerber & Gonzalez, 2013). With neuroimaging in particular, images of brains have an almost instinctive allure, even to well-trained scientists, that have been shown to give the impression of explanatory power even when they logically do not (Gewin, 2012; McCabe & Castel, 2008).

Given this, it becomes interesting from a history or sociology of science perspective to look at the way reviews of the neuroscience literature mirror contemporary perspectives about emerging adulthood, as discussed in this chapter. Many of the neuroscience studies or reviews of emerging adulthood focus on risky behavior and psychopathology, reflecting the emphasis in our culture on seeing emerging adults as poor decision makers at risk for various negative outcomes, including psychopathology. Meanwhile, it is true that emerging adulthood is a time when psychopathology is often first identified, though unclear whether this is more for social or neurodevelopmental reasons (Pharo et al., 2011; Victor & Hariri, 2016).

In their comprehensive review, Taber-Thomas and Perez-Edgar (2014) argue that development during emerging adulthood is on the same continuum as has been described in adolescents, moving toward "greater balance between bottom-up and top-down functioning as executive and self-regulatory mechanisms of the prefrontal cortex (PFC) develop to interact with reactive processes" (p. 127). As in the literature about adolescents, this process is tied to the development of the association cortices and frontolimbic systems. Finally, Taber-Thomas and Perez-Edgar link these processes with the appearance of psychopathology in adulthood and postulate that the "permissive environment" created by these dynamics underlies the vulnerability to disorders.

One uncontroversial observation from the neuroscience literature is that to date this area has been little studied in comparison with adulthood, childhood, and adolescence, and it is as yet unclear whether neuroscience will change what we know about emerging adulthood in meaningful ways (Marsh et al., 2008). As in the clinical realm, only time will tell if and when advances in neuroscience will have meaningful effects on diagnosis, prognosis, clinical recommendations, or assessment of change. Estimates of when such advances will be made, even by experts in the field, range from "the next few years" to "many decades away" (Daniel Pine, personal communication, 2019). In the meantime, further research will continue, hopefully with benefits worth the expense, and not detracting from other means of studying the psychosocial issues around emerging adulthood.

CONCLUDING THOUGHTS

Emerging adulthood is a pivotal developmental period that impacts long-term life trajectories. Choices made during this period can define personal biographies across the life span. Our decisions on marriage, partnership, parenthood, and/or career paths have enduring repercussions. It is no wonder that this stage of life, when we have the most autonomy with the fewest obligations, is fraught with anxiety, excitement, and loss. Tanner (2006) asserts "that emerging adulthood is a critical juncture in life span development when the relationship between the individual and society takes on new meaning" (p. 22). This shift to becoming a responsible adult and contributing member of society involves the relinquishment of the exploratory self to a consolidated self, stabilized by adult roles and beliefs, with a sense, purpose, and life direction.

This chapter has delineated the developmental tasks, particularly continued self-definition, and the ensuing relational tensions of emerging adulthood. The hope is that a better appreciation of the intermingled internal, familial, relational, and societal reconfigurations that are occurring at this stage will lead to more empathy and understanding rather than the one-dimensional caricatures of "failure to launch." This is not to say that there are not individuals who struggle with meeting the internal and external demands of emerging adulthood. Our view is that we cannot limit our clinical conceptualizations to individual symptoms or facile explanations such as failure to launch or Peter Pan syndrome. A distressed or derailed emerging adult must be viewed through a developmental lens that has psychological, familial, relational, and social dimensions. Furthermore, a focus on individual failure and symptoms obscures the family system's role in psychopathology. It is our opinion that clinical approaches that include an assessment of the parental support for individuation and autonomy, degree of enmeshment, or lack of differentiation (from a Bowen family systems perspective) are imperative and will lead to more effective interventions.

One of the sociological determinants of emerging adulthood as a construct was the historical shift in industrialized countries from manufacturing economies to knowledge economies. A knowledge economy required a more educated workforce and a greater percentage of college-educated individuals, and college became an important context of emerging adulthood. Though the socioeconomic and cultural changes over the last 50 years have provided emerging adults, especially women, more choices, they have magnified structural inequalities and barriers to successful adulthood. The cost of college, for example, has increased so significantly that it is not accessible for those from low-income backgrounds. For those who fund college, partially or wholly, with student loans, college debt can also be so burdensome for some emerging adults that the path to economic stability may be longer and more precarious.

We also included in this chapter two clinical vignettes with the hope of illustrating the ways in which Arnett's psychosociological model can seamlessly incorporate psychodynamic thought and practice. The first vignette, Justin (who could easily have been labeled "failure to launch"), illustrated how ambivalence, anxiety, and loss contributed to his impasse. Justin's therapy highlighted the gradual relinquishment of the exploratory self to the more stable adult self capable of making a work commitment.

The second vignette, Elizabeth, elucidated the psychoanalytic construct of separation-individuation and the corresponding relational conflict and anguish that can accompany the maturation of the self. It is our hope that these vignettes illuminated the richness and complexity of emerging adulthood as a stage of human development.

Francis Bartolomeo, PhD, LCSW, is Director of Adolescent Services at Silver Hill Hospital in New Canaan, Connecticut, where he works with adolescents, emerging adults, and families. He volunteers as a Consulting Editor, American Society of Group Psychotherapy and Psychodrama (ASGPP) and as a Senior Advisor to "Authentic Connections," a non-profit organization which strives to implement community-based support groups to help foster resilience in the face of high stress. He received his MSW from Boston University and his PhD from Simmons College School of Social Work.

Andrew J. Gerber, MD, PhD, is President and Medical Director of Silver Hill Hospital, a private non-profit psychiatric hospital in New Canaan, Connecticut. Dr. Gerber serves as associate clinical professor in the Division of Child and Adolescent Psychiatry at Columbia University Medical Center and the Child Study Center, Yale University. He completed his medical and psychiatric training at Harvard, Cornell, and Columbia medical schools and his PhD in psychology at University College, London. Dr. Gerber is past Director of the Magnetic Resonance Imaging Program at the New York State Psychiatric Institute and past Medical Director and CEO of the Austen Riggs Center.

Anna-Lee Stafford, PhD, is a postdoctoral resident working in a community health center in Connecticut. She provides individual, family, and group psychotherapy to clients across the lifespan, and specializes in treating trauma in children and adolescents. Dr. Stafford's research has focused on child cognitive development, parent–infant interactions, and the impact of attachment on adult interpersonal functioning.

REFERENCES

Allen, J. G., & Fonagy, P. (2006). (Eds.). *Handbook of mentalization-based treatment*. John Wiley and Sons.

Arnett, J. J. (2000). Emerging adulthood: A theory of development from the late teens through the twenties. *American Psychologist, 55*(5), 469–480.

Arnett, J. J. (2007). Emerging adulthood: What is it, and what is it good for? *Child Development Perspectives, 1*(2), 68–73.

Arnett, J. J. (2016). Does emerging adulthood theory apply across social classes? National data on a persistent question. *Emerging Adulthood, 4*(4), 227–235.

Arnett, J. J., Žukauskienė, R., & Kazumi, S. (2014). The new life stage of emerging adulthood at ages 18-29 years: Implications for mental health. *Lancet Psychiatry, 1*(7), 569–576. doi:10.1016/S2215-0366(14)00080-7

Arnstein, R. (1984). Young adulthood: Signs of maturity. In D. Offer & M. Sabshin (Eds.), *Normality and the life cycle* (pp. 108–145). Basic Books.

Blos, P. (1967). The second individuation process of adolescence. *Psychoanalytic Study of the Child, 22*(1), 162–186.

Casey, B. J., Jones, R. M., & Hare, T. A. (2008). The adolescent brain. *Annals of the New York Academy of Sciences, 1124*(1), 111–126.

Colarusso, C. A. (1995). Traversing young adulthood: The male journey from 20 to 40. *Psychoanalytic Inquiry, 15*(1), 75–91.

Colarusso, C. A. (2000). Separation-individuation phenomena in adulthood: General concepts and the fifth individuation. *Journal of the American Psychoanalytic Association, 48*(4), 1467–1489.

Erikson, E. H. (1950). *Childhood and society.* Norton.

Erikson, E. H. (1968). *Identity: Youth and crisis.* Norton.

Gerber, A. J., & Gonzalez, M. Z. (2013). Structural and functional brain imaging in clinical psychology. In J. S. Comer & P. C. Kendall (Eds.), *The Oxford handbook of research strategies for clinical psychology* (pp. 165–187). Oxford University Press.

Gewin, V. (2012). Turning point: Craig Bennett. *Nature, 490*(7420), 437–437. https://doi.org/10.1038/nj7420-437a

Hauser, S. T., & Greene, W. M. (1991). Passages from late adolescence to early adulthood. In S. I. Greenspan & G. H. Pollock (Eds.), *The course of life: Adolescence* (pp. 377–405). International Universities Press.

Karpel, M. (1976). Individuation: From fusion to dialogue. *Family Process, 15*(1), 65–82.

Koepke, S., & Denissen, J. J. (2012). Dynamics of identity development and separation-individuation in parent–child relationships during adolescence and emerging adulthood: A conceptual integration. *Developmental Review, 32*(1), 67–88.

Lapsley, D., & Woodbury, R. D. (2016). Social cognitive development in emerging adulthood. In J. J. Arnett (Ed.), *The Oxford handbook of emerging adulthood* (pp. 142–159). Oxford University Press.

Mahler, M. S., Pine, F., & Bergman, A. (1975). *The psychological birth of the human infant.* Basic Books.

Marsh, R., Gerber, A. J., & Peterson, B. S. (2008). Neuroimaging studies of normal brain development and their relevance for understanding childhood neuropsychiatric disorders. *Journal of the American Academy of Child and Adolescent Psychiatry, 47*(11), 1233–1251. https://doi.org/10.1097/CHI.0b013e318185e703

McCabe, D. P., & Castel, A. D. (2008). Seeing is believing: The effect of brain images on judgments of scientific reasoning. *Cognition, 107*(1), 343–352. https://doi.org/10.1016/j.cognition.2007.07.017

Miller, J. M. (2017). Young or emerging adulthood: A psychoanalytic view. *Psychoanalytic Study of the Child, 70*(1), 8–21.

Nelson, L. J., & Padilla-Walker, L. M. (2013). Flourishing and floundering in emerging adult college students. *Emerging Adulthood, 1*(1), 67–78.

Pharo, H., Sim, C., Graham, M., Gross, J., & Hayne, H. (2011). Risky business: Executive function, personality, and reckless behavior during adolescence and emerging adulthood. *Behavioral Neuroscience, 125*(6), 970–978. https://doi.org/10.1037/a0025768

Pollock, G. C. (1998). Aging or aged: Development or pathology. In G. H. Pollock & S. I. Greenspan (Eds.), *The course of life: Completing the journey* (pp. 41–86). International Universities Press.

Steinberg, L. (2008). A social neuroscience perspective on adolescent risk-taking. *Developmental Review, 28*(1), 78–106.

Steinberg, L. (2014). *Age of opportunity: Lessons from the new science of adolescence.* Houghton Mifflin Harcourt.

Syed, M. (2016). *Emerging adulthood: Developmental stage, theory, or nonsense?* In J. J. Arnett (Ed.), *The Oxford handbook of emerging adulthood* (pp. 11–25). Oxford University Press.

Taber-Thomas, B., & Perez-Edgar K. (2016). Emerging adulthood brain development. In J. J. Arnett (Ed.), *The Oxford handbook of emerging adulthood* (pp. 126–141). Oxford University Press.

Tanner, J. L. (2006). Recentering during emerging adulthood: A critical turning point in life span human development. In J. J. Arnett & J. L. Tanner (Eds.), *Emerging adults in America: Coming of age in the 21st century* (pp. 21–55). American Psychological Association.

Victor, E. C., & Hariri, A. R. (2016). A neuroscience perspective on sexual risk behavior in adolescence and emerging adulthood. *Development and Psychopathology, 28*(2), 471–487. https://doi.org/10.1017/S0954579415001042

Intimacy Versus Isolation Revisited

Some New Ways to Think About Early Adulthood in the Light of Cultural and Technological Change

STEVE TUBER AND KAREN TOCATLY

For 70 years, the series of eight paradigms developed by Erik Erikson (1950) to describe the ebb and flow of human development have provided a remarkably useful heuristic from which to understand processes of change over the life span. Erikson describes each of the eight life stages as crises defined by the relation between individual development and functioning within society. In each paradigm, individuals are thought to struggle with intense personal strivings in the face of the societal and institutional requirements associated with a given life stage. Each challenge is therefore characterized by a goal and its converse developmental pitfall—with a favorable emergence from each crisis building upon successful negotiation of previous paradigms.

Framed as a series of relational alternatives throughout the life span, each of Erikson's stages aims to describe dimensions of experiencing, behaving, and unconscious inner states shaping one's ways of being within one's environment. In the first paradigm of basic trust versus basic mistrust, the infant negotiates ongoing testing of the relation between the internal and external, with the goal of this stage defined as attaining basic trust in the continuity of external caretakers, as well as one's own body's ability to endure urges. If the infant is fortunate enough to live within the sanctuary of much more trust than mistrust, there is then a greater likelihood that relations with others (and with one's self) will be marked by more *ruth* than ruthlessness (Tuber, 2008, p.

181). This, in turn, sets up the child to take on the world as a benign place of exploration and likely satisfaction. Each of the subsequent crises—autonomy versus shame and doubt, initiative versus guilt, industry versus inferiority, identity versus role confusion, intimacy versus isolation, generativity versus stagnation, and ego integrity versus despair—employs the gains of every earlier stage, intertwined with physiological and psychic change, to bolster individual progress from infancy to late adulthood.

While much of Erikson's work on the earliest stages of childhood has gone largely unquestioned, there have been enough societal and cultural changes over the past seven decades to suggest that some aspects of his theorizing may need refinement. We believe this is especially true regarding his two paradigms that attempt to capture the essence of the adolescent (identity versus role confusion) and young adult (intimacy versus isolation) developmental processes. For Erikson, the adolescent years provided the primary forum for the development of a work identity, as his notion of role is almost exclusively linked to finding a vocation that clarifies one's sense of what one is and will become.

Erikson describes the crisis of identity versus role confusion as a period in which adolescents, faced with impending adult duties and responsibilities, grapple with the tension between the way they are perceived by their surroundings and the way they feel themselves to be. He explains that this period is defined by a challenge to form a sense of ego identity—an integrated sense that one's previously established sense of inner continuity matches one's identity in the eyes of others. Such congruence between one's view of oneself and the perception of others is described as the prerequisite for the development of an adult vocation.

Accordingly, Erikson suggests that the inability to settle on a vocation is the primary source of disturbance for young people at this stage, who then, in an attempt to maintain a sense of cohesion, tend to overly identify with others. He describes this phenomenon as a particular, immature type of adolescent "falling in love" that is not primarily relational, but more an attempt to define one's image by projecting one's more diffused, murky identity onto others and gradually gaining clarity through the image reflected in return.

His young adult paradigm, by contrast, is almost exclusively a relationship identity paradigm, as it is devoted to whether we can love another and develop intimacy with them. It is only upon the emergence from the prior stage of identity formation that Erikson describes a young adult's readiness to merge a hard-won sense of identity with that of others. He posits that, upon the successful completion of the stage of identity versus role confusion, a young adult is prepared for the challenge of creating intimacy with another.

Erikson describes the goals of this latter stage as embedded in Freud's assertion of the goal of psychoanalytic treatment: To love and to work. He explains that Freud's reference to love means a mutual sexual connection, and a concomitant ability to work productively, developed in a previous life stage, which does not interfere with one's love relationships. At the end of this young adult stage one should be able to find a partner with whom one is willing to accompany through cycles of work, procreation, and recreation. The converse danger embedded in this challenge is isolation, defined as the avoidance of interactions that might potentiate intimacy.

We will first argue that the time frame Erikson posited for these two paradigms is no longer as relevant as it once was, given today's cultural vicissitudes. We will then speak to a number of cultural and technological changes in our society that play a role in how and why these paradigms should be amended. Further, we will argue that these identity paradigms now occur at the same time and that this merger accounts for much of the stress regarding young adulthood. We will also offer some ways in which the current cultural climate also enhances psychological well-being and thus fortifies the young person's quest for an authentic identity.

We must begin with a very large caveat. Almost all of what we will suggest in this chapter is derived from assumptions regarding social class. That is, persons raised in socioeconomically marginalized conditions often do not have the luxury to be responsive to a large number of the points we will be making about cultural changes, and thus they might react to them in very different ways than what we are suggesting here. Even more fundamentally, there are aspects of the attenuation of the early adult process that are simply not possible without economic viability. It is beyond the scope of this chapter to do more than speak broadly to the role that social class "injuries" (Cobb & Sennett, 1993) often play in defining young adulthood. We ask your indulgence while we focus in this chapter on understanding young adulthood largely through a middle-class to affluent-class prism, although we will point out on occasion where socioeconomic status issues intercede in the process of becoming a viable adult. We must also add that, due to the systemic racial inequities in America for over 400 years and counting, it is impossible to disentangle socioeconomic status from race in America, and thus this theorizing is also limited in its capacity to reflect on being impoverished, Black, and Brown as well.

IMPEDIMENTS TO A FULLY AUTHENTIC LIFE: THE ROLE OF CULTURAL FORCES THAT MERGE ERIKSON'S TWO PARADIGMS

Erikson wrote in an era in which a far smaller percentage of the population went to college, and thus a work identity was more likely to be established beginning in middle to late adolescence. Employment choices were often initiated while in high school or instead of high school, with the expectation that one's chosen occupation coalesced by one's late teens to early 20s. Those going to college were also expected to finalize the choice of a profession during their college years—such that one's work identity was essentially a prerequisite for early adulthood and not a process begun in early adulthood. It is thus no coincidence that Erikson's fifth stage of development, the working through of issues regarding identity versus role confusion, was seen as an inherently adolescent process. One used the latency phase, described by Erikson as the fourth stage, to develop the capacity for work (industry), and then this capacity was shaped into a specific field of study or vocation that defined one's role or work identity. Those persons who had not sufficiently mastered earlier phases of development and/or were arrested psychologically during this adolescent process were described as suffering from role confusion. What is most salient from our point of view is that the splitting of work identity from relationship identity that Erikson's paradigms depict is not nearly as viable in the developmental process of today's young adult. There has been a shift in time such that neither work nor relationship identity are settled prior to young adulthood but rather are struggled with in tandem throughout one's 20s and 30s. Rather than seeing this ongoing struggle as an extension of adolescence, which we feel gives a negative connotation to the teenage years, we prefer to describe the linking of work and love identities as a dual task that has made young adulthood more complex and thus more likely to take a greater amount of time to work through.

A socioeconomic reality that can impact simultaneously both the work and relationship identity process lies in the greater difficulty in recent years of a large swath of the late adolescent and early adult population in being able to afford to pay for their own autonomous housing separate from their parents. Relying on parents for housing and/or food makes problematic the notion of creating a financially independent identity in the private space necessary for a critical part of adult development to take root. It simultaneously limits the privacy necessary for intimate relationships to prosper, thus affecting both aspects of identity development. A good part of what allows young adults to feel separate from their parents sufficiently to more clearly determine what aspects of their parents they wish to identify with or away from is a feeling of financial independence. The greater the financial dependence upon one's parents, all things being equal, the harder it will be to engender a truly sep-arate sense of self, thus making the early adult process still more attenuated.

TIME SPEEDS UP

Paradoxically, while the dual dilemmas of establishing both work and inti-mate identities as a young adult may slow down and attenuate these develop-mental issues well into one's 30s, people reaching adolescence in this age of internet-driven technologies cannot help but be sped up by having access to enormously inflated arenas of information at lightning speed. The degree to which information is just a few clicks away has altered what it means to find out about the world and to be found out by others.

FINDING OUT ABOUT THE WORLD
IN THE CLICK OF AN EYE

Having that kind of near-immediate access to information allows no time to maintain the illusion that one's ideas are unique and cannot be questioned. If we can be fact-checked in real time, what does this do to the need of young adults to define themselves independently from the ideas of others? An ado-lescent may read a brief article on communism, as an example, and become infatuated with its promise of equality; posting this stance on social media, however, can be met within moments by a barrage of negative reaction. There is a real need, we believe, to have at least some moments when one's ideas can stand unquestioned or unchallenged. At the very least, this time lag allows for a period of reflection on what has been said or not said. The relentless availabil-ity of information and the implicit or explicit need to respond immediately to information received impinges on our capacity to be alone (Winnicott, 1965a). Feeling safe and vibrant when alone is a result of endless opportunities, begin-ning in infancy, to take the secure base of caretakers for granted—therefore allowing for a focus on one's inner life in relation to the world of objects. This focus takes time and, thus, a lack of time to reflect negates the space to sit with one's own ideas and lessens the capacity to feel practiced in the useful art of being alone at times.

As the first author has argued elsewhere (Tuber, 2008), the diminution of the capacity to be alone has adverse effects on the development of a capacity for playfulness, which in turn hinders the development of a sense of vitality so necessary to a sense of authentic identity. The ability to stop and reflect on what others have said or done and our responses to them provides a unique imperative to establish what Winnicott (1965b) called "going on being," a state of mind that allows reverie, promotes immediacy, and sustains a sense of uniqueness—all variables critical to feeling comfortable in one's own skin. Losing this reflection time in the midst of high-speed digital communication places a young adult at risk for assimilating herself into modes of communication that estrange, rather than solidify, identity formation. In the abovementioned example of a young "communist" adult sharing ideological excitement that she has not yet had the space to reflect upon on her own, there is a risk of possibly being shaped by others' reactions more than her own authentic mind. In this vein, it is striking to wonder what the ongoing quarantine in the face of the COVID-19 pandemic can do to both impair and propel one's capacity for aloneness. Winnicott (1965a) speaks of how solitary confinement might be bearable for someone with the capacity to be alone, but catastrophic for someone without that capacity. Is such a confinement akin to being quarantined alone? Or is the capacity for solitude that makes quarantine bearable, and even enhancing, reflected in the capacity to feel good about being alone?

THE NEED FOR A TRANSITIONAL SPACE IN THE 21ST CENTURY

There are of course many times when having information at our fingertips is vital, defining, and capable of augmenting our sense of self. But the need for a transitional space (Winnicott, 1971; Tuber, 2019), a place that is both not fully real yet not simply fantasy, is a uniquely powerful mechanism that allows the self to feel authentic and private even while in the midst of others. Winnicott describes the notion of a transitional space in a way that has direct relevance to our discussion of early adulthood:

> It is usual to refer to reality testing and to make a clear distinction between perception and apperception. I am here staking a claim for an

intermediate state between a baby's inability and his growing ability to recognize and accept reality. I am therefore studying the substance of illusion, that which is allowed to the infant, and which in adult life is inherent in art and religion, and yet becomes the hallmark of madness when an adult puts too powerful a claim on the credulity of others, forcing them to acknowledge a sharing of illusion that is not their own. (Winnicott, 1965a, p. 3)

How is this relevant to the processes of early adulthood? This gap between perception and apperception is a dilemma that each of us struggles with and acknowledges to different degrees, in which the greater the comfort with acknowledging this gap, the greater the comfort with the ability to play with inner versus outer realities. This capacity to play needs time and space to develop, and is fragile enough that it needs to be nurtured throughout life.

This need for playfulness to be continually protected and nurtured is exactly why the maintenance of transitional space is still crucial in the early adult years. If such a space is squeezed shut by what can feel like a bombardment of information coming in rapid-fire fashion, how does the young adult keep their sense of self intact and alive?

Taken from a nonclinical perspective, the need to daydream (Singer, 2009) is similarly an inherent part of the human experience, allowing us to master present problems as well as to sit with alternative realities that comfort and excite us. What happens to fostering daydream time or cultivating transitional-space time when there is almost literally no time between a question and a response? We are all also familiar historically with how the demands in the workplace have sped up—the changes from handwritten, posted letters to telephone conversations to reduce downtime was a profound enough shift through the mid-19th and early 20th centuries. But the shift from telephone calls to the immediacy of email, text, or tweet has prompted further expectations that one needs to respond to queries immediately and hence in an almost nonstop fashion. Indeed, working from home during the pandemic may render the distinction between home as a time for respite, and work as being outside the home, irrevocably transformed. Has the pace of information outdistanced the capacity to take note of ourselves, so that we may provide or receive answers to our questions but without sufficient time to check in with ourselves about what our answers actually say about us, or what they might mean to us? If what young adults lose, in their access to quantum leaps in information to aid decision making, is their capacity to be alone in a transitional space of their own making, do they lose precious aspects of identity making? We believe that this is certainly a risk that needs further exploration.

Related to this potential consequence of a lack of transitional experience and aloneness due to the overly rapid flow of information to process are the exacting standards it places on what is communicated. Constant fact-checking also can distort the sense of what is adequate or good enough and place the young adult in a seemingly never-ending spiral of constantly striving for perfection, that the work produced can never be fast enough or complete enough. What does this do to the developing work identity of a young adult? One can easily speculate as to the impact on one's self-esteem of this ratcheting up of demands for increased exactness. The most obvious danger is the internalization of the feeling that one is never good enough. We can further speculate that this feeling of constant shortcomings at work may interfere with the self-confidence necessary to create and sustain intimacy, although it is also quite possible that both partners may use their alienation from work as a means to forge a more intimate sharing of the alienation work induces—leading to a shared misery that brings greater closeness. In either case, we posit that it is this potential diminution of transitional space that may lie at the heart of disturbance in the process of establishing both a work and a love identity. We will discuss the clinical implications of this loss in our last section.

BEING FOUND OUT IN THE CLICK OF AN EYE

The greater rapidity of information processing is challenging enough to our work identities, but the application of this processing power to our social identities is perhaps even more unsettling to the development of a capacity for intimacy. As unpleasant as blind dates set up by friends might be, or family-arranged marriages in an earlier era, or even going to a bar to meet others, what has the advent of social media applications done to the decision-making process of whom to be intimate with? Online bios for dating apps place young adults' superficial self-descriptions in an arena open to millions. They also have the illusory side effect of allowing the fantasy of seeking ever-greater perfection in a mate because there is such a plethora to choose from. Of course, if one is not being chosen despite the proliferation of possibilities, the assault on one's self-esteem can also be markedly greater than if one is rejected on a one-on-one basis. The idea that there is always another potential date available to be conjured up in moments cannot help but place an inordinate burden on first impressions and a concomitant illusion that a perfect choice is just another click away. To put this dilemma in a way that Winnicott would have liked, the more we are so readily and publicly found, the more difficult it is to have periods of necessarily being lost in ourselves, a loss that is ultimately a necessary precondition for authenticity. Paradoxically, to never have the feeling of being lost, even if only in one's thoughts, makes it far more difficult to feel firmly found to one's self, the true precondition for identity formation. Being comfortable with transitory feelings of being lost is another way of saying that the capacity for being comfortable with aloneness is an invaluable tool in the identity-making process.

Yet another aspect of this complex sense of being lost and found is related to those digital social media that allow one to post pictures of oneself to an immediate large audience. While this ability to share one's life experiences with others has many positive dimensions, it also raises the specter of a carefully curated false self. This curated quality feeds on itself so that it fosters the presentation of a coherent, if biased, self—capable of generating envy in others and/or hiding a less than glamorous lifestyle. If young adults must assume that such glamour is a vital part of one's digital media presentation, it leaves open the possibility that a vicious cycle emerges where one feels compelled to respond to others' glamorous posts with an even more heavily curated post of one's own. The notion that these media thus enhance the possibility of more crystalized false selves is not without merit. The implications of this vicious cycle suggest that for those persons struggling most powerfully with the coming together of their identity into a coherent whole, the potential for being dominated by digital media rather than seeing it as a tool for self-expression is manifest and problematic.

THE ROLE OF AUTONOMY IN THE IDENTITY FORMATION PROCESS

One of Erikson's great contributions is how his earlier stages continue to play out across the life span. One can especially see a link between the development in Stage Two of a sense of autonomy and the pairing of this autonomy with the capacity for industry in Stage Four, and then on to the early adult issues of work and relationship identities. The capacity to want to do things on one's own terms cultivates a sense of competence and mastery (White, 1960), while the notion of practice and repetition building ever more capable competencies is a virtuous cycle that makes work (industry) a vital part of one's identity. This industry then leads to further competence if one is able to choose a vocation in one's early adult years that builds on the intrinsic motivation of competence via the extrinsic motivation of getting paid and/or appreciated for what one can do. Erikson's stage model thus is still fundamentally sound in its depiction of current stages being bolstered or harmed by previous stages. What is being posited here is that early adulthood in the 21st century has become an amalgam of both a work and love identity that Erikson saw as separate processes that begin in adolescence, but which may now be more accurately viewed as reaching their crucial period in early adulthood.

Adolescence is no longer the prime era for the consolidation of a work role. With the many changes in the workplace as a result of artificial intelligence, globalized markets, and internet technologies, it is increasingly less likely that a single career choice will capture the experience of young adults. Instead, a larger number of occupations, driven more by skill than by job title, will make it far more likely that young adults will have multiple work identities all through their 20s and 30s, with the real possibility that a coalesced, singular work identity will become the exception rather than the rule across a lifetime. What impact will this have on young adult development? It is hoped that a work identity will come to be seen as a process more than the attainment of specific content. One can envision, in the best-case scenario, that young adults can come to enjoy the process of burnishing new skills throughout their adult lifetimes and view this openness and flexibility as evidence of a more vital, creative life rather than as a confusing, disruptive series of new challenges.

CHANGES IN THE EXPERIENCE OF SPACE

While we have discussed the ways in which a sense of time has simultaneously been both sped up and slowed down by shifts in culture and technology, it is also important to note the difference in conceptions of space and distance as compared to the era in which Erikson created his eight paradigms for development. It is certainly well within the first author's lifetime that a long-distance call to Europe or elsewhere was a major event, costing a significant amount of money and used only for a special occasion or in an emergency. Comparing that to the currently effortless linking of persons around the world by both voice and picture creates the sense that the world is indeed an ever-smaller place. Once again, however, a paradox reigns. The globalization of economic markets and industries also carries with it the very real possibility that one may have to travel or move halfway around the world to maintain or enhance one's employment prospects. While the now-displaced person can far more easily contact those left behind than could be done in earlier eras, there is still the reality that they cannot be readily touched or held by those left behind. The increasing likelihood that multiple generations of families may no longer live in the same city or even country may simultaneously enhance separateness but at the cost of losing intimate contact with family members. If an autonomous identity is made too autonomous by necessary moves far from home, one can speculate as to what is lost in intimacy despite what might be gained in separateness.

ONE POSITIVE CONTRIBUTION OF THE DIGITAL AGE TO IDENTITY FORMATION

Although it is relatively easy to wax eloquent on the dangers of the digital age to the consolidation of a sense of both a work and an intimate self, it is necessary to speak to cultural changes that enhance identity formation. One positive contributor also has to do with the way time has been shaped by technological enhancements.

This is especially apparent for women, with advances in the technology behind storing and freezing eggs and embryos so that pregnancy can be fostered in ways that stretch out the biological clock, giving women more time to decide when and how to have a child or children. On the one hand, if technology permits women to more easily have children into their 40s, it certainly gives them far more time to both enhance and develop their professional aspirations, as well as more time to decide upon a mate to raise the child with, if such a mate is desired. On the other hand, this added time stretches out and hence attenuates the time without children, which may have adverse effects on the increased maturity that parenthood often brings. To the extent that parenthood may enhance one's capacity for devotion and altruism, such an attenuation may increase the time it takes to fully cohere an adult identity. It is essential to stress here that the capacity for intimacy that Erikson describes is not linearly related to the desire to have children for either men or women. However, the stretching of the biological clock may make it easier for some women to figure out ways to balance career and family that did not exist prior to the 21st century.

We must again raise the role that social class plays in this depiction of how reproductive technologies may make young adulthood an easier place from which to derive both work and relationship identities. Having access to these very expensive technologies is far beyond the financial capacities of most middle-class and poor people. Indeed, at present only a very small percentage of the population can afford such procedures, rendering it a true luxury only for those that can.

THE EFFECT OF THESE SHIFTS IN EARLY ADULTHOOD ON PARENTS

In an earlier work (Tuber, 2016), the first author spoke to the changes that occur over the adult life span vis-à-vis one's experience of being essential to one's children. The utter dependency of infants on caretakers sets up a rubric whereby parents may derive a large portion of their self-esteem from their caretaking prowess, yet must be ever alert for allowing, and indeed fostering, the emerging autonomy of their children. The first author then proposed a continuum from pure essentialness, to being essential on call, to being relevant to one's children as they move across the life span into their own adulthood. This continuum may be usefully linked to our discussion here about young adults' need for their parents' financial care, as the cost of independent housing may be too high for young adults after finishing their education (or pursuing graduate education). If a work and love identity is formed, ideally, in the cauldron of autonomous living, how does living in a home with one's parents and/or being financially dependent upon them for rent affect this emerging identity? Perhaps of equal importance, how does this attenuated parent–child relationship affect the parent and their ability to allow their child the freedom to be on their own? Does it extend the parent's wish to be essential? Does it offend the parent's wish not to be burdened by their child's needs? It is of course likely to be a measure of both points on this parenting continuum. In either case, it speaks to the vital need for parents and their young adults to have the ability to speak together openly about these issues and suggests a useful content area for therapists to explore in their work with either young adults or older adults who live with adult children in their homes. The first author and his wife have, at the time of this writing (June 2020) been spending the past three months with their eldest son, his wife, and their now six-month-old daughter. Many an evening has been spent with the four adults speaking to the pluses and minuses of this arrangement, with the consensus so far that the pluses have outweighed the minuses!

THE ROLE OF SOCIAL CLASS AND WELL-BEING IN CAREER AND FAMILIAL TRAJECTORIES

A decision to forge one's work identity before one focuses on a relationship is very much affected by the ability to easily pay for the cost of higher education or internships that foster later career choices. With familial financial support, a decision to go to graduate school, for example, becomes far less an exercise in debt collection and far more a process of exploring different fields before finding the vocational choice one feels most vitalized by. In a world where money is no or little object, the luxury of taking the time to consolidate a work identity over the better part of one's 20s and then to have the similar luxury of using reproductive technologies to allow one to safely and effectively become a parent in one's 30s or 40s markedly changes the dynamics involved in consolidating an identity capable of intimacy. To the extent that such choices are largely outside the realm of possibility for poor or working-class people, it once again reifies the concept of how race and class create very different possibilities and options in the working through of life's challenges across the life span.

Another potential effect of social class on early adulthood is that for affluent people, this time may also be viewed as a time for emotional growth operationalized by the far greater prevalence and awareness of the importance of focusing on emotional well-being as a necessary part of one's identity. While we may cynically note that the greater pressures and alienation of the work space that we defined above can wreak havoc on the formation of an authentic, private self in the first place, it is also striking to note how our culture has made an industry out of ways of promoting inner calmness, whether through yoga, meditation, or psychotherapy, and the focus on wellness in general as an expectation in the workplace and in college settings.

Similarly, the greater emphasis on emotional happiness has made choosing a mate more of a psychological phenomenon than in earlier eras. A focus on a couple's capacity to engage in conflict clearly and openly without lingering resentments has become part of the world of self-help books, podcasts, and television. We are thus in the paradoxical position of creating cultural and technological forces that impair authenticity at the same time as we have far greater awareness of the toxicity of these forces. Yet another paradox exists in terms of the implicit messages in the pursuit of well-being. For some, this pursuit becomes a holy grail of sorts, with the need to be increasingly perfect at "well-beingness" or self-care simply another burden to feel inadequate about. These two paradoxes suggest questions on both micro and macro levels. On the microlevel of individual development, does the balance between estrangement and greater self-awareness tilt in the direction of pathology or healthy adaptation for the young adult? On the macrolevel of societal development, does the balance between environmental estrangement (climate change, as one example) and globalizing centrifugal forces on the one hand, and enhanced connectivity and greater individual choice on the other, tilt toward the alienation of society or a greater awareness that we are all in this together? It truly remains to be seen how this balance will tip on both individual and societal levels.

CLINICAL IMPLICATIONS OF THESE EARLY ADULTHOOD DILEMMAS

We have hinted earlier at the many repercussions of technological and cultural changes for society at both the individual and collective levels. From a clinical perspective, it seems most relevant to stress how the condensation of time and the expansion of space may both play a disturbing role in the malformation of both work and intimacy identities for young adults. These changes in time and space, moreover, may be contradictory, creating a push–pull on the psyche that can leave a given individual abuzz with anxiety or gripped by assaults on self-esteem that make dysthymia an ever-present threat.

Late adolescence and early adulthood have always been a period in which existential threat and/or confusion can and even should be of powerful import. Finding one's place in the worlds of work and love are the two most primary and hence daunting tasks of our lifetimes, and it is only in young adulthood that the latitude to explore these feelings first goes beyond solely an internal struggle to that of its implementation in the adult world. This taking off beyond the limits of one's family of origin has always placed significant stress on the working through of separation from family at the same time as one focuses on finding peers to replace many of those familial ties. Developing a perspective on the strengths and limitations of one's family (especially one's parents) provides the impetus to become aware of what aspects of these family members one wishes to identify with and what aspects to identify away from. It is also essential to stress in this context that the changes we have described were not present when the young adult's parents were growing up. Therefore, the aspects of one's parents that the young adult may internalize simply did not contain the impact of the digital age. Thus, many of the implications of this era, with which the young adult wrestles daily, are often beyond the ken of their parents. This provides a likely potential disconnect between parent and young adult exactly at the phase of life when the wisdom of parental experience ought to be helpful to the young adult's emerging autonomy. The stress of an attenuated financial dependence on parents who truly don't get what their children are going through is a definite obstacle to the process of fully individuating. To the extent that the young adult has happily internalized aspects of their parent's values, wishes, and needs and yet finds that these internalizations do not necessarily apply to the digital age, there is still another possible obstacle to working through this phase of development. It also suggests another reason why the capacity to be alone and comfortable with transitional space/reverie is so crucial to emotional well-being, for if the child is indeed disconnected from their parents in these arenas, the need to rely upon one's own inner resources is that much more salient.

These dilemmas existed well before the idea of an internet even crossed the minds of the pioneers of this new way of communicating. But the advent of these technologies has largely transpired much faster than anyone has been able to anticipate the psychological consequences of these advances. As clinicians, we must recognize that for people now in their 20s and 30s, these technological advances were simply not there during their early childhood, so that they have not had ample time to digest their implications. If we look at these advances from the viewpoint of their potential assaults on (1) the capacity to be alone, (2) the capacity to maintain a psychological space neither purely reality based nor delusional, and (3) the capacity for reverie and reflection, we can better appreciate the meaning behind some of the symptoms these young people may bring to our consulting rooms. Certainly the feeling that one can never be good enough to keep pace with technological changes may be the emotional manifestation of an underlying failure to feel competent and hence to derive an intrinsic satisfaction from working. Similarly, the sense that one must be the perfect mate or be forever digitally looking to find the perfect mate can easily be the manifestation of underlying malformations in the capacity to be alone. The constant need to produce at work, moreover, can be a function of a flight from reverie that speaks to a deficit in the capacity to find reflection both comforting and growth enhancing. The fear of reverie can also be a function of the fear of maintaining the ability to conjure a transitional space that provides the spawning ground for creativity and spirituality. It is imperative that clinicians see these symptoms as wholly understandable consequences of technologies that have fundamentally altered how time and space are processed, and hence how these changes have altered the phenomenological experience of everyday living for these young people. It is also crucial to note how the disconnects between these new cultural imperatives and the disparate experiences of the parents of these young adults in these technological arenas may be necessary aspects of therapeutic work with both parents and their adult children. The need for therapists to become more culturally fluent in order to appreciate their young patients' dilemmas is certainly relevant.

It is hoped that the depiction of the impact of these cultural and technological changes makes plain how the adolescent and early adult phases that Erikson described as sequential in 1950 have needed alteration to fit these changing times. In particular, it is important to link the attainment of a work identity and its vicissitudes to the parallel vicissitudes of the development of a capacity for intimacy. Both these processes are more clearly seen as part of a push-pull dialectic that may indeed take up the bulk of one's 20s and 30s and cannot be usefully seen as separate phenomena. While more affluent folks can more luxuriously place either work or love as something to develop first and thus keep the sequence Erikson described (albeit during young adulthood and not during adolescence) intact, even the most affluent are far from immune to the intrinsic difficulties of the new work environment, nor can affluence guarantee that finding a mate who is good enough can be felt to be sustainable. Certainly, for the vast majority of young adults who are not affluent, the pressure to have it all, both job and mate, can be truly disabling. This can be especially exhausting to Black men and women, for whom the battle against the insidious effects of systemic racism place additional demands on the already daunting tasks of creating viable work and love habitats.

A FINAL NOTE

If one can see the merits of our arguments regarding how these technological and cultural shifts can wreak havoc on the capacity to feel authentic, alone and yet comfortable with reverie, one can also see how a psychodynamically-oriented talk therapy could be a compelling antidote to many of the difficulties that arise for these young adults, particularly if they are affluent enough to afford it.

The idea of a regular, predictable, calm, slow-paced interaction with a caring, concerned other that promotes reverie, creativity, and looking inward seems, at face value, to be a compelling partial remedy to these existential threats facing young people. The fact that psychotherapy in general is viewed with far less stigma than in the past and is now seen more often as part of a wellness plan, as opposed to a place for mental illness to be ameliorated, further increases the chances that such a psychotherapy experience may be increasingly valued. This does, however, beg the question of whether these changes have also induced such a fear of self-reflection that any type of psychotherapy process would be seen as taking too long, or not being perfect enough, making in-depth psychotherapy feel especially dangerous.

Steve Tuber is Professor of Psychology, Director of Clinical Training, and Program Head of the doctoral program in clinical psychology at the City College of New York. He is the author and/or editor of 12 books and over 150 papers in the intertwining fields of the assessment and treatment of children and adults. He has won or been nominated for numerous awards in these fields, as well as for his contributions to the doctoral program he has run for over 20 years.

Karen Tocatly is a doctoral student in the clinical psychology program at the City College of New York. She is a therapist in training at the Psychological Center, where she treats children and adults.

REFERENCES

Cobb, J., & Sennett, R. (1993). *The hidden injuries of class.* Norton.

Erikson, E. (1950). *Childhood and society.* Norton.

Singer, J. (2009). Researching imaginative play and adult consciousness: Implications for daily and literary creativity. *Psychology of Aesthetics, Creativity and the Arts, 3*(4), 190–199.

Tuber, S. (2008). *Attachment, play, and authenticity: A Winnicott primer.* Rowman and Littlefield.

Tuber, S. (2016). *Parenting: Contemporary clinical perspectives.* Rowman and Littlefield.

Tuber, S. (2019). *Attachment, play, and authenticity: Winnicott in clinical context.* Rowman and Littlefield.

White, R. (1960). Motivation reconsidered: The concept of competence. *Psychological Review,* 66, 297–333.

Winnicott, D. (1965a). The capacity to be alone. In *Maturational Processes and the Facilitating Environment.* International Universities Press.

Winnicott, D. (1965b). The theory of the parent-infant relationship. In *Maturational Processes and the Facilitating Environment.* International Universities Press.

Winnicott, D. (1971). Transitional objects and transitional phenomena. In *Playing and Reality.* Tavistock.

CHAPTER 3

Substance Use and Young Adults

The Good, the Bad, and the Not So Ugly

CHANTEL T. EBRAHIMI, ALEXANDRIA G. BAUER,
AND DENISE HIEN

H istorically, when the words *substance use* and *young adults* were paired together in the literature or media, it usually suggested a public health concern, a problem, and/or a bad, unhealthy behavior. Research has shown that substance use during this developmental period is considered a harmful, negative, risky behavior that is correlated with unfavorable physical, economic, and mental health outcomes (Moss et al., 2014; Jessor et al., 2006; Aarons et al., 1999). Although we recognize and acknowledge past research, the ongoing opioid epidemic affecting the majority of young people in both rural and urban US settings (Center for Behavioral Health Statistics and Quality, 2020), and that overall substance misuse and addiction is a societal issue that is highly criminalized, this chapter's goal is not to outline what we already know, which is all the harmful ways in which substances interact with the self. Rather, our goal is to provide alternate explanations for why young people engage in substance use and their motivations for continued use through adulthood—explanations that honor their identity development, their autonomy, their desire for exploration, and their need to socialize. Arnett (2000) coined the term *emerging adults* to define this unique developmental period, from the late teens through the 20s, primarily focusing on ages 18–35, which is characterized by exploration, identity formation, role changes, and then ultimately the settling-down period, which usually occurs during the late 20s or early 30s. A unique aspect of this period of life is that it looks different demographically from the beginning to the end—young adults go from living with their parents to cohabitating with partners to forming a family. Further, five main social domains have been identified during this period: education, living situation, employment, cohabitation/marriage, and parenthood (Cadigan et al., 2019), and this chapter explores each of these domains and domain changes with respect to substance use behaviors. We do want to clarify that we acknowledge the differences in emerging adulthood across individuals, racial and ethnic groups, and socioeconomic status and that this chapter follows Arnett's (2000) broad theory of this developmental period.

PREVALENCE RATES

Before we explore the "not so ugly" part of young adult substance use patterns, it is important to understand the reality, the good and the bad, of the situation. It comes as no surprise that rates of alcohol and substance use among youth and young adults are high (Grucza et al., 2018). There are disparities in use, though. Young adults in rural areas are more likely to use than their urban peers (Lambert et al., 2008). Males report greater sustained levels of substance use through young adulthood (Chen & Jacobson, 2012). Historically, men have drunk more alcohol than women, but more recent studies show that drinking prevalence rates are increasing faster for women than for men (Grucza et al., 2018), thus closing the gap in gender differences (White, 2020). Sexual minorities use substances more than their heterosexual peers (Schuler et al., 2018). Substance use increases rapidly from early adolescence to emerging adulthood in white youth, but substance use rates peak in African Americans during the later part of young adulthood, where after the age of 30 African Americans continue to show higher levels of cigarette smoking and marijuana use (Chen & Jacobson, 2012). And last, Hispanic youth show a peak in substance use during early adolescence, but a decline in emerging adulthood (Chen & Jacobson, 2012). We will now outline the prevalence rates of substances commonly used among the young adult population as follows: alcohol; cigarettes, with a particular emphasis on e-cigarettes/vaping; cannabis; and illegal drugs, with a focus on cocaine, heroin, and prescription drugs.

Alcohol

It comes as no surprise that young adults drink alcohol. Lee and Sher (2018) observed the highest peak in drinking rates during the early 20s, which maps well with college entrance and the legal age for drinking in the United States. But as suspected with both the "maturing out" hypothesis and prefrontal cortex development, drinking rates slowly decline with age. For example, statistics show that in 2019, 35.7% of young adults 18–20 years of age used alcohol. The number almost doubled to 66.2% between ages 21 and 25, then decreased slightly between ages 26 and 29 to 64.9% (Elflein, 2020). Results for binge drinkers looked a little different, but a similar decline was also observed— binge drinking after the age bracket 21–25 (41.6%) decreased to 36.5% for 30- to 34-year-olds (Elflein, 2020).

Cigarettes

In 2019, 14% of adults aged 18 years or older smoked cigarettes—nearly 7% lower than in 2005 (CDC, 2020). Current cigarette smoking was lowest among people aged 18–24 years (8%), but highest among those 25–44 years of age (16.7%). Cigarette smoking rates do not include e-cigarettes or vapes.

Vaping

The prevalence of vaping marijuana and nicotine has been increasing over the years, and young adults aged 18–22 are among the highest users. Monitoring the Future (MTF), an ongoing, annual set of surveys of a nationally representative sample of US youth and young adults, noted that in 2018 "the annual and 30-day increases in vaping marijuana and nicotine, especially among those aged 19–22, [were] among the largest in MTF history for any substance" (Johnston et al., 2019, p. 8). And in 2019, the MTF study showed that 22% of young adults reported having vaped marijuana at least once in the past year, and 13% reported vaping marijuana at least once in the past 30 days (Schulenberg et al., 2020). The rates are a little higher for nicotine: 25% reported having vaped nicotine at least once in the past year, and 15% reported vaping at least once in the past 30 days. Although cigarette smoking rates are relatively low between the ages of 18 and 25, e-cigarette use rates are high, indicating that these youth are more likely to choose e-cigarettes or vapes over cigarettes. The bit of good news is that the 30-day prevalence of e-cigarette smoking decreased in 2020, according to MTF (Johnston et al., 2021).

Cannabis

After tobacco and alcohol, marijuana is the next most commonly used drug for young people—in 2018, 11.8 million young adults reported using marijuana in the past year (NIDA, 2021). In 2019, marijuana use increased to all-time highs for young adults (ages 19–28), where 40% used marijuana at least once in the past year, 27% used at least once in the past 30 days, and 9.4% used marijuana daily in the past 30 days (Johnston et al., 2020). Another data set shows that nearly a quarter (22%) of all 18- to 29-year-olds currently smoke marijuana and 11% of 30- to 49-year-olds smoke marijuana (Statista Research Department, 2020), suggesting that marijuana is a drug that's commonly used among younger adults, and its use tapers out over time.

Illicit Drugs: Ecstasy, Cocaine, Nonprescription Opioids

Although the opioid epidemic is ongoing, rates of heroin use (1.6%) for adults aged 18 to 25 was lower than lifetime cocaine use (11.3%) in 2016. But when looking at heroin use combined with opioid pain reliever misuse, 7.3% of young adults used in the past year, compared to 5.6% who used cocaine (Center for Behavioral Health Statistics and Quality, 2017). In 2016, the use of cocaine (1.4%), heroin (0.3%), and opioids (4.0%) decreased in persons aged 26 or older. According to the MTF study, annual use of illicit drugs from 2014 to 2019 remained steady, with a slow decline observed in 2019 (Schulenberg et al., 2020). But annual cocaine use increased to 6.5% and annual use of non-medical narcotics other than heroin, amphetamines, sedatives, tranquilizers, and MDMA all decreased significantly between 2014 and 2019.

Prescription Drug Sharing

It is also important to note the increasing prevalence of prescription sharing, as almost 25% of 12- to 44-year-olds share or borrow prescription medications (Goldsworthy et al., 2008; Petersen et al., 2008). Overall, prescription drug sharing was higher among young adults (18–35), peaking around the early 20s (Petersen et al., 2008). Stimulant drugs like Adderall, prescribed for attention-deficit/hyperactivity disorder (ADHD) patients, are commonly shared and borrowed between young adult college students to help with focus and attention. Adderall is now colloquialized as the "study drug." In 2016, Adderall was the most abused prescription drug in the United States, where nearly 20% of all college students had shared and borrowed this study drug (Benson, 2006). In fact, statistics show that Adderall was more abused than OxyContin in 2016 (Mikulic, 2021)—which begs the following question: will our next drug crisis be the Adderall crisis?

THE CHANGING LEGAL LANDSCAPE

It is important to consider the current legal and political context around substances, including evolving drug policies that result in decriminalization or legalization of drugs. At the time of this writing, at least 34 states have legalized cannabis for medicinal or recreational purposes, although its use remains illegal at the federal level. Furthermore, Oregon recently became the first state to decriminalize possession of all substances. This is a distinct shift from the way that substance use has historically been considered, which greatly stigmatized people who used substances, traditionally focused on punitive strategies to discourage use, and greatly contributed to disparities in incarceration—particularly among Black and African American communities (Joyce et al., 2019). There have also been calls to overhaul substance use policies following the COVID-19 pandemic, with opportunities to promote greater equity and innovation in our approach to substance use (del Pozo & Beletsky, 2020; Hien et al., 2021).

Researchers, policy makers, and public health experts continue to research and discuss best practices and strategies for avoiding harms related to substances and ensuring public health and safety (Shover & Humphreys, 2019; Bowles et al., 2017; Vicknasingam et al., 2018; Husak, 2003; Hall & Lynskey, 2016; Caulkins & Reuter, 2021). Researchers have also examined the impact of decriminalization on indirect outcomes that may influence use, such as pricing of illicit substances (Félix & Portugal, 2017). Recommendations have centered on coordination between multiple sectors to plan and implement regulations; oversight from the medical and scientific communities, particularly for medicinal substance use; and continued epidemiological monitoring of public health outcomes. Nationally, attitudes toward decriminalization and legalization have varied across populations and by type of substance (Hammond et al., 2020), although attitudes may be more favorable among young adults (Parnes et al., 2018; Rudy et al., 2020; Wen et al., 2019; Amroussia et al., 2020). It has also been suggested that drug policies contribute to national migration patterns, with some people being willing to relocate to states where substances have been legalized (Zambiasi & Stillman, 2020). This is also true of college students, who may make the decision to attend a college based on local laws (Parnes et al., 2018).

One key consideration, particularly for young adults, is whether these changing attitudes and policies lead to changes in use (Leung et al., 2018; Budney & Borodovsky, 2017), particularly given risks for adverse outcomes during development (Hall et al., 2020). Young adults such as college students, who are more strongly influenced to migrate by states' relaxed drug policies, have shown greater substance use (Parnes et al., 2018). Early research has suggested differential impacts of medical versus recreational cannabis legalization, but both types of policy change have been associated with increases in young adult cannabis use (Smart & Pacula, 2019; Parnes et al., 2018; Stormshak et al., 2019; Cerdá et al., 2020). However, some studies have shown that these increases may be small (Melchior et al., 2019; Salas-Wright et al., 2015; Doran et al., 2021), and researchers are continuing to investigate the impacts of these legislative changes.

Another consideration for young adults, regardless of changes in frequency of use, is the larger pattern of how, when, and why substances are used. For example, research has demonstrated that greater cannabis use has been associated with greater concurrent use of other substances, such as tobacco (Doran et al., 2021; Temple et al., 2017), and young adults who obtained cannabis from legal sources (e.g., medical dispensaries) were more likely to meet criteria for a substance use disorder (D'Amico et al., 2020). Problematic or unhealthy substance use is discussed in greater detail later in this chapter, but it is important first to consider the unique context of substance use in young adulthood.

WHAT IS OUR FRAMEWORK?

Despite the annually increasing prevalence rates of substance and alcohol use among young adults, the "maturing out" hypothesis (Lee & Sher, 2018) suggests that the majority of this problematic use actually becomes unproblematic over time. There are exceptions, of course, but the vast majority of studies found that there is a steep decline over development among young adults who use in their early 20s (Lee & Sher, 2018; Chen & Jacobson, 2012; Chassin et al., 1996; Chen & Kandel, 1995; Muthén & Muthén, 2000). Binge drinkers, for example, follow a downward trend, where the rate of binge drinking is 45% in their early 20s, 38% by their late 20s, 29% by their late 30s, and so on. The same pattern of decline is observed among nonbinge drinkers, as they also experience a spike in drinking in their early 20s and then a steady decline throughout their life span. So, the not-so-ugly truth is that binge drinking, and other forms of substance use, do decrease as young adults age, and heavy use is really just a characteristic of the first half of this period of young adulthood. In other words, as young adults experience increases in stability, school and work-related responsibilities, marriage, parenthood, and overall personal growth, they mature out of heavy substance use.

Why is this the case? One explanation can be the development of the prefrontal cortex (PFC). The PFC is located in the frontal lobe, right behind the forehead, and is scientifically shown to be the last region of the brain to develop. Researchers suggest that this region isn't fully developed until the age of 25 (Arain et al., 2013). The PFC is responsible for executive functioning,

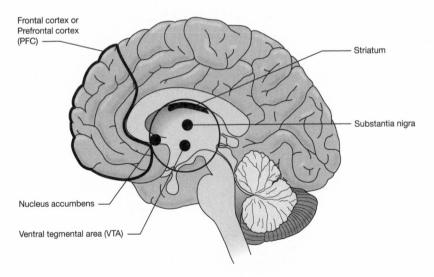

Figure 3.1: Diagram of neural pathway between prefrontal cortex (PFC) and reward center of the brain (nucleus accumbens).

decision making, organization, and planning behaviors (Di Chiara, 2000), which might explain why late teenagers' or early college-age students' decisions seem illogical or risky.

How does the PFC then relate to substance use? There is a direct track from the PFC to the nucleus accumbens, the reward processing center of the brain primarily responsible for the maintenance of addiction via sensation-seeking behaviors consisting of reward-seeking and inhibitory control constructs (Di Chiara, 2000; Perry et al., 2011). The key structures of the reward center are the nucleus accumbens, striatum, ventral tegmental area (VTA), and the substantia nigra (Haber & Knutson, 2010; see Figure 3.1). After a person uses a substance, dopamine, a neurotransmitter, rushes into the reward center's synapses, reinforcing the positive feelings associated with drug use (Volkow et al., 2004). This reinforcement then influences the PFC to make decisions to reengage in drug-seeking behaviors. With greater reinforcement comes more drug-seeking behaviors like cravings, triggers, and a compulsive drive toward drug use and reduced impulse control (Adinoff, 2004). Lack of impulse control at the reward center overpowers and influences many of the decisions made in the PFC, which results in a propensity for unhealthy decisions. In conclusion, the spike observed in substance use patterns and risky behaviors during early adulthood can be explained by the development of the PFC. In alignment with both the maturing-out hypothesis and PFC development, young adults emotionally and socially mature to determine which roles and responsibilities are primary through role conflict resolution and which others, like drinking or substance use, become secondary or tertiary and slowly decrease their substance use behaviors.

SUBSTANCE USE AND DEVELOPMENTAL CHALLENGES IN EMERGING ADULTHOOD

Young adulthood is a period of development that is characterized by a developing sense of self in relation to other people and the world. During this time of life, young adults are also developing their relationship to substances, including attitudes toward use and patterns and types of substances used. Similar to other areas of emerging adulthood, these attitudes and behaviors are influenced by one's social and environmental context in early life and adolescence (Kogan et al., 2017; Liga et al., 2017), as well as social and media-based influences (Jackson et al., 2018).

Personal Financial Stability and Exploration

Young adulthood is a unique time of life marked by developing autonomy or "launching" away from one's family. For most, this means increased responsibility and new roles, such as moving away from home, going to college, starting a career, or becoming a parent, which can all be stressors that prompt substance use (Arnett, 2005; Krieger et al., 2018; Goodman et al., 2016; Welsh et al., 2019; Jordan & Andersen, 2017; Perry et al., 2018). As young adults navigate this period, financial resources can also vary, with resulting impacts on substance use.

As demonstrated by the prevalence rates discussed earlier in this chapter, many young adults are buying and using substances despite financial instability—or perhaps because of it. For example, being unable to meet financial obligations (also called financial strain) has been associated with greater alcohol use, potentially as a means of coping, while living at home and having greater parental support were associated with lower alcohol use among young adults (Serido et al., 2014). Similar findings have been documented for young adults who use cannabis, with lower likelihood of employment and financial independence, and higher likelihood of financial problems, associated with longer-term use among individuals transitioning into young adulthood (Brook et al., 2013). However, family wealth and greater resources in childhood have also been associated with increased alcohol and cannabis use among young adults (Patrick et al., 2012), which suggests that many other factors influence whether (and how) young adults decide to use substances.

One such motivator is personal exploration and self-discovery (Arnett, 2005). Experimentation was cited by young adults as a reason for using cannabis and tobacco (Berg et al., 2018. Other studies have described continued likelihood of psychedelic use among young adults (Krebs & Johansen, 2013), most recently in the form of "microdosing," or using small amounts of a psychedelic substance to achieve improvements in mood, memory and attention, or physical functioning, without the hallucinogenic effects (Anderson et al., 2019; Ona & Bouso, 2020). Microdosing has grown in popularity among young adults (Cameron et al., 2020). However, young adults have also described concerns about obtaining psychedelics, particularly given their status as an illegal drug (Cameron et al., 2020), and the research on risks and benefits is still developing (Ona & Bouso, 2020).

Development of Relationships

Key social aspects of young adult development include identifying potential partners for long-term romantic relationships, maintaining previous friendships from early life and adolescence, and developing new friendships that align with an individual's burgeoning independence and multiple roles. At the same time, young adults are navigating their transition away from their families into independence. These social influences greatly contribute to whether, how, and for how long young adults engage in substance use.

Romantic Partners

For many young adults, substance use is closely tied to dating and the development of long-term romantic relationships, including finding and approaching potential partners, spending time together, and coping with relationship-related distress. For instance, going out for drinks is oftentimes the first contact for romantic relationships, and research has demonstrated greater risk for substance use when young adults are focused on short-term dating (Vincke, 2017). Young adults may also use substances to enhance sexual activity (Boys, 2001). However, there are complex associations between relationship status and substance use outcomes, particularly as relationships fluctuate over time (Fleming et al., 2018; Fleming, White, & Catalano, 2010).

Romantic partners can increase risk for substance use, particularly if the person's partner engages in antisocial behavior (Angulski et al., 2018) or heavy substance use (Fleming, White, Oesterle, et al., 2010). In contrast, romantic relationships have also been associated with lower substance use for cannabis, tobacco, alcohol, and illicit drugs, particularly as relationships become more established or progress to marriage (Fleming, White, Oesterle, et al., 2010; Whitton et al., 2018; Braithwaite et al., 2010; Merrin et al., 2020; Rauer et al., 2016). Notably, young adults have also reported increases in alcohol, tobacco, and cannabis use following a breakup or ending of the relationship (Fleming, White, & Catalano, 2010; Larson & Sweeten, 2012). Thus, it may be that a person finding and starting a romantic relationship has greater substance use, which decreases in frequency and amount over time, only to increase again when the relationship ends and they seek a new partner. However, it is also likely that romantic relationships impact substance use through multiple factors beyond duration, such as quality of the partnership, partner substance use behaviors, and other social and environmental influences (Rauer et al., 2016).

Of course, as is the case for other aspects of young adult development, romantic relationships are influenced by many intersectional characteristics including age, race/ethnicity, gender identity, and sexual orientation. The full impact of these multiple, intersectional identities on romantic relationships and substance use is beyond the scope of this book chapter, but we would like to highlight some of the broad patterns of substance use among diverse young adults and pathways that lead to greater or lesser substance use. For example, 2016 national estimates from the Substance Use and Mental Health Services Administration (SAMHSA) have demonstrated increased illicit substance use among LGBT+ adults, aged 18 and older, compared to heterosexual adults in the same age range (Medley et al., 2015). Researchers have also suggested greater illicit substance use among men who have sex with men, acknowledging that LBGT+ populations are not monolithic (Bourne & Weatherburn, 2017). In contrast, another study that further compared individuals, using a more detailed spectrum of sexual orientation, found equivalent rates of alcohol use between "mostly heterosexual" participants and LGBT+ participants, with lower use of nicotine and drugs among the latter group (Kuyper & Bos, 2016).

It is important to note, as with all considerations of diverse populations, that these differences are not due to any inherent characteristic, but rather depend on multiple other mediating influences. For example, in the study previously cited, greater substance use was associated with greater psychological distress. Studies have also demonstrated a powerful role of discrimination on substance use behaviors, and lifetime risk for developing substance use disorders, among LGBT+ populations (Lee et al., 2016; Slater et al., 2017; Demant et al., 2018b). In fact, one study found that smoking among the LGBT+ population signified a way of control—that is, taking control over an oppressor, controlling the effects of trauma and/or stress, and exerting control over the physical body in terms of protecting oneself from violence or one's mental health (Antin et al., 2018). Research has also suggested that greater engagement in the LGBT+ community (e.g., volunteering with related organizations, attending a Pride event) may be associated with greater substance use, possibly due to greater acceptance of substances among LGBT+ populations (Demant et al., 2018a, 2018b). Other factors overlap with the broader population of young adults—including the strong impact of friendships and platonic relationships on substance use, partially through availability and peer pressure.

Friendships

Evidence shows that the transition out of high school does increase the risk for higher levels of substance use and related issues (White et al., 2005) through development of new adult friendships and participation in college drinking activities. College is a unique time when emerging adults say goodbye to their old childhood friends, develop new friendships, and experience greater freedom and autonomy while branching away from their parental caregivers (Joy Jang et al., 2018; White et al., 2005). It cannot be denied that a great part of socialization, both in college and postgraduate, is drinking with friends—but this behavior doesn't necessarily lead to negative consequences. At each stage of their life course, young adults increase their social integration, creating systems of obligation and dependency that make it too costly to engage in harmful behaviors, like excessive substance use (Sampson & Laub, 1993; Green et al., 2010), and subsequently these behaviors decline or become less frequent.

Work Relationships

Most young adults adopt the social role of employment, which comes with its own set of roles and responsibilities. Happy hours, holiday parties, promotions, client and business meetings, and so on, often revolve around alcohol, and through drinking, employees socialize, bond, and build their networks. In fact, adoption of these traditional social roles can be a protective factor against midlife substance use and contributes to the phasing out of drug use during emerging adulthood due to role incompatibilities (Bachman et al., 1997; Merline et al., 2004; Newcomb & Bentler, 1988). In contrast, some studies show that young adults do continue to engage in heavy alcohol use as they enter the workforce (Chassin et al., 2002; Patrick et al., 2018). These young adults are more likely to work full time or longer hours (Lee et al., 2018) or have a heavy-drinking peer group that is less likely to disapprove of their drinking behaviors (Butler et al., 2010; Paschall et al., 2002). Although results are inconsistent, it cannot be denied that substance use, specifically alcohol, is inherently tied to work relationships.

Family

As young adults begin to develop their own self-identities and relationships with drugs and alcohol, it might pose a conflict with their parental guardians as they reconfigure their relationship to family (Simons-Morton et al., 2016; Cadigan et al., 2019; DiBello et al., 2018). Young adults might come home during the holidays and drink more often than their parents or caregivers anticipate or might use illegal substances that their parents disapprove of, creating family conflict and disputes.

It is important to also consider the relationship between family conflict, acculturation-related challenges, and substance use among young adults, especially racial and ethnic minoritized populations. Pew Research Center estimates the US immigrant population will almost double by 2065; thus, understanding the importance of acculturation and the potential conflict between parent and child is imperative in exploring the role of substances in a young person's life (Fry et al., 2020). Research shows that less acculturated Hispanic youth are at a higher risk for drug use (Rodriguez et al., 2007; Gil et al., 2004), which suggests that coping with the stress of acculturating to a new environment and the family conflict that arises out of it serves as a risk factor for drug use. Additionally, racial and ethnic minority youth might feel pressured to use drugs or drink alcohol as a means to socialize or fit in with the dominant peer group (Rodriguez et al., 2007; Myers et al., 2009). Not only does increased familial stress and strained parent–child relationships due to acculturation differences impact substance risk, but traumatic immigration experiences can also play a significant role. Migration to a new country that involves loss, trauma, and/or abuse may trigger traumatic stress to develop. If the youth does not develop strong coping skills or have access to appropriate care, the young adult might turn to drugs and alcohol to cope with distress (Rodriguez et al., 2007). Clearly, the impact of acculturation also extends beyond the household and is an important factor in understanding the role of substance use in a young adult's life.

COVID-19

Young adults were impacted by the coronavirus pandemic (COVID-19) in a unique way. In spring 2020, young adults from across the world abruptly uprooted themselves from their college campuses, roommates, and social lives that were usually characterized by a heavy-drinking culture and so on, and moved back home with their parents for the indefinite future. Pew Research Center estimates that nearly 52% of young adults moved back home with their parents due to the coronavirus pandemic in July 2020 (Fry et al., 2020). On top of the stressors associated with the pandemic, these young adults said goodbye to their friends, freedom, and socialization and had to learn to navigate their substance use around their parents. With increased parental supervision, young adult drinking and substance use behaviors were curtailed (Suffoletto et al., 2020; Steffen et al., 2021; White et al., 2020), potentially spiraling youth into withdrawal symptoms like anxiety, insomnia, vomiting, and irritability on top of the psychological impact of social isolation. Vaping behaviors among young adults who moved back home also decreased (Gaiha et al., 2020), likely due to social isolation, lack of accessibility, and increased parental monitoring.

Parenthood

Outside of the potential parental conflict generally observed during the earlier years of emerging adulthood, the later years are largely characterized by the young adult's own family formation. Research shows young adults, despite using substances in adolescence or early young adulthood, do mature out of drug use as they continue along this developmental timeline (Lee & Sher, 2018; White et al., 2005; Bachman et al., 1997). The fact of the matter is that experimentation during adolescence and early young adulthood is normal and is not indicative of a disrupted future or maladaptive health outcomes, although this is not observed among minoritized populations (White al., 2005; Schulenberg et al., 1996). One research study found that early substance use around ages 19–20 is associated with delayed marriage around ages 29–30, compared to nonusers (Joy Jang et al., 2018), suggesting that substance users might be deemed incompatible partners and are perceived as less suitable for marriage. As young adults become parents, naturally their substance and alcohol use patterns decrease as their responsibilities associated with parenthood and family life increase (Fergusson et al., 2012). In other words, young adult substance users age, or mature, out of their drinking and substance use behaviors as they begin to form their own families.

When Does Substance Use Become a Problem?

Leaving aside the changing legality of substances, with associated social and legal risks for obtaining and using illicit drugs, there is a wide spectrum of short- and long-term harms that can result from substance use, ranging from the physical (e.g., injury, sexual assault, impaired sleep) to cognitive (e.g., information processing, recall, planning) and emotional functioning (e.g., greater depression and anxiety) (Krieger et al., 2018). However, not all substance use results in a substance use disorder worthy of diagnosis by a clinician or health provider. Key considerations for substance use disorders are listed in the box below.

SIGNS OF PROBLEMATIC SUBSTANCE USE

- Using more of the substance than you meant to, or using longer than you'd planned
- Wanting to stop or cut down on your use, but not being able to
- Spending a lot of time getting the substance, using it, and/or recovering from it
- Feeling a craving or urge to use it
- Experiencing discomfort or distress after discontinuing the substance, which you may or may not resolve by taking more of it
- Failing to meet expectations at home, school, or work because of substance use
- Giving up activities that are important to you because of substance use
- Continuing to use substances even when it puts you in danger, causes a physical or emotional problem, or makes a problem worse for you
- Developing a tolerance to the substance—so that you need more of it to get the same effect

Notably, these criteria include physical outcomes, behavioral patterns, and how well an individual manages in multiple areas, which is an important consideration given the new and changing roles that are associated with young adulthood. Keep in mind that young adults do not need to meet all of these criteria to have a substance use disorder, and even experiencing a few of these signs may be cause enough to stop or substantially decrease substance use. Yet, changing attitudes toward substance use and lowering stigma of substance use disorders have led to diverse approaches for monitoring risk of problematic substance use, providing early diagnosis and treatment for these disorders, and conceptualizing recovery from a long-term perspective.

Treatment Options

Abstinence-based treatments, such as 12-step models, are a common method of both substance use prevention and intervention. These types of treatments are primarily a one-size-fits-all, top-down model with very little consideration for the user's contexts, which does not allow for the identification of healthy and safe substance use behaviors. Requiring abstinence creates multiple barriers to obtain and enter treatment, but a more liberal and tolerant treatment approach that is gaining popularity is harm reduction (Marlatt & Witkiewitz, 2002, 2010; Lee et al., 2011). Harm reduction is client-centered, meaning that its model is based on what size fits you; abstinence is only encouraged if and when the client chooses it (Marlatt & Witkiewitz, 2002). A harm reductionist approach aims to develop skills that reduce harm and decrease the adverse health, social, and economic consequences of drug use overall. Young adults are more accepting of harm reduction and rejecting of abstinence because it is more accessible and accommodates to their lifestyle needs—that is, a large part of their social identity revolves around drinking. For example, the Brief Alcohol Screening and Intervention for College Students (BASICS) is a harm reduction prevention approach for college students, as it focuses on aiding the student to reduce any risky behaviors and the harmful effects of heavy alcohol drinking (Dimeff et al., 1999; Marlatt et al., 1998; Baer et al., 2001). Young adults who underwent the BASICS intervention demonstrated a significant decrease in drinking rates, harmful consequences associated with drinking, and alcohol dependence than the control group. If you feel your drinking or substance use is beyond your control, yet abstinence is not your goal at the moment, we highly encourage you to look into these resources:

- American Addiction Centers (https://americanaddictioncenters.org /admissions)

- National Harm Reduction Coalition Resource Center (https://harm reduction.org/resource-center/harm-reduction-near-you/)
- SAMHSA's National Helpline: 1-800-662-HELP (4357)

If abstinence is your goal, and you are interested in joining a 12-step program, like Alcoholics Anonymous, please visit their website (https://alcoholics anonymous.com/find-a-meeting/). SAMHSA's National Helpline can also help identify other abstinence-based treatment services.

CONCLUSION

We hope this chapter has provided an overview of the good, the bad, and the not-so-ugly aspects of substance use among the young adult population. Research has supported the maturing-out hypothesis such that elevated drug and alcohol use is a characteristic of the earlier years of young adulthood, such that with increasing complexity in social roles, drug and alcohol use lowers in priority (Lee & Sher, 2018; White et al., 2005; Bachman et al., 1997). Parenthood is a common developmental period when substance use behaviors diminish as the role substances used to hold has less meaning, and the responsibility of parenthood holds greater meaning (Fergusson et al., 2012). Historically, alcohol has remained a major substance used in this age bracket (Elflein, 2020), and cigarette use has lowered, but e-cigarette use, which can include both nicotine and cannabis, has increased (Johnston et al., 2019; Schulenberg et al., 2020). Despite the tapering effect of substances throughout development, there is still the need for further advancement of early intervention approaches that follow both a harm reduction and sociocultural framework that acknowledges the meaning of substance use for young people. For instance, with the rise in vaping culture, harm reduction intervention approaches are needed to empower young adults to engage in healthy, safe smoking habits.

Alexandria Bauer, PhD, is a postdoctoral research associate at the Center of Alcohol & Substance Use Studies at the Graduate School of Applied and Professional Psychology, Rutgers University-New Brunswick. She earned both her master's degree and PhD in Clinical Psychology from the University of Missouri-Kansas City. Her work to date has focused on understanding and addressing health disparities, including trauma and substance use among diverse community populations. She is also invested in advancing culturally sensitive, tailored approaches to mental health treatment.

Chantel T. Ebrahimi is a Clinical Psychology PhD student at The New School for Social Research (NSSR). She completed her MA in Psychology with a Concentration in Mental Health and Substance Abuse Counseling at NSSR and her BS in Psychobiology at UCLA. Her research interests span the intersection of adolescents and young people, trauma, and addiction in communities of color.

Denise Hien, PhD, ABPP is Vice Provost of Research in the Chancellor-Provost's Office, Director and Helen E. Chaney Endowed Chair in Alcohol Studies of the Center of Alcohol & Substance Use Studies at the Graduate School of Applied and Professional Psychology, Rutgers University-New Brunswick. She also maintains longstanding adjunct appointments as Senior Research Scientist at Columbia University College of Physicians and Surgeons, Division on Substance Use Disorders and Adjunct Professor at the Graduate Center at the City University of New York. Considered a leader in the field, her body of work has contributed to the evidence base on the treatment of individuals with trauma-related psychiatric disorders and their comorbidity with addictions.

REFERENCES

Aarons, G. A., Brown, S. A., Coe, M. T., Myers, M. G., Garland, A. F., Ezzet-Lofstram, R., Hazen, A. L., & Hough, R. L. (1999). Adolescent alcohol and drug abuse and health. *Journal of Adolescent Health, 24*(6), 412–421. https://doi.org/10.1016/S1054-139X(99)00006-3

Adinoff, B. (2004). Neurobiologic processes in drug reward and addiction. *Harvard Review of Psychiatry, 12*(6), 305–320.

Amroussia, N., Watanabe, M., & Pearson, J. L. (2020). Seeking safety: A focus group study of young adults' cannabis-related attitudes, and behavior in a state with legalized recreational cannabis. *Harm Reduction Journal, 17*(1), 92. https://doi.org/10.1186 /s12954-020-00442-8

Anderson, T., Petranker, R., Christopher, A., Rosenbaum, D., Weissman, C., Dinh-Williams, L.-A., Hui, K., & Hapke, E. (2019). Psychedelic microdosing benefits and challenges: An empirical codebook. *Harm Reduction Journal, 16*, 1–10. https://doi .org/10.1186/s12954-019-0308-4

Angulski, K., Armstrong, T., & Bouffard, L. A. (2018). The influence of romantic relationships on substance use in emerging adulthood. *Journal of Drug Issues, 48*(4), 572–589. https://doi.org/10.1177/0022042618783490

Antin, T. M. J., Hunt, G., & Sanders, E. (2018). The "here and now" of youth: The meanings of smoking for sexual and gender minority youth. *Harm Reduction Journal, London, 15.* http://dx.doi.org.libproxy.newschool.edu/10.1186/s12954-018-0236-8

Arain, M., Haque, M., Johal, L., Mathur, P., Nel, W., Rais, A., Sandhu, R., & Sharma, S. (2013). Maturation of the adolescent brain. *Neuropsychiatric Disease and Treatment, 9*, 449–461. https://doi.org/10.2147/NDT.S39776

Arnett, J. J. (2000). Emerging adulthood: A theory of development from the late teens through the twenties. *American Psychologist, 55*(5), 469–480. https://doi.org/10 .1037/0003-066X.55.5.469

Arnett, J. J. (2005). The developmental context of substance use in emerging adulthood. *Journal of Drug Issues, 35*(2), 235–254. https://doi.org/10.1177/002204260503500202

Bachman, J. G., Wadsworth, K. N., O'Malley, P. M., Johnston, L. D., & Schulenberg, J. E. (1997). *Smoking, drinking, and drug use in young adulthood: The impacts of new freedoms and new responsibilities.* Mahwah, NJ: Lawrence Erlbaum.

Baer, J. S., Kivlahan, D. R., Blume, A. W., McKnight, P., & Marlatt, G. A. (2001). Brief intervention for heavy-drinking college students: 4-year follow-up and natural history. *American Journal of Public Health, 91*(8), 1310–1316. doi:10.2105/ajph.91.8.1310

Benson, J. (2006, February 24). When it comes to Adderall, sharing is not really caring. *Bowdoin Orient.* https://bowdoinorient.com/bonus/article/1617

Berg, C. J., Payne, J., Henriksen, L., Cavazos-Rehg, P., Getachew, B., Schauer, G. L., & Haardörfer, R. (2018). Reasons for marijuana and tobacco co-use among young adults: A mixed methods scale development study. *Substance Use and Misuse, 53*(3), 357–369. https://doi.org/10.1080/10826084.2017.1327978

Bourne, A., & Weatherburn, P. (2017). Substance use among men who have sex with men: Patterns, motivations, impacts and intervention development need. *Sexually Transmitted Infections, 93*(5), 342–346. https://doi.org/10.1136/sextrans-2016-052674

Bowles, N., Herzig, M., & Shea, S. (2017). Recent legalization of cannabis use: Effects on sleep, health, and workplace safety. *Nature and Science of Sleep, 9*, 249–251. https:// doi.org/10.2147/NSS.S152231

Boys, A. (2001). Understanding reasons for drug use amongst young people: A functional perspective. *Health Education Research, 16*(4), 457–469. https://doi.org/10 .1093/her/16.4.457

Braithwaite, S. R., Delevi, R., & Fincham, F. D. (2010). Romantic relationships and the physical and mental health of college students. *Personal Relationships, 17*(1), 1–12. https://doi.org/10.1111/j.1475-6811.2010.01248.x

Brook, J. S., Lee, J. Y., Finch, S. J., Seltzer, N., & Brook, D. W. (2013). Adult work commitment, financial stability, and social environment as related to trajectories of marijuana use beginning in adolescence. *Substance Abuse, 34*(3), 298–305. https://doi .org/10.1080/08897077.2013.775092

Budney, A. J., & Borodovsky, J. T. (2017). The potential impact of cannabis legalization on the development of cannabis use disorders. *Preventive Medicine, 104*, 31–36. https:// doi.org/10.1016/j.ypmed.2017.06.034

Butler, A. B., Dodge, K. D., & Faurote, E. J. (2010). College student employment and drinking: A daily study of work stressors, alcohol expectancies, and alcohol consumption. *Journal of Occupational Health Psychology, 15*(3), 291–303. https://doi .org/10.1037/a0019822

Cadigan, J. M., Duckworth, J. C., Parker, M. E., & Lee, C. M. (2019). Influence of developmental social role transitions on young adult substance use. *Current Opinion in Psychology, 30*, 87–91. https://doi.org/10.1016/j.copsyc.2019.03.006

Cameron, L. P., Nazarian, A., & Olson, D. E. (2020). Psychedelic microdosing: Prevalence and subjective effects. *Journal of Psychoactive Drugs, 52*(2), 113–122. https://doi .org/10.1080/02791072.2020.1718250

Caulkins, J. P., & Reuter, P. (2021). Ending the war on drugs need not, and should not, involve legalizing supply by a for-profit industry. *American Journal of Bioethics, 21*(4), 31–35. https://doi.org/10.1080/15265161.2021.1893064

CDC. (2020, December 15). *Current cigarette smoking among adults in the United States.* Centers for Disease Control and Prevention. https://www.cdc.gov/tobacco/data _statistics/fact_sheets/adult_data/cig_smoking/index.htm

Center for Behavioral Health Statistics and Quality. (2017). 2016 National Survey on Drug Use and Health: Detailed Tables. Substance Abuse and Mental Health Services Administration, Rockville, MD.

Center for Behavioral Health Statistics and Quality. (2020). Results from the 2019 National Survey on Drug Use and Health: Detailed tables. Rockville, MD: Substance Abuse and Mental Health Services Administration. https://www.samhsa.gov/data/

Cerdá, M., Mauro, C., Hamilton, A., Levy, N. S., Santaella-Tenorio, J., Hasin, D., Wall, M. M., Keyes, K. M., & Martins, S. S. (2020). Association between recreational marijuana legalization in the United States and changes in marijuana use and cannabis use disorder from 2008 to 2016. *JAMA Psychiatry, 77*(2), 165. https://doi.org/10.1001 /jamapsychiatry.2019.3254

Chassin, L., Pitts, S. C., & Prost, J. (2002). Binge drinking trajectories from adolescence to emerging adulthood in a high-risk sample: Predictors and substance abuse outcomes. *Journal of Consulting and Clinical Psychology, 70*(1), 67–78.

Chassin, L., Presson, C. C., Rose, J. S., & Sherman, S. J. (1996). The natural history of cigarette smoking from adolescence to adulthood: Demographic predictors of continuity and change. *Health Psychology, 15*(6), 478–484. https://doi.org/10.1037//0278-6133.15.6.478

Chen, K., & Kandel, D. B. (1995). The natural history of drug use from adolescence to the mid-thirties in a general population sample. *American Journal of Public Health, 85*(1), 41–47.

Chen, P., & Jacobson, K. C. (2012). Developmental trajectories of substance use from early adolescence to young adulthood: Gender and racial/ethnic differences. *Journal of Adolescent Health, 50*(2), 154–163. https://doi.org/10.1016/j.jadohealth.2011.05.013

D'Amico, E. J., Rodriguez, A., Dunbar, M. S., Firth, C. L., Tucker, J. S., Seelam, R., Pedersen, E. R., & Davis, J. P. (2020). Sources of cannabis among young adults and associations with cannabis-related outcomes. *International Journal of Drug Policy, 86*, 102971. https://doi.org/10.1016/j.drugpo.2020.102971

del Pozo, B., & Beletsky, L. (2020). No "back to normal" after COVID-19 for our failed drug policies. *International Journal of Drug Policy, 83*, 102901. https://doi.org/10.1016/j.drugpo.2020.102901

Demant, D., Hides, L., White, K. M., & Kavanagh, D. J. (2018a). Effects of participation in and connectedness to the LGBT community on substance use involvement of sexual minority young people. *Addictive Behaviors, 81*, 167–174. https://doi.org/10.1016/j.addbeh.2018.01.028

Demant, D., Hides, L., White, K. M., & Kavanagh, D. J. (2018b). LGBT communities and substance use in Queensland, Australia: Perceptions of young people and community stakeholders. *PLoS ONE, 13*(9), e0204730. https://doi.org/10.1371/journal.pone.0204730

DiBello, A. M., Benz, M. B., Miller, M. B., Merrill, J. E., & Carey, K. B. (2018). Examining residence status as a risk factor for health risk behaviors among college students. *Journal of American College Health, 66*(3), 187–193. https://doi.org/10.1080/07448481.2017.1406945

Di Chiara, G. (2000). Role of dopamine in the behavioural actions of nicotine related to addiction. *European Journal of Pharmacology, 393*(1), 295–314. https://doi.org/10.1016/S0014-2999(00)00122-9

Dimeff, L. A., Baer, J. S., Kivlahan, D. R., & Marlatt, G. A. (1999). Brief Alcohol Screening and Intervention for College Students (BASICS): A harm reduction approach. New York: Guilford.

Doran, N., Strong, D., Myers, M. G., Correa, J. B., & Tully, L. (2021). Post-legalization changes in marijuana use in a sample of young California adults. *Addictive Behaviors, 115*, 106782. https://doi.org/10.1016/j.addbeh.2020.106782

Elflein, J. (2020, September 17). *Current, binge, and heavy alcohol use in U.S. persons by age group, 2019*. Statista. https://www.statista.com/statistics/354265/current-binge-heavy-alcohol-use-among-persons-in-the-us-by-age/

Félix, S., & Portugal, P. (2017). Drug decriminalization and the price of illicit drugs. *International Journal of Drug Policy, 39*, 121–129. https://doi.org/10.1016/j.drugpo.2016.10.014

Fergusson, D. M., Boden, J. M., & Horwood, L. J. (2012). Transition to parenthood and substance use disorders: Findings from a 30-year longitudinal study. *Drug and Alcohol Dependence, 125*(3), 295–300. https://doi.org/10.1016/j.drugalcdep.2012.03.003

Fleming, C. B., Lee, C. M., Rhew, I. C., Ramirez, J. J., Abdallah, D. A., & Fairlie, A. M. (2018). Descriptive and prospective analysis of young adult alcohol use and romantic relationships: Disentangling between- and within-person associations using monthly assessments. *Substance Use and Misuse, 53*(13), 2240–2249. https://doi.org/10.1080/10826084.2018.1467455

Fleming, C. B., White, H. R., & Catalano, R. F. (2010). Romantic relationships and substance use in early adulthood: An examination of the influences of relationship type, partner substance use, and relationship quality. *Journal of Health and Social Behavior, 51*(2), 153–167. https://doi.org/10.1177/0022146510368930

Fleming, C. B., White, H. R., Oesterle, S., Haggerty, K. P., & Catalano, R. F. (2010). Romantic relationship status changes and substance use among 18- to 20-year-olds. *Journal of Studies on Alcohol and Drugs, 71*(6), 847–856. https://doi.org/10.15288/jsad.2010.71.847

Fry, R., Passel, J. S., & Cohn, D. (2020, September 4). A majority of young adults in the U.S. live with their parents for the first time since the Great Depression. https://

www.pewresearch.org/fact-tank/2020/09/04/a-majority-of-young-adults-in-the-u-s
-live-with-their-parents-for-the-first-time-since-the-great-depression/

Gaiha, S. M., Lempert, L. K., & Halpern-Felsher, B. (2020). Underage youth and young
adult e-cigarette use and access before and during the Coronavirus disease 2019
pandemic. *JAMA Network Open, 3*(12), e2027572–e2027572. https://doi.org/10.1001
/jamanetworkopen.2020.27572

Gil, A. G., Wagner, E. F., & Tubman, J. G. (2004). Culturally sensitive substance abuse
intervention for Hispanic and African American adolescents: Empirical examples
from the Alcohol Treatment Targeting Adolescents in Need (ATTAIN) Project. *Addiction (Abingdon, England), 99*(Suppl 2), 140–150. https://doi.org/10.1111/j.1360-0443
.2004.00861.x

Goldsworthy, R. C., Schwartz, N. C., & Mayhorn, C. B. (2008). Beyond abuse and exposure: Framing the impact of prescription-medication sharing. *American Journal of
Public Health, 98*(6), 1115–1121. https://doi.org/10.2105/AJPH.2007.123257

Goodman, I., Henderson, J., Peterson-Badali, M., & Goldstein, A. (2016). Youth perspectives on the transition to adulthood: Exploring the impact of problematic substance
use and treatment seeking. *Emerging Adulthood, 4*(2), 92–103. https://doi.org/10
.1177/2167696815601548

Green, K. M., Doherty, E. E., Reisinger, H. S., Chilcoat, H. D., & Ensminger, M. (2010).
Social integration in young adulthood and the subsequent onset of substance use and
disorders among a community population of urban African Americans. *Addiction,
105*(3), 484–493. https://doi.org/10.1111/j.1360-0443.2009.02787.x

Grucza, R. A., Sher, K. J., Kerr, W. C., Krauss, M. J., Lui, C. K., McDowell, Y. E., Hartz,
S., Virdi, G., & Bierut, L. J. (2018). Trends in adult alcohol use and binge drinking
in the early 21st-century United States: A meta-analysis of 6 national survey series.
Alcoholism: Clinical and Experimental Research, 42(10), 1939–1950. https://doi.org/10
.1111/acer.13859

Haber, S. N., & Knutson, B. (2010). The reward circuit: Linking primate anatomy and
human imaging. *Neuropsychopharmacology, 35*(1), 4–26. https://doi.org/10.1038/npp
.2009.129

Hall, W., Leung, J., & Lynskey, M. (2020). The effects of cannabis use on the development
of adolescents and young adults. *Annual Review of Developmental Psychology, 2*(1),
461–483. https://doi.org/10.1146/annurev-devpsych-040320-084904

Hall, W., & Lynskey, M. (2016). Evaluating the public health impacts of legalizing recreational cannabis use in the United States. *Addiction, 111*(10), 1764–1773. https://doi
.org/10.1111/add.13428

Hammond, A. S., Dunn, K. E., & Strain, E. C. (2020). Drug legalization and decriminalization beliefs among substance-using and nonusing individuals. *Journal of Addiction Medicine, 14*(1), 56–62. https://doi.org/10.1097/ADM.0000000000000542

Hien, D. A., Bauer, A., Franklin, L., Lalwali, T., & Pean, K. (2021, August 4). Conceptualizing the COVID-19, opioid use, and racism syndemic and its associations with
traumatic stress. *Psychiatric Services.* doi:10.1176/appi.ps.202100070

Husak, D. (2003). Four points about drug decriminalization. *Criminal Justice Ethics,
22*(1), 21–29. https://doi.org/10.1080/0731129X.2003.9992137

Jackson, K. M., Janssen, T., & Gabrielli, J. (2018). Media/marketing influences on adolescent and young adult substance abuse. *Current Addiction Reports, 5*(2), 146–157.
https://doi.org/10.1007/s40429-018-0199-6

Jessor, R., Costa, F. M., Krueger, P. M., & Turbin, M. S. (2006). A developmental study of heavy episodic drinking among college students: The role of psychosocial and behavioral protective and risk factors. *Journal of Studies on Alcohol, 67*(1), 86–94. https://doi.org/10.15288/jsa.2006.67.86

Johnston, L. D., Miech, R. A., O'Malley, P. M., Bachman, J. G., Schulenberg, J. E., & Patrick, M. E. (2019). *Monitoring the Future national survey results on drug use 1975–2018: Overview, key findings on adolescent drug use.* Ann Arbor: Institute for Social Research, University of Michigan.

Johnston, L. D., Miech, R. A., O'Malley, P. M., Bachman, J. G., Schulenberg, J. E., & Patrick, M. E. (2020). *Monitoring the Future national survey results on drug use 1975–2019: Overview, key findings on adolescent drug use.* Ann Arbor: Institute for Social Research, University of Michigan.

Johnston, L. D., Miech, R. A., O'Malley, P. M., Bachman, J. G., Schulenberg, J. E., & Patrick, M. E. (2021). *Monitoring the Future national survey results on drug use 1975–2020: Overview, key findings on adolescent drug use.* Ann Arbor: Institute for Social Research, University of Michigan.

Jordan, C. J., & Andersen, S. L. (2017). Sensitive periods of substance abuse: Early risk for the transition to dependence. *Developmental Cognitive Neuroscience, 25,* 29–44. https://doi.org/10.1016/j.dcn.2016.10.004

Joyce, M., Sklenar, E., & Weatherby, G. A. (2019). Decriminalizing drug addiction: The effects of the label. *Forensic Research and Criminology International Journal, 7*(4), 154–162. https://doi.org/10.15406/frcij.2019.07.00280

Joy Jang, B., Patrick, M. E., & Schuler, M. S. (2018). Substance use behaviors and the timing of family formation during young adulthood. *Journal of Family Issues, 39*(5), 1396–1418. https://doi.org/10.1177/0192513X17710285

Kogan, S. M., Cho, J., Brody, G. H., & Beach, S. R. H. (2017). Pathways linking marijuana use to substance use problems among emerging adults: A prospective analysis of young Black men. *Addictive Behaviors, 72,* 86–92. https://doi.org/10.1016/j.addbeh.2017.03.027

Krebs, T. S., & Johansen, P.-Ø. (2013). Psychedelics and mental health: A population study. *PLoS ONE, 8*(8), e63972. https://doi.org/10.1371/journal.pone.0063972

Krieger, H., Young, C. M., Anthenien, A. M., & Neighbors, C. (2018). The epidemiology of binge drinking among college-age individuals in the United States. *Alcohol Research: Current Reviews, 39*(1), 23–30.

Kuyper, L., & Bos, H. (2016). Mostly heterosexual and lesbian/gay young adults: Differences in mental health and substance use and the role of minority stress. *Journal of Sex Research, 53*(7), 731–741. https://doi.org/10.1080/00224499.2015.1071310

Lambert, D., Gale, J. A., & Hartley, D. (2008). Substance abuse by youth and young adults in rural America. *Journal of Rural Health, 24*(3), 221–228. https://doi.org/10.1111/j.1748-0361.2008.00162.x

Larson, M., & Sweeten, G. (2012). Breaking up is hard to do: Romantic dissolution, offending, and substance use during the transition to adulthood. *Criminology, 50*(3), 605–636. https://doi.org/10.1111/j.1745-9125.2012.00272.x

Lee, C. M., Cadigan, J. M., Fairlie, A. M., & Lewis, M. A. (2018). Transitions into young adulthood: Extent to which alcohol use, perceived drinking norms, and consequences vary by education and work statuses among 18–20 year olds. *Addictive Behaviors, 79,* 107–112. https://doi.org/10.1016/j.addbeh.2017.12.004

Lee, H. S., Engstrom, M., & Petersen, S. R. (2011). Harm reduction and 12 steps: Complementary, oppositional, or something in-between? *Substance Use and Misuse, 46*(9), 1151–1161. https://doi.org/10.3109/10826084.2010.548435

Lee, J. H., Gamarel, K. E., Bryant, K. J., Zaller, N. D., & Operario, D. (2016). Discrimination, mental health, and substance use disorders among sexual minority populations. *LGBT Health, 3*(4), 258–265. https://doi.org/10.1089/lgbt.2015.0135

Lee, M. R., & Sher, K. J. (2018). "Maturing out" of binge and problem drinking. *Alcohol Research: Current Reviews, 39*(1), 31–42.

Leung, J., Chiu, C. Y. V., Stjepanović, D., & Hall, W. (2018). Has the legalisation of medical and recreational cannabis use in the USA affected the prevalence of cannabis use and cannabis use disorders? *Current Addiction Reports, 5*(4), 403–417. https://doi.org/10.1007/s40429-018-0224-9

Liga, F., Ingoglia, S., Inguglia, C., Lo Coco, A., Lo Cricchio, M. G., Musso, P., Cheah, C., Rose, L., & Gutow, M. R. (2017). Associations among psychologically controlling parenting, autonomy, relatedness, and problem behaviors during emerging adulthood. *Journal of Psychology, 151*(4), 393–415. https://doi.org/10.1080/00223980.2017.1305323

Marlatt, G. A., Baer, J. S., Kivlahan, D. R., Dimeff, L. A., Larimer, M. E., Quigley, L. A., Somers, J. M., & Williams, E. (1998). Screening and brief intervention for high-risk college student drinkers: Results from a 2-year follow-up assessment. *Journal of Consulting and Clinical Psychology, 66*, 604–615.

Marlatt, G. A., & Witkiewitz, K. (2002). Harm reduction approaches to alcohol use: Health promotion, prevention, and treatment. *Addictive Behaviors, 27*, 867–886.

Marlatt, G. A., & Witkiewitz, K. (2010). Update on harm-reduction policy and intervention research. *Annual Review of Clinical Psychology, 6*(1), 591–606. https://doi.org/10.1146/annurev.clinpsy.121208.131438

Medley, G., Lipari, R. N., Bose, J., Cribb, D. S., Kroutil, L. A., & McHenry, G. (2015). *Sexual orientation and estimates of adult substance use and mental health: Results from the 2015 National Survey on Drug Use and Health.* Washington, DC: Substance Abuse and Mental Health Services Administration.

Melchior, M., Nakamura, A., Bolze, C., Hausfater, F., El Khoury, F., Mary-Krause, M., & Azevedo Da Silva, M. (2019). Does liberalisation of cannabis policy influence levels of use in adolescents and young adults? A systematic review and meta-analysis. *BMJ Open, 9*, 1–13. https://doi.org/10.1136/bmjopen-2018-025880

Merline, A. C., O'Malley, P. M., Schulenberg, J. E., Bachman, J. G., & Johnston, L. D. (2004). Substance use among adults 35 years of age: Prevalence, adulthood predictors, and impact of adolescent substance use. *American Journal of Public Health, 94*(1), 96–102. https://doi.org/10.2105/ajph.94.1.96

Merrin, G. J., Ames, M. E., Sturgess, C., & Leadbeater, B. J. (2020). Disruption of transitions in high-risk substance use from adolescence to young adulthood: School, employment, and romantic relationship factors. *Substance Use and Misuse, 55*(7), 1129–1137. https://doi.org/10.1080/10826084.2020.1729200

Mikulic, M. (2021, March 23). *20 most abused prescription drugs in the U.S. by revenue 2016.* Statista. https://www.statista.com/statistics/825766/most-abused-prescription-drugs-by-revenue/

Moss, H. B., Chen, C. M., & Yi, H. (2014). Early adolescent patterns of alcohol, cigarettes, and marijuana polysubstance use and young adult substance use outcomes in a nationally representative sample. *Drug and Alcohol Dependence, 136*, 51–62. https://doi.org/10.1016/j.drugalcdep.2013.12.011

Muthén, B. O., & Muthén, L. K. (2000). The development of heavy drinking and alcohol-related problems from ages 18 to 37 in a U.S. national sample. *Journal of Studies on Alcohol, 61*(2), 290–300. https://doi.org/10.15288/jsa.2000.61.290

Myers, R., Chou, C. P., Sussman, S., Baezconde-Garbanati, L., Pachon, H., & Valente, T. W. (2009). Acculturation and substance use: Social influence as a mediator among Hispanic alternative high school youth. *Journal of Health and Social Behavior, 50*(2), 164–179.

Neuroscience News. (2013, July 22). Scientists identify key brain circuits that control compulsive drinking in rats. https://neurosciencenews.com/neurobiology-neural -pathway-alcoholism-325

Newcomb, M. D., & Bentler, P. M. (1988). Impact of adolescent drug use and social support on problems of young adults: A longitudinal study. *Journal of Abnormal Psychology, 97*(1), 64–75. https://doi.org/10.1037/0021-843X.97.1.64

NIDA. (2021, April 20). What is the scope of marijuana use in the United States? National Institute on Drug Abuse. https://www.drugabuse.gov/publications/research-reports /marijuana/what-scope-marijuana-use-in-united-states on 2021

Ona, G., & Bouso, J. C. (2020). Potential safety, benefits, and influence of the placebo effect in microdosing psychedelic drugs: A systematic review. *Neuroscience and Biobehavioral Reviews, 119,* 194–203. https://doi.org/10.1016/j.neubiorev.2020.09.035

Paschall, M. J., Ringwalt, C. L., & Flewelling, R. L. (2002). Explaining higher levels of alcohol use among working adolescents: An analysis of potential explanatory variables. *Journal of Studies on Alcohol, 63*(2), 169–178. https://doi.org/10.15288/jsa.2002 .63.169

Parnes, J. E., Smith, J. K., & Conner, B. T. (2018). Reefer madness or much ado about nothing? Cannabis legalization outcomes among young adults in the United States. *International Journal of Drug Policy, 56,* 116–120. https://doi.org/10.1016/j.drugpo .2018.03.011

Patrick, M. E., Rhew, I. C., Lewis, M. A., Abdallah, D. A., Larimer, M. E., Schulenberg, J. E., & Lee, C. M. (2018). Alcohol motivations and behaviors during months young adults experience social role transitions: Microtransitions in early adulthood. *Psychology of Addictive Behaviors, 32*(8), 895–903. https://doi.org/10.1037/adb0000411

Patrick, M. E., Wightman, P., Schoeni, R. F., & Schulenberg, J. E. (2012). Socioeconomic status and substance use among young adults: A comparison across constructs and drugs. *Journal of Studies on Alcohol and Drugs, 73*(5), 772–782. https://doi.org/10 .15288/jsad.2012.73.772

Perry, C. L., Pérez, A., Bluestein, M., Garza, N., Obinwa, U., Jackson, C., Clendennen, S. L., Loukas, A., & Harrell, M. B. (2018). Youth or young adults: Which group is at highest risk for tobacco use onset? *Journal of Adolescent Health, 63*(4), 413–420. https://doi.org/10.1016/j.jadohealth.2018.04.011

Perry, J. L., Joseph, J. E., Jiang, Y., Zimmerman, R. S., Kelly, T. H., Darna, M., Huettl, P., Dwoskin, L. P., & Bardo, M. T. (2011). Prefrontal cortex and drug abuse vulnerability: Translation to prevention and treatment interventions. *Brain Research Reviews, 65*(2), 124–149. https://doi.org/10.1016/j.brainresrev.2010.09.001

Petersen, E. E., Rasmussen, S. A., Daniel, K. L., Yazdy, M. M., & Honein, M. A. (2008). Prescription medication borrowing and sharing among women of reproductive age. *Journal of Women's Health, 17*(7), 1073–1080. https://doi.org/10.1089/jwh.2007.0769

Rauer, A. J., Pettit, G. S., Samek, D. R., Lansford, J. E., Dodge, K. A., & Bates, J. E. (2016). Romantic relationships and alcohol use: A long-term, developmental perspective. *Development and Psychopathology, 28*(3), 773–789. https://doi.org/10.1017 /S0954579416000304

Rodriguez, R., Henderson, C., Rowe, C., Burnett, K., Dakof, G., & Liddle, H. (2007). Acculturation and drug use among dually diagnosed Hispanic adolescents. *Journal of Ethnicity in Substance Abuse, 6*, 97–113. https://doi.org/10.1300/J233v06n02_07

Rudy, A. K., Barnes, A. J., Cobb, C. O., & Nicksic, N. E. (2020). Attitudes about and correlates of cannabis legalization policy among U.S. young adults. *Journal of American College Health*, 1–8. https://doi.org/10.1080/07448481.2020.1713135

Salas-Wright, C. P., Vaughn, M. G., Todic, J., Córdova, D., & Perron, B. E. (2015). Trends in the disapproval and use of marijuana among adolescents and young adults in the United States: 2002–2013. *American Journal of Drug and Alcohol Abuse, 41*(5), 392–404. https://doi.org/10.3109/00952990.2015.1049493

Sampson, R. J., & Laub, J. H. (1993). Structural variations in juvenile court processing: Inequality, the underclass, and social control. *Law and Society Review, 27*(2), 285–311. https://doi.org/10.2307/3053938

Schulenberg, J. E., Johnston, L. D., O'Malley, P. M., Bachman, J. G., Miech, R. A., & Patrick, M. E. (2020). *Monitoring the Future national survey results on drug use, 1975–2019: Volume II, College students and adults ages 19–60*. Ann Arbor: Institute for Social Research, University of Michigan. http://monitoringthefuture.org/pubs.html#monographs

Schulenberg, J., O'Malley, P. M., Bachman, J. G., Wadsworth, K. N., & Johnston, L. D. (1996). Getting drunk and growing up: Trajectories of frequent binge drinking during the transition to young adulthood. *Journal of Studies on Alcohol, 57*(3), 289–304. https://doi.org/10.15288/jsa.1996.57.289

Schuler, M. S., Rice, C. E., Evans-Polce, R. J., & Collins, R. L. (2018). Disparities in substance use behaviors and disorders among adult sexual minorities by age, gender, and sexual identity. *Drug and Alcohol Dependence, 189*, 139–146. https://doi.org/10.1016/j.drugalcdep.2018.05.008

Serido, J., Lawry, C., Li, G., Conger, K. J., & Russell, S. T. (2014). The associations of financial stress and parenting support factors with alcohol behaviors during young adulthood. *Journal of Family and Economic Issues, 35*(3), 339–350. https://doi.org/10.1007/s10834-013-9376-x

Shover, C. L., & Humphreys, K. (2019). Six policy lessons relevant to cannabis legalization. *American Journal of Drug and Alcohol Abuse, 45*(6), 698–706. https://doi.org/10.1080/00952990.2019.1569669

Simons-Morton, B., Haynie, D., Liu, D., Chaurasia, A., Li, K., & Hingson, R. (2016). The effect of residence, school status, work status, and social influence on the prevalence of alcohol use among emerging adults. *Journal of Studies on Alcohol and Drugs, 77*(1), 121–132. https://doi.org/10.15288/jsad.2016.77.121

Slater, M. E., Godette, D., Huang, B., Ruan, W. J., & Kerridge, B. T. (2017). Sexual orientation-based discrimination, excessive alcohol use, and substance use disorders among sexual minority adults. *LGBT Health, 4*(5), 337–344. https://doi.org/10.1089/lgbt.2016.0117

Smart, R., & Pacula, R. L. (2019). Early evidence of the impact of cannabis legalization on cannabis use, cannabis use disorder, and the use of other substances: Findings from state policy evaluations. *American Journal of Drug and Alcohol Abuse, 45*(6), 644–663. https://doi.org/10.1080/00952990.2019.1669626

Statista Research Department. (2020, October 13). *U.S. consumers who use marijuana 2019, by age group.* Statista. https://www.statista.com/statistics/737849/share-americans-age-group-smokes-marijuana/

Steffen, J., Schlichtiger, J., Huber, B. C., & Brunner, S. (2021). Altered alcohol consumption during COVID-19 pandemic lockdown. *Nutrition Journal, 20*(1), 44. https://doi.org/10.1186/s12937-021-00699-0

Stormshak, E. A., Caruthers, A. S., Gau, J. M., & Winter, C. (2019). The impact of recreational marijuana legalization on rates of use and behavior: A 10-year comparison of two cohorts from high school to young adulthood. *Psychology of Addictive Behaviors, 33*(7), 595–602. https://doi.org/10.1037/adb0000508

Suffoletto, B., Ram, N., & Chung, T. (2020). In-person contacts and their relationship with alcohol consumption among young adults with hazardous drinking during a pandemic. *Journal of Adolescent Health, 67*(5), 671–676. https://doi.org/10.1016/j.jadohealth.2020.08.007

Temple, J. R., Shorey, R. C., Lu, Y., Torres, E., Stuart, G. L., & Le, V. D. (2017). E-cigarette use of young adults: Motivations and associations with combustible cigarette alcohol, marijuana, and other illicit drugs. *American Journal on Addictions, 26*(4), 343–348. https://doi.org/10.1111/ajad.12530

Vicknasingam, B., Narayanan, S., Singh, D., & Chawarski, M. (2018). Decriminalization of drug use. *Current Opinion in Psychiatry, 31*(4), 300–305. https://doi.org/10.1097/YCO.0000000000000429

Vincke, E. (2017). Drinking high amounts of alcohol as a short-term mating strategy: The impact of short-term mating motivations on young adults' drinking behavior. *Evolutionary Psychology, 15*(2), 147470491770707. https://doi.org/10.1177/1474704917707073

Volkow, N. D., Fowler, J. S., Wang, G.-J., & Swanson, J. M. (2004). Dopamine in drug abuse and addiction: Results from imaging studies and treatment implications. *Molecular Psychiatry, 9*(6), 557–569. https://doi.org/10.1038/sj.mp.4001507

Welsh, J. W., Shentu, Y., & Sarvey, D. B. (2019). Substance use among college students. *Focus, 17*(2), 117–127. https://doi.org/10.1176/appi.focus.20180037

Wen, H., Hockenberry, J. M., & Druss, B. G. (2019). The effect of medical marijuana laws on marijuana-related attitude and perception among US adolescents and young adults. *Prevention Science, 20*(2), 215–223. https://doi.org/10.1007/s11121-018-0903-8

White, A. (2020). Gender differences in the epidemiology of alcohol use and related harms in the United States. *Alcohol Research: Current Reviews, 40*(2). https://doi.org/10.35946/arcr.v40.2.01

White, H. R., Labouvie, E. W., & Papadaratsakis, V. (2005). Changes in substance use during the transition to adulthood: A comparison of college students and their noncollege age peers. *Journal of Drug Issues, 35*(2), 281–306. https://doi.org/10.1177/002204260503500204

White, H. R., Stevens, A. K., Hayes, K., & Jackson, K. M. (2020). Changes in alcohol consumption among college students due to covid-19: Effects of campus closure and residential change. *Journal of Studies on Alcohol and Drugs, 81*, 725–730.

Whitton, S. W., Dyar, C., Newcomb, M. E., & Mustanski, B. (2018). Effects of romantic involvement on substance use among young sexual and gender minorities. *Drug and Alcohol Dependence, 191*, 215–222. https://doi.org/10.1016/j.drugalcdep.2018.06.037

Zambiasi, D., & Stillman, S. (2020). The pot rush: Is legalized marijuana a positive local amenity? *Economic Inquiry, 58*(2), 667–679. https://doi.org/10.1111/ecin.12832

CHAPTER 4

Widening the Cultural Lens of Suicide-Related Risk Among Racial/Ethnic Minority Emerging Adults With Acculturation Frameworks

LILLIAN POLANCO-ROMAN AND MARJORINE
HENRIQUEZ-CASTILLO

S uicide, an intentionally fatal act of self-directed harm, is the second leading cause of death in people ages 18–24 years old in the United States (Centers for Disease Control and Prevention, 2019). Thus, suicide in emerging adults is a major public health concern. Over the past decade, suicide deaths in emerging adults have continued to rise, despite decreases in overall mortality (Khan et al., 2018). Though suicide deaths remain more prevalent in young men, the increase is disproportionately higher in young women (Ruch et al., 2019). Not surprisingly, increases in suicidal thoughts and behaviors in emerging adults are also evident (Han et al., 2018), which are, paradoxically, more prevalent in young women compared to young men. For instance, the National Survey on Drug Use and Health (NSDUH) shows that about 13.7% of young women and 9.8% of young men (up from 7.1% and 5.0% in 2009, respectively) ages 18–25 years had serious thoughts of suicide in the year prior to the survey, and 2.3% of young women and 1.3% of young men (up from 1.3% and 1.0% in 2009, respectively) made a suicide attempt (U.S. Department of Health and Human Services, 2019).

The current COVID-19 pandemic has also disproportionately impacted suicide-related risk. Though complete suicide data are not available at the time of publication, early findings from a national survey conducted in June 2020 indicated that up to 25% of young adults ages 18–24 years seriously considered suicide in the 30 days prior to the survey, compared to the national average of 10.7%. Similarly, higher rates of suicide ideation were detected in individuals of Hispanic/Latinx (18.6%) and Black (15.1%) backgrounds compared to white (7.9%) and Asian (6.6%) backgrounds (Czeisler et al., 2020). The racial and ethnic disparities in suicide risk allude to the critical role of social determinants of health that have been exacerbated and brought to the fore by the COVID-19 pandemic, though rooted in years of inequitable distribution of societal resources via systemic racism.

Suicidal ideation (thoughts), a consideration or desire to end one's own life, can range from passive thoughts such as a wish to die to more active thoughts involving a plan of action with strong intent. Suicide attempts (behaviors) are intentional acts of self-directed harm that are nonfatal. About one-third of youth who think about suicide will make an attempt, though 24 in 25 attempts are nonfatal (Cha, Franz, et al., 2018). This makes it difficult to accurately identify youth at greatest risk for attempting and dying by suicide. Despite the low lethality of suicidal thoughts and behaviors, these nonfatal manifestations of suicide remain the strongest indicators of suicide-related risk.

Although adolescence is a high-risk period for the emergence of suicidal thoughts that, on average, transition to behaviors within 1 year (Nock et al., 2013), the severity of risk increases through emerging adulthood, as suicidal thoughts and behaviors become more frequent, impairing, and lethal (Goldston et al., 2015). This is due, in part, to a lack of early intervention, as the majority of youth at high risk for suicidal behaviors do not seek mental health care (King et al., 2019). The suicide literature abounds with information on intrapersonal risk factors such as psychiatric disorders, personal or family history of suicidal behaviors, and demographics (Franklin et al., 2017). The consistent demographic differences in suicide (e.g., age, gender, socioeconomic status, race/ethnicity) allude to ecological influences, yet our understanding of suicide risk in a sociocultural context remains limited. In fact, suicide deaths among racial/ethnic minority populations are most prevalent in emerging adulthood, as individuals from Black, Hispanic, Asian, and Native American backgrounds are most likely to die by suicide before the age of 30. This is in contrast to white populations, for whom middle age (40s–50s) is the highest-risk period for suicide deaths. Importantly, the majority (50–75%) of suicide deaths in people under age 25 are first attempts (McKean et al., 2018), signaling a real urgency in identifying and preventing risk, particularly in racial/ethnic minority emerging adults.

Racial/ethnic minority emerging adults in the United States may be at greater risk for thinking about and attempting suicide than their white peers, according to findings from a large national college survey (Sa et al., 2020), though this was not supported by the data from NSDUH. There is also evidence to suggest racial/ethnic differences in the risk factors (Cheref et al., 2019), and in the developmental course of suicidal thoughts and behaviors (Kim et al., 2019; Erausquin et al., 2019), as well as in the antecedents of suicide (Lee & Wong, 2020). Further exacerbating suicide-related risk, racial/ethnic minority youth are also less likely to disclose their suicidal thoughts and behaviors to others (Morrison & Downey, 2000) and less likely to seek mental health services compared to their white peers (King et al., 2019). Together, these findings highlight the disproportionate burden of suicide-related risk on racial/ethnic minority youth and allude to the important role of cultural influences along the suicide spectrum. Although the racial/ethnic disparity in youth suicide risk has prompted calls for cultural considerations in our understanding of suicide-related risk (Goldston et al., 2008), the cultural context of suicide risk, particularly in emerging adults, remains poorly understood. Identifying these cultural influences could inform preventive strategies by providing novel targets for intervention to reduce suicide-related risk in racial/ethnic minority emerging adults.

A better understanding of how cultural development may impact suicide-related risk may provide important insight about the racial/ethnic disparities in suicidal behaviors in emerging adults. This chapter describes early and contemporary models of acculturation frameworks in the context of emerging adulthood. We also highlight theoretical models of suicide that could be applied within an acculturation framework. The chapter follows with a select review of the literature identifying cultural risk and protective factors linked to suicidal thoughts and behaviors. Finally, we conclude with clinical implications for emerging adults by describing several programs that have integrated acculturation frameworks into suicide prevention to reduce risk in racial/ethnic minority youth.

ACCULTURATION HISTORY AND THEORY

Population estimates in the United States project a multicultural-majority country (based on ethnic and racial composition) by the year 2050 (Vespa et al., 2020). As the country becomes increasingly racially and ethnically diverse, most youths will experience navigating two (heritage and mainstream) or more cultures (Gladding, 2006, p. 40).* Acculturation, or the psychological changes associated with navigating two or more cultural environments, can be a challenging process that results in distress (Berry, 2006; Schwartz et al., 2015). Though largely examined in immigrant groups, acculturation is relevant in the lives of marginalized individuals, including racial and ethnic minority emerging adults. A better understanding of how acculturation impacts the development of emerging adults, particularly of racial and ethnic minority backgrounds, could inform health preventive and intervention strategies to promote well-being among this growing US population.

The sociopolitical context and changing demographics of the United States have shaped conceptual and methodological approaches of acculturation research over time. Early studies focused on the cultural experiences of Native Americans, who were forced to discard their heritage culture and adopt the Anglo culture of white Europeans following colonization (i.e., assimilation; Garrett & Pichette, 2000). In the early 20th century, the research involved examining the assimilation process of new waves of immigrants from Southern and Eastern European countries (e.g., Germany, Italy, Ireland; Schwartz et al., 2010). Like Native Americans, the recent Western European immigrants were expected to adopt US culture and maintain white racial homogeneity. Assimilation was promoted as a healthy acculturation experience, whereas maintenance of heritage culture (i.e., enculturation) was deemed harmful and associated with identity diffusion, psychic conflict, and other mental health disorders (for a review, see Rudmin, 2009). This ideology was especially detrimental to racial and ethnic minority groups, particularly descendants of enslaved Africans and Native Americans, as they were not able to integrate into mainstream US society with subsequent generations, as observed with white immigrants (Alba, 2009).

By the mid-20th century, the civil rights movement and the Immigration Act of 1965 helped shift the assimilation ideology toward embracing multiculturalism and opened the door to an influx of non-European immigrants (Smokowski et al., 2017). Incoming immigrants at this time were largely from African, Latin American/Caribbean, and Asian countries (also known as the global south), whose race, values, practices, and languages differed from the majority white, Anglo, and English-speaking population in the United States

---

* The shared values, beliefs, expectations, worldviews, symbols, and appropriate learned behaviors of a group that provide its members with norms, plans, traditions, and rules for social living. Culture is transmitted from one generation to the next.

(Deaux, 2006). Racial discrimination and language barriers made assimilating to mainstream US society difficult for these new immigrants, which prompted greater attachment to their heritage culture (Ferguson & Birman, 2016).

An alternative acculturation theory emerged and proposed that, contrary to findings associated with assimilation theory, heritage and mainstream cultures can coexist independently of each other and promote mental well-being (Berry et al., 2006). This bidimensional model outlined four acculturation strategies: assimilation (reject heritage and adopt mainstream culture), separation (maintain heritage and reject mainstream culture), marginalization (reject heritage and mainstream cultures, and integration or biculturalism (embrace both cultures). This approach noted the protective effects of maintaining one's heritage culture (e.g., strong racial or ethnic identification), as well as negative experiences such as acculturative stress, or stress reactions resulting from navigating distinct cultures (Berry, 2006). Findings further point to biculturalism as the most protective strategy for racial and ethnic minorities living in multicultural contexts, whereas loss of heritage culture (regardless of orientation to mainstream culture) was associated with the poorest outcomes, including symptoms of depression and anxiety (Berry, 2017).

Contemporary models of acculturation expanded on this fourfold model to encompass independent and interrelated cultural dimensions such as values, practices, and identification across both mainstream and heritage cultures (Schwartz et al., 2010). This multidimensional model conceptualized acculturation as a dynamic and developmental process to better understand its impact on health outcomes. Studies using racial/ethnic minority adolescent samples indicate that changes toward maintenance of heritage culture in practices (e.g., language use) and values (e.g., collectivism, familism), but not identity (e.g., ethnic pride) are linked to fewer depressive symptoms and lower risk for substance use (Cruz et al., 2017; Schwartz et al., 2015), suggesting differential effects on mental health across cultural dimensions. Little remains known, however, about how acculturation may impact health in emerging adulthood.

ACCULTURATION AND HEALTH IN EMERGING ADULTHOOD

Emerging adulthood is conceptualized as a transition period between adolescence and adulthood (i.e., ages 18–29 years) and characterized by continued identity exploration and delayed entry into adulthood commitments (e.g., college, employment, marriage, parenthood; Arnett, 2000). Some scholars have argued, however, that this developmental period is a luxury of the white middle class that may not apply to the poor and working class (who are disproportionately racial/ethnic minority individuals). Racial/ethnic minority youth may not have the option to delay their adulthood commitments due to societal barriers such as racial/ethnic discrimination and financial instability (Syed & Mitchell, 2014). Additionally, emerging adulthood is centered around individualistic values (i.e., autonomy, independence) that may contrast with more collectivistic values that may lead to family conflict about how and when an individual enters adulthood (LeBrón & Viruell-Fuentes, 2020; Schwartz, 2016). The tension between these opposing cultural demands may exacerbate the vulnerability resulting from role changes and transitions typical of emerging adulthood. Thus, examining culture-specific experiences (e.g., racial/ethnic discrimination, cultural values) during emerging adulthood may provide critical insight into the health and well-being of racial/ethnic minority emerging adults.

Emerging adulthood is marked by high levels of health risk behaviors, including unprotected sex, substance/alcohol misuse, and suicidal behaviors (Arnett, 2000, p. 20). Racial/ethnic emerging adults undergoing dual cultural processes may be particularly vulnerable to these risk behaviors, yet very little is known about acculturation in emerging adulthood. Frameworks drawn from multicultural psychology (i.e., cultural experiences), developmental sciences (i.e., age periods), and child psychopathology (i.e., mental health) highlight the role of acculturation in development and health (Causadias, 2013). Early evidence suggests that the acculturative effects observed in adolescents continue into emerging adulthood, as individuals enter adulthood commitments while navigating heritage and US cultural expectations.

Findings on the association between acculturation and health risk behaviors in emerging adults have revealed complex relationships based on the dimensions, outcomes, and groups examined. For instance, Schwartz and colleagues (2011) found no significant association between cultural dimensions and health risk behaviors among white college students, but differential effects among racial/ethnic minority students were observed. Specifically, endorsement of heritage cultural values (i.e., collectivism) was associated with more safe-sex practices among East Asians, less hazardous alcohol use among South Asians and Blacks, and less illicit drug use among Hispanics.

Studies about cultural practices and health risk behaviors produced mixed findings. In one study, greater endorsement of US practices (assessed as language and friend/romantic relationships) was linked to higher likelihood of unsafe sex among East Asians, whereas greater endorsement of heritage practices was associated with less illicit drug use among Hispanics (Schwartz et al., 2011). No association between US and heritage cultural practices (via language use) and alcohol misuse were detected among Hispanic emerging adults from Texas (Cano et al., 2020; Perrotte et al., 2019) though other studies conducted in Arizona and Florida have shown bicultural social networks was associated with less alcohol use severity (Cano et al., 2020). Additionally, high levels of Hispanic cultural practices in adolescence from Southern California were linked to lower cigarette, alcohol, and marijuana use in emerging adulthood (Unger et al., 2014). Thus, type of cultural practices, timing, and context play an important role in the impact of acculturation on health.

Similarly, studies on identification and health risk behaviors have also yielded mixed findings. For example, no association was found between ethnic identity and substance use as adolescents transitioned into emerging adulthood (Unger et al., 2014). Meanwhile, identification with US culture was associated with more alcohol use among East Asians and less illicit drug use among Black immigrants, whereas heritage culture identification was associated with less alcohol use among South Asians, but greater likelihood of unsafe sex among Hispanics (Schwartz et al., 2011). More recent research found differential effects of fluctuations in cultural identification on daily psychological well-being within a 12-day period between US and heritage culture. A greater sense of belonging to heritage culture was associated with positive well-being on that same day (Meca et al., 2018), but at the end of the 12-day period, fluctuations in bicultural hybridity (i.e., sustaining two or more cultural identities) was linked to negative psychological well-being and internalizing symptoms (Schwartz et al., 2019). Thus, how an individual reconciles the juxtaposition between conflicting cultures may have immediate and distal effects on health.

Taken together, these findings indicate that assessing acculturation among racial and ethnic minority emerging adults could greatly inform our understanding of how cultural factors are implicated in health and well-being during emerging adulthood, despite the limitations of these studies that include largely Hispanic and college student samples, compromising the generalizability of the findings. Employing a developmental and multidimensional perspective could provide a clearer picture of how specific cultural values (e.g., collectivism, self-construal), practices (e.g., linguistic, relationships), and identification (e.g., pride, exploration) relate to a variety of health outcomes including substance use and abuse, internalizing symptoms, stress physiology, sexual risk behaviors, and other health outcomes yet to be explored through a cultural lens during emerging adulthood, such as suicide risk.

ACCULTURATION AND SUICIDE-RELATED RISK

Suicide models drawing from ecological perspectives intersect with acculturation frameworks to inform our understanding of suicide-related risk. One of the earliest models of suicide comes from Durkheim (1897/1951), who used a sociological lens to explain the higher prevalence of suicide deaths in Protestants compared to Catholics, citing social disintegration. Decades later, Trautman (1961) offered an account of the possible role of migration and acculturation to help explain the high volume of young Puerto Rican women presenting with suicidal behaviors at a public hospital in the Bronx, NY. Contemporary models have since shifted to focus on more intrapersonal factors such as psychiatric disorders, cognitive vulnerability, stressful life events, and impulsive behaviors (Barzilay & Apter, 2014). This has yielded studies focusing on the same risk factors (Franklin et al., 2017), and using predominantly white, adult samples (Cha, Tezanos, et al., 2018). This narrow approach has impeded our understanding of suicide-related risk within a sociocultural context, as culture-specific experiences were often overlooked in the study of suicide.

The cultural model and theory of suicide of Chu and colleagues (2010) is one of the few suicide models to highlight the role of culture. This model proposes that cultural experiences may impact suicide-related risk across the spectrum through various avenues. Specifically, cultural experiences may influence the nature of stress exposure, as evidenced by racial/ethnic discrimination, minority stress, and acculturative stress. Cultural experiences may also impact the ways in which individuals evaluate, manifest, and respond to stressful experiences. Last, cultural experiences may impact attitudes about and expressions of suicidal thoughts and behaviors.

There is growing evidence to support the cultural model of suicide, as culture-specific risk (e.g., racial/ethnic discrimination, acculturative stress, minority stress) and protective (e.g., ethnic identity, ethnic density) factors are linked to suicidal thoughts and behaviors, particularly across racial/ethnic minority adults (Odafe et al., 2016) and adolescents (Goldston et al., 2008). Findings also show physiological changes associated with chronic social stress (e.g., cortisol, heart rate) may also be elicited by culture-specific stressors like racial/ethnic discrimination (Berger & Sarnyai, 2015). This is consistent with another suicide model, one of the few to apply a developmental approach to understanding youth suicide-related risk, and cites a disruption in the stress response system as a potential underlying cause. Specifically, this model proposes early exposure to chronic stress, such as culture-specific stressors, may overwhelm the arousal system and render the youth vulnerable to future stressors, which in turn may increase vulnerability to thinking about or attempting suicide in the future (Miller & Prinstein, 2019).

CULTURE-SPECIFIC RISK FACTORS FOR SUICIDAL THOUGHTS AND BEHAVIORS

Research consistently points toward the effect of acculturation on suicide-related risk in youths in the United States. Specifically, more acculturated Black (Joe et al., 2009), Hispanic (Peña et al., 2008), and Asian (Wong & Maffini, 2011) adolescents, via greater exposure to mainstream US culture, are more likely to attempt suicide than their less acculturated peers, particularly girls. Despite the narrow approach in assessing acculturation (e.g., country of origin, generation status), these findings suggest the acculturative process may impact suicide-related risk in racial/ethnic minority youth. The underlying mechanisms of how acculturation may impact suicide-related risk remain poorly understood. Nevertheless, such findings have prompted questions about whether abandoning the practices, values, and identity of the heritage culture in exchange for practices, values, and identity tied more to the mainstream culture was harmful. For instance, Zayas and colleagues (2009) found that the degree to which Latina adolescents culturally orient toward mainstream US or Hispanic heritage was not associated with a history of suicide attempts. This finding highlights the complex and dynamic nature of acculturation processes and indicates that the impact of the cultural environment on suicide-related risk is much more nuanced. Individual differences in the acculturative experience, specifically distress associated with navigating cultural environments, may be helpful in clarifying how acculturation may impact suicide-related risk.

Acculturative stress is one type of cultural stressor that has garnered some attention in the suicide literature. Such experiences commonly result from migration and acculturation processes, and may involve not only novel encounters of discrimination, but also pressures to assimilate to the mainstream culture, language, and other culture-specific barriers, and intrafamilial conflict arising from conflicting expectations. Though scarce, research shows increases in acculturative stress are associated with increases in suicidal ideation and attempts in racially/ethnically diverse groups of adolescents and emerging adults (Hovey & King, 1996; Gomez et al., 2011; Polanco-Roman & Miranda, 2013; Walker et al., 2008), though some studies found no association (Cho & Haslam, 2010; Chesin & Jeglic, 2016).

Another type of cultural stressor that has garnered some attention in the suicide literature is racial/ethnic discrimination, or unjust treatment predicated on an individual's racial or ethnic group affiliation. The harmful effects of racial/ethnic discrimination on mental health are well documented (Williams, 2018). According to a national survey conducted by the American Psychological Association (2016), the majority of Black (71%), Hispanic (56%), and Asian (64%) adults reported day-to-day racial/ethnic discrimination. This report also indicated that, compared to older adults, emerging adults were less likely to deal well with experiences of racial/ethnic discrimination. Thus, emerging adults, particularly from racial/ethnic minority backgrounds, may be particularly vulnerable to the harmful effects of racial/ethnic discrimination.

There is growing evidence to suggest that racial/ethnic discrimination may increase suicide-related risk. Using nationally representative samples of Black, Hispanic, and Asian adults in the United States, researchers found that racial/ethnic discrimination was positively associated with suicidal thoughts and behaviors (Oh et al., 2018). Similar findings were also reported in adolescents (Assari et al., 2017; Madubata et al., 2019) and emerging adults (Gomez et al., 2011; Polanco-Roman & Miranda, 2013), though other studies found no association (Chesin & Jeglic, 2016; Castle et al., 2011). Thus, the relation between racial/ethnic discrimination and suicide-related risk is complex.

The mixed findings detected in the relation between cultural stressors (i.e., acculturative stress, racial/ethnic discrimination) and suicide-related risk may be due, in part, to the indirect nature of the relation. Indeed, research indicates that acculturative stress may impact risk for suicide ideation to the extent that it impacts feelings of hopelessness (Polanco-Roman & Miranda, 2013) and difficulties in emotion regulation (Mayorga et al., 2018). Similarly, several potential pathways through which racial/ethnic discrimination may impact risk for suicidal thoughts and behaviors have been identified, such as cognitive factors like hopelessness (Polanco-Roman & Miranda, 2013) and rumination (Cheref et al., 2015); interpersonal factors like perceived burdensomeness (Hollingsworth et al., 2017), symptoms of depression (Walker et al., 2017; O'Keefe et al., 2015; Polanco-Roman & Miranda, 2013), anxiety (Kwon & Han, 2019), and posttraumatic stress (Polanco-Roman et al., 2019).

Scholars have largely focused on cultural stressors, particularly racial/ethnic discrimination, in the form of interpersonal manifestations of overt displays of racial/ethnic biases and prejudices. However, discrimination in other manifestations may also impact suicide-related risk. Microaggressions, or more covert, subtle, and chronic slights (O'Keefe et al 2015; Madubata et al., 2019) as well as institutional discrimination, or racial/ethnic bias in practices and policies (Kwon & Han, 2019), have also been linked to suicidal thoughts and behaviors in racial/ethnic minority youth. The effects of racial/ethnic discrimination may even extend beyond the individual to the next generation. For instance, in a clinical sample of African American mothers in treatment for substance abuse, maternal experiences of racial discrimination were associated with suicidal thoughts and behaviors in their adolescent and young adult offspring, independent of the offspring's personal discrimination experiences (Arshanapally et al., 2018). In sum, the harmful effect of cultural stressors on suicide-related risk is well supported.

Considering the important role of family dynamics in youth development, research has also identified ways in which acculturative processes may influence family relations to impact suicide-related risk. For instance, parents acculturate at a slower pace than their youth offspring (Phinney et al., 2000), resulting in an acculturation gap. This acculturation gap may create discord within the family, and the resulting disruption may increase vulnerability to suicidal thoughts and behaviors. For instance, one study found that increases in the acculturation gap in a group of Latina mother-daughter dyads were associated with lower parent-youth mutuality and greater risk for psychiatric disorders in youth, which in turn was associated with suicide attempts (Baumann et al., 2010). The acculturation gap may be further exacerbated by changes in societal norms around gender roles and scripts and familial scripts, particularly for girls and young women. For instance, a qualitative study found that themes of secrets and silence about experiences of gendered oppression and sexual violence were prevalent in Latina adolescents with suicide attempt history (Szlyk et al., 2018). Studies also identified intrapersonal (individual-level) factors such as hopelessness and emotional reactivity (Ortin et al., 2018) and stress resulting from an acculturation gap (Cervantes et al., 2014), through which an acculturation gap may potentially impact suicide-related risk.

CULTURE-SPECIFIC PROTECTIVE FACTORS FOR SUICIDAL THOUGHTS AND BEHAVIORS

The higher rates of suicidal thoughts and behaviors in more acculturated racial and ethnic minority youth also allude to potential culture-specific factors that may protect against suicide-related risk. Such factors identified involve collectivistic (versus individualistic) values and practices that promote a sense of belonging or connection via ethnic identity, family cohesion, ethnic density, and religiosity or spirituality.

A neighborhood context that is representative of an individual's ethnic background, also referred to as ethnic density, may protect against suicide-related risk. For instance, in a study examining suicide deaths among Hispanic individuals from various metropolitan areas across the United States, Wadsworth and Kubrin (2007) found that immigrants (i.e., individuals born outside the US) overall had higher rates of suicide than US-born Hispanics, but not among immigrants who lived in ethnic enclaves of Hispanic immigrants. Though it remains unclear what it is about living in an ethnic enclave in particular that may be protective against suicide risk, one possible explanation is a sense of community and belonging, as well as access to social networks and support. Indeed, ethnic identity, or the degree to which an individual feels connected to their ethnic group, is associated with lower suicide-related risk. Using nationally representative samples of Asian (Cheng et al., 2010) and Hispanic (Perez-Rodriguez et al., 2014) adults in the United States, researchers found that a stronger ethnic identity was associated with lower lifetime rates of suicidal thoughts and behaviors. Ethnic identity may protect against suicide-related risk by buffering the harmful effects of cultural stressors such as racial/ethnic discrimination (Polanco-Roman & Miranda, 2013; Cheref et al., 2019; Walker et al., 2008). Further, developing a strong sense of ethnic pride may help ward off feelings of isolation and loneliness, provide a strong social network and source of emotional support, and foster healthy adaptive strategies to more effectively manage culture-specific stressors such as racial/ethnic discrimination (Neblett et al., 2012).

The protective effects of religiosity on suicide-related risk in racial/ethnic minority groups have also been documented in racial/ethnic minority populations. These effects may function through the promotion of negative attitudes toward suicide (Anglin et al., 2005), fostering more effective coping styles (Molock et al., 2006), and, as observed with ethnic identity, buffering the harmful impact of culture-specific stressors (Walker et al., 2014). Although this research has largely focused on African American populations in an attempt to address the historically low rates of suicide deaths compared to white populations, research has reported similar findings in Latinx/Hispanic adolescents (Boyas et al., 2019).

Cultural values with more collectivistic ideologies that prioritize the needs of the family over the needs of the individual may also protect against suicide-related risk, particularly to the extent that they promote family cohesion and attenuate conflict. In a group of Latina mother-daughter dyads, Zayas and colleagues (2009) did not find a direct relation between familism and suicide attempts. Upon further examination, however, they found that there was an indirect association through influences on mother-daughter mutuality (Baumann et al., 2010), family conflict (Kuhlberg et al., 2010), and family cohesion (Peña et al., 2011). This research has largely focused on Latina adolescents, or the "dutiful daughters" within the lens of Marianismo, in attempt to address the appreciably high rates of suicidal behaviors in this population, and warrants further attention.

A clinical vignette is provided to help illustrate how acculturative processes may impact suicide-related risk in racial/ethnic minority emerging adults. Wilma is a 20-year-old Latina from Puerto Rico who relocated to the mainland United States with her mother following displacement due to Hurricane Maria in 2017. Wilma was reluctant to leave Puerto Rico, as she was in college with professional aspirations, and where she had a strong support network of family and friends. But her family's precarious financial situation was acute and derailed her future plans. Wilma had little choice but to work a low-wage job, given her limited transferable skills and social network in the United States. Wilma's fair skin had previously protected her from the racism her darker-skinned mother had faced growing up in Puerto Rico. But her accented English has made her a new target of discrimination that she is faced with navigating unguided. She is growing acutely aware of the added challenges, coupled with the reduced support, accessible to her in the United States. She is having a difficult time adjusting to her new life and meeting new people, and has grown increasingly isolated and withdrawn. Wilma doesn't want to give her already highly stressed mother further stress and concern, so she keeps her worries to herself. Wilma and her mother are disheartened by the slow governmental response to aid Puerto Rico's recovery, which they had hoped would expedite their return home. They feel abandoned. Wilma starts developing hopeless thoughts about ever returning to her family and friends back home in Puerto Rico or returning to college as she had planned. She starts to feel like a burden to her mother and believing that she would be better off dead. She begins to miss too many days of work and is unable to keep up with her household chores, which now become points of tension between Wilma and her mother. After a contentious dispute in which Wilma's mother mischaracterizes her depression as "laziness," Wilma waits for the first opportunity when she is home alone to attempt suicide by overdosing on sleeping pills.

CULTURAL APPROACHES TO SUICIDE PREVENTION

The knowledge obtained in recent years about acculturation and suicide-related risk has offered critical, though limited, insight into the suicidal process within a cultural context and has informed several suicide prevention programs. These interventions geared toward racial/ethnic minority youth often rely on community-based approaches and target culture-specific risk and protective factors. This approach is particularly important in working with racial and ethnic minority youth at risk for suicide, who are less likely to seek mental health care services than their white peers (King et al., 2019). Thus, culture-specific approaches to suicide prevention may be an effective strategy to address suicide-related risk in racial and ethnic minority emerging adults as well.

There are several suicide prevention strategies tailored toward Latinx youth that address culture-specific processes. For instance, Life Is Precious is an after-school, community-based program in New York City (Humensky et al., 2017) that promotes coping skills, targeting cultural stressors like discrimination and family conflict. Though it is intended to supplement mental health services, early evidence suggests it may help reduce suicide-related risk in Latinx youth (Humensky et al., 2017). Familias Unidas was originally developed to reduce substance misuse and sexual risk behaviors in Latinx youth (Vidot et al., 2016), but its effects may cross over to reduce suicide-related risk as well. Despite a lack of suicide-specific targets, this family-based intervention targets communication between parents and adolescents to reduce family conflict, particularly resulting from acculturation differences. Another example is the Sociocognitive behavior therapy for suicidal behaviors (SCBT-SB; Duarté-Velez et al., 2016), is a culturally adapted psychotherapy developed to reduce risk for suicidal behaviors in Puerto Rican adolescents. In addition to targeting maladaptive thoughts and behaviors as traditionally done in cognitive-behavioral therapy, SCBT-SB also addresses family and ecological processes by targeting family conflict, minority and discrimination stressors, and identity development.

Community-based approaches highlighting culture-specific factors have prevailed as suicide prevention strategies within Native American/American Indian populations. Drawing on the effectiveness of a community- and school-based skills training program to reduce alcohol and substance use in American Indian adolescents, the American Indian Life Skills Development Curriculum was created (LaFromboise et al., 2008). This curriculum targeted self-regulation, stress coping, and problem solving via modeling by adults from the community who reinforced themes of perseverance in the face of colonization and gatekeeping by tribal community members who promoted cultural values and pride. Similarly, the consistent finding that strong American Indian values and a strong ethnic identity are robust protective factors against suicide-related risk in American Indian youth spurred the creation of the Elders Resilience Curriculum (Cwik et al., 2019). This community-led approach to suicide prevention for American Indian youth has leveraged the wisdom of community elders to promote cultural pride, practices, and values to reduce risk for suicidal behaviors. The elders participated at every stage of the intervention, from the development of the curriculum to its implementation in middle schools.

Suicide prevention strategies targeting Black youth have leveraged the relationship between the Black communities and their church (Molock et al., 2008). Through this model, the church served to bridge the gap between the Black community and traditional mental health services, specifically through providing information about mental health services in an attempt to normalize attitudes toward them. Some advantages noted in using the church as a gatekeeper for mental health care include reducing the stigma of seeking help, increasing accessibility and reducing barriers to services, and promoting religious coping as a protective factor against suicide-related risk.

The early evidence for culture-specific strategies in suicide prevention tailored toward racial/ethnic minority youth seems promising, though they have largely targeted adolescents. Nevertheless, it is possible that some of the benefits may cross over to emerging adults, though further research is warranted. There is also a paucity of suicide research and culture-specific suicide prevention strategies tailored toward Black and Asian American youth.

CONCLUDING REMARKS

Integrating acculturation frameworks into our current understanding of the suicide process is essential for reducing suicide-related risk in emerging adults, particularly those from racial and ethnic minority backgrounds. Research has identified culture-specific risk and protective factors, alluding to the role of acculturation in the development of suicidal thoughts and behaviors. Several suicide prevention programs have leveraged this information in applying culture-specific strategies to reduce risk in racial and ethnic minority adolescents. These strategies seem promising in their ability to engage and deliver culturally sensitive services and may also benefit emerging adults.

Further research is warranted to better understand the ways in which cultural experiences may impact suicide-related risk in emerging adults. Specifically, research needs to move beyond the context of a college setting and broaden the study of cultural stressors to include discrimination on a more structural and societal level. Additionally, a more intersectional approach could provide critical insight about the influence of race, ethnicity, socioeconomic status, immigration status, sexual orientation, religion, and other social identities on acculturation and suicide-related risk (LeBrón & Viruell-Fuentes, 2020). Intergenerational processes may also provide important insight as acculturation experiences may impact development across the life span and also across generations. Such directions would broaden the cultural lens of understanding of suicide-related risk in racial and ethnic minority emerging adults.

Lillian Polanco-Roman is an Assistant Professor of Psychology and the director of the Mental Health Equity Lab at The New School. Dr. Polanco-Roman is a licensed clinical psychologist. She obtained her doctoral degree in clinical psychology at The Graduate Center, CUNY (City College) and completed a Postdoctoral Research Fellowship at Columbia University Irving Medical Center/New York State Psychiatric Institute. Her research aims to examine the developmental and mental health consequences of race-based stress and trauma in racially and ethnically minoritized and immigrant youth, specifically in relation to suicidal thoughts and behaviors.

Marjorine Henriquez-Castillo is a PhD Candidate in the Developmental Psychology Doctoral Program at The Graduate Center, City University of New York. She's also an NIH Diversity Supplement Predoctoral Research Fellow at Columbia University Medical Center/New York State Psychiatric Institute through the Environmental influences on Child Health Outcomes Program. Her research focuses on using latent variable modeling to examine the changes associated with navigating multiple cultural experiences (acculturation) and how it shapes the psychological health (psychopathology and well-being) of parents and their children. Additionally, she examines how different social factors (race, ethnicity, socioeconomic status, nativity) impact this relationship, particularly among Latinx youth.

REFERENCES

Alba, R. D. (2009). *Remaking the American mainstream: Assimilation and contemporary immigration.* Harvard University Press.

American Psychological Association. (2016). Stress in America: The impact of discrimination. *Stress in America Survey.* American Psychological Association.

Anglin, D. M., Gabriel, K. O., & Kaslow, N. J. (2005). Suicide acceptability and religious well-being: A comparative analysis in African American suicide attempters and non-attempters. *Journal of Psychology and Theology, 33*(2), 140–150. https://doi.org/10.1177/009164710503300207

Arnett, J. J. (2000). Emerging adulthood: A theory of development from the late teens through the twenties. *American Psychologist, 55*(5), 469–480. https://doi.org/10.1037/0003-066X.55.5.469

Arshanapally, S., Werner, K. B., Sartor, C. E., & Bucholz, K. K. (2018). The association between racial discrimination and suicidality among African-American adolescents and young adults. *Archives of Suicide Research, 22*(4), 584–595. https://doi.org/10.1080/13811118.2017.1387207

Assari, S., Moghani Lankarani, M., & Caldwell, C. H. (2017). Discrimination increases suicidal ideation in black adolescents regardless of ethnicity and gender. *Behavioral Sciences, 7*(4), 75–85. https://doi:10.3390/bs7040075

Barzilay, S., & Apter, A. (2014). Psychological models of suicide. *Archives of Suicide Research, 18*(4), 295–312. https://doi.org/10.1080/13811118.2013.824825

Baumann, A. A., Kuhlberg, J. A., & Zayas, L. H. (2010). Familism, mother-daughter mutuality, and suicide attempts of adolescent Latinas. *Journal of Family Psychology, 24*(5), 616–624. https://doi:10.1037/a0020584

Berger, M., & Sarnyai, Z. (2015). "More than skin deep": Stress neurobiology and mental health consequences of racial discrimination. *Stress, 18*(1), 1–10. https://doi.org/10.3109/10253890.2014.989204

Berry, J. W. (2006). Acculturative stress. In P. T. P. Wong & L. C. J. Wong (Eds.), *Handbook of multicultural perspectives on stress and coping* (pp. 287–298). Springer US. https://doi.org/10.1007/0-387-26238-5_12

Berry, J. W. (2017). Theories and models of acculturation. In S. J. Schwartz & J. Unger (Eds.), *The Oxford handbook of acculturation and health*. Oxford University Press. https://doi.org/10.1093/oxfordhb/9780190215217.013.2

Berry, J. W., Phinney, J. S., Sam, D. L., & Vedder, P. (2006). Immigrant youth: Acculturation, identity, and adaptation. *Applied Psychology: An International Review, 55*(3), 303–332. https://doi.org/10.1111/j.1464-0597.2006.00256.x

Boyas, J. F., Kim, Y. J., Villarreal-Otálora, T., & Sink, J. K. (2019). Suicide ideation among Latinx adolescents: Examining the role of parental monitoring and intrinsic religiosity. *Children and Youth Services Review, 102*, 177–185. https://doi.org/10.1016/j.childyouth.2019.04.026

Cano, M. Á., Sánchez, M., De La Rosa, M., Rojas, P., Ramírez-Ortiz, D., Bursac, Z., Meca, A., Schwartz, S. J., Lorenzo-Blanco, E. I., Zamboanga, B. L., Garcini, L. M., Roncancio, A. M., Arbona, C., Sheehan, D. M., & de Dios, M. A. (2020). Alcohol use severity among Hispanic emerging adults: Examining the roles of bicultural self-efficacy and acculturation. *Addictive Behaviors, 108*, 106442. https://doi.org/10.1016/j.addbeh.2020.106442

Castle, K., Conner, K., Kaukeinen, K., & Tu, X. (2011). Perceived racism, discrimination, and acculturation in suicidal ideation and suicide attempts among black young adults. *Suicide and Life-Threatening Behavior, 41*(3), 342–351. https://doi.org/10.1111/j.1943-278X.2011.00033.x

Causadias, J. M. (2013). A roadmap for the integration of culture into developmental psychopathology. *Development and Psychopathology, 25*(4, pt. 2), 1375–1398. https://doi.org/10.1017/S0954579413000679

Centers for Disease Control and Prevention. (2019). Fatal injury reports, national, regional and state, 1981–2019. U.S. Department of Health and Human Services. http://www.cdc.gov/injury/wisqars/fatal_injury_reports.html

Cervantes, R. C., Goldbach, J. T., Varela, A., & Santisteban, D. A. (2014). Self-harm among Hispanic adolescents: Investigating the role of culture-related stressors. *Journal of Adolescent Health, 55*(5), 633–639. https://doi.org/10.1016/j.jadohealth.2014.05.017

Cha, C. B., Franz, P. J., M. Guzmán, E., Glenn, C. R., Kleiman, E. M., & Nock, M. K. (2018). Annual research review: Suicide among youth—epidemiology, (potential) etiology, and treatment. *Journal of Child Psychology and Psychiatry, 59*(4), 460–482. https://doi .org/10.1111/jcpp.12831

Cha, C. B., Tezanos, K. M., Peros, O. M., Ng, M. Y., Ribeiro, J. D., Nock, M. K., & Franklin, J. C. (2018). Accounting for diversity in suicide research: Sampling and sample reporting practices in the United States. *Suicide and Life-Threatening Behavior, 48*(2), 131–139. https://doi.org/10.1111/sltb.12344

Cheng, J. K. Y., Fancher, T. L., Ratanasen, M., Conner, K. R., Duberstein, P. R., Sue, S., & Takeuchi, D. (2010). Lifetime suicidal ideation and suicide attempts in Asian Americans. *Asian American Journal of Psychology, 1*(1), 18-30. https://doi: 10.1037/a0018799.

Cheref, S., Lane, R., Polanco-Roman, L., Gadol, E., & Miranda, R. (2015). Suicidal ideation among racial/ethnic minorities: Moderating effects of rumination and depressive symptoms. *Cultural Diversity and Ethnic Minority Psychology, 21*(1), 31-40. https:// doi: 10.1037/a0037139

Cheref, S., Talavera, D., & Walker, R. L. (2019). Perceived discrimination and suicide ideation: Moderating roles of anxiety symptoms and ethnic identity among Asian American, African American, and Hispanic emerging adults. *Suicide and Life-Threatening Behavior, 49*(3), 665–677. https://doi: 10.1111/sltb.12467

Chesin, M. S., & Jeglic, E. L. (2016). Factors associated with recurrent suicidal ideation among racially and ethnically diverse college students with a history of suicide attempt: The role of mindfulness. *Archives of Suicide Research, 20*(1), 29–44. https:// doi: 10.1080/13811118.2015.1004488

Cho, Y. B., & Haslam, N. (2010). Suicidal ideation and distress among immigrant adolescents: The role of acculturation, life stress, and social support. *Journal of Youth and Adolescence, 39*(4), 370–379. https:// doi: 10.1007/s10964-009-9415-y

Chu, J. P., Goldblum, P., Floyd, R., & Bongar, B. (2010). The cultural theory and model of suicide. *Applied and Preventive Psychology, 14*(1–4), 25–40. https://doi.org/10.1016/j .appsy.2011.11.001

Cruz, R. A., King, K. M., Cauce, A. M., Conger, R. D., & Robins, R. W. (2017). Cultural orientation trajectories and substance use: Findings from a longitudinal study of Mexican-origin youth. *Child Development, 88*(2), 555–572. https://doi.org/10.1111/cdev.12586

Cwik, M., Goklish, N., Masten, K., Lee, A., Suttle, R., Alchesay, M., O'Keefe, V., & Barlow, A. (2019). "Let our Apache heritage and culture live on forever and teach the young ones": Development of the elders' resilience curriculum, an upstream suicide prevention approach for American Indian youth. *American Journal of Community Psychology, 64*(1–2), 137–145. https://doi.org/10.1002/ajcp.12351

Czeisler, M. É., Lane, R. I., Petrosky, E., Wiley, J. F., Christensen, A., Njai, R., Weaver, M. D., Robbins, R., Facer-Childs, E. R., Barger, L. K., Czeisler, C. A., Howard, M. E., & Rajaratnam, S. M. W. (2020). Mental health, substance use, and suicidal ideation during the COVID-19 pandemic—United States, June 24–30, 2020. *MMWR, Morbidity and Mortality Weekly Report, 69*, 1049–1057. https://www.cdc.gov/mmwr/volumes /69/wr/mm6932a1.htm?s_cid=mm6932a1_w

Deaux, K. (2006). Setting the stage: Policies, demography, and social representations. In *To be an Immigrant* (pp. 12–39). Russell Sage Foundation; JSTOR.

Duarté-Vélez, Y., Torres-Dávila, P., Spirito, A., Polanco, N., & Bernal, G. (2016). Development of a treatment protocol for Puerto Rican adolescents with suicidal behaviors. *Psychotherapy, 53*(1), 45–56. https://doi.org/10.1037/pst0000044

Durkheim, E. (1951). *Suicide: A study in sociology* (J. A. Spaulding & G. T. Simpson, Eds.). Free Press. (Original work published 1897).

Erausquin, J. T., McCoy, T. P., Bartlett, R., & Park, E. (2019). Trajectories of suicide ideation and attempts from early adolescence to mid-adulthood: Associations with race/ethnicity. *Journal of Youth and Adolescence, 48*(9), 1796–1805. https://doi: 10.1007 /s10964-019-01074-3

Ferguson, G. M., & Birman, D. (2016). Acculturation in the United States of America. In D. L. Sam & J. W. Berry (Eds.), *The Cambridge handbook of acculturation psychology* (2nd ed., pp. 396–416). Cambridge University Press. https://doi.org/10.1017 /CBO9781316219218.023

Franklin, J. C., Ribeiro, J. D., Fox, K. R., Bentley, K. H., Kleiman, E. M., Huang, X., Musacchio, K. M., Jaroszewski, A. C., Chang, B. P., & Nock, M. K. (2017). Risk factors for suicidal thoughts and behaviors: A meta-analysis of 50 years of research. *Psychological Bulletin, 143*(2), 187–232. https://doi: 10.1037/bul0000084

Garrett, M. T., & Pichette, E. F. (2000). Red as an apple: Native American acculturation and counseling with or without reservation. *Journal of Counseling and Development, 78*(1), 3–13. https://doi.org/10.1002/j.1556-6676.2000.tb02554.x

Gladding, S. T. (2006). *The counseling dictionary: Concise definitions of frequently used terms* (2nd ed.). Pearson.

Goldston, D. B., Daniel, S. S., Erkanli, A., Heilbron, N., Doyle, O., Weller, B., Sapyta, J., Mayfield, A., & Faulkner, M. (2015). Suicide attempts in a longitudinal sample of adolescents followed through adulthood: Evidence of escalation. *Journal of Consulting and Clinical Psychology, 83*(2), 253–64. https://doi: 10.1037/a0038657

Goldston, D. B., Molock, S. D., Whitbeck, L. B., Murakami, J. L., Zayas, L. H., & Hall, G. C. N. (2008). Cultural considerations in adolescent suicide prevention and psychosocial treatment. *American Psychologist, 63*(1), 14–31. https://doi: 10.1037/0003-066X.63.1.14

Gomez, J., Miranda, R., & Polanco, L. (2011). Acculturative stress, perceived discrimination, and vulnerability to suicide attempts among emerging adults. *Journal of Youth and Adolescence, 40*(11), 1465–1476. https://doi: 10.1007/s10964-011-9688-9

Han, B., Compton, W. M., Blanco, C., Colpe, L., Huang, L., & McKeon, R. (2018). National trends in the prevalence of suicidal ideation and behavior among young adults and receipt of mental health care among suicidal young adults. *Journal of the American Academy of Child and Adolescent Psychiatry, 57*(1), 20–27. https://doi: 10.1016/j. jaac.2017.10.013

Hollingsworth, D. W., Cole, A. B., O'Keefe, V. M., Tucker, R. P., Story, C. R., & Wingate, L. R. (2017). Experiencing racial microaggressions influences suicide ideation through perceived burdensomeness in African Americans. Journal of Counseling Psychology, *64*(1), 104-111. https://doi: 10.1037/cou0000177

Hovey, J. D., & King, C. A. (1996). Acculturative stress, depression, and suicidal ideation among immigrant and second-generation Latino adolescents. *Journal of the American Academy of Child and Adolescent Psychiatry, 35*(9), 1183–1192. https://doi: 10.1097/00004583-199609000-00016

Humensky, J. L., Coronel, B., Gil, R., Mazzula, S., & Lewis-Fernández, R. (2017). Life is Precious: A community-based program to reduce suicidal behavior in Latina adolescents. *Archives of Suicide Research, 21*(4), 659–671. https://doi: 10.1080 /13811118.2016.1242442

Joe, S., Baser, R. S., Neighbors, H. W., Caldwell, C. H., & Jackson, J. S. (2009). 12-month and lifetime prevalence of suicide attempts among Black adolescents in the National

Survey of American Life. *Journal of the American Academy of Child and Adolescent Psychiatry, 48*(3), 271–282. https://doi: 10.1097/CHI.0b013e318195bccf

Khan, S. Q., de Gonzalez, A. B., Best, A. F., Chen, Y., Haozous, E. A., Rodriquez, E. J., Spillane, S., Thomas, D. A., Withrow, D., Freedman, N. D., & Shiels, M. S. (2018). Infant and youth mortality trends by race/ethnicity and cause of death in the United States. *JAMA Pediatrics, 172*(12), Online only. https:// doi: 10.1001/jamapediatrics.2018.3317

Kim, J., Pike, K., McCauley, E., & Vander Stoep, A. (2019). Ethnic variations of trajectories in suicide ideation and attempt: From middle school to high school. *Suicide and Life-Threatening Behavior, 49*(2), 432–443. https://doi: 10.1111/sltb.12441

King, C. A., Brent, D., Grupp-Phelan, J., Shenoi, R., Page, K., Mahabee-Gittens, E. M., Chernick, L. S., Melzer-Lange, M., Rea, M., McGuire, T. C., Littlefield, A., Casper, T. C., & Pediatric Emergency Care Applied Research Network. (2019). Five profiles of adolescents at elevated risk for suicide attempts: Differences in mental health service use. *Journal of the American Academy of Child and Adolescent Psychiatry, 59*(9), Online First. https://doi: 10.1016/j.jaac.2019.10.015

Kuhlerg, J. A., Peña, J. B., & Zayas, L. H. (2010). Familism, parent-adolescent conflict, self-esteem, internalizing behaviors and suicide attempts among adolescent Latinas. *Child Psychiatry and Human Development, 41*(4), 425–440. https://doi: 10.1007/s10578-010-0179-0

Kwon, S., & Han, D. (2019). Discrimination, mental disorders, and suicidal ideation in Latino adults: Decomposing the effects of discrimination. *Journal of Immigrant and Minority Health, 21*(1), 143–150. https://doi: 10.1007/s10903-018-0726-5

LaFromboise, T. D., & Lewis, H. A. (2008). The Zuni life skills development program: A school/community-based suicide prevention intervention. *Suicide and Life-Threatening Behavior, 38*(3), 343–353. https://doi: 10.1521/suli.2008.38.3.343

LeBrón, A. M. W., & Viruell-Fuentes, E. A. (2020). Racial/ethnic discrimination, intersectionality, and Latina/o health. In A. D. Martínez & S. D. Rhodes (Eds.), *New and emerging issues in Latinx health* (pp. 295–320). Springer International. https://doi.org/10.1007/978-3-030-24043-1_14

Lee, C. S., & Wong, Y. J. (2020). Racial/ethnic and gender differences in the antecedents of youth suicide. *Cultural Diversity and Ethnic Minority Psychology, 26*(4), 532–543.

Madubata, I., Spivey, L. A., Alvarez, G. M., Neblett, E. W., & Prinstein, M. J. (2019). Forms of racial/ethnic discrimination and suicidal ideation: A prospective examination of African American and Latinx youth. *Journal of Clinical Child and Adolescent Psychology*, Online First. https://doi.org/10.1080/15374416.2019.1655756

Mayorga, N. A., Jardin, C., Bakhshaie, J., Garey, L., Viana, A. G., Cardoso, J. B., & Zvolensky, M. (2018). Acculturative stress, emotion regulation, and affective symptomology among Latino/a college students. *Journal of Counseling Psychology, 65*(2), 247–258. https:// doi: 10.1037/cou0000263

McKean, A. J., Pabbati, C. P., Geske, J. R., & Bostwick, J. M. (2018). Rethinking lethality in youth suicide attempts: First suicide attempt outcomes in youth ages 10 to 24. *Journal of the American Academy of Child and Adolescent Psychiatry, 57*(10), 786–791. https://doi: 10.1016/j.jaac.2018.04.021

Meca, A., Cobb, C. L., Schwartz, S. J., Szabó, Á., Moise, R., Zamboanga, B. L., Lee, T. K., Klimstra, T. A., Soares, M. H., Ritchie, R., & Stephens, D. P. (2018). Exploring individual differences in the relationship between cultural identity processes and well-being. *Emerging Adulthood, 9*(1), 11–21. https://doi.org/10.1177/2167696818817168

Miller, A. B., & Prinstein, M. J. (2019). Adolescent suicide as a failure of acute stress-response systems. *Annual Review of Clinical Psychology, 15*, 425–450. https://doi: 10.1146/annurev-clinpsy-050718-095625

Molock, S. D., Matlin, S., Barksdale, C., Puri, R., & Lyles, J. (2008). Developing suicide prevention programs for African American youth in African American churches. *Suicide and Life-Threatening Behavior, 38*(3), 323–333. https://doi: 10.1521/suli.2008.38.3.323

Molock, S. D., Puri, R., Matlin, S., & Barksdale, C. (2006). Relationship between religious coping and suicidal behaviors among African American adolescents. *Journal of Black Psychology, 32*(3), 366–389. https://doi: 10.1177/0095798406290466

Morrison, L. L., & Downey, D. L. (2000). Racial differences in self-disclosure of suicidal ideation and reasons for living: Implications for training. *Cultural Diversity and Ethnic Minority Psychology, 6*(4), 374–86. https://doi: 10.1037/1099-9809.6.4.374

Neblett, E. W., Rivas-Drake, D., & Umaña-Taylor, A. J. (2012). The promise of racial and ethnic protective factors in promoting ethnic minority youth development. *Child Development Perspectives, 6*(3), 295–303. https://doi.org/10.1111/j.1750-8606.2012.00239.x

Nock, M. K., Green, J. G., Hwang, I., McLaughlin, K. A., Sampson, N. A., Zaslavsky, A. M., & Kessler, R. C. (2013). Prevalence, correlates, and treatment of lifetime suicidal behavior among adolescents: Results from the National Comorbidity Survey Replication Adolescent Supplement. *JAMA Psychiatry, 70*(3), 300–310. https://doi:10.1001/2013.jamapsychiatry.55

Odafe, M. O., Talavera, D. C., Cheref, S., Hong, J. H., & Walker, R. L. (2016). Suicide in racial and ethnic minority adults: A review of the last decade. *Current Psychiatry Reviews, 12*(2), 181–198.

Oh, H., Stickley, A., Koyanagi, A., Yau, R., & DeVylder, J. E. (2019). Discrimination and suicidality among racial and ethnic minorities in the United States. *Journal of Affective Disorders, 245*, 517–523. https://doi.org/10.1016/j.jad.2018.11.059

O'Keefe, V. M., Wingate, L. R., Cole, A. B., Hollingsworth, D. W., & Tucker, R. P. (2015). Seemingly harmless racial communications are not so harmless: Racial microaggressions lead to suicidal ideation by way of depression symptoms. *Suicide and Life-Threatening Behavior, 45*(5), 567–576. https://doi.org/10.1111/sltb.12150

Ortin, A., Miranda, R., Polanco-Roman, L., & Shaffer, D. (2018). Parent-adolescent acculturation gap and suicidal ideation among adolescents from an emergency department. *Archives of Suicide Research, 22*(4), 529–541. https://doi.org/10.1080/13811118.2017.1372828

Peña, J. B., Kuhlberg, J. A., Zayas, L. H., Baumann, A. A., Gulbas, L., Hausmann-Stabile, C., & Nolle, A. P. (2011). Familism, family environment, and suicide attempts among Latina youth. *Suicide and Life-Threatening Behavior, 41*(3), 330–341. https://doi.org/10.1111/j.1943-278X.2011.00032.x

Peña, J. B., Wyman, P. A., Brown, C. H., Matthieu, M. M., Olivares, T. E., Hartel, D., & Zayas, L. H. (2008). Immigration generation status and its association with suicide attempts, substance use, and depressive symptoms among Latino adolescents in the USA. *Prevention Science, 9*(4), 299–310. https://doi: 10.1007/s11121-008-0105-x.

Perez-Rodriguez, M. M., Baca-Garcia, E., Oquendo, M. A., Wang, S., Wall, M. M., Liu, S. M., & Blanco, C. (2014). Relationship between acculturation, discrimination, and suicidal ideation and attempts among US Hispanics in the National Epidemiologic Survey of Alcohol and Related Conditions. *Journal of Clinical Psychiatry, 75*(4), 399–407. https://doi: 10.4088/JCP.13m08548

Perrotte, J. K., Zamboanga, B. L., Lui, P. P., & Piña-Watson, B. (2019). Pregaming among

Latina/o emerging adults: Do acculturation and gender matter? *Journal of Ethnicity in Substance Abuse, 18*(4), 530–548. https://doi.org/10.1080/15332640.2017.1417187

Phinney, J. S., Ong, A., & Madden, T. (2000). Cultural values and intergenerational value discrepancies in immigrant and non-immigrant families. *Child Development, 71*(2), 528–539. https://doi: 10.1111/1467-8624.00162

Polanco-Roman, L., Anglin, D. M., Miranda, R., & Jeglic, E. L. (2019). Racial/ethnic discrimination and suicidal ideation in emerging adults: The role of traumatic stress and depressive symptoms varies by gender not race/ethnicity. *Journal of Youth and Adolescence, 48*(10), 2023–2037. https://doi:10.1007/s10964-019-01097-w

Polanco-Roman, L., & Miranda, R. (2013). Culturally related stress, hopelessness, and vulnerability to depressive symptoms and suicidal ideation in emerging adulthood. *Behavior Therapy, 44*(1), 75–87. https://doi: 10.1016/j.beth.2012.07.002

Ruch, D. A., Sheftall, A. H., Schlagbaum, P., Rausch, J., Campo, J. V., & Bridge, J. A. (2019). Trends in suicide among youth aged 10 to 19 years in the United States, 1975 to 2016. *JAMA Network Open, 2*(5), e193886–e193886. https://doi: 10.1001/jamanetworkopen.2019.3886

Rudmin, F. (2009). Constructs, measurements and models of acculturation and acculturative stress. *International Journal of Intercultural Relations, 33*(2), 106–123. https://doi.org/10.1016/j.ijintrel.2008.12.001

Sa, J., Choe, C. S., Cho, C. B. Y., Chaput, J. P., Lee, J., & Hwang, S. (2020). Sex and racial/ethnic differences in suicidal consideration and suicide attempts among US college students, 2011–2015. *American Journal of Health Behavior, 44*(2), 214–231. https://doi: 10.5993/AJHB.44.2.9

Schwartz, S. J. (2016). Turning point for a turning point: Advancing emerging adulthood theory and research. *Emerging Adulthood, 4*(5), 307–317. https://doi.org/10.1177/2167696815624640

Schwartz, S. J., Meca, A., Ward, C., Szabó, Á., Benet-Martínez, V., Lorenzo-Blanco, E. I., Sznitman, G. A., Cobb, C. L., Szapocznik, J., Unger, J. B., Cano, M. Á., Stuart, J., & Zamboanga, B. L. (2019). Biculturalism dynamics: A daily diary study of bicultural identity and psychosocial functioning. *Journal of Applied Developmental Psychology, 62*, 26–37. https://doi.org/10.1016/j.appdev.2018.12.007

Schwartz, S. J., Unger, J. B., Zamboanga, B. L., Córdova, D., Mason, C. A., Huang, S., Baezconde-Garbanati, L., Lorenzo-Blanco, E. I., Rosiers, S. E. D., Soto, D. W., Villamar, J. A., Pattarroyo, M., Lizzi, K. M., & Szapocznik, J. (2015). Developmental trajectories of acculturation: Links with family functioning and mental health in recent-immigrant Hispanic adolescents. *Child Development, 86*(3), 726–748. https://doi.org/10.1111/cdev.12341

Schwartz, S. J., Unger, J. B., Zamboanga, B. L., & Szapocznik, J. (2010). Rethinking the concept of acculturation. *American Psychologist, 65*(4), 237–251. https://doi.org/10.1037/a0019330

Schwartz, S. J., Weisskirch, R. S., Zamboanga, B. L., Castillo, L. G., Ham, L. S., Huynh, Q.-L., Park, I. J. K., Donovan, R., Kim, S. Y., Vernon, M., Davis, M. J., & Cano, M. A. (2011). Dimensions of acculturation: Associations with health risk behaviors among college students from immigrant families. *Journal of Counseling Psychology, 58*(1), 27–41. https://doi.org/10.1037/a0021356

Smokowski, P. R., Bacallao, M., & Evans, C. B. R. (2017). Acculturation. In R. J. R. Levesque (Ed.), *Encyclopedia of adolescence* (pp. 1–12). Springer International. https://doi.org/10.1007/978-3-319-32132-5_300-2

Syed, M., & Mitchell, L. L. (2014). *How race and ethnicity shape emerging adulthood*

(J. J. Arnett, Ed.; Vol. 1). Oxford University Press. https://doi.org/10.1093/oxford
hb/9780199795574.013.005

Szlyk, H. S., Gulbas, L., & Zayas, L. (2019). "I just kept it to myself": The shaping of Latina
suicidality through gendered oppression, silence, and violence. *Family Process, 58*(3),
778–790. https://doi: 10.1111/famp.12384

Trautman, E. C. (1961). The suicidal fit: A psychobiologic study on Puerto Rican
immigrants. *Archives of General Psychiatry, 5*(1), 76–83. https://doi: 10.1001/arch
psyc.1961.01710130078009

Unger, J. B., Schwartz, S. J., Huh, J., Soto, D. W., & Baezconde-Garbanati, L. (2014).
Acculturation and perceived discrimination: Predictors of substance use trajectories from adolescence to emerging adulthood among Hispanics. *Addictive Behaviors,
39*(9), 1293–1296. https://doi.org/10.1016/j.addbeh.2014.04.014

U.S. Department of Health and Human Services, Substance Abuse and Mental Health
Services Administration, Center for Behavioral Health Statistics and Quality. (2019).
National Survey on Drug Use and Health 2019. Retrieved from https://datafiles
.samhsa.gov/

Vespa, J., Medina, L., & Armstrong, D. M. (2020). *Population estimates and projections.*
U.S. Census Bureau.

Vidot, D. C., Huang, S., Poma, S., Estrada, Y., Lee, T. K., & Prado, G. (2016). Familias
Unidas' crossover effects on suicidal behaviors among Hispanic adolescents: Results
from an effectiveness trial. *Suicide and Life-Threatening Behavior, 46,* S8–S14. https://
doi: 10.1111/sltb.12253

Wadsworth, T., & Kubrin, C. E. (2007). Hispanic suicide in U.S. metropolitan areas:
Examining the effects of immigration, assimilation, affluence, and disadvantage.
American Journal of Sociology, 112(6), 1848–1885. https://doi.org/10.1086/512711

Walker, R., Francis, D., Brody, G., Simons, R., Cutrona, C., & Gibbons, F. (2017). A
longitudinal study of racial discrimination and risk for death ideation in African
American youth. *Suicide and Life-Threatening Behavior, 47*(1), 86–102. https://doi
.org/10.1111/sltb.12251

Walker, R. L., Salami, T. K., Carter, S. E., & Flowers, K. (2014). Perceived racism and suicide ideation: Mediating role of depression but moderating role of religiosity among
African American adults. *Suicide and Life-Threatening Behavior, 44*(5), 548–559.
https://doi.org/10.1111/sltb.12089

Walker, R. L., Wingate, L. R., Obasi, E. M., & Joiner, T. E., Jr. (2008). An empirical investigation of acculturative stress and ethnic identity as moderators for depression and
suicidal ideation in college students. *Cultural Diversity and Ethnic Minority Psychology, 14*(1), 75-82. https://doi.org/10.1037/1099-9809.14.1.75

Williams, D. (2018). Stress and the mental health of populations of color: Advancing our
understanding of race-related stressors. *Journal of Health and Social Behavior, 59*(4),
466–485. https://doi.org/10.1177/0022146518814251

Wong, Y. J., & Maffini, C. S. (2011). Predictors of Asian American adolescents' suicide
attempts: A latent class regression analysis. *Journal of Youth and Adolescence, 40*(11),
1453–1464. https://doi.org/10.1007/s10964-011-9701-3

Zayas, L. H., Bright, C. L., Álvarez-Sánchez, T., & Cabassa, L. J. (2009). Acculturation,
familism and mother-daughter relations among suicidal and non-suicidal adolescent Latinas. *Journal of Primary Prevention, 30*(3–4), 351–369. https://doi: 10.1007
/s10935-009-0181-0

Section II

BECOMING AN ADULT IN TODAY'S WORLD

PART 1

Not All Young Adults Are the Same

CHAPTER 5

Protect Your Energy

A Clinical Psychologist and Her Clients' Racial Identity Development During the Pandemic and the Black Lives Matter Movement

KATHLEEN ISAAC

Self-transformation commences with a period of self-questioning. Questions lead to more questions, bewilderment leads to new discoveries, and growing personal awareness leads to transformation in how a person lives. Purposeful modification of the self only commences with revising our mind's internal functions. Revamped internal functions eventually alter how we view our external environment.

—KILROY J. OLDSTER, *DEAD TOAD SCROLLS*

The tasks of adolescence and young adulthood are to solidify your identity and form lasting relationships with others (Hamman & Hendricks, 2005; Lawford et al., 2020). But what does that look like when the world is falling apart around you? Young adults' lives have been significantly challenged and impacted by an ongoing global pandemic as well as social and political crisis and conflict. And yet, in spite of these challenges, it has been a time of growth, realization, and transformation.

I am a first-generation Haitian American, cisgender female, heterosexual, Christian, partnered, clinical psychologist who works for an academic institution and has a part-time private practice. As a Millennial psychologist, I work primarily with BIPOC and LGBTQ+ young adults in their 20s and 30s. I specialize in trauma and culturally informed psychotherapy, incorporating themes of race, gender, sexuality, spirituality, and other aspects of identity into my approach. I often rely on my own experience as a young, Black, professional woman to inform the work that I do, and it has been particularly salient as I've supported my clients and coped with my own challenges in the wake of the pandemic and civil rights movement. This chapter examines the growth edges and conflicts that young adults are facing during this time, with particular emphasis on how culture and social location shape those experiences. I draw on my experiences working with medical trainees and young adults in private practice to illustrate these dynamics.

SOCIAL UNREST, ACTIVISM, AND SOCIAL RESPONSIBILITY: COVID-19 AND THE BLM MOVEMENT

In March 2020, the United States was suddenly in the midst of a global pandemic. Thousands of individuals became ill with coronavirus, and the country was ravaged by the rapid spread of the virus and the loss of lives. Stay-at-home orders were enforced—those who sometimes worked from home as a job perk were now working from home every day. Many others faced job insecurity and job loss due to having jobs that could not be performed remotely. Social contact was limited, and the constant threat of contracting the virus or spreading it to others filled the minds of everyone. As the world panicked with job insecurity and the threat of the virus, I saw an uptick in requests for therapy as people struggled with significant anxiety. While many of my clients expressed fears regarding the virus, a significant stressor was adjusting to working from home with limited social contact. For individuals who cope with their stress by socializing, this posed a significant challenge, as people could no longer spend time with friends or family. In addition, suddenly losing control over your schedule and having unlimited time at home, with an unclear expectation for how long it would last, created a lot of anxiety because there was now too much time available to stress and worry about the pandemic. Clients also struggled with the loss of family members, as well as the loss of their freedom and sense of safety and control. Many people mourned the loss of connection and sank into a depressed state, feeling hopeless and uncertain about the future.

Having narrowly missed contracting the virus at a conference I attended where multiple people tested positive for COVID-19, I quarantined at home in the beginning of March. My adjustment to working from home was not as challenging as I expected it to be, which I attributed to my introverted nature and the break I received from my commute. When it came to therapy, I began phone sessions with my own therapist and transitioned all of my clients to video sessions. I already had experience seeing clients virtually due to past training experiences, so my main challenge was to adjust to having my entire caseload be virtual. I had always taken an eclectic approach to my work, blending psychodynamic and cognitive-behavioral therapy (CBT) techniques, but I soon realized that I had to be even more active and directive with my clients, primarily to keep them engaged with the virtual platform, but also to respond to their needs that changed during this time. Many of my clients were struggling with the loss of structure that work and school provided. I transitioned from my typical neutral, listening stance to active problem solving during sessions and assigning things to work on between sessions. I offered psychoeducation about anxiety and trauma and the various coping techniques that could help clients manage their thoughts and emotions. I worked with my clients to identify ways to add more structure to their day, making suggestions for activities to fill up their time, and encouraged the discovery of new hobbies and interests. My clients shared a range of activities they engaged in, including exercising, baking, learning how to play instruments, and gardening. For those who struggled with social distancing, we came up with creative ways to mix up virtual hangouts, including phone and video chats and conducting virtual group activities, such as game nights. I combined psychodynamic exploration with techniques from CBT, dialectical behavior therapy, and acceptance and commitment therapy to help clients monitor their anxious and depressive thoughts, identify their catastrophic thinking, and challenge themselves to redirect their thoughts and practice acceptance. At the same time, I would simply hold space for them and encourage them to express their feelings as they came. I normalized and validated the intense anxiety and sadness that we were all feeling and encouraged healthy expression of those feelings while identifying concrete strategies to cope with those feelings so that clients would not feel stuck. Shifting my focus in this way worked well for my clients, with a select few who continued to have a difficult time keeping perspective and adjusting. I often used myself as an example to model healthy coping behaviors and to normalize and validate the challenges of the time.

As the country continued to struggle through the pandemic, we were startled by the release of a video that showed the state-sanctioned murder of George Floyd on May 25, 2020. In a time when everyone was struggling to cope with the ongoing challenges of social distancing and the disproportionately higher death rate from COVID-19 among Black individuals, the outrage of knowing that an unarmed Black man was killed by police when we were all stuck inside of our homes proved to be the catalyst that added fuel to the Black Lives Matter movement, which started in 2013 after the murder of Trayvon Martin. The image of the cop's knee on George Floyd's neck as he struggled to breathe was seared into the minds of many and illustrated the experience of so many Black and Brown individuals who have continued to be subjected to oppression and violence since the foundation of this country. Additional cases were highlighted at this time, including the shooting deaths of Ahmaud Arbery and Breonna Taylor, both of whom were also unarmed. It was most upsetting that Black lives were still in danger even when we were all restricted to being at home, and this resulted in collective outrage among many individuals. Those who were outraged by the injustice of white supremacy and police violence felt compelled to resist and protest against the long-standing inequalities and oppressive policies that resulted in the deaths of Black and Brown people at the hands of police. Young adults led the charge as people left the safety of their homes and took to the streets to protest these injustices. In true Millennial fashion, activism became a trending topic, and social media became flooded with calls for true allyship from whites and non-Black people of color to denounce systemic oppression. Seemingly overnight, demonstrations of activism and commitments to antiracism became the trending topic, with countless hashtags and retweets of posts and videos calling for change. Individuals and organizations scrambled to show their support and solidarity to avoid being called out as racist. Every institution suddenly felt the pressure to demonstrate their commitment to diversity and inclusion as people were forced to reckon with long-standing systemic barriers that limited opportunities for Black lives. The movement finally had a wider audience, and people were moved in ways that they previously had not been before. This showed the power of social media and the impact of this current generation to push everyone to wake up and make a difference.

ACTIVISM IN TREATMENT

These calls to action were processed by my clients who struggled with feeling the collective loss and trauma of another Black life lost, and/or figuring out how they could best show their support and solidarity during this time. Many individuals had conflicts about participating in the protests, given their ongoing concerns about the pandemic. I worked with my clients to expand their ideas about what protest and activism could look like. For example, one of my clients who identifies as white shared her desire to be more active and engaged in antiracist work. Antiracism, the philosophy which calls for dismantling the belief that there are any differences behaviorally, socially, or genetically between the races (Kendi, 2019), became a buzzword during this time. I shared my belief that while social media was filled with people showing how much they were reading about race and protesting structural racism, there was a significant amount of individualized emotional and psychological work to be done to challenge white supremacist structures. My client became overwhelmed when I challenged her to think about additional strategies on her own and encouraged her to focus more of our session time on unpacking her relationship to her whiteness and explore what it meant to her. She was tearful as she described feeling lost and unsure about what I was asking of her. I invited her to think about early memories of encountering race, and she acknowledged that it was not explicitly talked about in her family. She soon started to recall her different racialized experiences throughout her teen and college days. I also explored her feelings about me challenging her in the way that I did. I had my own conflicting feelings about pushing her, as I was working through my own complicated feelings about a white client seeking support and guidance from me at a time when I was hurting myself. I felt encouraged, however, knowing that I was using my platform as a therapist to challenge white supremacy and encourage racial identity exploration for all of my clients. This was my way of honoring a personal commitment to being an antiracist therapist.

I had similar conversations with my Asian and South Asian clients, who struggled with figuring out their place in the fight against racism. Caught between feeling invisible in larger conversations about race and feeling conflicted about their relative success compared to other marginalized groups, Asian individuals often find it difficult to navigate their identity and what it means in the larger social context (Eng & Han, 2000). In sessions, we explored how the model minority myth (Eng & Han, 2000) and expectations of success felt like a burden. My clients discussed how their parents pushed assimilation for survival, teaching them to keep their heads down and focus on academic success and upward mobility as a way to compensate for existing in a country that was not their home due to their immigrant status. They shared how they still experienced discrimination but did not feel empowered to challenge it, instead choosing to ignore and attempt to assimilate as best they could. I challenged comments that questioned why Black individuals felt compelled to continue protesting. I invited my clients to consider the parallels between the discrimination they described and the racism that Black and Latino individuals face in this country. If they could acknowledge what was harmful about the discrimination they faced, could they connect to the plight of other groups? I shared my knowledge about how white supremacy created hierarchies that pitted marginalized groups against each other. If they could realize that the root issue is white supremacy and resist the urge to blame and critique other racial groups that are below them in the hierarchy, then we could truly make progress. I offered, "If you work on fighting for equal rights for those at the bottom of the hierarchy, you benefit too." One of my patients remarked, "Wow, I never thought of it that way," and began to explore what her identity as a Brown person meant to her as well as how she could use her experience to connect with other minorities. Another patient explored how her immigrant status and identity as a South Asian woman from a country with its own oppressive norms and caste system informed her experience of the current crises. She shared how she struggled to reconcile her family relationships, noting how her awareness of her family's beliefs diverged from her activist beliefs. This particular client also struggled with her fears of attending protests and posting things on social media, for fear of retribution given her immigrant status. While one could interpret this as paranoia, I validated her concerns and explored the reality of the current political climate and encouraged her to identify ways to safely show her solidarity.

Working with non-Black clients during this time and seeing their commitment to exploring their racial identity in sessions was enlightening and meaningful for me. I have been most stretched, however, in my work with Black clients. Because I identify with my clients, many of whom are similar in age to me and are going through similar challenges, I tend to see myself in them and feel like I am speaking to myself when I'm helping them navigate their conflicts. This became a significant challenge for me after the sudden loss of a Black female client at the beginning the pandemic. She was in her 30s, and her death was completely unexpected. While I never found out the specific cause of her death (non-COVID related), those who knew her spoke of how tirelessly she (over)worked and wondered whether this exacerbated her health problems. Her loss was devastating and traumatic for me and served as a wake-up call, because we were so close in age. I started reflecting on the fragility of life, considering how my hectic schedule and overextension of myself to meet the needs of my clients and others in my life was ultimately hurting me. As I struggled with managing my grief, I found a renewed desire to protect myself and my mental health, while exploring how capitalism, patriarchy, and white supremacy had indoctrinated me into the grind culture that kept me overworked and tired all of the time.

My fatigue left me resentful and angry, and I was struck by how many of my Black clients were also processing similar feelings. I began working with a Black, queer medical student who specifically requested to meet with me a few weeks after the murder of George Floyd. He described feeling upset, sad, and angry about the current racial climate and noted that it was becoming increasingly difficult to cope with his strong emotions. Our sessions centered on processing his feelings of anger, despair, and fatigue, connecting these feelings to his concerns about how to navigate social and academic difficulties that emerged as he wrestled with his overwhelming emotions. We also explored his identity as a first-generation Caribbean person and the conflicts of navigating racism and American culture when his family had traditional values from their home country. I resonated with a lot of the challenges he explored and used my own experience growing up in a similar Caribbean culture to inform my approach. He often shared his appreciation that I could speak from actual experience in addition to exploring psychological theories and processes with him. As we explored these themes, he uncovered deeper conflicts about solidifying his sense of self and improving his self-esteem.

We explored similar themes in my Underrepresented in Medicine (URM) support group for Black and Latinx medical students (Isaac, 2019). Throughout the pandemic, the URM group was a space where students could vent, yell, and cry as they processed their rage and grief about the pandemic and the Black Lives Matter movement. The group served as a safe haven for the members to collectively mourn the perpetual loss of Black lives, process their anger, and support each other in their activism on campus. The group sessions were heavy, but the members also used a lot of humor to counteract their sadness. It became a group norm for me to comment on the levity, with someone reminding me that "we laugh to keep from crying." The students used their voices to organize and push their fellow students as well as the administration to recognize the impact of systemic oppression on their lives. The students reflected on feeling pressured to take on the charge to end systemic racism in their institution. While they had already been involved in campus activism, there was the added pressure of making an immediate change as everyone knew that the popularity of activism would not last long. Their frustration increased as they shared how traumatic it was to share their personal experiences with racism to move others to empathize with their plight. They became angrier as they realized that the change would still be slow and how deeply ingrained institutional norms that perpetuate racism can be. I resonated with the urgency they felt to see change happen immediately, recognizing that their activism was a central part of their identity development as they strove for autonomy and mastery.

Group therapy has been such an important outlet for my clients over the past few months. My success with the URM group inspired me to start an affinity group for Black women. I left my own therapy group due to feeling misunderstood and at times unsupported as the only Black woman in the group and was inspired to create a safe space for other Black women to come together, share their experiences, and find support and community. My group, which started a few weeks before the murder of George Floyd, turned out to be just as therapeutic for me as it was for the group members. As a Black woman, there are few spaces where I can share my experience without having to educate or explain my experience to others. The women in the group immediately connected on how powerful it was to come together and see other Black women (including me) nodding their heads in understanding and agreement. Since its inception, the group has explored various topics that encompass the lives of Black women, including processing feelings of anger and sadness about the ongoing executions of Black and Brown individuals at the hands of police, working on relationships with family, friends, and romantic partners, balancing work and personal commitments, and navigating personal and professional spaces as Black women. Additional themes include colorism (i.e., discrimination based on skin color/shade), parent–child relationships, and trauma. The women in the group shared that being in a group of all Black-identified women removed the burden of explanation that is often felt in mixed-race dialogues. They also noted how powerful it has been to collectively sigh and cry together about what is happening in society. I have felt emotionally moved by the group even in my leader role, as the topics explored and feelings expressed mirrored my own thoughts and feelings. As the average age of the women in the group is around 30 years, they are often going through things that I am currently dealing with myself. I often speak from my own experience when I provide interventions and also learn from their collective wisdom. During this time, it has been critical for me to explore the various reactions I have to the group in my own therapy sessions due to the themes that come up in our sessions.

Processing my feelings as I supported my clients and grappled with my own challenges with coping was essential. As the country confronted its long-standing history of racism and state-sanctioned violence against Black and Brown people, I felt sad, angry, and frustrated. Even though I knew that the work I had been doing as an essential worker during the pandemic and the Black Lives Matter movement was important, I still felt as if it wasn't enough. I pushed past my fears about contracting COVID-19, donned a mask, and joined my church community to protest the deaths of George Floyd, Ahmaud Arbery, Breonna Taylor, and the hundreds of others who preceded them. Chanting "Black Lives Matter!" throughout the streets of Harlem was powerful, and seeing the outpouring of support by the surrounding neighborhood was encouraging. At the same time, I struggled with my own feelings of hopelessness, knowing how deeply ingrained racism is in our society. I still had to make myself available to support my clients and try to offer them hope during this time of uprising, however. While I talked about race as a general practice with clients, I was suddenly flooded with back-to-back sessions processing the trauma of racial violence, the protests for Black lives, and racial identity with my clients. Some of my clients would check in on me and ask how I was doing, sharing concerns about having to process their feelings about race with me, a Black woman, which showed their awareness of how challenging it was to hold space for them in the midst of my own grief and anger. One client offered to not meet, as a way to give me back time to myself. I explored this with her and shared my appreciation for her generosity, but this also led to a discussion about sacrificing herself and putting her needs aside for others, which was also tied to her cultural background as an Asian woman. We also processed her desire to take care of me and the guilt she felt about bringing further harm to me during a time of collective grief and unrest. Although I would often feel exhausted after a long day of sessions about racial identity, I would also feel invigorated and encouraged by the desire to dig deeper and explore, and welcomed ongoing dialogue about our therapeutic relationship and how race impacted our experience of each other.

INTERVENTIONS FOR TREATING YOUNG ADULT CLIENTS

Separation and Individuation

While a central focus of my work with my clients has been racial identity, we have also explored the intersections of other aspects of identity such as gender, sexuality, spirituality, and so on, and how it relates to their journey toward defining their overall personhood and identity. A significant achievement of young adulthood, according to Erikson, is to consolidate one's identity, that is, to solidify one's roles as an adult and work toward a grounded, integrated sense of self (Hamman & Hendricks, 2005; Lawford et al., 2020). The path toward identity consolidation includes working through various relationship conflicts, improving self-esteem, and becoming more assured in the choices that we make for how we want to live our lives.

One of the primary conflicts to resolve during adolescence and young adulthood is separating from your parents (Blos, 1967; Grotevant & Cooper, 1985). Once the pandemic hit, many of the students and young adults I work with suddenly had to leave campus or their apartments and return home to live with their parents. While a significant number of young adults were already living at home (Bialik & Fry, 2019), the transition to home was a challenging one for many of my clients. Living away from their parents afforded my clients the freedom to live life on their own terms. One client of mine was suddenly unable to spend time with his girlfriend, with whom he had practically been living beforehand. Another had a challenging time trying to make decisions about his academic plans due to fears about disappointing his parents and diverging from their expectations for him. He noted that it was much easier to make decisions when he wasn't physically in the home with his parents, as the physical distance somehow made their controlling nature less powerful for him. For many of my Asian and South Asian clients, deference to parents and other authority figures is one of the most important values that they must adhere to. In sessions, we explored how meaningful it was to practice asserting themselves and taking small liberties for themselves when they moved away from home. Moving back home during the pandemic therefore felt like a regression to childhood, and many of my clients described feeling childlike and shared their concerns about upsetting their parents. In sessions, we explored how cultural norms differed from their present desires and discussed ways to navigate parent–child conflicts.

For those who did not live with their parents, the pandemic created what felt like a reprieve from relationships that were enmeshed and toxic. Many of my clients have relationships in which their parents manipulate and control them, and they are often made to feel guilty when they make any decisions that deviate from their parents' expectations. Some parents would take any exercise of autonomy as a personal affront, which made it difficult for my clients to assert themselves. As I previously mentioned, these relationships would be complicated by cultural expectations to defer to parents. I worked with one medical resident who shared how stressful it was to have to deal with her mother's repeated intrusions and emotional abuse after long days and nights at the hospital treating COVID-19 patients, noting how this added to her feelings of being overwhelmed and stressed. In sessions, I would challenge my clients to reflect on the emotional experience of feeling locked into the roles that they took on when dealing with their parents, which would frequently be at odds with who they saw themselves to be in other areas of their lives as well as who they aspired to be.

Setting and Maintaining Boundaries

One of the most significant interventions to address these relationship challenges was to encourage my clients to set boundaries with their parents and with others in their lives. Many clients would comment that they did not even consider what their needs were, as they would typically prioritize the needs of others over their own. While I would often empathize with and validate my clients' challenges with navigating these relationship dynamics, I challenged them to confront these conflicts through effective communication. Often my clients would struggle with confronting others, for fear of creating conflict or disrupting the relationship. The pandemic and the BLM movement brought these conflicts to the forefront in ways that forced my clients to confront how harmful tolerating these relationships was to their emotional well-being. I worked with clients to articulate what their needs were, particularly as they emerged during this time and discussed ways to communicate them to parents, friends, and colleagues.

For example, I had several clients who identified as biracial who discussed how they avoided sharing their feelings about the BLM movement, systemic oppression, and police violence with a white parent. They noted that they felt unsupported by parents who either did not bring it up or would minimize the impact of this time on their experience. I encouraged clients to push past their fears and start difficult conversations, sharing how let down they felt by parents who did not make space for their emotions about race. Many of my clients shared their experiences of having these conversations, and the results ranged from hopefulness about beginning racial dialogue with parents who were more receptive than they anticipated to disappointment with parents who still were unable to rise to the occasion. For those who continued to feel unsafe and misunderstood by parents or other individuals in their lives, they considered whether setting boundaries and creating emotional distance was warranted or not. I maintained the stance that intolerance for racism was an important personal and emotional boundary that should be honored, and they should not feel guilty about figuring out for themselves what their personal limits and boundaries are.

Setting and maintaining boundaries extends beyond race and has been a core theme in many of my sessions with young adult clients. Identifying boundaries and communicating them effectively without feeling guilty about it marks an important step in honoring one's values and needs. In doing so, individuals feel more empowered, which helps to reinforce one's sense of self. In a capitalistic society, where productivity often supersedes individual limits and needs, setting boundaries about work has also become important. For many individuals, working from home has meant that people no longer have the physical separation that commuting to a different office space created. Working with clients to figure out ways to re-create that separation for themselves, and deciding when to end their work day or take breaks, has been an ongoing task.

Radical Self-Care

> Caring for myself is not self-indulgence, it is self-preservation, and that is an act of political warfare.
>
> —AUDRE LORDE, *A BURST OF LIGHT*

Setting boundaries is closely related to another important theme in my work with young adults. Working from home and having limited social contact throughout the pandemic, as well as the overwhelming emotional toll of ongoing activism and exposure to racialized violence and oppression from the government, left us feeling drained. However, this conflicted with the expectation to constantly be working. In the wake of ongoing protests and calls for activism, this translated to pressure to continue to participate in the fight against racism and oppression for fear of contributing to the problem rather than being part of the solution. This resulted in many of my clients feeling overburdened with responsibility and guilt and feeling overworked and physically and emotionally exhausted. People also struggled with poor sleep, unhealthy eating habits, and hypervigilance (e.g., closely tracking news and social media to stay abreast of rapid developments).

My suggestions to protect and preserve one's energy by taking breaks and focusing on self-care were not easily heeded by my clients, who felt as if they could not afford to take a break or look away for a second so that they did not miss anything. As time passed and things seemed only to get worse with each passing week, clients became more receptive to the idea that prioritizing self-care was a way to honor their limits and boundaries. Taking breaks from social media, which was becoming too emotionally activating and triggering for some, limiting contact with individuals who made them feel unsafe, spending more time with those who were supportive, and identifying activities and self-affirmations that would help them recharge and improve their mood all became strategies for prioritizing their self-care. I would also reinforce that radical self-care (Lorde, 2017), which emphasizes the responsibility to take care of oneself first before taking care of others as a way to support our collective healing efforts, is also an act of protest and activism. Many of my clients, particularly my Black clients, struggle with this due to the urgent reality of oppression and the threat against their lives and their community. It has been powerful for me to reconcile my own desire to overextend myself as the therapist to meet the needs of my clients, and I use myself as an example in sessions, sharing awareness of the competing demands and how hard it is to prioritize the self in a time of significant social crisis. When I took a few weeks off for vacation toward the end of the summer, one of my clients shared that this was a good model for her own self-care needs, and this remains an ongoing goal for myself and for my clients.

The Work Continues

In considering what has been most effective in my work with young adults, I offer the following:

1. Young adults are very knowledgeable and have access to so much information that it can become overwhelming. As a result, they still struggle to integrate everything they are learning as they try to figure out how to accommodate their awareness into their growing identity. Therapists can help consolidate information by challenging them to think critically about what they absorbing and keeping in mind their fluctuating identity.

2. Young adults need safe spaces to express their full range of emotions. Therapists can help with identifying and naming emotions and, most importantly, validating their experiences.

3. Understanding the intersections of racism, capitalism, white supremacy, patriarchy, and so on, and how it affects the lives of young adults is essential. Young adults are much less tolerant of the status quo and push us all to be uncomfortable and strive for change.

4. A significant task of young adulthood is figuring out to how to balance the personal and professional. Self-care and boundary setting are essential life skills that should be encouraged and practiced.

5. As therapists, we are also part of the systems that our clients live in, and it is important to reflect on our own developmental needs personally and professionally. Appropriate self-disclosure is an important way to model self-awareness and encourage deeper exploration.

CONCLUSION

Our collective stamina for coping with what has been one of the most defining moments of this generation's life experience waxes and wanes. As I write this, social distancing rules continue to be relaxed and people are taking more and more risks to spend time with others, as the thought of indefinite physical distance seems unbearable. However, the threat of a resurgence of the virus in the coming months remains a reality. The fight for social justice presses on as we continue to experience significant polarization in regards to addressing race and racism, ongoing police violence, and perceived threats to civil rights and democracy. As a society, we will continue to navigate differing beliefs, with varying individual limits when it comes to the risk of contracting and spreading the virus as well as varying limits and expectations when it comes to eradicating oppression at its many levels. Making meaning of this time is a work in progress, and we have yet to see the long-term impact of what we have witnessed and experienced during this time. I remain encouraged and motivated to continue working toward personal growth for myself and with my clients.

Kathleen Isaac, PhD, is an African American, cisgender female, licensed Clinical Psychologist, and Clinical Assistant Professor at NYU Langone Health, where she provides individual, couples, and group psychotherapy to medical students, residents, and hospital employees. She also has a part-time private practice focused on serving BIPOC and LGBTQ+ clients with integrative treatment approaches, specializing in trauma, health psychology, and cultural issues. Additionally, Dr. Isaac is an adjunct lecturer and offers consultation and training to organizations to increase racial literacy and promote racial dialogue. She is committed to promoting the use of mental health treatment and reducing mental health stigma.

REFERENCES

Bialik, K., & Fry, R. (2019). Millennial life: How young adulthood today compares with prior generations. *Pew Research Center, 14.*

Blos, P. (1967). The second individuation process of adolescence. *The Psychoanalytic Study of the Child, 22*(1), 162–186.

Eng, D. L., & Han, S. (2000). A dialogue on racial melancholia. *Psychoanalytic Dialogues, 10*(4), 667–700.

Grotevant, H. D., & Cooper, C. R. (1985). Patterns of interaction in family relationships and the development of identity exploration in adolescence. *Child Development, 56*(2), 415–428.

Hamman, D. & Hendricks, C. B. (2005) The role of generations in identity formation: Erikson speaks to teachers of adolescents. *Clearing House: A Journal of Educational Strategies, Issues and Ideas, 79*(2), 72–76

Isaac, K. S. (2019) Lifting as we climb: The development of a support group for underrepresented minority medical students. *Group, 43*(2–4), 101–112.

Kendi, I. X. (2019). *How to be an antiracist.* One world.

Lawford, H. L., Astrologo, L., Ramey, H. L., & Linden-Andersen, S. (2020). Identity, intimacy, and generativity in adolescence and young adulthood: A test of the psychosocial model. *Identity, 20*(1), 9–21. doi:10.1080/15283488.2019.1697271

Lorde, A. (2017). *A burst of light and other essays.* Courier Dover.

Schwartz, S. J., Zamboanga, B. L., & Weisskirch, R. S. (2008). Broadening the study of the self: Integrating the study of personal identity and cultural identity. *Social and Personality Psychology Compass, 2*(2), 635–651.

CHAPTER 6

Asians Emerging in America

ELISA LEE

sian Americans as a perceived collective maintain a particular position in the United States. Despite being a rapidly growing population in the United States, Asian Americans remain underrepresented and underserved by the mental health field compared to other racial groups (Wong et al., 2017; Lee et al., 2011). In contrast to the lived experience of Asian Americans, which is ever shifting, the psychological literature regarding this group, with a few notable exceptions, focuses on mental health concerns as being culturally based, that is, based on Asian culture. This often leads to a flattening of the turbulent dynamics between Asians and America and overemphasizes distress as being rooted in Asian culture.

Given that emerging adulthood is a time of identity exploration and instability, it is important to examine the historical factors that have influenced Asian American emerging adults as well as notable current events that have continued to affect their sense of identity and place within this country. As I write this, we are living in a particularly anxiety-ridden time as the 2020 presidential election draws near alongside the ongoing impacts of the COVID-19 pandemic—an event which for many, if not all, Asian Americans has shown the stark reality that acceptance of Asians in America is a conditional state, all too vulnerable to political change. Case examples will serve to illustrate themes manifesting in the therapy room for Asian American emerging adults, notably legacies of the model minority stereotype and more recently the upheavals due to COVID-19 and the resurgence of the Black Lives Matter movement after the murder of George Floyd.

The cases I describe in this chapter are composites of various patients I have seen in private practice. They are also notably all US-born Asian Americans of East Asian descent whose parents immigrated to the United States, some parents during their own emerging adulthood. I make this distinction as the term "Asian American" often encompasses several distinct cultures from Asia as well as Asians recently immigrated to the United States alongside US-born Asians. In doing so, one can often ignore the different stressors and nuances that are present depending on one's specific cultural background and immigration story. To that end, while certainly the themes seen here are not exclusive to US-born East Asians, they will be the focus at least in this snapshot of a much larger, diverse community.

BRIEF HISTORY: FROM YELLOW PERIL TO MODEL MINORITY

As a group, Asians have often remained on the fringes of racial discourse in America. While frequently considered "honorary whites" who wield more socioeconomic capital and privilege than other racial minority groups, Asians are also simultaneously cast as perpetual foreigners who, by phenotypic and perceived cultural differences, are persistently thought of as the Other. As such, Asians remain vulnerable to flutters and shifts in the political atmosphere, at times praised for their industrious contribution to this country's capitalist framework and at other times ejected from the country's borders with persistent doubts of their nationality ("Where are you from? Where are you *really* from?"). In this sense, the ground is always shifting beneath their feet. To appreciate how Asian Americans were placed, or rather remain displaced, one would need to understand the historical context by which Asians settled in the United States and how the interactions of political and economic factors came to position Asians within the public consciousness.

The United States saw the first wave of Asian immigrants in the 1800s as the Chinese immigrated to work in labor-intensive jobs. This arrival was soon met with a hostile reception as laws were quickly established to restrict their freedoms. Labeled the "yellow peril," Asians were depicted as unassimilable "Orientals" who would cause social and economic disruption within the United States. Indeed, the idea of yellow peril seemed largely born from what white European Americans took to be a vast cultural and physical difference between the United States and East Asia. By and large, Asians were portrayed as cunning, greedy, and devious, their industrious nature to be viewed with suspicion. The Chinese Exclusion Act of 1882 placed a moratorium on Chinese immigration for a decade as well as prohibiting current Chinese residents from naturalizing. Subsequent government action legalized the discrimination of Chinese Americans, an entire generation remaining ineligible for citizenship or property ownership. By the time the Chinese Exclusion Act was being repealed in 1943, the United States had moved to legalizing Japanese internment camps, taking Japanese and Japanese Americans out of their homes, stripped of their legal rights as World War II raged on.

The eventual lifting of the immigration ban in 1965 made way for the second major wave of Asians arriving in America. Most notably, the group arriving in the 1960s was largely composed of highly educated professionals (e.g., engineers) because the United States granted visa exceptions to those who could demonstrate a sought-after discipline in order to stimulate the economy. With this latest immigration soon arose the idea of Asian Americans as the model minority. The model minority was a sign of the American Dream, as immigrants and children of immigrants could achieve academic and economic success through hard work. The success of the generations of Asian Americans following World War II suggested an acceptance of cultural differences and proof that America was a land of equality. However, a closer examination of the characteristics assigned to the model minority image showed that many of its features were simply a reworking of characteristics attached to the yellow peril stereotype. Asian Americans, with their quiet diligence and strong work ethic, were exemplary minorities who were able to rise economically and socially. In effect, the model minority stereotype created a less threatening version of the yellow peril, where the industriousness and ambition of Asian Americans made them productive citizens of the United States (Kawai, 2005); symbols of the American Dream and its promise of success through hard work.

The model minority remains one of the most enduring stereotypes associated with Asian Americans. The reasons for its continued persistence can be attributed to the term's usefulness in upholding systematic racism. To the effect that the myth places Asian Americans as examples of immigrant success, it places other races as examples of immigrant failure, effectively driving a wedge between Asian Americans and other minority groups (Wu, 2013). If taken as a sign that America is a country of opportunity and meritocracy, the model minority suggests the reasons for other minority groups not succeeding in the United States are a lack of effort on their part, rather than a system designed to uphold white supremacy by limiting upward mobility for other racial groups.

A significant cost of the model minority stereotype for Asian Americans has been the assumption that due to their supposed economic and academic success, Asians are less vulnerable to racism, socioeconomic stressors, and overall distress. In actuality, studies have shown that compared to their white counterparts, Asian American emerging adults experience higher levels of distress and suicidal ideation (Kim et al., 2016; Kisch et al., 2005) as well as more suicidal thoughts, intent, and attempts than other age groups (Duldulao et al., 2009). The model minority also posits that the majority of Asian Americans enjoy the benefits of strong academic performance and economic success, equal to white Americans. However, Asian Americans display the largest disparities within group in economic standing and higher education attainment. Relatedly, when education levels are accounted for, Asian Americans earn less than their white counterparts (Chen, 2018). Thus, while Asian Americans are perceived as having achieved equality, they do not share in equal benefits with the white majority, nor is there uniform achievement across separate Asian ethnic groups. Yet despite this, the label of the model minority and its false image of equality means Asian Americans are denied clear spaces to acknowledge and process experiences of oppression and racism.

Despite the falsehood of the model minority, it remains a lasting stereotype as it has been internalized by many Asian Americans. Through its role in giving Asians visibility in America, the model minority has been the main lens by which this country still views Asian Americans as a perceived whole. Any Asian American who does not fit the model minority stereotype is often left in a state of exclusion, not only from the general public but also from their own communities. That is, the model minority, having been such a strong framework in shaping Asian American identity, has meant that Asian Americans themselves have used it as a means by which they measure against and formulate their own sense of self and, for some, the lack thereof.

CASE EXAMPLE: DANIEL

Daniel, a second-generation Korean American cisgender male, entered into treatment with me at the start of his senior year of college for depression. He detailed that while he did have a job lined up after college, he felt largely directionless with little purpose. He lamented that at the end of college, he felt he had largely squandered his time, never having found anything that remotely interested him. While he speculated that some of that might be due to an appropriate level of anxiety one faces toward the end of senior year, he expressed never having an idea of what his interests were or how he envisioned himself one year, five years, or ten years from now.

Daniel's parents had immigrated to the United States for his father's graduate studies. After his education ended, Daniel's father kept his family in the United States but struggled to find secure employment. As a consequence, Daniel's family experienced financial hardship throughout most of his childhood. While Daniel's parents were traditional in that they wanted Daniel to do well in school, get into college, and get a good job, they gave him little direction or guidance as they remained predominantly preoccupied with supporting the family financially. Daniel described himself as an average student who did not excel in any particular subject. While he was surrounded by peers who were of similar financial standing as his own family, he was one of the few Asian students at his school. He recalled being teased by his classmates for his low academic performance. While Daniel was able to make a handful of friends, his experience of his early social life was a lonely one, not only with his peers, to whom he felt little connection, but also with his teachers, who seemingly ignored him. Daniel chose to attend college in a more racially diverse area, excited that he might be around a larger community of Asians for the first time. However, when he arrived, he found himself still struggling to find a peer group where he was comfortable. He noted that all around him were either academically minded Asians or wealthy Asians or a combination of both, none of whom he felt he could relate to. When I asked him if he really was not able to find any Asians like himself in the entire city, he replied with some humor that they must be hiding from him.

Daniel's half-joke that diverse Asians were potentially hiding from him is an accurately melancholic statement. Among career-oriented Asian Americans, he did not feel driven enough to have anything in common with them.

Among wealthy Asian Americans, the difference in their economic standing felt too great to overcome when socializing, and they in turn seemed almost perplexed and disinterested in Daniel's experiences of poverty growing up. This type of erasure and isolation from within the Asian American community felt more painful to Daniel than the casual rejection by his non-Asian peers who felt unable to place him given his lack of model minority abilities. So then, where were Daniel's Asians, the ones with a background similar to his, who, being neither career driven nor wealthy, were not part of the model minority? Surely they were out there. But they had become invisible even to Daniel's own eyes, erased not just from the mainstream but possibly from Daniel's own mind and imagination. If so, then how did Daniel see himself? Could he see himself at all?

As a stereotype, the model minority is perhaps more insidious to Asian Americans as it is at face value a positive stereotype, though its characteristics largely work to dehumanize them. It is a structure by which Asian Americans feel they can find their place in the United States, however much it may cost them. The internalization of the stereotype, like any other, for the Asian American is to deny and render invisible parts of the self and to make invisible others who cannot embody this caricature. For Asians Americans like Daniel, it leaves him unseen by others, including other Asian Americans and even at times himself.

ASIANNESS AS A DIAGNOSIS

> The most damaging legacy of the West has been its power to decide who our enemies are, turning us not only against our own people, like North and South Korea, but turning me against myself.
>
> —CATHY PARK HONG, *MINOR FEELINGS*

When the subject of Asian American mental health has been examined, the focus has largely been on cultural factors, such as stigmatization of mental health care and language barriers as reasons for impaired functioning as well as low help-seeking behavior (Ta et al., 2010; Abe-Kim et al., 2007; Kung, 2004). A common narrative that has emerged and to a large extent remains in place is that the children of Asian immigrant parents struggle under immense pressure to achieve academically in order to obtain educational and financial success. This is often coupled with the image of Asian immigrant parents being too emotionally remote and unfeeling toward their children's plight, simultaneously pushing them too far while denying them adequate support due to cultural intolerance of mental health concerns. And while threads of this narrative hold certain truths, a push toward academic achievement as well as cultural stigmatization of mental health is hardly exclusive to Asian cultures (Pong & Landale, 2012). Despite this, the image of hard, disciplining parents for the sake of upward mobility at the cost of children's emotional well-being remains a stereotype linked with Asian immigrant parents and Asian culture overall.

What is missing in the narrative that traditional Asian parents are the cause of their children's distress is the long history of racism, stereotyping, and trauma of immigration in the United States that continues to impact Asian Americans. In their writing, Eng and Han (2019) outline the phenomenon of racial melancholia by which to understand the protracted sadness of the Asian American experience. Racial melancholia is the process for Asians in America who, while holding onto the ideals and possibilities of equality, enter into a never-ending state of mourning as true acceptance remains impossible: "the inability to blend into the American melting pot, suggests that for Asian Americans ideals of whiteness are perpetually strained—continually estranged. They remain at an unattainable distance, at once a compelling fantasy and a lost ideal" (Eng & Han, 2019). With their description of racial melancholia, the authors offer a nonpathologizing lens by which to understand the depression that plagues Asian Americans as something created within a system that demands an internalization of whiteness as the ideal and pushes Asian Americans toward an impossible goal of achieving whiteness, in part by rejection of Asianness. The consequence of this for many Asian American emerging adults is the implicit message that their problems and their stressors are linked to their families and their Asian cultural values. In order to obtain mental health stability, one would need to divest themselves of their Asianness. As one of my patients joked while recalling their past therapies, "Apparently I'm too Asian to not be depressed."

Historically, a frequently depicted dynamic in Asian American stories has been the contention between US-born children and their immigrant parents as the children feel pulled by their parents to adhere to familial duty while simultaneously trying to be American and live for themselves.

It is a story that often pits children against their immigrant parents. It is a narrative that unfortunately can also find its way into therapy rooms as traditional Western models of health often stress the importance of individualism and independence. However, more recently, new narratives seem to be materializing.

One of the key features of emerging adulthood is that it is an age of self-focusing, a time when one is freed from parental-directed routines. It is also an age of identity exploration when children, having gained more distance from their parents, can perhaps more freely examine who they want to be and what they wish from their lives (Arnett, 2006). It is also a rich period in which Asian American children, having perhaps moved away from their parents both physically and psychically, can return to them as a matured version of themselves, capable of not only telling their own stories but listening and carrying the stories of their families.

CASE EXAMPLE: ELLEN

Ellen, a second-generation Chinese American cisgender female, came to me for treatment shortly after graduating from college. She reported that she had struggled with anxiety and depression for most of her life and had been in therapy before with various providers. During her initial contact with me, she stated that she felt it was important for her to work with an Asian American therapist, as she had never done so before. Throughout her childhood, Ellen had academically excelled. Tutored by her mother rigorously through her early education, Ellen had continued to achieve during her first semester of college before hitting a wall. She described becoming depressed and overtired by her constant, rigorous academic schedule, which she had maintained at the sacrifice of other college experiences during her first semester. She eventually decided to reinvent herself in college and refocused her efforts on socializing and getting involved in various student groups on campus. She noted that during this period, she pointedly cut off ties with her family, largely blaming her parents for putting too much pressure on her, detailing her weekly calls with her mother, who usually told Ellen to stay busy whenever Ellen spoke to her about her depression. She also did not date Asian men, nor did she have Asian friends, something which she stated she had purposefully done as she did not want to be thought of as an international Asian student whose social circle was only other Asians. When asked about this, Ellen stated that during that time in her life, she associated Asian culture, as personified by her parents, with the reasons for her anxiety and depression.

Ellen stated that what she now remembers about her early years in college was how lonely she had been, despite her socializing. While she had been the one to stop communicating with her parents, she felt the estrangement deeply. She also keenly felt being the only Asian American within her groups of friends, which were composed entirely of white peers, and the cultural gaps between them. Ellen had divested herself of her Asianness, and yet her depression and anxiety remained. It was only more recently that she had been able to articulate for herself that she was lonely because she yearned for peers of her own ethnic group, wanting to find a community where certain cultural norms would be understood and relished. As Ellen began to socialize more and more with other Asian Americans, she also reestablished her contact with her parents and began the process of reconciling with them. It was largely because of this that she had decided to reengage in therapy, wanting a place to process her still ongoing repair with her family as well as the Asian parts of her.

What stood out in my work with Ellen soon after our initial sessions was the stories she told, not just about herself but about her parents and their immigration to the United States. As she continued to reestablish contact with her parents, Ellen began to speak with them for the first time of the circumstances that prompted their immigration to the United States as well as their early years living in a new country. She shared stories of her parents living through China's Cultural Revolution and leaving for the United States in hopes of more opportunity as well as the early days of confusion and subtle racism they encountered as they worked to establish themselves in a new country. Ellen mused on how her parents had to maintain the belief in America as a system of meritocracy in order to make their lives here. And while Ellen herself did not share in their idealization of the United States, in hearing more about her parents' journey, she found greater connection with them as well as context by which she could understand their push for Ellen to succeed. It allowed her to be angry, not exclusively at her parents, but at a system that gave her parents little choice on how to parent her while telling them they had all the choices in the world.

There is a growing curiosity in Asian American emerging adults for their parents' stories and a connection to their parents' country that is also very much theirs alongside the United States. Rather than focusing exclusively on the pressures to achieve they felt from their parents, they seek spaces where connection to their families and the shared burden of trying to thrive in this country can be spoken about. Patients like Ellen ask for spaces where their families can also be with them in the room, rather than being implicitly told that to be in a space of restoration, one needs to leave family behind.

EXPOSURE IN THE WAKE OF COVID-19

On March 11, 2020, the World Health Organization officially declared COVID-19, a virus that reportedly originated from China, a worldwide pandemic. The following weeks marked a seismic shift in our day-to-day lives. Shelter at home orders, panic buying in stores, and a deluge of medical information began to pour into the collective consciousness. Amid statements of COVID-19's aggressiveness being over-sensationalized as well as denials of even its existence, the United States was soon forced into settling into a new way of life in isolation and fear. Soon the general panic and frustrations of the country started to find a target as the Trump administration began to refer to COVID-19 as the "Chinese virus" and "Kung flu." Reports of racially motivated attacks against Asians began to increase all over the country, ranging from people reporting being spat at in grocery stores to Asian American health care workers being verbally attacked by the very patients they were trying to treat (Jan, 2020; Loffman, 2020). In a matter of a few weeks, COVID-19 exposed the conditional acceptance afforded to Asian Americans as it thrust the model minority image back behind that of the yellow peril. While the administration's rhetoric pushed the xenophobia even more to the forefront, echoing the kinds of government-supported racism toward Asian Americans seen throughout various points in history, sentiments within the Asian American community also seemed to echo a return toward the model minority mentality. Former presidential hopeful Andrew Yang (2020) in his *Washington Post* op-ed called for Asian Americans to be "part of the cure" by being helpful to fellow Americans with acts of service so as to assuage any doubts about Asian Americans being patriotic; suggesting that through hard work, Asian Americans would be able to end the recent spike in racism toward their communities.

My Asian American patients met this initial wave of racism with a mixture of fear and sadness. Some reported personal experiences of being targeted on the streets, being pelted with racist slurs while outside. Others felt their anxieties increase as they stifled coughs, worried about what that might set off in the people whom they felt were watching them with wariness. For many, this was their first experience of feeling racially profiled as well as being exposed to the casual racism within their friend groups. Several Chinese American patients expressed their anger and hurt that even non-Chinese Asians seemed quick to make sure others knew they were not of Chinese descent, as if to try and spare themselves any racial targeting. It seemed at the start of this pandemic that we would be seeing a repeat of history; that with the rise of government-sanctioned villainizing of the Chinese, Asian Americans would again be told, even by each other, to cling to the model minority and that the problem was within their own communities.

What instead began to emerge in the therapy room was Asian American emerging adults speaking of a general disillusionment toward the false promises attached to the idea of being a model citizen, a model minority, as well as sharp criticism toward in-group distancing and fighting among Asian Americans. A number of them, who for a significant portion of their lives felt some identity alliance to aspects of the model minority stereotype, began to focus on the sacrifices they had made over the years to adhere to this image. They detailed the microaggressions and silencing they had experienced throughout their lives by not rocking the boat. However, microaggressions had become macroaggressions, and the exposure of the unstable acceptance of Asian Americans in the United States had given many young Asian Americans a solid ground by which they could talk about their own marginalized experiences. For them, their anger now felt justified and their grievances valid.

ALLIED ASIAN AMERICANS

On May 25, 2020, George Floyd, a Black man, was killed by white police officer Derek Chauvin. His murder sparked worldwide protests against police brutality and anti-Blackness. In the United States, the Black Lives Matter movement found itself back in the forefront of the nation's consciousness as hundreds of people marched in the streets. Asian Americans are often in the margins of racial discourse in the United States, which tends to focus on the Black-white model. While this has meant that Asian Americans struggle to find spaces to discuss their own experiences of racial prejudice, it has also contributed to Asian Americans struggling with allyship toward other racial minority groups. Certainly the legacy of the model minority stereotype has left Asian Americans with the framework that in order to advance in the United States, it would mean internalizing not just ideals of whiteness and Westernness but also anti-Blackness. All this has often left activism within Asian American communities for other minority groups complicated, underachieved, and unrecognized.

The resurgence of the Black Lives Matter movement in the public eye following the death of George Floyd came at the heels of anti-Asian sentiments in the wake of COVID-19. The timing of this felt particularly noteworthy as several of the Asian American emerging adults I was seeing in practice began to speak about joining protests and becoming involved in various organizations and movements against anti-Blackness. Many also expressed feelings of guilt regarding their lack of involvement when Black Lives Matter made headlines back in 2013 following the killing of Trayvon Martin as well as shame around the anti-Black sentiments they have seen from their parents and their own cultures. It appeared that with the recent dissolution of the fantasy that Asian Americans existed in a system of equality that truly benefited them, Asian Americans were finding their spaces in being allies and joining the BLM movement. As one patient succinctly stated, "Why were we helping a system that never cared about us? We need to all care about each other."

Alongside joining in protests, many young Asian American patients also discussed confronting their parents about contrasting political beliefs. Several detailed how this was an uncomfortable shift for them, as they usually left anti-Black sentiments and their parents' adherence to the model minority mentality (i.e., Black people are not succeeding because they aren't trying hard enough) unchallenged. Now they were motivated to engage with their parents around these viewpoints. In what felt like double fortuitous timing, young Asian Americans who had demonstrated greater curiosity about their parents' histories seemed better equipped to have these difficult conversations. Many expressed that having an understanding of what their parents sacrificed to make a life in the United States helped put into perspective their parents' difficulty in accepting that the United States has a flawed system based on upholding systemic racism: "My parents had to believe America is a land of equality." From this standpoint of empathy, they kindly but firmly continued to challenge and push their parents to recognize the importance of BLM, not just for Black communities but for all nonwhite communities, including Asian communities. And while no one spoke about easy resolutions, many spoke of hope and greater connection, not just with their families but with other minority communities and, to that extent, with this country.

CONCLUSION

While the model minority seemingly continues to impact the identity formation of Asian American emerging adults, its legacy has begun to shift as more Asian Americans begin to find spaces to better understand the sacrifices that are being asked of them to adhere to the stereotype and how it has worked to maintain a system of inequality rather than equality for all. The recent impacts of COVID-19 have seemingly only furthered the critical thinking and curiosity among Asian American emerging adults around their relationship to their families and their cultural heritage as well as their place in this country as a racial minority. In doing so, there has been a greater push for Asian Americans to align themselves with Black communities during the BLM movement. What may have begun as Asian Americans attempting to find their place in this country through an idealization of whiteness has begun to reform as Asian Americans ally themselves with other oppressed groups in hope of finding a true realization of the equality that America once promised.

Elisa Lee, PhD, is a New York City-based clinical psychologist in private practice. She earned her doctorate at the City University of New York and completed a postdoctoral fellowship at Harvard Medical School/ Cambridge Health Alliance. In addition to private practice, Dr. Lee is a supervising psychologist for doctoral trainees and has presented at various training seminars. While Dr. Lee treats a range of concerns, she specializes in working with adults and emerging adults struggling with life transitions and racial/cultural concerns—in particular, the experiences of Asian Americans.

REFERENCES

Abe-Kim, J., Takeuchi, D. T., Hong, S., Zane, N., Sue, S., Spencer, M. S., Appel, H., Nicdao, E., & Alegría, M. (2007). Use of mental health-related services among immigrant and US-born Asian Americans: Results from the National Latino and Asian American Study. *American Journal of Public Health, 97,* 91–98. https://doi.org/10.2105/AJPH.2006.098541

Arnett, J. J. (2006). *Emerging adulthood: The winding road from the late teens through the twenties.* Oxford University Press.

Chen, S. (2018, May 10). *Racial wealth snapshot: Asian Americans.* Prosperity Now. https://prosperitynow.org/blog/racial-wealth-snapshot-asian-americans

Duldulao, A. A., Takeuchi, D. T., & Hong, S. (2009). Correlates of suicidal behaviors among Asian Americans. *Archives of Suicide Research, 13*(3), 277–290. doi:10.1080/13811110903044567

Eng, D. L., & Han, S. (2019). *Racial melancholia, racial dissociation.* Duke University Press.

Jan, T. (2020, May 19). Asian American doctors and nurses are fighting racism and the coronavirus. *Washington Post.* https://www.washingtonpost.com/business/2020/05/19/asian-american-discrimination/

Kawai, Y. (2005). Stereotyping Asian Americans: The dialectic of the model minority and the yellow peril. *Howard Journal of Communications, 16*(2), 109–130. https://doi.org/10.1080/10646170590948974

Kim, J. E., Park, S. S., La, A., Chang, J., & Zane, N. (2016). Counseling services for Asian, Latino/a, and white American students: Initial severity, session attendance, and outcome. *Cultural Diversity and Ethnic Minority Psychology, 22*(3), 299–310. https://doi.org/10.1037/cdp0000069

Kisch, J., Leino, E. V., & Silverman, M. M. (2005). Aspects of suicidal behavior, depression and treatment in college students: Results from the spring 2000 National College Health Assessment Survey. *Suicide and Life-Threatening Behavior, 35,* 3–13.

Kung, W. W. (2004). Cultural and practical barriers to seeking mental health treatment for Chinese Americans. *Journal of Community Psychology, 32,* 27–43. https://doi.org/10.1002/jcop.10077

Lee, S., Martins, S., Keyes, K., & Lee, H. (2011). Mental health service use by persons of Asian ancestry with *DSM-IV* mental disorders in the United States. *Psychiatric Services, 62,* 1180–1186. https://doi.org/10.1176/appi.ps.62.10.1180

Loffman, M. (2020, April 7). Asian Americans describe "gut punch" of racist attacks during coronavirus pandemic. PBS. https://www.pbs.org/newshour/nation/asian-americans-describe-gut-punch-of-racist-attacks-during-coronavirus-pandemic

Park Hong, C. (2020). *Minor feelings.* One World.

Pong, S.-L. & Landale, N. (2012). Academic achievement of legal immigrants' children: The roles of parents' pre- and postmigration characteristics in origin-group differences. *Child Development, 83,* 1543–1559. doi:10.1111/j.1467-8624.2012.01790.x

Ta, V. M., Holck, P., & Gee, G. C. (2010). Generational status and family cohesion effects on the receipt of mental health services among Asian Americans: Findings from the National Latino and Asian American Study. *American Journal of Public Health, 100*(1), 115–121. doi:10.2105/AJPH.2009.160762

Wong, E. C., Collins, R. L., Cerully, J., Seelam, R., & Roth, B. (2017). Racial and ethnic differences in mental illness stigma and discrimination among Californians experiencing mental health challenges. *Rand Health Quarterly, 6*(2), 6. doi:https://doi.org/10.7249/RR1441

Wu, E. D. (2013). *The color of success: Asian Americans and the origin of the model minority.* Princeton University Press.

Yang, A. (2020, April 1). We Asian Americans are not the virus, but we can be part of the cure. *Washington Post.* https://www.washingtonpost.com/opinions/2020/04/01/andrew-yang-coronavirus-discrimination

CHAPTER 7

Exploring White Supremacy With Emerging Adults in Psychodynamic Therapy

CAROLINA FRANCO

D uring the 2020 New York City pandemic-related lockdown and social justice uprising, I provided weekly teletherapy from my bedroom office to 22 patients under the age of 25. Sequestered with my own reactions to the inequality displayed in the news and outside my window, I was intrigued but not surprised by my young patients' interest in exploring white supremacy, defined by Merriam-Webster (n.d.) as the belief that the white race is inherently superior and should have control of other races. I routinely examine societal issues in therapy, but rarely does my practice coalesce around one theme, and never before had the exploration of one issue fit the therapeutic needs of my diverse patient population. Specifically, older adolescents and emerging adults reported "feeling better" when they confronted and explored the systemic problems laid bare by a national crisis.

Witnessing my young patients become more secure in their identity and experience containment during a chaotic time brought up conflicting but familiar sentiments. It reaffirmed my confidence in the therapeutic value of psychodynamic treatment. And it reinforced my belief that psychodynamic exploration is limited by theories of health and pathology developed for and by people who were predominantly white, cisgender, straight, male, and upper class.

This passage from Alice Miller's (2008) book *Drama of the Gifted Child* depicts ideas that shaped me as a psychologist as well as attitudes I had to repudiate to practice authentically:

One can therefore hardly free a patient from the cruelty of his introjects by showing him how the absurdity, exploitation, and perversity of society causes our neuroses and perversions, however true this may be. Freud's patient Dora became sick because of society's sexual hypocrisy, which she was unable to see through. Things we can see through do not make us sick; they may arouse our indignation, anger, sadness, or feelings of impotence. What makes us sick are those things we cannot see through, society's constraints that we have absorbed through our mother's eyes—eyes and an attitude from which no reading or learning can free us. To put it another way: our patients are intelligent, they read in newspapers and books about the absurdity of the armaments race, about exploitation through capitalism, diplomatic insincerity, the arrogance and manipulation of power, submission of the weak and the impotence of individuals—and they have thought about these subjects. What they do not see, because they cannot see it, is the absurdities of their mothers at the time when they still were tiny children. One cannot remember one's parents' attitudes then, because one was a part of them, but in analysis, this early interaction can be recalled and parental constraints are thus more easily disclosed. (p. 100)

Miller highlights several enduringly applicable psychodynamic concepts that inform my work: primary relationships pass down harmful patterns in subtle and often invisible ways; insight alone is not curative; and the therapeutic relationship facilitates the uncovering and working through of toxic introjects (Ferenczi, 1909/1956; Freud, 1917).

Regrettably, Miller's insistence that psychopathology is transmitted through the "mother's eyes" disregards the influence of the caregivers' surroundings and that of the larger society. Furthermore, her description of human exploitation and political deception as absurdities that are easy to see, the discussion of which would waste our well-informed patients' time, illustrates old, but not relinquished, assumptions about whom we treat (articulate, educated people) and what we value (internal and intimate relational experiences). Miller's claims, at best, steer therapeutic dialogue away from harmful societal problems and, at worst, overlook, and consequently uphold, dehumanizing and oppressive systems.

I view Alice Miller's statement, "What makes us sick are those things we cannot see through," as a call to examine our patients' relationship to arguably the most invisible, unknowable, and unspeakable construct: white supremacy.

IN THIS CHAPTER

I propose that helping emerging adults identify the links between their experiences and the external forces that shape their worlds supports their identity development, adds nuance to how young adults understand this development, and gives greater clarity to their presenting problems. I will share how broadening the scope of my own analysis helped me understand and work through painful racial and ethnic identity conflicts. I will also share three case vignettes with emerging adults, where exploring the impact of systemic discrimination and white supremacy shed light on core conflicts and promoted intrapersonal and relational growth.

WHY IS EXPLORING IDENTITY IMPORTANT FOR EMERGING ADULTS?

The growing representation of marginalized groups in the mainstream, which often entails decentering whiteness, is undermined by the failure to educate the public about the violence of exclusion. Plainly speaking, without inclusion there is no peace in a multicultural society. Because our institutions have not sent a clear message, older generations often dismiss, dislike, or reject the evolving discourse about identity. And white people who experienced belonging to the "mythical norm" often experience the expectation to use different language or to consider the needs of previously marginalized groups as coercive and threatening.

Campbell (2011) argues that people of all backgrounds have been conditioned to view whiteness as the "mythical norm": normal, ubiquitous, and universally understood. The mythical norm also requires everything diverging from whiteness to be identified and explained. Because emerging adults' central concerns are related to their identity (Arnett, 2000), and older adults are ill equipped to discuss their concerns, many young people report talking about their identities away from home. Young people who grow up in religious or tight-knit ethnic communities tend to be secure in those identities, but still benefit from exploring race, gender, and sexuality. Black American youth's racial identity development is supported by the

long-established practice of racial socialization in African American families (Boykin & Toms, 1985; Spencer, et al., 1996; Peters, 2002, Rodriguez,
Mckay, & Bannon, 2008).

I experienced the racialization of my identity as a young immigrant alone.
The adults around me did not acknowledge that they engaged in discrimination based on race; they refused to identify racially; and they seemed unaware
of being racialized by the society at large.

IDENTITY STRUGGLES WHEN ETHNICITY IS RACIALIZED

I was born in the Dominican Republic. Dominican identity has been shaped
by colonial and white supremacist forces that benefited from pitting Dominican people against their genetically and historically similar Haitian neighbors,
with whom we share the island of Hispaniola. My family's relationship to race
and privilege was influenced by the dictatorship of Rafael Leonidas Trujillo
Molina (1930–1961), termed the most brutal Latin American dictatorship of the
20th century (Farid, 2016). The women in my maternal line, like many Black
and Brown Dominicans, lacked basic rights, economic opportunity, and access
to education. They survived through a combination of intergenerational family
support, manual labor, and sporadic government assistance. In contrast, born
to Spanish immigrants and the president of the family business, my father was
married and had six children with an affluent woman of European descent.

In a patriarchal Dominican society, my father made a second home with
a poor 20-year-old Brown single mother without experiencing societal con-
demnation. The local community, which shunned my mother for having a
child with a neighborhood boy, viewed her second, this time a light-skinned,
illegitimate daughter, as a blessing from God. The gleeful approval of their
sinful union revealed the hypocrisy of their morals and the power of a wealthy
white male.

At my father's instruction, I was treated the same way as his other children. My "feet never touched the floor," my mother once said to illustrate
my charmed infancy, which, unlike that of my older half-sister, was spent in
someone's arms or propped up in a miniature rocking chair. In 1979, David,
the only category 5 hurricane that made landfall in the Dominican Republic
in the 20th century, destroyed Santo Domingo and nearly bankrupted my
father's business. That same year, exactly one month after my fourth birth-

day (celebrated extravagantly), my father died of a heart attack. Following his death, we saw his family twice, first at the funeral mass, where, after everyone left, my paternal grandmother let us in to see his body. Later, his brother came to our house to collect items he deemed valuable. Overnight, like every woman in her lineage, my mother was on her own. There was no space for regret.

Less than one year after my father's death and before my fifth birthday, my mother joined the Dominican diaspora, moving first to Venezuela, then Puerto Rico. Finally, after seven years, we reunited in New York City. Suarez Orozco et al. (2002) found that 85% of Latino families come to the United States as we did, through serial migration. This process is characterized by extended parent–child separations, which increases the risk for traumatic experiences in the children (Zentgraf & Chinchilla, 2012). The lack of communication about our constantly changing living situation stands out among the many painful events of this time. As an example, after securing a well-paid job and countless talks about our imminent move to Puerto Rico, my mother called my sisters and me to say, "This is not the place for us; we are not wanted here." We all made it to New York one year later and never discussed those years of separation. A randomized controlled trial showed that improving communication about experiences of separation and loss in recently reunited families significantly reduced parent–child conflict and emotional distance, and improved understanding of each other's perspectives (Greenfield et al., 2020).

Studying the diaspora later in life helped me understand my mother's previous cryptic and disappointing statement. By the early 1980s, Dominican identity had been racialized in Puerto Rico (Duany, 2006). Duany built upon Howard Winant's (1997) definition of racialization as the extension of racial meaning to a previously racially unclassified relationship, social practice, or group. The fellow islanders, with whom Puerto Ricans shared many cultural traditions and history, started experiencing anti-Dominican bias in the 1970s. During this time, Dominicans were associated with low occupational status, dark skin color, irregular legal status, low intelligence, nonstandard dialect, and poor morals. Many social woes were blamed on the influx of Dominican immigrants: drug trafficking, increasing crime rates, prostitution, and unemployment. Ironically, these images of Dominicans in Puerto Rico resemble those of Haitians in the Dominican Republic and those of Puerto Ricans in the United States (Duany, 2006, p. 234).

The family reunion was bittersweet. We were finally together, but everyone was too overwhelmed to enjoy it. Adjusting to the receiving culture at age

11 marked the beginning of my identity confusion. In terms of my identity development, in the Dominican Republic, I was in the Pre-encounter phase, or thinking that "white was right." Back in the Dominican Republic, I had made friends with slightly older kids who idolized American and British punk rock. We used words like "anarchy" and phrases like "fuck the police," but we were mostly attracted to very white subcultures, because we saw them as the antithesis to the sexist, racist, and classist Dominican society we despised. We never thought that only listening to white musicians was racist, because we did not identify racially with white people. We were just Dominican, and we hated it.

Through the gaze of New Yorkers, I experienced the Encounter phase. American kids labeled me "Spanish girl," because, I guessed, I spoke Spanish. The differences between Dominicans, Puerto Ricans, Colombians, and whoever else were evident only to us. And young Dominicans dutifully adhered to all the stereotypes, lest they be confused with a different islander. It was the rest of the country that racialized our ethnicity and categorized us as brown Latin American immigrants—or Spanish for short.

Things changed when I met a diverse group of teenagers who braved the consequences of resisting stereotypes. For me, this was a time of connection with my Caribbean, African, and Latin American heritage, and of distancing myself from white underground cultures. As I attempted to confront my internalized racism, I directed my self-hate onto some white people, whom I viewed as racists. Learning about American systemic anti-Black oppression helped me to take the focus off individuals and to start thinking structurally. Understanding systemic racism softened the black-and-white split that I had internalized and later projected onto individuals.

In therapy, I explored immigration-related losses, painful family dynamics, and internal conflicts. But I did not bring up many encounters with oppressive systems, or explore my racial identity or sexual orientation. I remember the one session when my analyst, uncharacteristically, asked why I embraced my Latina identity and claimed Dominican nationality, but felt disconnected from Dominican culture. At age 19, I had no trouble answering this question. I cared about this issue and believed the difference between identifying as Dominican or Latina was enormous. I believed that Dominican ethnicity had been racialized and reduced to limiting stereotypes, while Latinx identity offered the freedom to be anything.

Because my family experienced significant discrimination in the United States, it was tempting to use my marginalized identities in what Eve Tuck and

Wayne Yang (2012) call "a move toward innocence." To authentically own my Dominican identity, I had to understand how white supremacy lived within my family's psyche. My white father was a patriarch who enjoyed unquestioned membership in the Dominican ruling class. My Black great-grandmother was the matriarch who, despite her indisputable subjugation, resisted the push to migrate to hostile places, thus maintaining a rightful connection to the land. From my childhood point of view, my white father was a benevolent patriarch whose generosity inspired loyalty and affection, and my chocolate-brown great-grandmother was long braids, bare feet on a clean shiny floor, and the smell of oranges and cloves in her soft bed. Both the white princess and the Black servant are in me, as is the trauma they experienced and inflicted.

WORKING WITH EMERGING ADULTS DURING A PANDEMIC AND SOCIAL UNREST

Six months in, and the year 2020 was already a punchline. I cringed at the "Worst Year Ever" jokes, but I understood the need to separate 2020 from normal life. Therapy was also different in 2020. The lockdown created a sense of timelessness that made the work harder but also forced patients to reckon with their most painful symptoms.

I have chosen three examples of emerging adults whose psychological problems were exacerbated by pandemic-related stressors. After a period of stabilization, when we focused on expressing and regulating feelings of impotence, loss, and fear, patients were able to deepen their exploration into long-standing symptoms. White supremacy emerged as an influential factor affecting their family histories, social worlds, and self-concepts. The combination of a reliable therapeutic alliance and insight-oriented therapeutic interventions provided the safety and space necessary for a meaningful exploration of an overwhelming concept.

Black–White Savior

Jen was a cisgender, heterosexual woman of mixed race in her mid-20s. She presented with symptoms of complicated grief, related to the recent and unexpected death of her father. She also wanted to resolve concerns about her biracial, Latina and white, identity. She reported that she felt like an impostor around people of color.

Jen's white American mother fell in love with a dark-skinned Dominican man while volunteering for a charitable organization in the Dominican
Republic. There they lived happily until the birth of their son, when they
moved to a large city in the Midwest. Jen was told that her father was unhappy
in the United States and wanted to move the family back to the Dominican
Republic. Jen's mother did not want to leave the United States. Her parents
divorced, and the children never saw their father again. Jen grew up feeling
abandoned by her father, half-believing the family narrative that she was better off without him.

When Jen was 18, her mother became quite ill and decided to share letters Jen's father had sent over the years. Jen's mother explained that she cut
off communication because she believed it would be easier for the children.
Perhaps because of her mother's illness, Jen did not dwell on her mother's
actions and made arrangements to meet her father. Despite the significant
language barrier, they made an easy connection. Jen reported that suddenly,
her hair, skin color, body type, and even natural charisma made sense. She
liked him right away, and he was clearly smitten, stopping people in the street
to introduce his daughter and brag about her accomplishments. She made
plans to live with him after college. But he died unexpectedly while she lived
in Colombia, where she was learning Spanish to better communicate with
her Dominican family.

During the coronavirus lockdown, Jen worked for a government agency
that focused on immigrant health. Extremely effective, she outperformed her
superiors and pushed them to expand their reach. She worried constantly
about the undocumented community in New York and felt limited by her position. Jen felt a lot of pressure to save lives, due in part to her father's death. She
revealed secret fantasies that had she gone straight to Dominican Republic,
her father might be alive. Her mother's professional expectations were also
notable. She described her mother's priorities: "She prepared me to run for
president, but never learned to do my hair."

After the murder of George Floyd, Jen read the *New York Times* article
(June 27, 2020) by Kim Barker about Alex Kueng, a 24-year-old Black police
officer who reportedly "joined the police force to fix it from within." Instead,
on his third day on the job, he actively participated in the slow murder of an
unarmed Black man. Jen self-deprecatingly noted that, without therapy, she
would "be like Alex Kueng, a Black–white savior." I was curious about the idea
of a Black–white savior. She noted that she did not relate to Mr. Kueng's choice

to join an institution known for its history of racial violence. But she identified with what she imagined was Mr. Kueng's unconscious enactment of his white mother's white saviorism. The biracial officer, like Jen, was raised by a white liberal single mother, who was involved in social justice and charity work, but did not seem to understand the experiences of her Black children.

As we worked together, it became clear that Jen was quite secure in her biracial, Latina identity. But she needed a space to imagine her white family's relationship to their own identities. As we explored her maternal family's context and history, a struggle with white European identity and class came into view. Her family avoided any talk of race or class, and only acknowledged Jen's mixed-race identity as an asset in a postracial world or as a manifestation of the absence of racism in the family. We wondered if it was too threatening to acknowledge that she and her brother were Black and experienced racism. Even more untouchable was the idea that separating the children from their father and their culture was a racist act. Since Jen's family refuses to talk about race, we hypothesized that their difficulty understanding Jen and her siblings' racial identity, as well as their rejection of nuanced or systemic definitions of racism, served to protect their fragile sense of goodness. To view their actions as self-protection rather than attacks on her Dominican identity did not excuse the hurt they caused. But she felt less victimized, which calmed her rage enough to let her be curious about the worlds that produced such privileged people, who would sooner emotionally abandon a child than own that they acted based on racism. Jen's work includes understanding narcissistic structures, and disruptions in attachment, trauma, and racism. All of these concepts add layers of nuance and coherence to her experiences.

Eve Tuck and Wayne Yang (2012) note that decolonization is not just symbolic but means the repatriation of indigenous land and life, and therefore by definition is unsettling, and does not promise a path to reconciliation or forgiveness. Recognizing that racism is internalized and enacted within families often has a similar effect. Jen came to therapy knowing that she did not grow up with her father because of racism, and yet accepting this idea changed her perception of her whole life. It unsettled her and, without her family's acknowledgment, left no path to reconciliation. In decolonization, the first step is to return that which was stolen (Tuck & Yang, 2012). Jen's father died, but she retains her right to have a connection to the Dominican Republic. She has a right to her Dominican heritage, to her father's family history, to Latina identity and culture. This is true whether or not Jen chooses to claim it.

Internalized American Exceptionalism

Reese, a white, straight, cisgender 24-year-old woman, sought therapy to address depressed moods, excessive crying, and low self-esteem, triggered by fears of failure. Talented and hardworking, she had been a top acting student and moved to New York to pursue her dream. Disillusioned by rejections and financial hardship, she described herself as "one more white girl in a sea of white girls."

At first, she theorized that her lack of opportunities reflected the industry's preference for nonwhite and/or queer people. Turning red, she expressed feeling ashamed to say this to me, a Brown Latina. She explained that the art community needs to attract artists of diverse backgrounds to remain relevant. Still, she felt that her identity put her at a disadvantage in auditions. I offered that those arguments had been part of her consciousness long before she had any use for them. She then noted that the successful white cisgender female actors all seemed to have financial security. They had connections to important people in the industry as well as time for classes and auditions. She was again embarrassed, this time by her envy as well as her naïveté. She had never thought of the professional advantages that come with wealth. I proposed that she might feel aggrieved because she followed the rules of a meritocracy, which promises talented people success in return for hard work. It was not fair, but who was to blame?

The disconnect between the way Reese described herself and her presentation was striking. The referring clinician aptly described Reese as "a ray of sunshine." She was attractive, stylish, and likable, and had an active artistic life. She was in a healthy relationship and worked to support herself and pay her student loans. I asked why she expected immediate success in such a competitive and often nonlucrative field. She admitted she had never thought about monetizing her craft. Then she repeated that her lack of success was due to competing with girls just like her. Blaming herself was painful, but it protected the worldview her family inculcated.

Reese described her childhood as idyllic, at first. She had a doting stay-at-home mom and an authoritarian but generous father, as well as a tight-knit church community. In therapy, she noted that her father sternly shut down conversations about money or social issues, two areas she struggled to think or talk about. During the first outbreak of coronavirus in New York City, Reese left the city to work remotely from her parents' home. She expressed concern about her father's identification with right-wing ideology, which she evaded until he tried to convince her that the pandemic was a hoax. Rather than arguing, she gave him a well-sourced article. He responded by angrily ordering her to leave his house.

Reese called from her home in New York, terrified of getting sick and shocked that her father put her in danger. At home, her roommate refused Reese's request to stop socializing at home, and told her to save her "white tears" and go back home. She decided that a group of queer people of color did not need to know why she came back to New York. Feeling attacked from the right and the left, she felt sorry for herself. I felt the injustice of the situation, but I struggled to empathize with her sadness. The disavowed anger beneath Reese's sadness obstructed a genuine connection. When she completely shut down, I sat in silence while she cried. Her parents had not prepared her for a world not moved by her tears. Thus we focused on her tears. She had used them to ward off aggression and to get comfort, even to evade responsibility. But in that moment she was angry, and her tears were tears of frustration. She felt misunderstood, victimized, and abandoned, and it was easy to empathize with all of those feelings.

In addition to engaging in conventional therapeutic exploration, Reese was interested in discussing American history, sexism, white supremacy, and capitalism. The sessions felt like the conversations she wished had taken place at the family dinner table. She was learning about ideas like internalized American exceptionalism, which explained the unbearable shame she experienced when faced with the slightest rejection. She became curious about the social and political environment that shaped her parents. They were both given a set of rules for success, and they followed them, but they did not achieve the financial security they felt entitled to.

The idea that institutional oppression is invisible to those who are not explicitly oppressed and/or who benefit from the exploitation of others helped her understand her parents. However, as her understanding of systemic problems evolved, so did her father's focus on blaming groups of people, and they grew apart. Leaving the family bubble behind came with immense relational losses that had to be mourned alongside fantasies of fairness. Therapy, education, and antiracist activism have played a role in Reese's treatment. With a more coherent view of the world, she became more secure in her white identity. Being grounded in her identity has helped her figure out what she wants to do, who she wants to be with, and how she wants to live. She is not a paper doll in a sea of paper dolls anymore.

Tolleson (2009) argues that the psychoanalytic engagement of the subjective effectively services the demands of capitalism by employing soothing techniques that calm people and quell dissent; by reframing social problems in terms of individual psychopathology; by displacing blame for suffering onto local objects, like parents, particularly mothers; and by tranquilizing human distress through pharmacology. Tolleson noted that psychotherapy outcomes like improved self-esteem, reduced suicidal ideation, and stable employment and relationships are in essence commodities that skew the focus of treatment and promote Western ideals as a measurement of success. She finally argues that the decision to interpretively disregard the potency of the broader social world in the forming of subjectivity, expunging political meaning from the therapeutic discourse, is as political an act as any other.

A Good Life in a Terrible World

Mario, a 24-year-old Mexican, straight, married, cisgender man, was brought to the United States at age 3 and grew up undocumented. He sought treatment for anxiety with insomnia and constant worry about making mistakes at work, as well as relationship issues which he attributed to depressed moods and difficulties identifying and communicating his thoughts and feelings to his partner. He also reported feelings of guilt about "leaving his undocumented family members behind" when he adjusted his documentation status to United States resident through marriage at age 23. Mario grew up in a mixed-status family. His parents were undocumented. He and his older sibling had Deferred Action for Childhood Arrival status (DACA), and his younger siblings were born in the United States.

As soon as the pandemic hit, Mario's symptoms changed. He reported anxiety attacks, numbing, and sleep problems triggered by intrusive thoughts that the coronavirus would lead to death and extreme poverty, which would unleash more police violence on vulnerable communities. Even if a Democratic candidate were to be elected (his best-case scenario), he feared the election and the months before the transition of power would trigger massive social unrest and destruction. His concerns were notable because he reportedly never worried. He explained that he had never had optimistic, pessimistic, or even neutral thoughts of the future. As an example, he was surprised by his college graduation, because had not thought of graduating or about what he would do after. We understood his difficulty planning for the future as a survival mechanism aimed at protecting him from loss and disappointment. Mario realized that when he tried to think of the future, he felt anxious and hopeless, two feelings he seldom experienced because he tended to stay in the present, his comfort zone. The problem was that this present offered no comfort.

Mario succeeded academically and professionally because of his calm approach to problems and his perseverance. But he was not always so even-tempered. Mario's parents obsessively warned him about getting in trouble with the police. He grew up with what then seemed to be an exaggerated fear that he would make a mistake that would destroy his family, so he rarely left the house. Mario's parents never discussed their or their older children's undocumented status, and they did not explain that the police were targeting young Latinos in his neighborhood. Mario's parents' frightening warnings about children being taken away and teenagers getting arrested confused and annoyed Mario, who was an athlete and a straight-A student his whole life. He internalized his anger, experienced a quiet numbing, and shut everyone out. In session, we examined his dissociation and his parents' anxieties in relation to the sociopolitical climate surrounding his upbringing.

Abrego et al. (2017) examined the processes that produce the notion of "criminal aliens" by reviewing the legal history, enforcement programs, and practices at the border and interior, as well as by exploring the consequences for immigrants and their families living in the United States. They outlined legislative changes that paved the way for the criminalization of immigration and explored the importance of the Illegal Immigration Reform and Immigration Responsibility Act (IIRIRA) and the Antiterrorism and Effective Death Penalty Act (AEDPA) in 1996. They explained how specific programs and practices have turned people and whole communities into objects of law enforcement. And, finally, they described how the criminalization of immigrants affects power dynamics within families and outside the home.

Mario's home was regulated by a strict code of conduct. As we explored the impact of their mixed documentation status, his parents' insistence that their children be exceptionally well behaved and respectable seemed more like a desperate effort to protect them from deportation and consequent family separation. Their "unreasonably" high standards for the children, contrasted with a lack of ambition for themselves, took on new meaning when Mario thought that they might have been preparing the children to live without them. Mario had witnessed the targeting of immigrants in the United States but never thought how anti-immigrant policies and rhetoric affected him and his family. Outside the home, despite doing everything right, Mario never felt safe. He remembered not quite believing stories of neighborhood teenagers getting arrested and deported for jaywalking. We discovered that he had many fears that were never acknowledged or validated. I communicated that I understood why he refuses to be hopeful by asking, "Can you have a good life in a terrible world?" This question lingered in the air for a while.

One of the biggest problems I see with young people is that their reality has been constantly denied. For a time I worked in palliative care, and in that work the root of suffering is denial. While working with terminally ill children and their families, I was amazed that the end-of-life treatment was radical acceptance. We often told patients and families, "You have six months: how do you want to spend that time?" The very Western concepts of never-ending progress and quarterly gains have turned psychological treatment into a commodity. The pressure to yield observable results leads to our focus on changing behavior and our avoidance of unsolvable or overwhelming problems, like death and climate change. Paradoxically, the acceptance of scary truths allows for realistic and sustainable actions to improve situations. It is not uncommon for terminally ill people to use their precious time generously repairing relationships and comforting others. Mario ended the session saying he wanted to take time to think about how he might have a good life in this world. This intention was important in two respects: he was considering how to live well in an unjust world, and he felt ready to imagine himself in the future.

RECKONING WITH THE PAST IN THE FIELD OF PSYCHOLOGY

To achieve a more inclusive psychodynamic orientation, we need to recognize that our foundational theories are not ahistorical or unbiased, and may not be generalizable to today's youth. Asking if some of our long-held assumptions are irrelevant or even toxic to our patients is a good start, as is a thorough investigation of the ways psychology has been used to buttress systems of oppression.

Most contemporary therapists would regard Alice Miller's language as outdated and offensive. But her accurate depiction of many consulting rooms shows that inclusive discourse does not always translate into practical change. Malcolm Harris's (2017) book *Kids These Days: Human Capital and the Making of Millennials* argues, from a materialist viewpoint, that "the most educated, hardest working generation in American history, has less money, more debt, reports more anxiety and depression, and is more medicated than their parents and grandparents" because of the political, economic, and social institutions that regulate their environment. His argument echoes concerns expressed by most of my young patients. Simply put, emerging adults are doing too much; they don't know why they are doing it all; and they can't stop. I propose we respond with an attitude change. I would like to retire the antipathy for the concrete and get curious about the material issues driving young people to exhaustion.

EXPANDING THE SCOPE OF PSYCHODYNAMIC EXPLORATION

Many young people have sophisticated, even expert, knowledge about identity, because they are genuinely interested and have access to unlimited information. Also, Generation Z and Millennials tend to support meaningful inclusion of historically marginalized people, and their young brains integrate new language and changes in social norms rather easily. There is a significant and threatening backlash against this progress, but these societal gains are undeniable.

Therapists who are cisgender, straight, older, conservative, religious, or from immigrant backgrounds may feel intimidated in the presence of a young expert. We should not confuse theoretical or cutting-edge knowledge about culture and identity with an understanding of the patient's relationship to those concepts. We can assist the achievement of a coherent sense of self by encouraging the integration of intellectual, physical, and emotional experiences. With genuine curiosity, respect, and a willingness to venture into unknown territory, we can provide that space.

Therapy and life experiences did not help me understand why I had rejected my identity so intensely. For that, I needed to understand the story beyond my family. Ethnographer Milagros Ricourt (2016) explained that Dominicans were indoctrinated to identify as Hispanic, Catholic, and rarely as Black, and to dehumanize Haitians, because the ruling class needed Dominicans and

Haitians to be adversaries. To that end, Africa needed to be erased from the official Dominican racial imaginary. However, Ricourt's research reveals an unacknowledged fight to preserve African heritage, a present reckoning with anti-Black racism, and murderous xenophobia, which is strengthening the perpetual movement to fight white supremacy in the Dominican Republic.

The first purpose of forging a national Dominican identity was to antagonize Haitian nationals. That is the identity I yearned to separate from. However, running away from colonial anti-Black discrimination kept me from learning about the continuous fight for liberation and justice. Clinicians can help patients enter adulthood with a nuanced picture of who they are and the capacity to think critically about their identities and values. By expanding therapeutic exploration to include social context and history, insight-oriented therapy can help emerging adults locate themselves and their role, however small, in the much bigger—often terrifying—story of the world.

Carolina Franco, PhD, is a psychologist in private practice and a clinical supervisor for the doctoral program at City College, City University of New York. Dr. Franco has a strong psychodynamic foundation and vast experience implementing manualized, innovative, and evidence-based interventions in outpatient clinics, hospitals, and university settings. Dr. Franco has clinical, research, and teaching experience in the areas of trauma, addictions, immigration, and minoritized identities psychology. She aims to contribute to the movement toward more inclusive, socially conscious, and progressive psychological theories and practices.

REFERENCES

Abrego, L., Coleman, M., Martinez, D. E., Menjivar, C., & Slack, J. (2017). Making immigrants into criminals: Legal processes of criminalization in the post-IIRIRA era. *Journal on Migration and Human Security, 5*(3), 694–715.

Arnett, J. J. (2000). Emerging adulthood: A theory of development from the late teens through the twenties. *American Psychologist, 55*(5), 469–480.

Barker K., (2020, June 28). The Black officer who detained George Floyd had pledged to fix the police. *New York Times.* Section A, Page 1.

Boykin, A. W., & Toms, F. D. (1985). Black child socialization: A conceptual framework.

In: McAdoo, H. P., McAdoo, J. L., editors. *Black children: Social, educational, and parental environments*, pp. 33–51. Thousand Oaks, CA: Sage Publications, Inc.

Campbell, D. (2011). Oppression of the different: Impact and treatment. *International Journal of Applied Psychoanalysis Studies, 8*(1), 28–47.

Duany, J. (2006). Racializing identity in the Spanish-speaking Caribbean. *Latin American and Caribbean Ethnic Studies, 1*(2), 231–248.

Farid, S. (2016). Rewriting the Trujillato: Collective trauma, alternative history, and the nature of dictatorship. *International Journal of Communication and Linguistic Studies, 14*(3), 39–51. doi:10.18848/2327-7882/CGP/v14i03/39-51

Ferenczi, S. (1956). Introjection and transference. In *Sex in psychoanalysis* (pp. 30–79). Dover. (Original work published 1909)

Freud, S. (1915). Instincts and their vicissitudes. In J. Strachey (Ed. & Trans.), *Standard edition of the complete psychological works of Sigmund Freud* (Vol. XIV, pp. 109–140). Hogarth.

Freud, S. (1917). Mourning and melancholia. In J. Strachey (Ed. & Trans.), *Standard edition of the complete psychological works of Sigmund Freud* (Vol. XIV, pp. 243–258). Hogarth.

Gill, M. (1994). The analysis of transference. In G. Bauer (Ed.), *Essential papers on transference analysis* (pp. 109–138). Jason Aronson.

Greenfield, P. M., Espinoza, G., Monterroza-Brugger, M., Ruedas-Gracia, N., & Manago, A. M. (2020). Long-term parent–child separation through serial migration: Effects of a post-reunion intervention. *School Community Journal, 30*(1), 267–298.

Harris, M. (2017). *Kids these days: human capital and the making of millennials*. First Edition. Little, Brown and Company.

Kroger, J. (1998). Adolescence as a second separation-individuation process: Critical review of an object relations approach. In E. E. A. Skoe & A. L. von der Lippe (Eds.), *Personality development in adolescence: A cross national and life span perspective* (pp. 172–192). Routledge.

Merriam-Webster. (n.d.). *Merriam-Webster.com dictionary*. Retrieved March 10, 2021, from https://www.merriam-webster.com/dictionary/white%20supremacy

Miller, A. (2008). *The drama of the gifted child: the search for the true self.* 30th anniversary ed., rev. and updated. Basic Books/Perseus Books Group.

Murji, K., & Solomos, J. (2005). Introduction: Racialization in Theory and Practice. In K. Murji & J. Solomos (Eds.), *Racialization: Studies in theory and practice* (pp. 1–12). Oxford University Press.

Ricourt, M. (2016). *The Dominican racial imaginary: Surveying the landscape of race and nation in Hispaniola*. Critical Caribbean Studies. Rutgers University Press.

Rodriguez, J. A., Mckay, M., & Bannon, W. M. (2008). The role of racial socialization in relation to parenting practices and youth behavior: An exploratory analysis. *Social Work in Mental Health, 6*, 30–54.

Spencer M. B., Dupree D., & Swanson D. P. (1996). Parental monitoring and adolescents' sense of responsibility for their own learning: An examination of sex differences. *The Journal of Negro Education, 65*(1), 30–43.

Suarez-Orozco, C., Todovora, I., Louie, J. (2002). Making up for lost time: The experience of separation and reunification among immigrant families. *Family Process, 41*(4), 625–643.

Tolleson, J. (2009) Saving the world one patient at a time: Psychoanalysis and social critique. *Psychotherapy and Politics Intl., 7*(3), 190–205.

Tuck, E., & Yang, W. K. (2012). Decolonization is not a metaphor. *Decolonization: Indigeneity, Education and Society, 1*(1), 1–40.

Vaillant, G. (1994). Ego mechanisms of defense and personality psychopathology. *Journal of Abnormal Psychology, 103*(1), 44–50. https://psycnet.apa.org/doi/10.1037/0021-843X.103.1.44

Zentgraf, K. M., & Chinchilla, N. S. (2012). Transnational family separation: A framework for analysis. *Journal of Ethnic and Migration Studies, 38,* 345–366.

CHAPTER 8

Veterans and Emerging Adulthood

Contemporary Veteran Identity and Clinical Concerns

ANNELISA PEDERSEN AND PETER LEMONS

P erhaps it is telling that within the broad literature on emerging adulthood (EA), there is a dearth of writing specifically about veterans. This gap might suggest that, as a concept, EA does not readily apply to veterans. At the very least, veterans do not seem to experience EA in the same way as their age-matched peers. For one thing, EA, according to Arnett, tends to be characterized by "obtaining a broad range of life experiences before taking on enduring—and limiting—adult experiences" (2000, p. 474). Service members do sometimes join because they wish to see the world or seek adventure. But in actuality, military service tends to be more limiting than broadening, as service members are assigned specific roles and compelled to obey the military chain of command.

It is possible veterans simply interpret their responsibilities differently as members of a subculture, and, if so, nonconformity might look different in this population and therefore go undetected. On the other hand, such a phenomenon may stem from the fact that many veterans are more likely to have been asked to take on outsized responsibility for others than those who have not served in the armed forces, perhaps especially during wartime. Although direct research has not quantified the effect of taking responsibility for the lives of others on an individual's experience of EA, Arnett states that parenthood, which also involves taking responsibility for the life of another, "thrusts [young parents] into adulthood immediately and abruptly, as they are suddenly required to change their lives to care for their newborn child" (2015, p. 320). He characterizes this as a singular event that serves to truncate EA for those who experience it, despite their age (Arnett, 2015, p. 319). In other words, though features of EA may draw some young people into military service (e.g., adventurousness, an opportunity to change the direction of one's life trajectory), the strict guidelines of military life seem more likely to decommission the exploratory process that is most often associated with this phase of life.

Arnett (2015, p. 265) himself has begun enumerating the ways in which conventional cultural dividing lines do not necessarily inhibit the broader features of EA, and as such, without more research on military and veteran populations, it is difficult to claim with confidence that service members do not experience EA. Before being able to make a definitive claim about the presence or absence of EA within the experience of military veterans, systematic studies would need to be conducted examining features of EA among younger veterans, designed to compare this population with their civilian peers and older veteran cohorts. To our knowledge, no such studies have been undertaken. It therefore seems worthwhile to consider how aspects of EA might be relevant for this group, and how navigating the transition into a stable and fulfilling civilian life might require some level of engagement with the process of emerging adulthood. After all, most recruits join the service in their late teens and early 20s, and the average duration of service with the armed forces is seven years (Clever & Segal, 2013). Demographically, that means that many, if not most, service members who complete their service end up doing so at some point in their 20s, when they are still likely to be finding their way into longer-term adult commitments. At minimum, this overlapping trajectory that interweaves developmental milestones with total institutionalization in the armed forces makes former service members a special case to be considered through the theoretical lens of emerging adulthood.

If for no other reason, looking into the many factors facing young veterans as they transition into civilian life gives those of us working clinically with veterans—especially those of us who are not veterans ourselves—the chance to enhance our understanding of the challenges veterans face, and to help them navigate the transition between the military and civilian worlds.

Because few Americans serve and understand military culture or the pressures veterans face as they reintegrate,* veterans experience an increased risk of social isolation and marginalization as they establish their civilian identities (Smith & True, 2014). Veterans who return home to reintegrate with their civilian peers have at minimum missed out on roughly the first half of this period, characterized by fluidity of identity and creative expression, which their peers back home have been experiencing, often without the constraints of concrete responsibility. As identity conflict is so often related to diagnosable mental health concerns, it is our duty as clinicians to be aware of, and sensitive to, the ways in which military veterans in particular are vulnerable to developing mental health challenges because they are so much more likely to experience such conflict upon their return home.

Before continuing, we feel it is prudent to clarify the scope of our clinical experience, as there is reason to believe that the population of veterans being treated at Veterans Health Administration facilities, and especially those electing treatment within behavioral health, is not representative of the veteran population at large. As a whole, the data suggest veterans who utilize VA services are more likely to experience lifetime psychopathology, to be combat exposed or to have physical disabilities, to make less than $60,000 per year, and are less likely to be employed than veterans who do not utilize such care (Meffert et al., 2019). In sum, the subset of veterans we discuss below, based on our experience working at VA, cannot be taken to represent all veterans. As with many subsequent observations in this chapter, further research will need to be completed before we fully understand the meaning of the differences between those who opt for VA care and those who do not.

In this chapter, we first briefly review the existing literature exploring the role of military service in emerging adulthood. Then we explore how findings from the research on veteran identity may shed light on how young veterans engage with aspects of emerging adulthood. Here we also integrate composite case material, generalized from our experiences, to illustrate ways in which we have witnessed themes related to emerging adulthood in our clinical work.

---

* The portion of the US population serving in the active-duty military today remains relatively low, at less than half a percent of the total population (1.3 million; Council on Foreign Relations, 2020). Compare this to the early 1970s when the military draft ended and nearly 2 million men and women—or 1% of the population at the time—were engaged in active service (Council on Foreign Relations, 2020).

Finally, we explore clinical concerns that commonly emerge with young veterans and offer ideas and recommendations for future research based on our experiences.

IDEAS FROM THE EXISTING LITERATURE

Of the existing literature on emerging adulthood, there is a small segment that speaks directly to the experience of military service as a component of early adulthood and identity formation. This literature comes primarily out of Israel, where the great majority of young men and women serve in the Israeli Defense Forces beginning in their late teens. A 2016 study interviewed 72 Israeli emerging adults to examine their developmental processes (Schulman et al., 2005). Because military service is such a common experience for young Israelis, the authors acknowledge the developmental influence the military may have exercised on their sample—both fostering independence and simultaneously hindering it. On the one hand, military service enhances maturity by encouraging responsibility, developing impulse control, and fostering independent decision making; and on the other, it imposes a "demanding, rigid, and authoritarian system that controls the life of the individual" (Schulman et al., 2016, p. 580). In another Israeli study, Scharf and Mayseless (2004) explore attachment-related concerns among emerging adults, integrating variables related to military service to their quantitative analyses. They consider how specific experiences acquired during military service may function as a moderating influence on the lives of emerging adults, in some cases bolstering feelings of efficacy and individuation, and in others contributing to preexisting insecure vulnerabilities (Scharf & Mayseless, 2004). The findings of their study suggest that the underlying attachment style of emerging adults (e.g., secure vs. dismissing) in Israel may indeed influence how or whether they experience an enhancement of healthy identity formation during their military service. While these findings do not necessarily generalize to the US population of young service members and military veterans, they do offer helpful ideas around the ways in which military service may influence the trajectory of a young person's life while also accounting for how underlying psychological factors may interact with military experiences to influence development during emerging adulthood.

VETERANS AND IDENTITY DEVELOPMENT

Arnett's (2000) theory suggests that emerging adulthood concludes as individuals find themselves entering longer-term roles in marriage, parenthood, and in careers they see themselves remaining in for years to come. Emerging adulthood is a stage defined by identity exploration "in the areas of love, work, and worldviews" (Arnett, 2000, p. 473), when individuals understand themselves to be between childhood and adulthood, and when risk behaviors are likely to peak. While for many this period ends in the mid-20s, for some it lasts through the late 20s. If we understand this period as more of a developmental stage of life, aspects of it may indeed last much longer. For emerging adults in the general population, this time is also characterized by considerable amounts of stress, anxiety, and depression, and at the same time, "The fact that so many emerging adults often feel anxious or depressed should not lead to the conclusion that they are unhappy with their lives" (Arnett, 2015, p. 278). Arnett goes on to state, "although a majority of 18–29-year-olds often feel anxious, and about one-third often feel depressed, an even higher proportion agrees that 'I am satisfied with my life' (81%) and that 'this time of my life is fun and exciting' (83%)" (2015, p. 278). In this way, emerging adults may be uniquely prone to feeling that their foibles—no matter how distressing—are meaningful. This inconsistency of attitude may be especially consequential for those who experience trauma and moral injury, as the potential for associating a time perceived as full of meaning and purpose with emotional devastation may be high.

For veterans who discharge from military service in their 20s—either voluntarily, due to medical complications, or due to disciplinary action—and who identify with aspects of emerging adulthood, making the transition not only into adulthood but into civilian adulthood may be an additionally burdensome process. Not unlike individuals who transition out of other "total institutions" (Smith & True, 2014, p. 149) such as prison, veterans are tasked with accounting for their former identity (i.e., military service member) while forging their unique sense of self as adults in the civilian world. Furthermore, veterans must execute this assimilation in the context of peers who have been experiencing a period characterized by identity exploration and freedom from responsibility, and who have generally moved toward more liberal worldviews that stand in contrast to the institutional, conservative norms to which veterans have grown accustomed.

Case Composite 1: For example, consider Joe, a 28-year-old white, Latino, male combat veteran who served multiple tours of duty in Iraq with a Marine Corps unit. He described his approach to dating and meeting new people upon his return to the United States: "I just try to avoid talking about [the war], but it's hard because you get three sentences in and they start to ask you, 'What do you do?' I say, 'I sell cars.' Then it's, 'How long have you been doing that?' And then I'm screwed. I can make something up, but I sound sketchy. I can say, 'Six months,' and then it's, 'What were you doing before that?'"

In therapy sessions, Joe shared the suspicion he feels he encounters in these situations, and it is easy to understand how this might be the case. He has reentered civilian life at a time when others his age have hit the end or are approaching the end of their emerging adulthoods and have come to expect standard answers to questions about job history, for example. Joe is unable to provide the expected answers, and his life at age 28 more closely resembles that of someone much younger and simultaneously much older. He is casually dating and has not had many relationships, as he was deployed for most of his 20s. He is also separated and has part-time custody of two small children from a marriage that began around the time he enlisted as an infantry Marine. He is working at a car dealership, a job he has no interest in for the long term, and does not know what he wants to do. He has also already completed a career in which he received exemplary commendations for his leadership of younger Marines in battle. As one might expect, Joe frequently described feeling he could no longer relate to his friends from high school, and he had to work quite hard to "force [him]self to go out and be social," as he had to spend a lot of time strategizing his approach to casual interactions in order to simultaneously hold the boundaries he needed to feel safe and also appear transparent enough not to arouse suspicion.

It is important to note that Joe's tours of duty were characterized by intense fighting, and he was diagnosed with PTSD, which led to his discharge when he would have preferred to stay in the Marines, where he hoped to have a full career. His story nevertheless illustrates how veterans can easily find themselves trapped in conversations with their peers who have had much more time to discover themselves, and who are more likely to be willing to share the narrative of their discovery.

We know from the literature on individual identity development how fundamental a coherent identity is for mental health, and furthermore, how identity
adjustment difficulties are reported to be a common concern for veterans coming out of the military conflicts of the early 21st century (Orazem et al., 2017).
While there is a robust literature on the prevalence of PTSD, depression, and
other comorbid clinical concerns among young veterans today, there have also
been a number of studies conducted in recent years focusing on the reintegration experiences of veterans. These studies demonstrate a new consensus
around the importance of identity in supporting mental health in this cohort
(Demers, 2011; Smith & True, 2014; Rumann & Hamrick, 2010). In outlining
the dimensions of adjustment difficulties facing veterans, Orazem and his
colleagues (2014, p. 4) note that two-thirds of their 100-person study sample,
composed of both men and women, endorsed problems including feelings of
not belonging in the civilian world, missing the structure provided by the military lifestyle, "feeling left behind" in comparison with civilian counterparts,
having negative views of civilian life, and also having trouble finding meaning in civilian society. Historically, concerns about the identity adjustment of
veterans coming out of the Vietnam War have also been documented, with
articles written about chronic identity diffusion among those conscripted for
combat (Silverstein, 1994). Whereas veterans returning from Vietnam faced
significant social stigma and professional discrimination, those completing
their service in the early 21st century have experienced a much more positive reception. Indeed, being a former service member is often highly valued
among veterans and their family members, even if this identity often brings
with it a burdensome transition out of military life (Smith & True, 2014).

Case Composite 2: To illustrate, consider Lalo, a 33-year-old white,
Latino, Army infantry combat veteran who described being fired
from multiple jobs since his separation from the Army. He said he
missed deployment every day despite what he had faced in combat.
He saw his best friend and fellow infantryman die in battle, and also
remembered deployment as "the most meaningful time in [his] life."
He said, "I knew what we were doing every day, and yeah, it was a clus-
terfuck, but it was also really fun and exciting. Leadership was usually
bad, and I don't know what we were really doing over there, but my job
was simple—I had to look out for my guys." He mentioned feeling he

had a purpose and was invaluable as a member of his group: "That's
the bond. You have each other's back. It's different here—everyone's
in it for themselves." Lalo added, "The only time I felt like I did there
since being back was during [Hurricane] Harvey. I drove my boat over
to Houston and just went through the neighborhoods grabbing people
off their houses and bringing them to safety. I've been thinking maybe
I could do something like that, that would make a difference, but you
only get hurricanes every so often. That's not a job."

Lalo expressed feelings of disillusionment with the civilian world
and worried that he might never find secure footing again: "It's like I
have to figure out who I am all over again." He identified ways in which
he felt his experiences didn't match his age: "At the restaurant, I work
with so many 22-year-olds, and they just don't get me!" He also lamented
that in managing his diabetes and preparing for a knee replacement,
he felt much older than his years. Lalo was also in the early stages of
recovery from years of heavy drinking and was intensely experiencing
many of the emotions, both positive and negative, that the alcohol had
been numbing since his discharge. In therapy, he struggled to identify
goals or things he desired for his future, specifically around work and
family. As treatment progressed and he began to process childhood
and combat-related trauma, gradually his depression diminished and
his self-confidence improved, yet his struggles with identity persisted
as he considered how to arrive at a path that would provide him the
meaning he longed for from his years in service.

Arnett (2000) himself acknowledges how the work of Erik Erikson contributes to the theory underlying emerging adulthood. Erikson observed that
adolescence can be prolonged, especially in industrial societies, during
which young people are given a psychological moratorium when they can
experiment with their identities and roles in society (Arnett, 2000; Erick-
son, 1968). If we are to consider emerging adulthood as a hybrid of or stage
between Erikson's fifth psychosocial stage of adolescence and sixth stage of
young adulthood, it is worthwhile to consider the developmental achievements Erikson mapped onto this period. If individuals in the fifth stage are
tasked with developing a coherent sense of self (identity vs. role confusion),
when they struggle in this developmental stage they are at risk of develop-

ing problems in their intimate relationships and professional lives, and they may also face legal problems resulting from aggressive or impulsive actions (Silverstein, 1994; Erikson, 1956). Indeed, the challenges facing young men and women during military service may place unrealistic demands upon their still-forming identities and set them up for a tough transition back into the civilian world.

Another way in which the transition from military life to civilian life can prove challenging from the perspective of identity development is in the cultural shift veterans must make from the military world back into the civilian world. Schulman and his colleagues (2005, p. 580) also address this in their studies of Israeli emerging adults in describing how the "demanding, rigid, and authoritarian" milieu of the Israeli Defense Force can interfere with the natural experimentation of emerging adulthood and result in increased dependency on authoritarian structures. In writing about their research with US veterans of the wars in Iraq and Afghanistan, Smith and True (2014, p. 147) describe the mental health challenges veterans face when they are expected to adapt to "identity expectations of autonomy, self-advocacy, and being rational" in the civilian world after having been acclimatized to the "deindividuation, obedience, chain-of-command, and dissociation" of the military. In our own clinical work with veterans in the United States, we have witnessed these very difficulties: a sense of bewilderment with the civilian world and a longing for the structure and camaraderie the military service built into everyday life. It is no wonder that some veterans struggle to fully emerge into the roles of adulthood Arnett describes.

SPECIFIC CLINICAL CONCERNS OF VETERANS IN EMERGING ADULTHOOD

As clinicians working with young veterans, we must be sensitive not only to the myriad ways in which they may be facing challenges in forging a coherent identity in the civilian world, but also to the many other and likely related clinical concerns that may bring them to treatment. We address some of these clinical concerns here: PTSD, military sexual trauma (MST), sexual orientation discrimination, substance and alcohol use, and suicidality. We also address ways in which experiences with military discharge, marriage, parenthood, education, and professional concerns may emerge and require attention when working therapeutically with this population.

PTSD

Epidemiological studies of PTSD among returning service members from the wars in Iraq and Afghanistan suggest that as many as 20% to 30% of veterans screen positive for PTSD (Eber et al., 2013). While it is difficult for methodological reasons (Wolf et al., 2012) to determine relative rates of PTSD among veterans of the wars in Iraq and Afghanistan and those of previous conflicts, it is worth acknowledging how the use of IEDs (improvised explosive devices) and guerrilla warfare tactics may make service members more vulnerable to developing PTSD from combat-related events (Reisman, 2016). What has been noted consistently is the increased number of combat tours service members have been subject to during the conflicts in Iraq and Afghanistan, with young soldiers often signing up for three or more tours overseas, thereby greatly increasing the chances of exposure to traumatic events that could later result in a diagnosis of PTSD (Institute of Medicine, 2010). Additionally, battlefield medicine has become more sophisticated and, as a result, more casualties of war survive grievous physical injuries and return to civilian life after medical discharge, only to discover the path to recovery is not limited to physical functioning alone (Bollinger et al., 2015).

It goes without saying that due to its high prevalence, PTSD should be screened for among younger veterans who could identify with aspects of emerging adulthood. Clinical care for these young men and women is enhanced when their providers are also sensitive to the many ways in which young veterans carry this specific diagnosis. Some veterans have clearly benefited from awareness campaigns and efforts to destigmatize seeking treatment. Others may even wear their diagnosis as a badge of honor, representing the psychological toll of their service to their country. Yet others, through no fault of their own, may live for many years unaware of how trauma has impacted them and might resist receiving a diagnosis of PTSD due to the stigma they perceive. Ultimately, each of these pathways carries the risk of harm: for the former, the veteran who is proud of his psychological scars, it can be hard to choose to embark on a difficult journey through treatment that is expressly designed to help veterans move beyond a diagnosis with which they have become strongly identified. For the latter, the veteran who will not seek treatment for fear of stigma, the avoidance process often engenders years of ineffective or destructive attempts at symptom control, leading veterans into years of repetitive coping with no real sense of growth or meaning. Exploring what a diagnosis of PTSD means to each individual can be a valuable therapeutic intervention, yielding countless different responses. It can also provide helpful information as to each veteran's readiness to begin treatment for PTSD.

When veterans are ready to engage in trauma-focused therapy, VA practitioners often recommend so-called gold-standard approaches such as cognitive processing therapy (Resick et al., 2017) and prolonged exposure (Foa et al., 2019). Such therapies have the potential to help patients heal from their traumas and learn new ways of coping emotionally, cognitively, and behaviorally; however, there is evidence suggesting that the therapeutic effects of short-term cognitive-behavioral therapies (e.g., for depression, anxiety) diminish over long periods of time (Shedler, 2010). There is limited evidence about longer-lasting positive effects (e.g., beyond one year) of manualized treatments for PTSD based on randomized controlled trials, so it is difficult to judge the effectiveness of such approaches longitudinally. Along these lines, we have found that as stand-alone treatments, the manualized treatments for PTSD are often insufficient in promoting rapid recovery in patients facing chronic psychiatric concerns (e.g., chronic or complex PTSD). We have found that these treatments are most effective when provided in the context of a longer-term therapeutic relationship that also allows room for veterans to receive supportive psychotherapy in which they can explore and process current stressors as well as the traumas of the past, and in which they can learn how to integrate new skills for coping with PTSD into their lives more broadly. In sum, we have noticed treatments benefit veterans more when tailored specifically to their experiences, drawing upon the gold-standard techniques noted above while allowing room for flexibility (e.g., via common factors such as trust building or rapport building within the therapeutic relationship, as emphasized by Wampold et al., 1997).

Military Sexual Trauma and Sexual Orientation Discrimination

Military Sexual Trauma encompasses sexual harassment to sexual assault and has increasingly come into focus as a long-standing significant problem within military culture. It is well established that, due to a culture involving heavy weekend drinking and leadership structures that have historically turned a blind eye to predatory behavior (Myers, 2020), young service members of all genders experience sexual assault and harassment at higher rates than their civilian counterparts, with 25–33% of women reporting a history of MST and 1.1% of male service members reporting (Turchick & Wilson, 2010; Gurung et al., 2018). These numbers, however, should be taken with a grain of salt because the rate of reporting for both men and women is likely suppressed due to stigma associated with coming forward about sexual assault and harassment, not to mention the risk of retaliation of perpetrators (Department of Defense, 2016). As for PTSD, the Veterans Health Administration has been making new efforts to screen for MST and attend to its many repercussions, both psychologically and physically.

When working in a clinical setting specifically designed to serve veterans, such as the VA, it is also critical to be sensitive to ways in which the act of accessing treatment could be triggering for victims of MST due to exposure to an environment aligned with military service. Treatment options should vary, as some may prefer individual over group settings, and some might prefer seeking treatment outside VA or veteran-focused organizations entirely. It is also worth highlighting studies suggesting that veterans identifying as LGBTQ face an increased risk of MST in comparison with non-LGBTQ service members (Gurung et al., 2018), indicating that clinicians should be especially sensitive to the experiences of LGBTQ-identified veterans around any experiences of harassment and assault during their military service.

Substance and Alcohol Use

Arnett (2015) writes specifically about the increased use of alcohol and experimentation with drugs during emerging adulthood in his piece "Wrong Turns and Dead Ends." He describes how substance use and abuse, like other risk-taking behaviors, peaks in the late teens and early 20s and consistently declines by the late 20s. In part this is attributed, he writes, to the stress and emotional instability so many emerging adults experience and may seek to self-medicate. In part he attributes it to the natural sensation seeking of this age and to social norms. For many, risky use of drugs and alcohol, characterized by binge drinking and use of illicit substances, may resolve over time and never emerge again. Yet for others, developing consistent and risky use of alcohol and other substances early on may establish a pattern that becomes persistent for many years to come, well beyond late adolescence and into adulthood (Moffitt, 2007).

Veterans completing their service with the US military at a young age, therefore, may be doubly at risk for developing problems with drug and alcohol use, due to the natural, developmental risk factors related to their young age, along with the challenges that accompany reintegration to civilian society. Indeed, service members leaving the military are more likely than their peers who remain to use substances and to engage in problematic drinking behaviors (Hoopsick et al., 2017). Due to the zero-tolerance policy currently in place regarding the use of controlled substances in the US armed forces, there are significant incentives for active-duty members not to use. But when service members finish their military service, these disincentives disappear, and risky use of drugs and alcohol may intensify or emerge for the first time. According to a 2011 study, approximately 11% of veterans presenting to establish care with the Veterans Health Administration met criteria for a substance use disorder (Seal et al., 2011). Young males carry additional risks for meeting criteria for a substance use disorder, and veterans ages 18–25 demonstrate higher rates of substance abuse than their civilian counterparts (Teeters et al., 2017). What's more, substance use disorders among veterans of all ages continue to rise, despite efforts by the VA and others to reduce their prevalence (Teeters et al., 2017). Of course, experiences unique to former service members such as deployment, combat exposure, increased risk of sexual harassment and sexual assault, and the demands of reintegrating into civilian life may all make veterans more likely to turn to alcohol and drugs as an outlet or escape.

When working therapeutically with young veterans presenting for concerns related to risky use of drugs and alcohol, we have found in many cases that normalizing the use of drugs and alcohol within the cohort is helpful to reduce the shame and stigma associated with accessing support. In addition, encouraging young veterans to be both self-compassionate and curious about the factors motivating their use can further soften shame around understanding their behaviors. We have also found basic psychoeducation around the long-term physical and psychological effects of alcohol and drugs to be useful as a way of empowering veterans to make more informed choices about their use. Finally, using harm reduction methods to address problematic use of substance and alcohol use seems to have a broader appeal to younger veterans, though some may inevitably find that an abstinence-based approach to treatment is what they need and eventually decide to pursue.

Risk for Suicide

It is well known that veterans complete suicide at a rate far greater than the general population. As of 2018, military veterans were 50% more likely to die by suicide than the broader population, and it was estimated that an average of 17.6 veterans completed suicide each day (US Department of Veterans Affairs, 2020). While suicide has been on the rise across the United States in general since 1999, veterans may face a significantly greater risk of suicide due to many factors including greater access to lethal means such as firearms, familiarity with others who have completed suicide, and higher rates of psychiatric disorder and comorbid substance use among some age groups. It is worth noting that, according to the Department of Veterans Affairs, the age group demonstrating the most dramatic increase in suicides since 2012 has been veterans ages 18–34, with a rate of 45 suicides per 100,000 as of 2017 (US Department of Veterans Affairs, 2019). Preventing suicide continues to be challenging, though new research has increased our knowledge about extant risk factors that can be used in the formulation of better risk detection algorithms; for example, one study found that physical health problems among veterans may elevate suicide risk (Wood et al., 2020).

Clinically, attending to the risk for suicide among young veterans remains of the utmost importance. Because veterans engaging in mental health care within the VA and other veteran-oriented agencies are assessed for suicide risk so frequently, they may find ways of dismissing such questions by downplaying suicidal ideation.* Therefore, we have found that it is important to attend to suicide risk thoughtfully, patiently, and in a way that welcomes reactions to the assessment itself, and that clarifies mandated risk management procedures in a way that supports veterans in feeling free to share openly. Due to the higher rates of suicide among younger veterans and regular use of social

---

* There is robust evidence about the limitations of current suicide prediction and assessment methods (Chan et al., 2018; Large et al., 2016). Researchers express concern that the ever-broadening use of suicide risk assessment may paradoxically limit the time available to address the clinical concerns causing patients' suicidal thoughts in the first place (Chan et al., 2018).

media, young veterans in particular often have direct knowledge or experience of fellow service members who have taken their own lives. Anniversaries of such suicides may be especially trying. As with any good risk assessment, supporting veterans by identifying protective factors against suicide is also a valuable strengths-based intervention to engage.

Discharge Status and Experiences

Another important component of supporting young veterans experiencing aspects of emerging adulthood is to explore the specific circumstances of their discharge. We have yet to meet a veteran seeking treatment who did not experience some degree of internal conflict around their departure from service. Some elected discharge after completing a standard contract, but may still have misgivings, wondering if remaining in service would have been preferable. Others may have been discharged for disciplinary reasons and may experience self-reproach or resentment toward their higher-ups for the circumstances that led to the early termination of a military career they had once wanted. Other veterans experience discharge for medical reasons beyond their control and may need to grieve the careers they enjoyed and wanted to continue. These are just a few examples, but each one carries with it material that may be ripe for therapeutic exploration, especially as young veterans negotiate the transition back to civilian life.

Veterans and Marriage

Men and women in military service tend to marry at a younger age than their civilian counterparts (Clever & Segal, 2013). One study conducted among active-duty Army personnel found the average age of marriage to be 22, in comparison to 27.4 among civilian women and 29.5 among civilian men (Lundquist & Xu, 2014). In part, this is attributed to family-friendly policies that benefit service members who are married and have children, as well as to the more traditional values often embraced by service members. Although military couples are more likely than civilian couples to remain together, once they leave the service they are three times as likely to become divorced as those who have never served in the military (Clever & Segal, 2013). Indeed, finishing military service and transitioning to civilian life can place significant strain on marriages and families. This highlights the importance of assessing young veterans for marital distress and exploring any relationship dynamics that may have emerged during reintegration.

Veterans and Parenting

Relative to civilians, men serving in the military tend to have their first child at the same age (at a mean of 25.0 and 25.1 years, respectively), whereas women in service tend to become mothers an average of 1.5 years earlier than women who have never served (at a mean age of 23.6 and 25.1 years, respectively; Kelty et al., 2010). For those veteran parents who finish their military service while still in their 20s, this may mean that they identify themselves in more established adult roles in some ways, but not in others. Just as with marital stressors, it is important to attend to the role parenthood plays in a veteran's overall identity. We have found that the responsibilities of parenting can provide a deep well of strength and a clear value system and focus on caring for children that motivates veterans to address their psychological and physical needs. In other cases, the stresses of parenting, especially when relations with a veteran's coparent are not amicable, can contribute to the destabilization of the reintegration period. Those who were geographically separated from their children due to deployments overseas may need to explore and process the impacts of their service on the family system and consider how they want to be as parents in civilian life. Former service members may not be aware of their ability to choose their style of parenting and may require guidance to understand where their default style comes from. Some may find themselves defaulting into an overly authoritarian style, for instance, treating their children as "little soldiers," as one veteran's wife described her husband's method of parenting, without considering alternatives.

Veterans, Education, and Work

Educational benefits such as access to the GI Bill, which provides money for tuition, books, and a living allowance during higher education, are one of the most well-known benefits of military service. Yet even with this financial support and incentive system in place, veterans tend to be less educated than their same-age civilian peers (Rothwell, 2016). Furthermore, most veterans will pursue employment in the civilian world at the conclusion of their service (Kelty et al., 2010). While many veterans make the transition to civilian employment successfully, others may struggle to find a foothold in the work-place as they face the psychological challenges of reintegration and coping with any lasting psychological or physical disabilities. Those younger veterans seeking treatment may feel as if military service did not live up to its prom-ises in terms of the value advertised in helping to secure a civilian job. Those veterans with more severe histories of PTSD may find themselves unable to secure work in law enforcement and other settings. Those dealing with active substance and alcohol use may find themselves at additional disadvantage in the workplace. Because problems at work are often a catalyst for seeking treat-ment among veterans, it is critical to attend to the professional sphere of their lives, to explore what their desires and goals may be, and to support them in accessing resources to help them further their education and careers.

CONCLUSION

In general, treatment with veterans experiencing any aspect of emerging adulthood should focus on supporting them integrating their life experiences prior to and during their military experiences with their next life chapter in the civilian world. Helping veterans in identifying and living by their values, to mourn losses and process traumas associated with their service, to build upon their strengths, and to develop healthy coping skills for navigating the inevitable challenges of readjustment are all central to good clinical work with this group. This work takes time and steady commitment and can be very rewarding.

Finally, given the notable dearth of research on experiences of emerging adulthood among young military veterans in the United States, we encour-age more research in this arena. There would be value in understanding to what extent veterans who have recently completed their service identify with the hallmark aspects of emerging adulthood, and to understand how their military service factors into their emerging adult identities. Furthermore, it would be equally compelling to do a similar study with active-duty service members to understand to what extent they identify with emerging adult-hood or not. Given the pronounced stress placed on identity formation vet-erans experience in transitioning out of military service, any research that provides a deeper understanding of identity in its developmental context is worthwhile—especially for such a unique, resilient, and multiply-stressed group of men and women.

Annelisa Pedersen, PhD, studied clinical psychology at the City University of New York andcompleted her pre-doctoral internship at Bellevue Hospital. She has previously worked with the Veteran community in San Francisco and the Rio Grande Valley of Texas, and her clinical andresearch interests have centered around treating trauma and addiction. She providespsychotherapy and clinical supervision in her private practice in Austin, Texas and is a member of Austin Psychoanalytic.

Dr. Peter Lemons completed his graduate training at Binghamton University after finishing his pre-doctoral internship at the New Jersey VA Medical Center. He works primarily with the Veteran population, and has focused primarily on treating trauma sequelae, anxiety, and mood disorders. Dr. Lemons currently practices psychotherapy in Austin, Texas, where he helps to raise his two daughters.

REFERENCES

Arnett, J. J. (2000). Emerging adulthood: A theory of development from the late teens through the twenties. *American Psychologist, 55*(5), 469–480.

Arnett, J. J. (2015). *Emerging adulthood: The winding road from the late teens through the twenties* (2nd ed.). Oxford University Press.

Bollinger, M. J., Schmidt, S., Pugh, J. A., Parsons, H. M., Copeland, L. A., & Pugh, M. J. (2015). Erosion of the health soldier effect in veterans of US military service in Iraq and Afghanistan. *Population Health Metrics, 13*(1), 8.

Chan, M. K. Y., Bhatti, H., Meader, N., Stockton, S., Evans, J., O'Connor, R. C., Kapur, N., & Kendall, T. (2018). Predicting suicide following self-harm: Systematic review of risk factors and risk scales. *British Journal of Psychiatry, 209*(4), 277–283. doi:10.1192/bjp.bp.115.170050

Clever, M., & Segal, D. R. (2013). The demographics of military children and families. *Future of Children, 23*(2), 13–39.

Council on Foreign Relations. (2020, July 13). *Demographics of the US military.* https://www.cfr.org/backgrounder/demographics-us-military

Demers, A. (2011). When veterans return: The role of community in reintegration. *Journal of Loss and Trauma, 16*, 160–179.

Department of Defense. (2016). *Department of Defense annual report on sexual assault in the military fiscal year 2016.* Government Printing Office.

Eber, S., Barth, S., Kang, H., Mahan, C., Dursa, E., & Schneiderman, A. (2013). The National Health Study for a New Generation of United States Veterans: Methods for a large-scale study on the health of recent veterans. *Military Medicine, 178*, 966–969.

Erikson, E. (1956). The problem of ego identity. *Journal of the American Psychoanalytic Association, 4,* 58–121.

Erikson, E. (1968). *Identity: Youth and crisis.* Norton.

Foa, E., Hembree, E. A., Rothbaum, R. O., & Rauch, S. A. M. (2019). *Prolonged exposure for PTSD: Emotional processing of traumatic experiences* (2nd ed.). Oxford University Press.

Gurung, S., Ventuneac, A., Rendina, H. J., Savarese, E., Grov, C., & Parsons, J. T. (2018). Prevalence of military sexual trauma and sexual orientation discrimination among lesbian, gay, bisexual, and transgender military personnel: A descriptive study. *Sexuality Research and Social Policy, 15*(1), 74–82.

Hoopsick, R. A., Fillo, J., Vest, B. M., Homish, D. L., & Homish, G. G. (2017). Substance use and dependence among current reserve and former military members: Cross-sectional findings from the National Survey on Drug Use and Health, 2010–2014. *Journal of Addictive Diseases, 36*(4), 243–251.

Institute of Medicine. (2010). *Returning home from Iraq and Afghanistan: Preliminary assessment of readjustment needs of veterans, service members, and their families.* National Academies Press.

Kelty, R., Kleykamp, M., & Segal, D. R. (2010). The military and the transition to adulthood. *Future of Children, 20*(1), 181–207.

Large, M., Kaneson, M., Myles, N., Myles, H., Gunaratne, P., & Ryan, C. (2016). Meta-analysis of longitudinal cohort studies of suicide risk assessment among psychiatric patients: Heterogeneity in results and lack of improvement over time. *PLoS ONE, 11*(6), e0156322. doi:10.1371/journal.pone.0156322

Lundquist, J., & Xu, Z. (2014). Reinstitutionalizing families: Life course policy and marriage in the military. *Journal of Marriage and Family, 76*(5), 1063–1081.

Meffert, B. N., Morabito, D. M., Sawicki, D. A., Hausman, C., Southwick, S. M., Pietrzak, R. H., & Heinz, A. J. (2019). US veterans who do and do not utilize Veterans Affairs health care services: Demographic, military, medical, and psychosocial characteristics. *Primary Care Companion for CNS Cisorders, 21*(1), 18m02350. https://doi.org/10.4088/PCC.18m02350

Moffitt, T. E. (2007). A review of research on the taxonomy of life-course persistent versus adolescence-limited antisocial behavior. In D. J. Flanner, A. T. Vazsonyi, & I. D. Waldman (Eds.), *The Cambridge handbook of violent behavior and aggression* (pp. 49–74). Cambridge University Press.

Myers, M. (2020, April 30). A culture that fosters sexual assaults and sexual harassment persists despite prevention efforts, a new Pentagon study shows. *Military Times.* https://www.militarytimes.com/news/your-military/2020/04/30/a-culture-that-fosters-sexual-assaults-and-sexual-harassment-persists-despite-prevention-efforts-a-new-pentagon-study-shows/

Orazem, R. J., Frazier, P. A., Schnurr, P. P., Oleson, H. E., Carlson, K. F., Litz, B. T., & Sayer, N. A. (2017). Identity adjustment among Afghanistan and Iraq War veterans with reintegration difficulty. *Psychological Trauma: Theory, Research, Practice, and Policy, 9*(S1), 4–11.

Reisman, M. (2016). PTSD treatment for veterans: What's working, what's new, and what's next. *Pharmacy and Therapeutics, 41*(10), 623–627, 632–634.

Resick, P. A., Monson, C. M., & Chard, K. M. (2017). *Cognitive processing therapy for PTSD: A comprehensive manual.* Guilford.

Rothwell, J. (2016, July 28). What's going on with young veterans in the labor mar-

ket? Brookings. https://www.brookings.edu/opinions/whats-going-on-with-young
-veterans-in-the-labor-market/

Rumann, C. B., & Hamrick, F. A. (2010). Student veterans in transition: Re-enrolling
after war zone deployments. *Journal of Higher Education, 81,* 431–458.

Scharf, M., & Mayseless, O. (2004). Adolescents' attachment representations and developmental tasks in emerging adulthood. *Developmental Psychology, 40*(3), 430–444.

Schulman, S., Feldman, B., Blatt, S. J., Cohen, O., & Mahler, A. (2005). Emerging adulthood: Age-related tasks and underlying self processes. *Journal of Adolescent Research,
20*(5), 577–603.

Seal, K. H., Cohen, G., Waldrop, A., Cohen, B. E., Maguen, S., & Ren, L. (2011). Substance use disorders in Iraq and Afghanistan veterans in VA healthcare, 2001–2010:
Implications for screening, diagnosis and treatment. *Drug and Alcohol Dependence,
116*(1–3), 93–101.

Shedler, J. (2010). The efficacy of psychodynamic psychotherapy. *American Psychologist,
65*(2), 98–109.

Silverstein, R. (1994). Chronic identity diffusion in traumatized combat veterans. *Social
Behavior and Personality, 22*(1), 69–80.

Smith, R. T., & True, G. (2014). Warring identities: Identity conflict and the mental distress of American veterans of the wars in Iraq and Afghanistan. *Society and Mental
Health, 4*(2), 147–161.

Teeters, J. B., Lancaster, C. L., Brown, D. G., & Back, S. E. (2017). Substance use disorders in military veterans: Prevalence and treatment challenges. *Substance Abuse and
Rehabilitation, 8,* 69–77.

Turchik, J. A., & Wilson, S. M. (2010). Sexual assault in the U.S. military: A review of
the literature and recommendations for the future. *Aggressive and Violent Behavior,
15*(4), 267–277.

U.S. Department of Veterans Affairs. (2019). *2019 national veteran suicide prevention annual
report.* https://www.mentalhealth.va.gov/docs/data-sheets/2019/2019_National
_Veteran_Suicide_Prevention_Annual_Report_508.pdf

U.S. Department of Veterans Affairs. (2020). *2020 national veteran suicide prevention annual
report.* https://www.mentalhealth.va.gov/docs/data-sheets/2020/2020-National-Veteran
-Suicide-Prevention-Annual-Report11-2020-508.pdf

Wampold, B. E., Mondin, G. W., Moody, M., Stich, F., Benson, K., & Ahn, H.-n. (1997).
A meta-analysis of outcome studies comparing bona fide psychotherapies: Empiri-
cially, "all must have prizes." *Psychological Bulletin, 122*(3), 203–215. https://doi
.org/10.1037/0033-2909.122.3.203

Wolf, D. A., Wing, C., & Lopoo, L. M. (2012). Methodological problems in determining
the consequences of military service. In J. M. Wilmoth & A. S. London (Eds.), *Life-
course perspectives on military service* (pp. 254–274). Routledge.

Wood, D. S., Wood, B. M., Watson, A., Sheffield, D., & Hauter, H. (2020). Veteran suicide
risk factors: A national sample of nonveteran and veteran men who died by suicide.
Health and Social Work, 45(1), 23–30.

CHAPTER 9

Gender Identity Development

Case Presentations of Clinical Work With Transgender Emerging Adults

ELIZABETH F. BAUMANN AND ZOË BERKO

G ender, like many identities, is a complex and shifting array of experiences—both internal and external—that exists both inside and outside of the psyche. Winnicott (1971) and other analysts tell us that gender starts before birth (as the parents learn and fantasize about the child), into infancy as bodily experience of the world begins and into a social sphere as development continues.

The last two decades have seen a proliferation of studies investigating contemporary gender-diverse, gender-expansive, and nonbinary identities (Meadow, 2011). This research has been paralleled by evolving theories of gender identity development and related standards of clinical care and what appears to be an ever-expanding array of signifiers to capture the complexity and plasticity of these identities (Ehrensaft, 2017). These shifts occur in the context of a recent increase of gender-diverse, gender-expansive, nonbinary adolescents, and young adults presenting for services as well as self-identifying as such in the general population (Ehrensaft, 2017). Gender identity development is thus very much a rapidly evolving landscape, and emerging adulthood offers a relatively unexplored context for its study, given that most research has been done on childhood and adolescence. There has been less writing on clinical work with transgender emerging adults and even less on the psychotherapeutic process with this population.

Arnett (2000, p. 469) coined the term "emerging adulthood" to refer to what he viewed as a "distinct developmental period demographically, subjectively and in terms of identity explorations" that occurs in industrialized societies from roughly ages 18 to 25. With its emphasis on identity exploration, emerging adulthood is very much rooted in Erikson's (1956/2007) psychosocial moratorium. Indeed, Arnett (2007) proposed five common (though not universal) features of emerging adulthood reflecting this emphasis: "it is the age of identity explorations, the age of instability, the self-focused age, the age of feeling in-between and the age of possibilities" (p. 69). These features and the related trying out of different roles and experiences that are characteristic of this developmental period underpin Arnett's (2007) conceptualization of emerging adulthood as "perhaps the most heterogenous period of the life course" (p. 69).

Emerging adulthood clearly offers an important and understudied context for the study of gender identity development and transgender identity development specifically. Indeed, Kuper et al. (2018) highlight that the majority of prior studies of gender identity development have been conducted with adult samples, despite findings from the large-scale 2015 US Transgender Survey ($N = 27,715$) showing that critical transitions take place during emerging adulthood. These transitions include alteration of names and pronouns, expressing one's identity through appearance, and seeking gender-affirmative medical care (James et al., 2016). The current chapter adds to the limited literature in this area through the presentation of two cases from the first author's clinical work with transgender emerging adults.

We would like to set the stage for the presentation of these cases with a brief overview of contemporary theory on gender identity. Historically, in most Western cultures, gender identity was a permanent binary assignment (male or female) made at birth on the basis of the external appearance of the infant's genitals. In contrast, contemporary theory conceptualizes gender identity as a "fluid spectrum" and importantly, "not a pathology but a normal human variation" (Malpas, 2011, p. 456). Indeed, recognizing the diversity of experiences, this treatment model does not view all gender-diverse, gender-expansive, and nonbinary individuals as needing clinical treatment. Indeed, interventions may be more appropriately focused on fostering a more gender-affirming environment around the adolescent or emerging adult. Gender identity development is conceptualized as a transactional and dynamic process: "Each child is presented with the task of weaving together the threads of nature, nurture and culture to establish

[a] unique authentic gender self" that is referred to as the "gender web" (Ehrensaft, 2017, p. 59).

The fourth dimension of this matrix is the temporal aspect of gender identity development (over a period of time). For clarity, it is important to highlight here that gender identity and sexuality are separate tracks, and the distinction between gender identity and gender expression is critical. As outlined above, there is an ever-expanding array of signifiers to capture the complexity and plasticity of these identities and diversity of lived experiences. This, of course, raises the question of what it means to group such diverse experiences of identity under the umbrella of a shared signifier in terms of research design and related implications for the generalizability of findings. Indeed, as one participant in Kuper et al.'s (2017) study observes, "gender is a spectrum—trans people are all different—no-one of us is alike" (p. 14).

Prior research has examined gender identity development among transgender individuals through the lens of both stage and narrative models (Bolin, 1998; Devor, 2004; Troiden, 1979). Stage models that originally outlined the identity development of lesbian, gay, and bisexual individuals were subsequently adapted to capture the experiences of transgender individuals, including social and medical transitions and emotional distress in response to the physical changes of puberty.

These stage models for transgender individuals focused primarily on the intrapersonal processes of gender identity development, namely, exploring, affirming, and integrating one's identity. The clinical cases presented below illustrate the ways in which interpersonal processes within the patient's social environment and within the therapeutic relationship alternatively hinder and support Mary and Max's intrapersonal journeys around their gendered selves.

Narrative approaches view making meaning of one's experience as critical to the process of identity development. Early narratives emphasized "being born in the wrong body" and the need to undergo gender reassignment surgery as the route to achieving a "true self" (Bolin, 1998, cited in Kuper et al., 2017). However, this narrative is now seen as overly simplistic by clinicians and trans activists alike (Kuper et al., 2017). Kuper et al.'s (2017) intersectional qualitative study examined gender identity development among transgender and gender-nonconforming emerging adults. One of the areas explored was the process of integrating one's gender identity (i.e., meaning making into one's larger sense of self). In discussing their findings, the authors highlight the occurrence of integration-related difficulties among transgender emerging adults due to barriers to social and medical transitions (e.g., lack of access to gender-affirming medical procedures or financial constraints requiring residence with one's unaccepting family of origin necessitating suppression of one's gendered self). Affirming psychotherapy and the development of a strong therapeutic relationship have been shown not only to be best practice but also necessary for psychotherapy to feel safe with this population (Baumann et al., 2020; Bettergarcia & Israel, 2018; Chang & Singh, 2016).

Contemporary literature on transgender and gender-nonconforming youth emphasizes the role that (gender-affirming) parents play in securing their children's desired gender identities. As Meadow (2011) outlines:

> Parents occupy a unique position in accounts of children's gender. They are, at moments, the ones demanding explanations of their children, yet they are also the proxy voices permitted (and often required) to make declarative statements in the medical and social environments their children inhabit. They "give gender" to their gender variable children (Ward, 2010), which is to say, they engage in affective, intellectual and bodily projects to assist their children in securing their desired gender identities. They become, in this way, the intermediaries between the entirely personal, emotional and cognitive experiences of their children and the larger surveilling glance of social institutions. (p. 730)

How does this process of accounting, which cisgender individuals (i.e., those who feel a congruence between their assigned and experienced gender) are not called upon to do, operate for emerging adults who developmentally must literally and figuratively move out of the parental home and into new relational contexts that call upon them to account for themselves? For emerging adults raised within or rejected by nonaffirming families, this developmental period may represent a first context for accounting for themselves and having their gendered selves seen by others. We see this in the case of Max, who feels affirmed in his gender identity when "sirred" but feels somehow less real when his accounts of his preferred pronouns are questioned and overtly rejected by his college classmates.

The gender-affirmative model of clinical care centers on "allowing children to speak for themselves about their self-experienced gender identity and expressions and providing support for them to evolve into authentic gender selves, no matter at what age" (Ehrensaft, 2017, p. 62). As Ehrensaft (2017) notes, the act of listening to the patient talk about gender is in itself an experience of mirroring and fundamental commitment to sitting with individuals exactly where they are. If we deny that, then we are denying their reality and subjectivity—and isn't that what psychoanalysis is about? Renik (2004) states, "To accept that clinical psychoanalysis is *intersubjective* means to recognize that the clinical analytic encounter consists of an interaction between two subjectivities—the patient's and the analyst's—and that the understanding gained through clinical analytic investigation is a product of that interaction." In these intersubjective therapeutic experiences, the first author takes the stance of first starting with an acceptance that the person who chooses to sit with a therapist and bear vulnerability has a subjectivity and sense of self that can be seen, explored, uncovered, and known from the inside out. The cases presented below illustrate the role of these interpersonal processes that facilitate formulating an account of one's gendered self and integrate this meaning into the larger sense of oneself. As Butler writes, "I begin my story of myself only in the face of a 'you' who asks me to give an account" (2005, p. 11).

CLINICAL CASE PRESENTATIONS

Before we hone in on the topic of gender identity with these two cases, we feel pulled to expand our lens outward and acknowledge that we are misled if we think that these concepts of gender identity are special topics in psychoanalytic work. Indeed, our training leads us to examine how these themes are universal, understandable, and applicable to all our work as relationally oriented psychotherapists.

What is gender but something that is hidden deep within us and expressed externally and interpersonally? Is that not the journey and core mission of psychotherapy—to go inward and find an ability to symbolize experience? Are we not all afraid that what we feel inside ourselves may not be understood, mirrored, and reflected back to us by our caretakers and then the larger world? Individuals who feel that the gender they were assigned at birth does not match their own internal gendered self come to psychotherapy with a large, sometimes bewildering, exploration. "There is something that is being judged, misunderstood or even hated by others." "Can I be seen?" "Will you see me and if so, how?" For young adults, at a time when their identity as self and in relation to other is being explored, this experience can be especially excruciating. Without pathologizing, diagnosing, or labeling, we can understand this experience as painful in its own right.

Mary

The first patient we discuss is Mary, a 19-year-old woman with whom Dr. Baumann worked in twice-weekly treatment for two years. Mary identifies as female, though she was assigned male at birth. At the beginning of our work together, she was a senior in high school who arrived in treatment due to significant depression in the context of gender dysphoria and declining grades. She had been working with the school counselor, who thought that she needed more intensive psychotherapy. When I first entered my waiting room to greet Mary, I saw a petite, mouse-like, young adult. She had shoulder-length hair that was unwashed and uncombed, and thick stubble across her face. She stood up and walked into my office, avoiding eye contact. She sat down in the middle of my couch, back upright, body stiff yet resigned at the same time. Everything about her looked and felt uncomfortable, and yet I immediately felt comfortable sitting with her—as if sitting quietly with her was the right and only place to start.

She knew that I worked with other transgender adolescents, and that her school counselor referred her for this reason to work with me. I asked her, as I do, how she identifies her gender identity. She said one word—"female"—then paused and looked at me, and slumped further into the couch. "OK," I said. And we started from there. Though she could tell me that she felt she identified as female for years, direct questions about her gender led to shrugs and downcast gazes. Words did little to symbolize the pain that Mary felt, and something as complex as gender identity was not yet accessible through language.

Quiet, compliant, and intellectually strong, she fell under the radar of her family—in other words, she wasn't seen, and thus she learned to turn away from looking at herself. It was not a surprise to me that Mary struggled to answer questions about why she knew she identified as a woman. Traditional concepts about treatment with transgender individuals prior to beginning hormone therapy would assume that a narrative about one's gender can be not only verbally expressed but coherently so. However, Mary had little access to a narrative—not about her life and especially not about her gender. "It has always been like this. I have always been a girl. It is not something I became. I was always this. I just could never say it or understand it."

Sitting with Mary meant sitting with what could not be symbolized. In this quiet with her, I found myself trying to do this for myself. Do I have a narrative, if someone were to ask me? As a cisgender person, I am privileged never to be asked this question or forced to tell someone else something so deep and preverbal about myself. Why do I feel female? Can I put my finger on it? What does that mean, other than a deep sense inside myself that I have never tried to articulate? As a cisgender woman, no one calls upon me to account for my deeply felt internal knowledge that I am female. These countertransferential musings led me to think about experiences when I had been asked to articulate why I am who I am. The countertransferential feeling I kept coming back to when sitting with Mary was one of "telling before the story can be told."

As our treatment deepened, Mary let herself be looked at, possibly even seen. As Bromberg (1993, 1996) would say, we "stood in the spaces" between her dissociated self and her known self, and we stood there together. "When things are quiet, I can notice my body," she stated. "In these moments, I think about whether I am the only one who knows I am female. If no one else knows, then is it real?" Mary's sense of herself as female without any mirroring left her on a dangerous ledge. For Mary, this mirror was just as real as it was symbolic. "I can't always shave because I can't look into the mirror, so it's hard," she told me. From a Winnicottian perspective, development of the self, and the gendered self, is made possible by accurate mirroring from others (Borden, 2009; Winnicott, 1971). What if the mirror was hidden for so long that even looking into it was too difficult? These thoughts were so intense that by the time Mary began working with me, she had collapsed into herself, hidden from the world. Slowly we began to construct a mirror.

The next months moved through, into, and out of a deep depression, trudging through college. By spring she was feeling better. She was showering and shaving more regularly. With great pride, she started to wear earrings and grow her hair to shoulder length. "I don't know how to brush it so it stays untangled," she said. For her 18th birthday and high school graduation, I bought her a present—a Mason Pearson hairbrush specifically for fine hair. Analytically trained, I thought long and hard about this gift. I had asked Mary to create her own narrative, symbolize her experience of gender—a journey that was so arduous that maybe my giving her a piece of my own gendered experience that was symbolized in an object, not words, would mean something. It felt important enough to risk. "Just because my gender identity is female, it doesn't mean I know a lot about makeup, as you can tell," I joked with her. "But I thought you could use this brush now that your hair is longer." Tears welled up in her eyes, and she immediately started brushing her hair.

That following summer, when Mary was feeling much less depressed, her team decided that she was ready to begin hormone replacement therapy. Her parents were well on board, happy that she was feeling better and knowing that starting medical treatment would only be a movement toward health for Mary. The day that she started hormone treatment was the first day I saw her smile, a real smile. It felt that her smile matched her hair, now growing longer and cared for. In many ways, Mary was starting to show her true self from the shoulders up—hair, face, and now smile. However, Mary's physiological journey, though started, was clearly going to be a long one, given her body composition, bone structure, and deep voice. Indeed, as the months continued on the hormone treatment, her body was slow to evidence any outward change. Though her skin appeared softer, and she began to develop breast tissue, other phenotypic markers did not appear. However, the hormone treatment led to a significant, marked improvement in her mood and ability to care for herself. "Why do you feel better if there is so little change on the outside?" I asked Mary one session. "Because the process has started and will take its course," she said. "It may be slow, but it has started, and that is better than before." Though getting past this initial stage of starting hormone treatment was extremely meaningful and clinically significant, it brought us into uncharted waters in Mary's relational world. But by fall, school started to become hard. By Thanksgiving, she had dropped out and was living at home again. Back home, our twice-weekly work resumed and was indeed the only time that Mary was leaving the house.

We started to examine what had happened—why she had backtracked just as she ventured into the world. This push to live in her affirmed gender meant taking this gendered part of herself out into the greater world where she could be seen. Slowly, we began exploring why this was so hard for her. "It's not that I can't go outside," she said. "It is that I can't go outside and say that I am Mary and not know how someone will react." "OK. I understand," I said. "It's good that you can say that. We will start from there."

Max

When I started working with him, Max was a 20-year-old college student at a local public college who presented for treatment due to increased depression. Assigned female at birth, Max also felt comfortable with the label transgender male. He was stocky and tall, with dyed hair, chunky glasses, and an anxious smile on his face that said so much. He was a precociously insightful young person and in many regards was a well-adjusted young adult.

From a large, very liberal, and, as he said, "queer" family, his parents, from the outset, were accepting of Max's gender identity when he started exploring it in later high school. It was not until he started at a local college that he began his coming-out process, noting that he needed a new space to make this shift, since he felt too known as a girl in his hometown.

As much as Max was extremely eager to try on how it felt to verbalize his gender identity to new peers in his college, he felt a nagging, hovering buzz of anxiety that he could not let go of or ignore. "I worry about people seeing me and thinking that I am a girl," he said in our first session. To him, this identity was secure, ego syntonic, and just felt right. In fact, from an outsider's perspective or to anyone walking past him on the college campus, he looked like someone who was at ease being very public about his transgender identity. He was quick to correct people who gendered him as female or used female pronouns. He felt proud of these daily experiences of coming out in the first semester of college. However, his knee-jerk reaction or self-protective act of correcting others started to take a toll. Every time he corrected someone, it was like he was counteracting a punch in the gut. Slowly he started to feel beaten down and depressed that people were not seeing him as he saw himself, as a young man.

A few months into our work, Max had an experience that was a punch too hard, knocking more than the wind out of him. In a class, a classmate used female pronouns to refer to him. As often happened, the teacher, who knew Max used male pronouns, did not correct the student, but rather ignored the statement and kept teaching. Max, as he was wont to do, took it upon himself to correct the peer and interrupted the class. "He. My pronoun is he," he said loudly and forcefully. The class became quiet, and someone in the back of the classroom said in an audible whisper, "Pinocchio." The class burst out into laughter. Again the teacher did nothing. Max's strong exterior began to crumble.

The peer's reference to a boy who is not "real" reverberated with Max's deepest fears of not being a real man. His worst fear was that he was not real. Brave and persevering, this incident did not stop him from correcting others when he was misgendered, but it pushed him over a precipice of self-doubt and vulnerability. He started to develop a hypervigilant stance around being misgendered and misunderstood. His voice felt false to him, his face not angular enough, his eyes too feminine. He started to struggle to be in school buildings without the intrusive thought that a look or perception by a peer or teacher would mean that he was not passing.

Max's painful experiences at school are the essence of Erving Goffman's (1963) half-century-old concept of passing. Goffman notes that for people who cannot pass in society, there is "a constant tension between their concealable differences which stigmatize them and 'out' them." This constant hypervigilance that Max would not pass as male was taking a toll on him psychologically. He stopped going to school regularly and started having panic attacks while in classes, fearing that someone was looking at him in a judgmental manner. "I just can't be in school without having these dysphoria attacks," he said. "I just can't do it."

In the months that followed, we started the process of getting Max started on hormone therapy. By the fall of his sophomore year of college, Max began taking testosterone. Hormone therapy led to the alleviation of many symptoms for Max. The commencement of hormone therapy significantly reduced his hypervigilance and concern about being misgendered. The physiological process in his body that had begun to take shape proved he was no longer Pinocchio. For Max, unlike Mary, physical changes immediately began to take place, including the deepening of his voice and the beginning of facial hair. "The process has started!" Max said excitedly, bouncing up and down on my couch. The lively, boisterous young man he was prior to the past year had room to emerge. "I can finally wear short sleeves! I have muscles now. I am getting 'sirred' " (called "sir" in public). These experiences did not just feel good to Max, they felt mirroring on the deepest level possible. How simple is it to want evidence that who you are is marked externally? If we see ourselves as strong and look in the mirror and see muscles on our body, we can feel strong. For Max, he needed this proof to feel real. Don't we all? A year past the start of hormone treatment, Max has had dips in his functioning but continues to do well. The shadows of self-doubt are diminishing. Recently, he decided to invite his boyfriend into my office to meet me. Kissing Max's hand gently, he said, "You're so cute. You're amazing. Please never change." Max said, "I want to believe you, but I can't. I can't believe you would feel that way about me." His boyfriend responded simply and warmly, "You're perfect as you are. You're not too much for me." And with that, Max's journey to being seen, to being real, has begun.

CONCLUDING THOUGHTS

"It was all so insignificant in the large scale of things," Max recently said when we were looking back, remarking on his progress post–hormone treatment, recalling the daily pain he felt when misgendered. We were in a discussion about the current political climate and current dangers for transgender individuals. "I mean, there are so many other larger things in the world that are harder than what I went through." Though he might be quick to downplay his experience, I gently, and with kind humor, disagreed. "You can think that, but I won't forget what you went through. It was real and it was hard." In her 2004 work, Judith Butler wisely asks us to consider: "What counts as a person? What counts as a coherent gender? What qualifies as a citizen? Whose world is legitimized as real?" For what else is primary in our development of self than being recognized by others and recognizing our own selves? For all us, just like for Max and Mary, who are we if we are not seen?

Elizabeth Freidin Baumann, PhD, is a part-time Instructor of Psychology in Psychiatry at Harvard Medical School/Cambridge Health Alliance where she teaches and supervises psychologists, psychiatrists, and social workers in clinical evaluation and practice. She is on the APA committee for Sexual Orientation and Gender Diversity (2019–2021). Dr. Baumann completed her post-doctoral training at McLean Hospital/Harvard Medical School. She has published on working clinically with transgender, gender variant and sexual minority children, adolescents, and families and she has a private practice in Cambridge, MA.

Zoë Berko, PhD, is a forensic evaluator with the Dutchess County NY Department of Behavioral & Community Health. She teaches in the MA Program in Forensic Mental Health Counseling at the John Jay College of Criminal Justice CUNY and is an adjunct clinical supervisor in the PhD program in Clinical Psychology at City College, CUNY. Her clinical and research interests center on the assessment and treatment of juvenile offenders, forensic psychotherapy, and Mentalization-Based Treatment (MBT).

REFERENCES

Arnett, J. J. (2000). Emerging adulthood: A theory of development from the late teens through the twenties. *American Psychologist, 55*(5), 469–480.

Arnett, J. J. (2007). Emerging adulthood: What is it, and what is it good for? *Child Development Perspectives, 1*(2), 68–73.

Baumann, E. F., Ryu, D., & Harney, P. (2020). Listening to identity: Transference, countertransference, and therapist disclosure in psychotherapy with sexual and gender minority clients. *Practice Innovations, 5*(3), 246.

Bettergarcia, J. N., & Israel, T. (2018). Therapist reactions to transgender identity exploration: Effects on the therapeutic relationship in an analogue study. *Psychology of Sexual Orientation and Gender Diversity, 5*(4), 423.

Bolin, A. (1998). Transcending and transgendering. *Current Concepts in Transgender Identity, 11*, 63–92.

Borden, William. 2009. *Contemporary Psychodynamic Theory and Practice.* Chicago: Lyceum Books, Inc.

Bromberg, P. M. (1993). Shadow and substance: A relational perspective on clinical process. *Psychoanalytic Psychology, 10*(2), 147.

Bromberg, P. M. (1996). Standing in the spaces: The multiplicity of self and the psychoanalytic relationship. *Contemporary Psychoanalysis, 32*(4), 509–535.

Butler, J. (2004). *Undoing gender.* Psychology Press.

Butler, J. (2005). Gender trouble: Feminism and the subversion of identity. *Political Theory, 4*, 4–24.

Chang, S. C., & Singh, A. A. (2016). Affirming psychological practice with transgender and gender nonconforming people of color. *Psychology of Sexual Orientation and Gender Diversity, 3*, 140–147.

Devor, A. H. (2004). Witnessing and mirroring: A fourteen stage model of transsexual identity formation. *Journal of Gay and Lesbian Psychotherapy, 8*(1–2), 41–67.

Ehrensaft, D. (2009). One pill makes you boy, one pill makes you girl. *International Journal of Applied Psychoanalytic Studies, 6*(1), 12–24.

Ehrensaft, D. (2017). Gender nonconforming youth: Current perspectives. *Adolescent Health, Medicine and Therapeutics, 8*, 57–67.

Erikson, E. (2007). The problem of ego identity. In D. Browning (Ed.), *Adolescent identities: A collection of readings* (pp. 225-242). Relational Perspectives Book Series. Analytic Press. (Original work published 1956)

Goffman, E. (1963). Embarrassment and social organization. *American Journal of Sociology, 62*(3), 264–271.

James, S. E., Herman, J. L., Rankin, S., Keisling, M., Mottet, L., & Ana, M. (2016). *The report of the 2015 US Transgender Survey.* Center for Transgender Equality.

Kuper, L. E., Wright, L., & Mustanski, B. (2018). Gender identity development among transgender and gender nonconforming emerging adults: An intersectional approach. *International Journal of Transgenderism, 19*(4), 436–455.

Lev, A. I. (2004). *Transgender emergence: Therapeutic guidelines for working with gender-variant people and their families.* Haworth Clinical Practice Press.

Malpas, J. (2011). Between pink and blue: A multi-dimensional family approach to gender nonconforming children and their families. *Family Process, 50*(4), 453–470.

Meadow, T. (2011). "Deep down where the music plays": How parents account for childhood gender variance. *Sexualities, 14*(6), 725–747.

Renik, O. (2004). Intersubjectivity in psychoanalysis. *International Journal of Psychoanalysis, 85*, 1053–1064.

Steiner, B. (1990). Intake assessment of gender-dysphoric patients. In R. Blanchard & B. Steiner (Eds.), *Clinical management of gender identity disorders in children and adults* (pp. 95–117). American Psychiatric Association.

Troiden, R. R. (1979). Becoming homosexual: A model of gay identity acquisition. *Psychiatry, 42*(4), 362–373.

Winnicott, D. W. (1979). *Playing and reality.* Psychology Press.

WPATH. (2011). *Standards of care of the health of transsexual, transgender, and gender nonconforming people* (7th version). World Professional Association for Transgender Health. https://www.wpath.org/publications/soc

CHAPTER 10

Like Me

Constructing Identity in the Age of Social Media

LEORA TRUB AND VENDELA PARKER

Who am I?
Come to my page and see
If you like what you see
Do you like me?
Do you see me?
Or something just like me?
Just like me!
Please!
Please?

Young adulthood has long been conceptualized as a critical period for identity development. Many spend this time exploring and trying on different identities as they move toward committing to a more stable and enduring sense of self (Erikson, 1968; Marcia, 1966). In the internet's earlier days, theorists focused on the likelihood that people would explore divergent identities using the anonymity of the internet as a protective shield for the (offline) self. In 2004, Sherry Turkle noted:

> [They] offer us many different contexts for presenting ourselves online. Those possibilities are particularly important for adolescents because they offer what Erik Erikson described as a moratorium, a time out or safe space for the personal experimentation that is so crucial for adolescent development. Our dangerous world—with crime, terrorism,

drugs, and AIDS—offers little in the way of safe spaces. Online worlds
can provide valuable spaces for identity play.

At that time, many people were gravitating towards online platforms that
offered a way to create personas from behind a pseudonym or avatar (e.g., blogging, chat rooms) that were often quite separate and distinct from their offline
selves (Amichai-Hamburger, Wainapel, & Fox, 2002; Gumbrecht, 2005; Hodkinson, 2007; Trub et al., 2014; Trub, 2016). But in the 18 years since Turkle's
essay, the scope of social media has moved steadily in the direction of developing an online presence that is consistent with people's offline identities (Davis,
2011). People now expect, and are expected, to maintain a digital presence that
is visible and searchable by anyone—from close friends and family to potential
employers, to romantic interests, to strangers. And with that, any real distinction between online and offline selves has been all but eradicated (Palfrey &
Gasser, 2008; Clough, 2018, 2019). This turned Turkle's observations on their
head—not only does the internet not provide a respite from general pressures
around cultivating identity, but the ubiquitous, public, and indelible nature of
social media makes it more challenging to find and prioritize private and low-
stakes spaces for exploring identity. This has produced some profound changes
to the already complicated processes of self-discovery and identity development.

This chapter explores these present-day challenges through the story of
a 21-year-old, mixed-race (white/Latinx) woman, Gabriella, who grew up in
a rural town in the Midwest and then moved across the country to attend a
university. While there is no typical social media user, Gabriella represents
many norms of her generation. Beginning at age 11, she has created profiles
on seven different social media sites. The number of people who follow her
social media is neither small nor large compared to others; her comments and
likes have always been commensurate in number with those of her peers. She
has a rich in-person life alongside her online interactions. And while she has
almost always preferred face-to-face interactions to those on social media,
she believes that maintaining an online presence is a necessity, not a choice,
given the culture and time in which she was raised. This sense of necessity
provides the backdrop for her young adult life, even as her social media use
has changed and lessened over time.

We begin by exploring the genesis of Gabriella's social media use and
identity in preadolescence and follow her story through the present. In the
final section, we discuss her use of less commonly used social media sites to

shed light on the use of certain social media to explore and inhabit marginalized parts of identity. All three sections are split into two parts: a narrative
account of Gabriella's experiences, followed by an analysis aimed at illuminat-
ing dynamics at play for young adults today as they navigate identity development amid social media culture.

SECTION I: THE EARLY YEARS

Developing a Digital Identity/From the Self to the Other

Gabriella was born in 2000. She grew up playing around on her father's
PalmPilot. He showed her how to download apps, and when she was 11, she
was the first among her friends to download Instagram and Twitter. With her
father's input, she identified some people to follow, including pop stars like
Ariana Grande and Justin Bieber. But her primary focus was on her own posts.
She snapped and posted lots of photos of anything she found interesting—
an outfit she had laid out for the first day of school, a gymnastics pose, her
family's dog, pictures with friends, and, of course, selfies. As was common,
she reposted and retweeted posts of others that she liked. She took part in
popular Instagram trends, like posting pictures of friends engaged in group
challenges (e.g., gymnastics poses) and reposting pictures of women that she
admired using the hashtag #womencrushwednesdays.

A more social dynamic evolved slowly in middle school, in which she
and her friends started to fashion their own profiles by examining the posts
of high school freshmen. People talked about how many followers they had,
and how many likes they got on posts. Gabriella started caring more about
these things too, and found herself thinking about how she compared with
the older girls she followed at school. She began to follow some YouTubers,
including Ashley, who posted about makeup, lifestyle, and fashion. A friendship began between them, in which they chatted directly and commented
publicly on each other's videos. Suddenly, Ashley's YouTube channel took off.
Within a period of several months, thousands of tween and teenage girls
began following Ashley, while only a few dozen people followed Gabriella's
channel. It wasn't long before Ashley stopped responding to Gabriella, as she
became "YouTube famous," got sponsorships and brand deals, and eventually
decided to homeschool so she could focus on her YouTube channel and related
pursuits. Eventually she reached millions of followers and made millions of

dollars in endorsements and advertisements, and now has her own fashion line. Gabriella easily recalls her talks with Ashley and has continued to follow her career trajectory. In retrospect, she noted that the sting of Ashley's rejection was about having to reckon with the realization that "people usually only communicate online with those of similar status or follower counts." Against the backdrop of this experience, she wasn't so shocked a few years later when a real-life friend from church stopped speaking to her when her Instagram account reached 10,000 followers. But the hurt of that rejection was greater.

Gabriella remained focused on her own internet pursuits. She had a You-Tube channel where she posted videos about anything that struck her fancy—book reviews, clothing hauls, room tours, routines, the occasional random comedic video. She showed her friends these videos, and they had a laugh. Her friends often left positive and encouraging comments. Occasionally, a stranger would happen upon a video and leave a negative comment complaining about their poor quality. She paid these comments little mind. But this didn't last long.

In 2013, Gabriella created a social media profile on the platform Tumblr. She was mainly looking for material related to fashion, photography, inspirational quotes, and healthy eating and exercise. But what she often found were posts of emaciated girls with quotes like, "skip dinner, wake up thinner," and "nothing tastes as good as skinny feels." The promotion of behaviors related to anorexia (known as pro-ana) is prevalent across social media platforms, though it has become more well-regulated after calls were made to censor this content. But for 13-year-old Gabriella, the fact that posts about self-starvation techniques were subtly threaded between posts about healthy eating and exercise created confusion and left her questioning whether some amount of starvation was appropriate. She watched as friends got swept up in the pro-ana messages and began engaging in new behaviors like drinking black coffee, smoking to suppress their appetites, and focusing intently on keeping their weight under 100 pounds. Gabriella did some dieting, but ultimately recognized the toxicity of these messages and was able to shift her focus toward healthier behaviors.

By the time Gabriella entered high school, everyone she knew had profiles on Instagram, Twitter, YouTube, and Snapchat (a social media app whose original defining feature is that messages and photos disappear as soon as they are read). In-person conversation at school often focused on people's Snapchat "streaks"— the number of days two people had "snapped" each other. It was socially competitive, especially if romantic interest was involved. Sometimes a girl would get very angry if another girl had a streak with the guy she liked, or if a guy broke a streak by not responding one day. Gabriella didn't have romantic relationships in high school, so she didn't do this. She found Snapchat confusing and pointless, and instead focused on her Instagram account, where the comments didn't disappear. But she recognized that Snapchat seemed to be an important indicator of popularity, as measured by a person's snap score (the number of snapchats someone had sent and received, listed directly on the profile).

Gradually, social media clout began to extend beyond the online world, influencing the day-to-day politics of her high school. People were reactive to the content on each other's profiles. People often posted about each other without using names but in a way that was obvious, which generated anger and frustration. Cultivating successful social media profiles (measured in followers, likes, positive comments, retweets, etc.) was a primary pastime. The popular guys posted photos of themselves and their buddies holding up the fish they caught, the deer they shot, the girls they were dating, their vehicles, and their sports teams. A popular girl's posts of photos showing off her body and pictures of herself and her friends partying with much older boys became the object of controversy and jealousy. Less popular kids at school had somewhat less active social media profiles. Some of them posted about their more fringe hobbies or extracurricular groups. Some pretended not to care. Very few—those who were self-assured in their outsider status—actually didn't care. Otherwise, social media was ever-present—at school, at home, every place that the phone was in operation (in short, everywhere). Though Gabriella had more self-control than her peers when it came to prioritizing school over social media, it was difficult not to get swept away in the social pressure to maintain an active and popular digital existence.

Analysis

> No soul can grow to its full stature without spells of solitude.
>
> —MARIE STOPES

While Gabriella's story focuses on social media, the dynamics of her early experiences largely overlap with predigital preadolescence. The fun of trying new things, of being silly, of showing off and caring little about what others think. The trivialities that make up a friendship. The excitement of new friends and the pain of rejection. The cultivation of one's own style by emulating older kids. Social media offers a platform for experimenting with identity amid one's peers while also within a larger, networked world where the distance and space between people are neutralized. Being able to maintain a connection over Facebook with a friend who lives abroad can expand a young adult's exposure and build a wider perspective. Being able to follow the posts of a favorite singer is exciting and invites identifications that can support development.

Gabriella's early positive experiences tend to coincide with the moments when she is more focused on posting her own content than on what others are doing. This is consistent with research findings that link active posting to self-esteem, and passive viewing to experiences of social envy and poorer psychological well-being (Verduyn et al., 2017). Gabriella experienced an early rupture upon the recognition that social status can surpass a friendship. Certainly, such examples of childhood innocence being shattered long predate the digital world. But there is something unique to social media about watching a fellow 12-year-old become a celebrity practically overnight. And there seems to be a randomness to why one girl trying to make it on YouTube fails to become popular while another succeeds beyond her wildest dreams. Internet celebrities, also known as influencers, are a product of the way that social media has enabled regular people to reach a large audience. It is easy for anyone to become preoccupied by the desire for recognition and feedback. It is addictive—the more likes people get, the more they want. For many people, the gratifying nature of these experiences is tempered by reality. But for those who gain significant popularity, reality doesn't serve to contain the self. In fact, it does the opposite: Negative comments and criticisms can be consuming and undermine a sense of self, particularly because they are cemented in writing and visible to all. Meanwhile, even the positive sentiments—while gratifying in the short term—often fail to buffer a person against the loneliness that can come from not being fully recognized (Balick, 2018).

Based on interviews with internet celebrities (i.e., regular people who managed to attract a large number of followers), Rockwell and Giles (2009) described how "becoming a celebrity alters the person's being-in-the-world. Once fame hits, with its growing sense of isolation, mistrust, and lack of personal privacy, the person develops a kind of character-splitting between the 'celebrity self' and the 'authentic self,' as a survival technique in the hyperkinetic and heady atmosphere associated with celebrity life." Even the social media platforms have recognized the need for additional protection in such situations, by taking measures such as instituting blocks on direct messaging and offering ways for people to verify their identity against potential scammers. While useful, these measures do little to address the fact that most adolescents and young adults are insufficiently prepared to protect themselves from this onslaught of feedback and to navigate the experience of hyperrecognition, exposure, and not enough time for the self.

This disorientation and preoccupation with managing a public self is not limited to celebrities. Many young adults grapple with the same questions. How real to be? How many average and quirky photos must be inserted between the polished and perfect ones to be considered authentic? Conversely, how many beautification filters (readily available on most apps) can a photo have before it becomes susceptible to accusations of being fake? Even the number of likes on a post can be suspect, as likes and followers can be purchased from apps in bundles. So a lot of attention is spent trying to strike an impossible balance of authenticity and putting one's best foot forward.

On social media, acts of recognition offer a boost to the ego, a sense of validation of a person's experience of themselves—or, perhaps more accurately, a reflection of how they want others to perceive them. But this ego recognition is not equivalent to the need for recognition of the parts of self that one does not actively choose to share or reveal to others (and sometimes—often—even to oneself). These are usually the more vulnerable or painful aspects of a person's experience, be it a difficult personality trait, a personal struggle, a traumatic event that triggers feelings of shame, and so on. These different needs for recognition are often in tension, and there is a danger that the deeper needs for recognition get sacrificed for those at the surface. It can be easy to forget that what a person posts on Instagram is not an indicator of their internal life. In extreme examples, a college student ends up in the hospital for a suicide attempt, and people are shocked because the person's social media profile was filled with inspirational quotes and status updates broadcasting contentedness and happiness. (Balick, 2012) writes:

> Social media comes to the service of the ego (possibly at the expense of the self) and the ego interacts with the social network as an extension of the ways in which our individual egos negotiate the world in any case. The ego likes to maintain familiar patterns, and that's

not always in the service of the self. The self seeks recognition from others (full, honest, authentic, and non-judging recognition)—the ego, however, likes its recognition to be conditional upon its own expectations and desires.

On social media, ego recognition comes in the form of followers, likes, positive comments, or invitations to join elite groups. It is often in tension with damages to the ego, which come in the form of not enough likes, negative comments, failing to gain the popularity a person thinks they deserve. As Gabriella entered adolescence, she was more susceptible to all of these experiences. On social media, the self-comparison that is already so pervasive in adolescence can become particularly insidious due to attribution biases—people tend to assume that a person's Instagram photos are a reflection of their real life, rather than a carefully cultivated presentation of self. When looking at photos of a friend attending parties, events, and vacations, it is easy to assume that they don't have bad hair days, or lonely days, or spend most of their time engaged in the mundane and uninteresting details of daily life. This can end up enhancing feelings of shame, self-doubt, and self-criticism during a critical developmental period when many people are already quite vulnerable to such feelings.

It strikes us that the word *social* is an odd modifier for what is most often a solitary activity. People commonly look at their social media while they are alone and, perhaps, lonely. And in those states, the combination of passive social media browsing and self-comparison tends to lead to feelings of jealousy and envy, poor self-esteem, depression, and other challenges (Lup et al., 2014; Latif et al., 2020; Verduyn et al., 2017). Developmentally, adolescence and emerging adulthood are marked by a tendency to overestimate the extent to which other people are paying attention and noticing every little thing—a phenomenon known as the spotlight effect (Gilovich et al., 2000). Getting out of the spotlight offers a much-needed opportunity to refuel and take a break from the pressures of self-definition. For those who came of age before social media, cultivating and presenting oneself to the world was mainly an embodied task, bound by time and place. Not anymore. While the physical body may be asleep, the digital self is open for business—receiving likes and comments and judgments from a wide network of others. Already, the continuous presence and endless distractions offered by technology present an exceptional challenge to people's need for alone time, and for the self-awareness and personal growth that can come from it (Bermingham et al., 2021; Essig et al., 2018; Carr, 2015; Turkle, 2011). Social media is an extension of this challenge. Without spaces for solitude in between public presentations of self, there is an impoverishment of opportunities to be alone and therefore to develop the capacity to be with oneself. The implications for identity development are stark, as our psychological and spiritual traditions tell us.

In 2015, young adults tried to take this into their own hands through developing fake Instagram accounts (known as Finstas). In reaction to the pressures of cultivating a polished profile, people began to create secondary accounts that they only shared with close friends and which were intended to be free of thoughts and anxieties about how they would be perceived. No more worrying about posting too many photos, or ugly pictures. Interestingly, it was these (ostensibly more authentic) accounts that were referred to as "fake"; the more public accounts were considered real. Something about this confusion captures the conundrum of identity development and presentation in digital space. People still have the need for spaces free of judgment to cultivate a self, and Finstas were an attempt to find that space. In some ways, it works. But can a problem really be fixed from within the very system which has created it?

SECTION II: THE LATER YEARS

Disillusionment, Reprioritization, Taking Back Control

Gabriella had always been socially conscious, which was at least in part a reaction to her upbringing in a strongly white and Republican rural town. As a 19-year-old in 2019, she posted a link to a story about the murder of a Black trans woman by the police on her Instagram story (which lasts for 24 hours) with the tag, "Black Lives Matter." This received some negative replies, in which people questioned this phrase and wrote things like, "duh, obviously all lives matter wtf." She responded to each of these comments through DMs (direct messages) and provided relevant statistics regarding police violence against people of color. She thought it was important to raise awareness about this movement, which at the time was relatively unknown. At the time, most people did not engage her in this conversation.

A year later, the murder of George Floyd brought the Black Lives Matter (BLM) movement onto the national radar. Gabriella found herself inundated by conversations about the role of social media in spreading the word about the BLM movement and social justice issues like racism and homophobia. All around her, people were switching their photos to the BLM flag or inserting BLM into their bio or name, in attempt to make their support of the movement a central part of their self-presentation. Instagram and Twitter were abuzz with debates and conflicting information. Consistent with the political climate of this moment, people's opinions came out strong, facile, and reproachful. Some people in her feed held the position that it is an ethical imperative to post on social media about social justice issues, through messages like, "If you don't post about BLM then unfollow me because I don't want to be friends with racists" and "Being silent means being complicit with a racist system." Others expressed opposing opinions, such as "Posting things on Instagram is performative and you shouldn't do it, you should go out and protest." Those who participated in #BlackOutTuesday posted a black square and the corresponding hashtag (in an attempt to show allyship with the Black community or simply to join with the crowd) often received blowback in their comments section from those who felt this was performative activism. Meanwhile, as she was watching infighting among the liberal side of her social media, her Republican peers from high school did not mention anything about George Floyd, Black Lives Matter, COVID-19, Asian hate crimes, or any other topics that were front and center on the social media of her liberal friends.

She was befuddled. How had a movement that few people she knew had even heard of come to be at the heart of how people were defining themselves—at least publicly? People were posting and reposting news articles, "facts," and advice like wildfire, and it was difficult to ascertain the accuracy of anything, including the legitimacy of causes or businesses that were asking for donations. There seemed to be no way to bow out of the politics of this moment. Amid the debates and intense pressure, people were targeting each other for what they posted as well as what they did not post. "Nobody wants to see your selfies right now" was a common critique of people who tried not to get involved. Gabriella watched as some people started posting a lot more, while others stopped posting or got off social media altogether to get a break from the intensity and pressure of this moment. She noted, "in today's highly virtual world, talking about things in real life seemingly isn't enough anymore. You have to post about something to have it be ingrained in your virtual identity, which overlaps with your actual identity. Can you be a young liberal and NOT post about social justice issues on social media? Will you be regarded as inactive or performative? What is the right thing to do?"

After this moment, Gabriella found herself more tuned into the complexities and downsides of social media. She noticed how scrolling through Instagram's explore page could make an hour go by in no time, that seeing social media stars and even her friends with their highly edited photos could make her feel badly about herself. So, in a moment of wisdom and self-restraint, she decided to set some rules for herself: (1) Go on Instagram only once per day (sometimes twice); (2) quickly check notifications and then scroll through close friends' posts to like or comment on their pictures; and (3) leave the app before starting to scroll aimlessly or stalk strangers' pages, knowing that doing so can pose a losing proposition for her own self-worth. This was especially true if she was already feeling insecure for other reasons, like finding out a crush was dating someone else, or feeling lonely on a given evening when nobody was around to hang out.

Meanwhile, she also decided to quit spending time on social media other than Instagram. This action quickly offered a sense of relief. When TikTok entered the scene, she decided not to get on it, despite feeling some social pressure from her peers, and from her awareness of its high level of influence in society. Some of her friends were getting real enjoyment out of taking part in the singing challenges and dancing trends. Despite this, her perception that it would be a huge time waster made her hold to her decision. She wanted more time for other things like socializing, writing, exercising, and drawing.

Currently, Gabriella has 1,467 Instagram followers. She typically spends less than an hour on the app over the course of the week. This is quite low when compared with the average Gen Z user, who spends 53 minutes per day. She posts lots of photos of herself and her friends. In her view, Instagram is a public scrapbook of the highlights of her life. But she is keenly aware that everything she posts sends a message about her identity and her life. This makes her think twice (or three or four times) about the perceptions that others are likely to have, from family to employers to the general public. So she keeps it clean—she doesn't swear, she avoids photos of partying, drinking, and more provocative outfits. She also doesn't post photos of people she is starting to date, having learned the hard way that it's pretty awkward to have to go back and delete them. Additionally, she keeps her controversial opinions to in-person conversations, where she can focus on how the person in front of her is perceiving her and not have to open herself to the varied and conflicting reactions of her almost 1,500 followers.

Analysis

Care about what other people think and you will always be their prisoner.

—LAO TZU

Virtue signaling, a term coined in 2015, refers to "the popular modern habit of indicating that one has virtue merely by expressing disgust or favor for certain political ideas or cultural happenings" (Cambridge Dictionary). The expression of opinions, especially on social media, is an attempt to show other people that you are a good person. The past few years have been beset by events that have drawn indignation and impassioned responses. And with that has come social pressure to express such views publicly. A (somewhat ironic) backlash to that has been anger and judgment toward those who are seen as being inauthentic in their self-expression.

In addition to the social and emotional ramifications as experienced by Gabriella and those around her, the notion of virtue signaling illustrates a core dilemma of social media. Even when our actions come from an authentic place, the publicness of demonstrating and sharing them makes them strategic—whether consciously or not (Jordan & Rand, 2019). Certainly, it can be tempting to judge the authenticity of people's public displays. And sometimes, it feels quite warranted, as in response to stories that surfaced about celebrities who showed up at BLM protests and rallies with a sign, posted the requisite selfie, and immediately got back into the car that dropped them off. But it distracts us from recognizing a more fundamental reality—that is, by replacing private expressions of self with public ones, social media has redefined the very experience of identity for those growing up and defining themselves in this digital age.

This gets at an essential paradox of social media—self expression and self-presentation, both core elements of social media, can often be in tension. It is normal to want to highlight some traits and hide others. Social media has evolved to accommodate this by having different platforms serve different functions and cater to different audiences. People tend to cultivate profiles along these (usually unspoken) guidelines and norms. Meanwhile, the popular social media of the day is constantly changing based on ambiguous, mysterious factors, leaving many people clamoring to move on to a new platform where they can be in the know. A typical young adult college student might have five social media accounts, including three Instagram accounts: (1) a public account for friends, family, and strangers, including prospective dates; (2) a Finsta (fake Instagram) for friends that includes private, "dirty" content not for public consumption, such as underage drinking, partying, inside jokes, and rants; (3) a more polished Facebook account for family, friends, and older adults (e.g., prospective employers) that might come digging for information; (4) a LinkedIn account for employers and professional contacts; and (5) a Snapchat for friends and acquaintances. Some of these platforms also have the option of joining groups. Groups can be public or private, open or closed. They range in size from just a few people to millions of people. Coin collectors, Lolita fashion lovers (a subculture from Japan that relies on Victorian clothing to achieve the aesthetic of cuteness) and Moms Against Vaccines can all find others online who want to connect with people who share their interests and opinions.

If this many profiles sounds like a lot of effort, well, it certainly can be. In some ways, it mirrors a dynamic of predigital or offline life. We behave differently when talking to a professor than we do when at a party. Being exactly the same in all contexts and with all people would be considered by many to be overly rigid and potentially problematic. And yet, the freedom of being different selves in different contexts is a function of the spontaneity of a given moment. This cannot be replicated on social media, where all acts of self-presentation are available for consumption outside of actual human interaction. People's thoughts and feelings are usually received at a later time, out of context, without body language, and directed toward a crowd rather than an individual. This has turned relational acts of connection and communication into prolonged and often discordant (at least in terms of timing) back-and-forths between people.

Another major difference is that everything is in writing. It is indelible. Something that one writes in a fleeting moment stays in existence as a representation of that individual, rather than a moment that is susceptible to recollection (or lack thereof), or to changing one's mind. This forces people to engage in a self-evaluative process in a moment that might otherwise be spontaneous and free of worry about how others will view that comment. Knowing that you will be judged based on your social media requires an extra level of thought. The many stories of people who get fired due to an employer seeing an inappropriate Facebook post serve as a warning and reminder that nothing is private (see Love, 2014), and companies have begun to try to counteract or prevent some of these situations by adopting clear social media policies about what their employees can and cannot do. But these attempts to prevent negative consequences may further obscure the fact that the pressure to be accountable for all acts of identity expression on social media can undermine the capacities for flexibility and adaptation in identity development. A feeling of needing to stay "on brand" can make it difficult to take risks when it comes to self-exploration. But, as the architect Rem Koolhaas warns, "The stronger the identity, the more it imprisons, the more it resists expansion, interpretation, renewal, contradiction."

Still, the current young generation is grappling more than those that have come before it with the realization of how powerful Facebook and other social media are in shaping who we are and how we think. Some people are angry at the notion that their attention is for sale, and at being manipulated by big technology companies for financial gain. Others are noticing that they don't have as much control as they might like over their use of social media and its impact on their lives. Social media operates like a mirror, hitting people in the places where they already carry their deepest wounds. It exacerbates feelings of body insecurity for someone who struggles with their appearance, triggers feelings about being left out for someone who struggles with rejection, triggers feelings of failure for someone who feels competitive or vulnerable about their achievements, and so on.

Gabriella was not alone in noticing the ways that social media was not serving her well. This generation has developed a variety of new norms aimed at countering the underbelly of social media. A recent trend has pushed people to clean their news feed by unfollowing accounts that cause negative feelings (e.g., people who post incessantly about politics, or society's many ills) or make people feel bad about themselves for whatever reason (e.g., a friend or ex that triggers strong feelings). Detoxing from social media by temporarily disabling accounts or deleting all apps from the phone became a phenomenon around 2013, as people recognized how much their waking life was governed by the apps and how unfathomable it had become to live without them. For many, the recognition of a need for separation from social media came in the wake of a breakup, as people realized how impossible it is to get over an ex and move on while being assaulted by status updates about that person's life (Safranova, 2017). Many people cannot resist the temptation to act out their postbreakup feelings in this domain—attempts to make the other jealous by posting photos of fun events or new partners, expressions of anger by unfollowing an ex (though at times continuing to secretly keep up with their lives by watching their news feed), self-imposed grief through incessant stalking, and so on. Taking a break from social media may be critical to moving on and enabling the internal work of mourning and/or resolution.

Another trend which has grown in popularity is to routinely purge one's social media profiles, which refers to deleting old posts that are not representative of how one wishes to be seen. For some, seeing old photos may trigger shame, embarrassment, or other negative feelings about an earlier version of oneself (e.g., before losing weight or changing one's appearance), or a previous part of one's life (e.g., before changing groups of friends or moving to a new place). But it also reflects a shift in how today's youngest generations are viewing the purpose of social media. Whereas older young adults (millennials) are at times already nostalgic for the past and want to flip through old photos, many Gen Zs use these purges to allow themselves to focus on the present, knowing that they won't have to account for previous expressions of self. After all, who would want a public record of daily thoughts and feelings from eighth grade? Sometimes, the psychology behind these purges mirrors that of an autocratic regime—any evidence of a previous life is seen as delegitimizing one's current self-presentation. Former friends get further informed (or reminded) of their drop in status. In an age when many are all too aware of digital surveillance, purges can also reflect an attempt to obtain a sense of privacy by preventing people from peeking into previous iterations of one's life. Whatever the motivations, it is worth noting that these norms evolve over time and often by the users themselves—in other words, social media creates both the need to develop a private scrapbook for public consumption and the need to go back and remove parts of the story.

Interestingly, despite the many tips and pointers available online about the benefits of getting off social media, no research has been conducted on the impact of deleting social media profiles or taking social media breaks. One study in 2004 highlighted how challenging it is to give them up, as one in three people who tried to give up Twitter for the month of Lent were unable to follow through with it (Shoenebeck, 2014). In the short term, such actions may increase people's anxiety, as research has found when people are separated from their iPhones (Clayton et al., 2015). But there is good news—these effects can reverse themselves during longer stretches of separation (Holte & Ferraro, 2018). Like any addiction, it is hard to break, but doing so can offer real freedom.

SECTION III: SECRETS, SECRET IDENTITIES, NICHE INTERESTS

Always having loved writing, Gabriella began writing stories at age 13. She started a profile on fanfiction.net and published her stories chapter by chapter. These stories were imaginary extensions or retellings of her favorite books, including *Twilight* and *Harry Potter*. In the beginning, only a few people read and commented on them, but over the years, as her writing ability and fan base grew, she gained a substantial group of readers. Sometimes she would reciprocate and read her followers' stories, and occasionally she would tell her favorite fanfiction.net authors about her stories. This online fan fiction community, which was also active on Archive of Our Own and Tumblr, gave Gabriella a platform for creative freedom and collaboration. On Tumblr she and other authors would assume a character's identity—replete with photos—and then write passages back and forth to each other from the various characters' perspectives to form collaborative stories. These stories usually dropped off as one or both contributors lost interest, but they nonetheless played a significant role in her identity development.

Around the same time, one of Gabriella's best friends, Bryan, was using Reddit to connect with people who were experiencing gender dysphoria. When they were 14, Bryan began to withdraw from Gabriella and their other friends. After Gabriella tried to connect with him for many months, Bryan shared with her that he thought he was transgender but was terrified of what his family and friends would think in their Republican, highly Christian community. He disclosed that he had been feeling hopeless and suicidal, until he had found an online community of other teens struggling with the same issues. Slowly, over the course of a few months, he began to feel better as he felt more validated in his struggle and realized he was not alone. After high school ended, Bryan changed his name to Anya and began using she/her pronouns, which became the topic of much gossip back home. As Anya feared, her family kicked her out, but luckily she found a friend whose family was accepting of her transition. Having a supportive online community to rally around her made a huge difference in helping Anya work through the shame and pain of these rejections.

Analysis

> In the social jungle of human existence, there is no feeling of being
> alive without a sense of identity.
>
> —ERIK ERIKSON

Before the advent of social media as we know it today—a series of platforms used by the vast majority of people in society, which mainly serve as extensions of their offline selves—several platforms were already in existence that operated largely through avatars or other anonymous representations of oneself. Certain people were drawn to these platforms precisely because they offered alternative spaces and ways to relate to others. Like Gabriella's collaborative online story writing, anonymous activities offer people freedom to say or do things they might not otherwise say or do. From behind a pseudonym, a person can unabashedly shout profanities and racial slurs, or forge true connections and create lifelong friends. Or both.

The world of immersive role-playing games (e.g., Dungeons and Dragons, World of Warcraft, PlanetSide, Grand Theft Auto) was one of the first to take advantage of internet capabilities, which for the first time allowed fantasy lovers to connect and play together in real time. Friendships are forged as players speak to each other through headsets and collaborate in teams. Subcultures are formed, with their own lingo and unique social conventions. Online games serve dual purposes in being both highly social and communal while also cognitively challenging. They served as a lifeline for many during the lockdowns of the COVID-19 pandemic, including people who hadn't used them before (Lufkin, 2020).

Other virtual worlds are more similar to offline life. Second Life was a virtual world created in 2003, where users developed avatars that could travel to faraway worlds and lands, participate in role-playing games, create and sell products, and socialize with others. Some people used it to live out an enhanced version of their own lives by creating an avatar of the same age, gender, culture, even profession, and then going about activities similar to their in-person lives. Others used it to experiment with identities very different from their own. The documentary *Life 2.0* (dir. Jason Spingarn-Koff, 2010), portrayed people for whom what began as a fun activity became extremely preoccupying when the virtual world became more real than the life it was meant to supplement. One man, who lived a seemingly normal life in the real world, became unexpectedly addicted to living virtually as a preteen school-girl, to the detriment of both his career and his marriage. It turned out that he had survived significant abuse during childhood and found it cathartic to live through this avatar. Ultimately, in recognition that he was unable to leave Second Life despite its potential to ruin his life, he decided he needed to get himself banned from the website. So he said goodbye to his virtual friends, gave away his avatar's belongings, and carried out multiple virtual suicide bombings until Second Life suspended him from their site.

When the internet meets unexplored or repressed parts of the psyche, the line between reality and virtual reality can become very blurry, or disappear altogether (Dryer & Lijtmae, 2007). For the man with the little-girl avatar, the opportunity to engage anonymously online allowed a rigid split between selves (see Trub, 2016), where online he became disinhibited and felt a diminished sense of accountability for a series of cruel and disturbing fantasies that he acted out there. Today, however, people do not have to create an avatar on Second Life to engage deeply in the darker or more disturbed parts of the psyche. YouTube has a plethora of videos dedicated to sharing ideas and worldviews that until recently had existed only on the fringes of society. Especially for young adults trying to find themselves, these ideas take hold and can become foundational in shaping identity. In 2018, a young unemployed man who was struggling with opiate addiction spent entire days in front of YouTube, linking from one conspiracy theory to the next. His fear, deep existential anxiety, and feelings of victimization found a home in the then little-known ideas about a conspiracy of those in power, including political figures and pop icons (ideas that are now widely recognized as part of QAnon). He began to identify as an "incel" (involuntary celibate, an online subculture of men who define themselves by their inability to find a romantic partner), which supported and intensified his rage and destructive urges toward women.

Reddit, a popular social media site, has dedicated groups for those who want to discuss a plethora of conspiracy theories, such as the idea that the world is actually flat (flat earthers), that the 2020 presidential election was stolen, that school shootings are fake events staged by proponents of gun control. The very nature of social media means that until a group comes under fire for being dangerous to others, it has a platform to offer community for like-minded individuals. And so, along with the groups touting conspiracies come the groups offering support and guidance, and a place to express parts of identity that previously were held on the sidelines because they were seen as weird and unacceptable. The list of secret identities explored online is endless: secret anorexia support groups, cancer support groups, porn addicts, people who want to share about mental health diagnoses. For people like Anya who are struggling with their sexual or gender orientation, simply entering the hashtag #LGBT into Tumblr or Instagram can open the door to support and camaraderie. They can follow people that post about LGBT topics, comment on relevant posts, and private message people who may best understand and empathize with their struggles. These groups can provide a lifeline for those dealing with rejection, isolation, and alienation.

Particularly in its early days, those who gravitated toward social media were looking for an outlet that they couldn't get in real life. But for many, turning online offered much more than that. Blogs, which set the framework for many modern social media that came after, were celebrated by many early adopters for playing dual roles in helping people carve out a space for themselves that is simultaneously highly individualized while enhancing a feeling of connectedness to others. One early blogger described being pleasantly surprised by how impactful blogging was to her sense of self:

> First, I discovered my own interests. I thought I knew what I was interested in, but after linking stories for a few months I could see that I was much more interested in science, archaeology, and issues of injustice than I had realized. More importantly, I began to value more highly my own point of view. In composing my link text every day I carefully considered my own opinions and ideas, and I began to feel that my perspective was unique and important. (Blood, 2004, para. 18)

Her words ring true today for the many people for whom a clearer and more solid sense of themselves was an outgrowth of taking advantage of the freedom to express themselves openly in an online forum.

CONCLUSION

For better and worse, discovering and presenting the self in an increasingly networked world can have an expansive effect on identity, as people stay more connected to each other as well as to wider political and social movements that can help shape their sense of self. For young people, social media can offer additional supports and resources for inhabiting parts of the self that might otherwise be buried or suppressed. That said, pressures abound when all acts of identity and selfhood occur in writing, in an indelible and always searchable fashion. Trends in social media coincide with and exemplify a culture of public confessions (see Foucault, 1978), where the value of sharing is often promoted at the expense of preserving a sense of privacy and solitude for the self. Many people who have grown up since the advent of Facebook unwittingly find themselves beholden to dynamics driven by social media—feeling a need to be "always-on" (Turkle, 2006), pursuing validation from a vast audience, all while experiencing continuous overstimulation and self-comparison against an impossible ideal. While, to some extent, these processes long predate modern technology, social media culture heightens many of the very dynamics that can undermine the capacity to develop a stable and secure sense of self. For young people, it is essential to find ways to stay connected to individual feelings, needs, desires, and priorities as one embarks on self-discovery and identity development in a highly networked and public sphere.

Leora Trub is an associate professor of psychology in the school/clinical-child PsyD program at Pace University, and a practicing psychologist based in New York City. She runs the Digital Media and Psychology lab, which explores how technologies affect our conceptions of ourselves and our relationships with others, as well as the underlying psychological and emotional needs they meet. Recent projects include a qualitative study of the perspectives and experiences of psychoanalytic clinicians on the impact of technology on psychotherapy practice, and the development of an app aimed at increasing mindfulness during text-based interactions.

Vendela Parker is a senior at Pace University in New York City, where she is studying psychology. She has been a member of Dr. Leora Trub's Digital Media and Psychology Lab for over a year now. She is currently applying to PhD programs and plans to conduct research in the field of social psychology in the future. In her free time, she enjoys exploring New York City and writing novels.

REFERENCES

Amichai-Hamburger, Y., Wainapel, G., & Fox, S. (2002). "On the internet no one knows I'm an introvert": Extroversion, neuroticism, and internet interaction. *CyberPsychology & Behavior, 5*(2), 125–128. doi: 10.1089/109493102753770507

Balick, A. (2018). The psychodynamics of social networking: Connected-up instantaneous culture and the self. Routledge.

Balick, A. (n.d.). Social media, the ego, and the self. *Dr.AaronBalick*. https://www .aaronbalick.com/news/social-media-the-ego-and-the-self/

Bermingham, L., Meehan, K., Wong, P. & Trub, L. (2021) Attachment Anxiety and Solitude in the Age of Smartphones. *Psychoanalytic Psychology*. https://doi.org/10.1037 /pap0000372

Blood, Rebecca. (2000, Sept. 7). Weblogs: A History and Perspective, Rebecca's Pocket. Message posted to http://www.rebeccablood.net/essays/weblog_history.html.

Cambridge Dictionary. (n.d.) Virtue signalling. In https://dictionary.cambridge.org / *dictionary*. Retrieved August 21, 2021, from https://dictionary.cambridge.org/us /dictionary/english/virtue-signalling.

Carr, N. (2015). *The glass cage: How our computers are changing us* [Ebook edition]. W. W. Norton & Company. https://www.amazon.com/dp/B00J9PQXOE/ref=dp-kindle -redirect?_encoding=UTF8&btkr=1

Clayton, R. B., Leshner, G., & Almond, A. (2015). The extended iSelf: The impact of iPhone separation on cognition, emotion, and physiology. *Journal of Computer-Mediated Communication, 20*(2), 119–135. https://doi.org/10.1111/jcc4.12109

Clough, P. T. (2018). The other-than-human and the "user unconscious". *Studies in Gender and Sexuality, 19*(1), 73–80, doi: 10.1080/15240657.2018.1419683

Clough, P. T. (2019). Notes on psychoanalysis and technology, the psyche and the social. *Studies in Gender and Sexuality, 20*(2), 75-83, doi: 10.1080/15240657.2019.1594043

Davis, K. (2011). Tensions of identity in a networked era: Young people's perspectives on the risks and rewards of online self-expression. *New Media & Society, 14*(4), 634–651. doi:10.1177/1461444811422430

Dryer, J. A., & Litmaer, R. M. (2007). Cyber-sex as twilight zone between virtual reality and virtual fantasy: Creative play space or destructive addiction? *Psychoanalytic Review, 94*(1), 39–61. http://dx.doi.org/10.1521/ prev.2007.94.1.39.

Erikson, E. H. (1968). *Identity: Youth and crisis.* New York: Norton.

Essig, T., Magaldi, D. & Trub, L. (2018). Technology, intimacy and the simulation of intimacy in G. Kanwal. & S. Akhtar (Eds.), Intimacy: Clinical, cultural, digital and developmental perspectives. Routledge.

Foucault, M. (1978). *The history of sexuality.* Pantheon Books.

Gilovich, T., Medvec, V. H., & Savitsky, K. (2000). The spotlight effect in social judgment: an egocentric bias in estimates of the salience of one's own actions and appearance. *Journal of personality and social psychology, 78*(2), 211–222.

Gumbrecht, M. (2005). Blogs as 'protected space'. Reprinted in D. Satish & K. R. Prabhakar (Eds.), *Blogs: Emerging Communication Media,* 79–91. Hyderabad, India: ICFAI University Press.

Hodkinson, P. (2007). Interactive online journals and individualisation. *New Media and Society, 9*(4). https://doi.org/10.1177/1461444807076972

Holte, A. J., & Ferraro, F. R. (2018). Tethered to texting: Reliance on texting and emotional attachment to cell phones. *Current Psychology, 40,* 1-8. doi:10.1007/S12144-018-0037-Y

Jordan, J., & Rand, D. (2019). Are you 'virtue signaling'? *The New York Times.* https://www.nytimes.com/2019/03/30/opinion/sunday/virtue-signaling.html

Koolhaas, Rem. (1994). *The generic city.* Introduction. In Macdonald, E. & Larice, M., *The urban design reader.* (2013). Taylor & Francis.

Latif, K., Weng, Q., Pitafi, A. H., Ali, A., Siddiqui, A. W., Malik, M. Y., & Latif, Z. (2021). Social comparison as a double-edged sword on social media: The role of envy type and online social identity. *Telematics Informatics, 56,* 101470. https://doi.org/10.1016/j.tele.2020.101470

Love, D. (2014). 17 people who were fired for using Facebook. *Business Insider.* https://www.businessinsider.com/17-people-who-were-fired-for-using-facebook-2014-7

Lufkin, B. (2020). How online gaming has become a social lifeline. *BBC.* https://www.bbc.com/worklife/article/20201215-how-online-gaming-has-become-a-social-lifeline

Lup., K, Trub., L, Rosenthal., L. (2015). Instagram #instasad?: exploring associations among Instagram use, depressive symptoms, negative social comparison, and strangers followed. *Cyberpsychol Behav Soc Netw, 18*(5), 247–252. doi: 10.1089/cyber.2014.0560

Marcia, J. E. (1966). Development and validation of ego-identity status. *Journal of Personality and Social Psychology, 3*(5), 551–558. https://doi.org/10.1037/h0023281

McLuhan, M. (1994). *Understanding media: The extensions of man.* Introduction by Lewis Lapham. The MIT Press.

Palfrey, J., & Gasser, U. (2008). *Born digital: Understanding the first generation of digital natives.* Basic Books.

Pew Research Center. (2021, April 7). *Social media use in 2021: A majority of Americans say they use YouTube and Facebook, while use of Instagram, Snapchat and TikTok is especially common among adults under 30* [Report]. https://www.pewresearch.org/internet/2021/04/07/social-media-use-in-2021/

Rockwell, D., & Giles, D. (2009). Being a celebrity: A phenomenology of fame. *Journal of Phenomenological Psychology, 40,* 178–210. doi: 10.1163/004726609X12482630041889

Safranova, V. (2017). Instagram is now a dating platform, too. Here's how it works. *The New York Times.* https://www.nytimes.com/2017/12/21/style/instagram-thirst-traps-dating-breakups.html

Schoenebeck, S. Y. (2014). Giving up Twitter for Lent: how and why we take breaks from social media. In *Proceedings of the SIGCHI Conference on Human Factors in Computing Systems,* 773–782.

Spingarn-Koff, J. (Director). (2010). *Life 2.0* [Film]. Steve Rotfeld Productions.

Trub, L., Revenson, T. A., Salbod, S. (2014). Getting close from far away: Mediators of the association between attachment and blogging behavior. *Computers in Human Behavior, 41,* 245-252. https://doi.org/10.1016/j.chb.2014.08.003

Trub, L. (2016). A Portrait of the Self in the Digital Age: Attachment, Splitting, and Self-Concealment in Online and Offline Self-Presentation. *Psychoanalytic psychology, 34*(1). doi: 10.1037/pap0000123

Turkle, S. (2004). How computers change the way we think. *The Chronicle Review, 50*(21), 26. https://www.chronicle.com/article/how-computers-change-the-way-we-think/

Turkle, S. (2006). Always-on/always-on-you: The tethered self. http://sodacity.net/system/files/Sherry-Turkle_The-Tethered-Self.pdf

Turkle, S. (2011). The tethered self: Technology reinvents intimacy and solitude. *Continuing higher education review, 75,* 28–31.

Verduyn, P., Ybarra, O., Résibois, M., Jonides, J., & Kross, E. (2017). Do social network sites enhance or undermine subjective well-being? A critical review. Social Issues and Policy Review, *11*(1), 274–302. https://doi.org/10.1111/sipr.12033

PART 2

Love and Work

CHAPTER 11

The Wooing Web

Double Binds of Internet Dating

LEORA TRUB

L ove is as old as time. But dating as we know it today—when a couple takes time to get acquainted and freely decides whether to deepen their intimacy and commitment—is a relatively modern phenomenon, dating back about 100 years (Weigel, 2016). With the exception of people who come from more traditional communities that rely on professional or parental matchmakers, the job of creating couples has mainly fallen to friends, family, and coworkers since the mid-20th century in the United States (Rosenfeld et al., 2019). It was a model that worked well for many, particularly heterosexual people. But for others, there remained a need to expand the dating pool and to find people with similar interests and proclivities—not to mention more discretion than was often shown by well-meaning friends of one's parents (Rosenfeld et al., 2019). And with that need came opportunities to capitalize on it. The first computer-based matchmaking service began in 1966, when two Harvard students charged $3 for people to answer 75 questions and receive six matches based on their responses (Leonhardt, 2006).

THE FUNNY BUSINESS OF LOVE: A BRIEF HISTORY

Fast-forward 50 years, and online dating has proliferated to a multibillion-dollar business (Clement, 2020). One in three adults has used a dating site or app, and 12% have ended up married or in a committed relationship to someone they met online (Anderson et al., 2020). These numbers are significantly higher for LGBT individuals, and for younger adults ages 18–29, about half of whom have engaged in online dating and 20% of whom ended up in a committed relationship. This represents a big jump from just seven years earlier in 2013, when 11% of US adults had engaged in online dating, and only 3% had started a serious relationship with someone they met on an online platform (Anderson et al., 2020).

While these quickly increasing numbers make the internet appear to be a supreme instrument of modern love, for many, the lived experience of online dating is far more complex, cryptic, and enigmatic. In a survey of Americans who had used a dating app in the past year, the majority expressed feeling more frustrated than hopeful (Anderson et al., 2020). While some of this frustration is endemic to dating, aspects of online dating can both exacerbate and alter the complexity and uncertainty of dating. Indeed, almost half of American adults feel that dating is harder now than it was 10 years ago (Brown, 2020). As with many modern technologies, people can find themselves feeling trapped, controlled by the technology rather than the other way around, and unable to disentangle the good from the bad (Trub & Barbot, 2016; Turkle, 2011a).

How are we to understand the role of our modern technologies in facilitating phenomena that long predate them—intimacy, romance, companionship, sex, love? To what extent are the challenges of online dating inherent to finding a partner just played out in a new medium? Which dynamics are new, representative of how the instrument itself may be changing the very nature of dating?

DOUBLE BINDS AND LANDMINES

People commonly describe the world of online dating in contradictory terms— abundant and limited; promising and hopeless; safer and more exposed; high and low stakes; easier and more challenging than other forms of dating.

When teased apart, the particular conditions of online dating seem to present people with a variety of double binds: Too many options can leave people feeling saturated and overwhelmed at the task of sifting through potential matches to find appropriate candidates for dating. But restricting the search through the use of filters can mean that good ones fall through the cracks. There is pressure to create a profile that will catch people's attention in the instant that it takes to swipe right or left (interested or not). Yet investing less energy and effort may yield better results, especially as it can protect against feelings of vulnerability and exposure. People cultivate profiles that present themselves in the best, most attractive, way. But then, it can be profoundly disappointing when an online connection doesn't translate to an in-person one. On the flip side, it can engender a sense of deception and inauthenticity that starts a relationship off on the wrong foot.

As dating apps have proliferated, the variety of goals for using them has increased. While this can be quite freeing, it creates additional vulnerability in those who are looking for a committed romantic partner but cannot assume that others are looking for the same thing. Excitement about a new dating landscape allows people to soften their characteristic defenses and biases. But when a situation turns out badly, the defenses return, often with added vigor. Getting to know others at a distance can embolden people to share a lot about themselves. But this can engender feelings of overexposure and danger when it comes time to meet up.

This chapter focuses on the paradoxical nature of online dating. It aims to illustrate and explore these and other double binds that young adults find themselves in when they enter the modern dating landscape of swiping, chatting, catfishing, and ghosting. The chapter presents these double binds along four dimensions: the paradox of choice, a new game without rules, the pull to keep things casual, and negotiating safety with strangers. The content of this chapter is derived from several sources, including the research literature, a qualitative study of adults in New York City who discussed their online dating experiences in focus groups in 2018, and clinical cases of individuals who happened to be engaged in online dating. Direct quotes are mainly from young adults who represent a diverse racial makeup, including Black, white, Latinx, Asian, and mixed-race individuals. They include individuals who identify as heterosexual, bisexual, and gay/lesbian. As this chapter aims to probe common and everyday experience, each of the themes has been chosen for its repetition across domains.

THE PARADOX OF CHOICE

While online dating might be low stakes in theory (it's free and easy), the stakes are also high for those hoping to find the—or a—right person. In his 2004 book *The Paradox of Choice: Why More Is Less*, psychologist Barry Schwartz argued that we have created a culture of abundance that robs us of the possibility of satisfaction. Building on an earlier concept of choice over-load, he argues that being faced with too many choices tends to be a setup for developing unrealistically high expectations, causing us to question our decisions almost before we have a chance to make them.

Society has hardly heeded this warning. Fifteen years later, maximiza-tion, efficiency, productivity, and automation have become part and parcel of what we expect from our digital technologies, and the (increasingly large) role that technology plays in helping us maintain and manage relationships, even—especially, perhaps—when it comes to love and romance. The array of apps connecting us to a sea of possible mates invites both the fantasy of a per-fect partner and the tendency to want to hold out for something better. This can make the process of finding that special someone more difficult, when it is (supposedly) meant to be easier.

And in many ways, it is easier. It is efficient. You can date from anywhere, at any time. You can do it while doing other things. One woman noted, "You can put it within your busy life . . . be on your lunch break and just bored and, you know, swipe this person, swipe that person. . . . You don't have to actually be there to talk to that person or match with that person." Like other phone-based, social networking kinds of activity, swiping through matches can be a pastime of its own. While theoretically driven by the search for a partner, the habitual and addictive nature of swiping and messaging can make the moti-vations at play rather murky—it may be a way to escape oneself or to regulate states of boredom or anxiety (see Trub & Barbot, 2020), or a flight into a fantasy of the perfect mate, the perfect life.

Different apps offer different products—people tailor their profile differ-ently on apps known for generating hookups than on apps that emphasize the search for a committed relationship. "It just commodifies dating. It turns it into, like, another convenience. It's like Seamless for dating. It's like, yo, I need a burger and a 24-year-old who's into the same stuff," said one man. Heino and colleagues (2010) coined the phrase "relationshopping" to describe people's tendency to date online the way they shop—assessing the market worth of themselves and others, shopping around for perfect parts, maximizing inven-tory. Participants in our study likened scrolling through matches on apps to window shopping, compared personal dating profiles to professional promo-tional websites, and drew an analogy between the transition from chatting on an app to meeting someone in person to the disappointment that comes with realizing clothing from a catalog doesn't look as good at home. And shopping doesn't mean purchasing—just as some people shop online mindlessly or for fun, it is not uncommon to use apps to flirt or simply pass the time, with no intention of meeting a match in person.

We have grown accustomed to having our relationships mediated by our devices (Essig et al., 2018). Even after starting to date someone new, many people linger on dating apps, despite the threat it can pose to a budding relationship. Real people have flaws, and they almost inevitably fall short when compared to the fantasies generated by seeing a profile. Moreover, the sheer number of profiles out there contributes to compulsion and the impulse to keep looking. "You can keep shopping," said a young woman. "It does make you really picky. Because here you are now saying, this is what I want. Here's my shopping list, and you need to tick all of the boxes." A young man joked about doing it "until I fall asleep, until I collapse, until I die." Another young woman said of a friend, "She took over a year on dating apps before choosing someone to go on a date with. She said she was overwhelmed with the options and wanted to filter through until she found her 'perfect' guy. Of course, he didn't end up being perfect. If I remember correctly, I think he ghosted her."

The shopping metaphor only goes so far. While utilitarian methods may be best for sifting through an overwhelming number of options, such callous and calculated decisions can feel at odds with the search for love, connection, and intimacy. Talk of algorithms, automation, filters, and efficiency is hardly in line with the magic and spontaneity of romance. While filters are essential for sifting through lots of options to identify acceptable dating partners, fitting people into boxes is problematic. It can strip people of their humanity. It flattens out the distinctions between people. And it comes with serious consequences, as it eliminates potential partners from even being on the radar.

DATING 2.0: A NEW(ISH) GAME, WITH NO RULES

The paradoxical setup of online dating can be mystifying. It offers little room to take time and grieve the loss of a partner (or potential partner) when things don't work out. Having so many options to choose from can create expectations to get over disappointment and move on quickly. But the anonymity of it creates a parallel expectation of avoiding high hopes. "There's an overall skepticism about these apps. And it keeps people from having expectations," said a young man. This message—that people should expect so little from the apps in which they are investing a great deal of time and energy, and which have sophisticated algorithms designed to strategically deliver appropriate and eligible partners—is somewhat bewildering.

What is behind this? Why shouldn't people have expectations about something they deeply desire? And why are so many people using a medium from which they (supposedly) expect so little? After all, isn't the very promise of online dating one of having transformed a difficult, imperfect process into one which is streamlined, technologically sophisticated, and reliable?

It depends. First and foremost, it depends on how dating is defined. For many, that definition is an expansive one. While some use online platforms to look for a committed romantic partner, people also use these platforms to find strictly sexual partners or platonic friends, and to expand their social networks (Couch & Liamputtong, 2008). Some use them to enhance traveling experiences by meeting locals or to have a carefree sexual experience when away from a partner. Some use it for identity exploration and experimentation (see Blackwell et al., 2014). Some use it when healing from a breakup and in need of validation. A woman noticed herself back on the app while going through a rough breakup, even though she wasn't ready to date. She was pleasantly surprised to realize, "I still got it!"

In our New York–based study, when asked to check boxes indicating what they were looking to find through online dating, 50% of participants endorsed looking for a monogamous relationship. But they were open to a variety of potential arrangements: Half endorsed looking for someone to text with; 41% selected friends and nothing more; 41% selected a casual fling, just sex or a one-night stand; and 35% endorsed looking for a consistent, nonmonogamous hookup. National polling shows similar trends, with 58% of younger adults (ages 18–39) saying they are open to either a relationship or casual dates. The rest are split between those looking for a relationship only (27%) and those looking only looking for something casual (15%).

Some argue that these varied motivations are an exploitation of the affordances and conveniences of online dating (Hobbs et al., 2016). But they also represent the reality of the process. To navigate through the complexities and unknowns, people come up with rules for themselves to follow—about the pacing of dating, for example. How long one should wait before meeting in person? Or conversely, what length of time is unreasonable to wait for a first date? "Generally no sooner than 10 messages exchanged, and no later than 3 days after matching/texting," suggests someone on a Reddit thread. Others opt for a video chat before meeting in person, to get a better sense of appearance, chemistry, and personality in a more spontaneous format. These things do matter—research finds that more time before meeting in person is associated with greater perceptions of intimacy (Ramirez et al., 2014). On the flip side, though, many people describe that a long texting courtship tends to disrupt momentum that is crucial to the early stages of dating. It can be maddening, but not uncommon, to find oneself in a long-term texting relationship with someone who says they want to meet in person but somehow never allows that to happen. One is left to wonder who is sitting behind that screen.

Other rules include what kind of pictures are acceptable to post, off-limits hours for chatting, and deal breakers—everything from drinking and drug use to religiosity (or lack thereof). As of 2020, half of US adults put someone who voted for Trump on their dating blacklist; this was rivaled only by someone who has a lot of debt or someone who lives far away (Brown, 2020). Such rules can be vital for bringing a sense of organization and structure to the murkiness and chaos.

Dating apps are always proliferating. New apps reach for a greater market share by boasting newer and better methods—those that empower women to make the first move; that match based on exact location; that match you with people already in your social network; those for people in open relationships; for people interested in kink experimentation; for those who only want to date people of a certain religion, or a certain socioeconomic status, and so on. This allows people to experiment, play, and look for different things on different apps. A woman in her 40s described her setup: "So I have like one website that I deal with, that deals with a more mature crowd, more my age. And then I have the one that [has] everybody. I notice that young guys are always flirting with me."

What purpose does the second app serve? Perhaps it's for the ego boost she gets when young men are interested. Maybe she sees herself as better matched with the younger men, but is keeping the site for more mature people as a backup. She could be ambivalent about a more serious relationship right now, or ever. Or she might be hoping for a fun, light romance while also looking for the real thing. Such questions often surround and envelop the world of online dating, especially when it comes to others' motives. It can be a crazy-making guessing game.

This example also highlights a compelling, almost utopian, aspect of online dating. It can open doors—to new people, new experiences. It can break down stereotypes and disrupt assumptions about who you want to date and who wants to date you. A young woman described how online dating changed her outlook on people: "I've never really been open to other cultures. But I think, you know, it's at your fingertips . . . so that's pretty exciting." She is joined by the vast majority of single adults in the United States, 77% of whom say they would date someone of a different religion and 85% of whom say they would date someone of another race or ethnicity (Brown, 2020). The apps allow people to be less restricted to meeting those who are already within their social mileu, and to gain exposure to a diversity of people in terms of culture, race, socioeconomic background, and other demographic characteristics.

This expansiveness can transform into a sense of timelessness. "There's no real time limit. Someone could have messaged me a month ago and I may not have seen it, and I see it today, and that will set it into action," explained one man, who compared it to traditional dating: "If I fail to catch someone's attention now, in this room, it's just over." This laid-back attitude may not sit well with the person who is waiting for a reply. For one young woman, this is a clear warning sign: "I go into a story about you must be on the rebound, or starved for attention, or whatever. But usually I feel slighted and rejected, like I'm in your recycling bin. . . . "

Rejection is part and parcel of dating, of course. But the expansive and anonymous world of online dating brings about new contexts for rejection. "There's a lot of people who [I've] had a lot of very nice conversations with and, like, all of a sudden one day they just took them off the earth. They just disappear," a man described. This disappearance—known as ghosting—is extremely common in the world of online dating and quite unsettling. Almost half (42%) of young adults ages 18–29 report having been ghosted (Brown, 2020).

Why is ghosting so common? Certainly, a lack of accountability is enhanced by the anonymity and distance of online spaces (Runions & Bak, 2015; Trub et al., 2014). But beyond that, ghosting may also represent a dark underbelly of all of the freedom and novelty of dating apps. When a new partner loses appeal, there are always others to swipe and fantasize about. Especially before meeting in person, swiping on faces may feel a bit like a video game. It can be easy to forget (or ignore) that those on the other side of the app are real people with real feelings. Rejecting people without having to consider their feelings is by its very nature dehumanizing, which is a core feature of interacting online (Balick, 2018; Suler, 2004). It is a space where the Golden Rule does not apply. No matter how much people may hate being ghosted, the experience of being on the receiving end may paradoxically engender a tendency to normalize the behavior as acceptable. It is easy not to think about the potential implications for others when swiping out of boredom, or for fun, or for validation, or for sex, or with no intention of getting involved with someone. So begins a cycle in which people hurt silently when they are treated insensitively, and then rationalize acting toward others in the very ways that caused them pain. "It's wrong! And I've done it 37,000 times," said one man. How, then, do people contend with the fact that others may be swiping on them with a similar callousness?

There may be no escaping a basic reality—in love, and in life, we reap what we sow.

KEEPING IT CASUAL

Some people know they want a serious relationship and say so unequivocally. But dating, whether on- or offline, is nuanced and not governed by logic. Madame de Staël, a political theorist during the French Revolution, said, "In matters of the heart, nothing is true except the improbable." Psychologically speaking, then, the safest way to play the dating game may be to aim for the lowest common denominator, which usually means adopting a casual mindset and keeping expectations low. Even when people hope to end up in a serious relationship, the nature of online dating—the anonymity, disinhibition, deception, the sheer volume of it all—can pull people to downplay those desires. The heavy reliance on photos can make the whole enterprise feel superficial (Anderson et al., 2020). When asked what they hope to find, many people equivocate. "Hopefully to meet somebody. I don't—it's kind of iffy for me. Yeah, I don't have a lot of expectations for it, but I'm open-minded about it," said one man.

A casual outlook can help to bridge the gaps between those looking for relationships and those looking for a hookup, which are inherent to online dating. The dating culture of Gen Z—and to a lesser extent, Millennials—tends toward sexual flexibility and relationship fluidity, which can add complexity and confusion to the search for intimacy (Orchard, 2020). These new trends widen the landscape of what people want, and what they think others want from them. People adjust their expectations accordingly, which can then operate as a bit of a self-fulfilling prophecy: The overwhelming majority of adults looking for a committed relationship tend to feel dissatisfied with their dating life, while those who express an openness to casual relationships are more likely to express feeling satisfied (Brown, 2020).

While many people may in fact be open to a wide array of arrangements, for others the adoption of a casual attitude represents an attempt to keep both hope and disappointment at bay. As one young woman surmises, "Most people are, in the back of their mind, open to more, maybe marriage. But it's just not something they hold their breath for." Several people named fear as a main motivator: "I just don't think people go on with high hopes. You know, men and women, I think, don't communicate that they are looking for long-term [relationships] because they are afraid, or they feel like they're not gonna find what they're looking for."

The dampening of hopes or expectations—both outwardly and within oneself—can play out at almost every step of the way. How much effort and care should go into making a profile? What will get people to swipe right? How does one convey oneself realistically and authentically while also portraying the best and most attractive aspects of oneself? Hesitant to feel or show too much vulnerability, people come up with rules meant to maximize positive experiences and minimize unpleasant ones. People find themselves working hard to seem like they are not working hard. Desperation, longing, need— these are human qualities to keep hidden.

Further complicating matters is that the norms differ from one app to the next. In interviews about the use of Grindr, an app for gay, bisexual, transgender, and queer people, men discussed liking the fact that Grindr offers a platform for experimentation and manipulation of identity and self-presentation. At the same time, there exists a norm of posting photos rather than chatting, which creates pressure to cultivate the most attractive profile possible. Meanwhile, the feature which allows for searching based on proximity means that Grindr users may be more likely to be seen in person by those who have seen their profile online, which increases pressure to be accurate (Blackwell et al., 2014). This scenario typifies the confluence of seemingly contradictory factors at play when people make decisions about how to portray themselves.

All of this is set against yet another stumper, which is that people say they expect others to lie and deceive on dating apps (Anderson et al., 2020; Drouin et al., 2016; Gibbs et al., 2010; Hall et al., 2010). And people do lie—often along gender stereotypes, with men being more likely to misrepresent their personal assets, relationship intentions, personal goals, and personal attributes (height in particular), and women more likely to misrepresent their age and weight

(Cody et al., 2010). One young woman described it: "Many women wind up liking a guy and then finding out later that he is living with his parents, or married, or he has a kid, or he is jobless, etc. There is no regulation—you can say that you are a doctor on your profile and unless your date looks you up, no one will know any different."

Expecting the worst doesn't actually protect people from the pain of being deceived. To the contrary, being misled can be startling, troubling, painful— from small infractions like feeling the gap between someone's profile photos and their level of attractiveness in person is too wide, to larger ones, like being misled about basic and important details (for example, if someone is separated but not divorced, or if they have a child), or feeling that someone misrepresented their intentions. Catfishing, which refers to presenting the self inauthentically on a digital platform, is easy to achieve on dating apps, which come with the tools necessary to make major changes to appearance— pulling in the waist, clearing the face of acne, increasing the size of butt and breasts, and so on. "People who wind up on dates with those who do this may feel upset because in a way they were lied to," explained one young woman, who said that some men use this as a reason to engage in behavior that is further objectifying, like asking for "proof" of the woman's looks in the form of nude or body shots on Snapchat. "It's a sad process to watch," she said. These kinds of negative experiences are not limited to young women. After a couple of bad experiences, one young man found himself looking for any sign that "[a woman] could be snuggled up with her man while she's typing something or be upset. . . . You never know what a person's ulterior motives are."

No matter who you are, it can be challenging to bounce back from such situations and return to a healthy balance between high hopes and low expectations. If you've been burned enough times, it's easy to become disillusioned and skeptical—which can further undermine the ability to suss out whether someone is worth taking seriously or to be suspicious. There is a fine line between perception and reality, and people often tolerate different amounts of stretching the truth for themselves and others. How much embellishment and refinement, filters and beautification tools can one utilize before being vulnerable to being perceived as dishonest? The precise amount of lying and deception considered acceptable is elusive, and the stakes feel high when too much—and too little—deception are judged harshly.

In a world where people are left to figure out the rules on their own, it is common to yearn for more clarity and reciprocity. When others do not play by the same rules, it engenders frustration—with both the people and the process. Whereas profiles with more information tend to engender trust (High & Wotipka, 2016), a sparse profile can be interpreted as uncaring and uninvested. But these are simply assumptions. How to toe the line between honesty and putting your best foot forward is hardly an exact science—appearing too interested can make a person seem needy; the wish to commit can be perceived as desperate. But being too casual can be insulting or off-putting, especially to those looking for a relationship. In a focus group where people were vague or dismissive about whether or not they hoped to find a serious partnership, a woman was left feeling exasperated and frustrated: "It doesn't make sense to be looking for a relationship in a sea of people who have no interest in committing."

> Technology is seductive when what it offers meets our human vulnerabilities. And as it turns out, we are very vulnerable indeed. We are lonely but fearful of intimacy. Digital connections and the sociable robot may offer the illusion of companionship without the demands of friendship. Our networked life allows us to hide from each other, even as we are tethered to each other.
>
> —TURKLE, *ALONE TOGETHER*

In our digital culture, devices have become the fulcrum for presenting the self and connecting to others. The cultivation of an online profile necessitates a hyperfocus on the self, which is then exacerbated by a corresponding need for validation—via likes and swipes. At the same time, our devices engender an expectation to be constantly connected to others. But this connection is often at the surface and can leave us feeling increasingly alienated and alone. We accept it because it is easier than the alternative—that is, vulnerability.

> I define vulnerability as uncertainty, risk and emotional exposure. With that definition in mind, let's think about love. Waking up every day and loving someone who may or may not love us back, whose safety we can't ensure, who may stay in our lives or may leave without a moment's notice, who may be loyal to the day they die or betray us tomorrow— that's vulnerability.
>
> —BROWN, *DARING GREATLY*

As dating apps and websites have come to dominate the search for love, people find themselves in a sometimes impossible bind—to connect deeply in a world where protecting the self from vulnerability is a top priority, to find intimacy without exposure. There is a dark underbelly to such an existence. For when we deny our own vulnerability, we lose sight of the vulnerability of others. We drop compassion and kindness, and we forget to treat others as we want to be treated—even as we are searching for deep connection and love.

PLAYING IT SAFE WITH STRANGERS, IN AND OUT OF A PANDEMIC

Rules are a way to negotiate safety—both emotional and physical. When behind a screen in one's own space, online dating can seem as safe as it is convenient. Early stages of contact tend to build gradually, from chatting over the app, to texting on the phone, to (sometimes) connecting over social media, to meeting over video chat (Couch & Liamputtong, 2008). Profiles with a lot of information are particularly likely to be perceived as trustworthy (High & Wotipka, 2016). Being able to communicate with people (and if necessary, to end communication) before meeting face to face helps to create a sense of safety (Rosenfeld et al., 2019). Meanwhile, engaging in a lot of disclosure can help reduce feelings of anxiety and uncertainty in this early phase of getting to know a stranger (Gibbs et al., 2010).

Once people do decide to meet up, previous feelings of safety and security can suddenly feel illusory. The setup is often paradoxical—having shared a lot of private information during the early phase may lead to greater vulnerability and fear when preparing to meet a match for the first time. This leads many people to search online for information to restore a feeling of control (Brown, 2020; Gibbs et al., 2010), or to ask a friend in common (usually discovered through social media) for information. But this, too, can spiral out of control or backfire in various ways: It can take the spontaneity and excitement away. It can start someone down a rabbit hole of online stalking. It can turn up information that is unattractive or worrisome and put someone in a bind of having to decide how to deal with secondhand (and possibly inaccurate) information.

Location-based apps uniquely typify the balance between extreme convenience and being too close for comfort. This highlights an essential but paradoxical aspect of online dating, where people feel safe sharing sexual preferences, exact location, and other personal information with strangers, on a platform where disinhibition can reign. Apps offer people a somewhat unprecedented opportunity to name desires that might otherwise be considered unacceptable, and to do so in a relatively anonymous domain. They offer the option of trying to meet a wide range of needs, including the most carnal. To be risqué can be fun and exciting. To share about oneself openly from behind a screen can feel good. But when it comes time to meet, the façade of security can quickly disintegrate, leaving people feeling exposed, vulnerable, and unsafe—particularly young women. Six in 10 females ages 18–34 are contacted by people after they expressed disinterest in further contact, and 57% have received an uninvited sexually explicit message or image. Almost half (44%) have been called an offensive name, and 19% have had someone threaten to physically harm them (Anderson et al., 2020). Given this, it should be no surprise that women are twice as likely as men to name increased physical and emotional risk as a main reason why online dating is difficult (Brown, 2020).

And that was before the COVID-19 pandemic, which brought safety concerns and risk assessment to an entirely new level. During the pandemic, one-night stands and hookups were off the table for many people. But loneliness was very much on it. With limited options for entertainment, even more people turned to dating apps than before (Meisenzahl, 2020). But the pandemic changed fundamental aspects of dating, forcing people to rediscover more traditional modes of dating that tend to identify sexual activity as something to wait for. Virtual dates became commonplace. Going for a drink in a crowded bar was replaced by a socially distanced walk in the park—sometimes with masks. One woman brought a tape measure to measure out six feet on the steps of a museum that became her preferred place to meet up. Dates were less likely to end in a goodnight kiss. Some people agreed to do a COVID test before meeting up. Some people found themselves having cybersex for the first time. People found themselves having talks about monogamy with potential partners before sleeping with them.

These changes weren't universal, of course. There are those who did not believe in the virus or follow social distancing rules, and people who threw caution to the wind in a moment of desire or recklessness. But even these people contended with the changes to dating culture: pop-up messages on apps reminding people to take precautions. New features on apps to encourage virtual dates as a first step before meeting up. Profiles that included information about people's social distancing habits and expectations for the behavior of others. Pictures of people with their toilet paper stash, early in the pandemic, when fears of running out ran high. Later on, photos of people receiving the vaccine—its own sort of advertisement.

As safety issues became more salient, some people allowed themselves to be more vulnerable. For many, increased risk slowed down the pace of dating and lengthened the getting-to-know-each-other phase. For others, it enabled a relationship to become serious as people looked to settle down with a "pandemic partner." While dating apps may have offered an escape from any of the myriad horrors of 2020, many found themselves compelled toward committing to giving things a try with a single partner for any number of pandemic-related reasons—for better or worse. Only time will tell how these changes to dating culture will impact online dating in a post-pandemic era.

CECE'S STORY: THE TRIALS AND TRIBULATIONS OF ONLINE DATING

Cece is a 20-year-old college junior who identifies as bisexual and is interested in finding a committed partner. She started with a Tinder profile, as is common among her age group. Immediately, she observed that more than half of the people she matched with never returned a message, or messaged her once before disappearing. She described it as feeling like "a game, or sorting through a haystack to find a needle."

As a bisexual woman, Cece faced a conundrum: Male matches replied quickly. But they often wanted casual sex, apparently undeterred by the explicit "no hookups" message in her profile. "Not very many young men actually will go through dating in real life the normal way, and they are usually older/more mature. Also, they often have an expectation that the woman they match with will hookup with them." Cece is right about this—four out of ten women report having been pressured to have sex by someone they went out with on a date (Brown, 2020).

Meanwhile, while she matched with plenty of women, they almost never messaged her. When they did message her, they often expressed an interest in friendship, not dating. "Because I don't appear to be a lesbian, or so I'm told, sometimes girls match with me expecting a straight friend. Very confusing stuff." She tried to set the record straight by being extremely explicit about her sexual orientation on her profile, to little avail.

When Cece did set up an in-person date, she often found herself waiting at the agreed-upon spot. She would send a message to see if the woman was running late, only to get the reply, "Oh, I can't make it," or "I'm not comfortable meeting someone from Tinder in real life. Sorry." This was after the woman agreed to a date, set it up, and let Cece wait for 20 minutes, sometimes in a restaurant. This process repeated itself many times over two years. "I actually gave up dating women for a while and stuck to guys because this process is so infuriating." She chalked much of it up to her appearance, concluding that "appearing straight" seems to cause confusion and makes it difficult to find a female partner.

Then came COVID-19. Cece moved home to live with her mother, who doesn't know she is bisexual. In a world where virtual dates were becoming more commonplace due to the risks of meeting in person, Cece's options became even more limited. How could she get into the headspace necessary to be on a date with a woman while worrying that her mother would crash the date and be confronted with the potentially devastating reality of Cece's sexual preferences?

And it's not just that. "It just doesn't feel like the time for dating. Not when people are dying every day and the country is a mess because of the violence with MAGA. It doesn't feel like a romantic time. At least not to me."

When the pandemic finally ends, Cece says she expects to be back on the apps, despite all of the frustrations, because it feels like the only option for finding what she wants. In the meantime, it's been a long year.

APPS AS EVOCATIVE OBJECTS

Ours has been called a culture of narcissism. The label is apt but can be misleading. It reads colloquially as selfishness and self-absorption. But these images do not capture the anxiety behind our search for mirrors. We are insecure in our understanding of ourselves, and this insecurity breeds a new preoccupation with the question of who we are. We search for ways to see ourselves. The computer is a new mirror, the first psychological machine. Beyond its nature as an analytical engine lies its second nature as an evocative object.

—TURKLE, *EVOCATIVE OBJECTS*

More than a tool, dating apps have become a powerful force to reckon with when negotiating needs for love, sex, romance, and friendship. They have become a pastime to distract from boredom and loneliness. Or to offer a dopamine rush at the gratification of being found attractive and appealing. Or to lift someone from loneliness. Or to offer validation. Or to avoid the anxiety at the beginning stages of a new relationship. In these moments, it can be the apps—rather than the partners they are meant to provide—that become the object of people's love, hate, and everything in between. People blame the app when love is not found, delete it in exasperation, then begin anew from a place of desperation, or renewed hope, or sexual desire.

While some try to hold out some hope in a process that so often feels hopeless, others maintain high levels of skepticism even as they continue to engage in the activity. Every method has its benefits; no method is foolproof. Rules meant to protect can backfire. Anticipating double standards, mixed messages, and hidden agendas causes cynicism and mistrust toward the very individuals from whom love and romance are sought. The medium itself can pull for disinhibition, dehumanization, and a lack of accountability. Even when people have felt the pain of being deceived, ignored, or disrespected, many still resist the obligation to be sensitive about the needs of others.

There is a flip side to this. In a busy world, the apps are opening new portals for meeting people. They offer freedom to engage new people and new experiences without worrying so much about the consequences or reverberations within the safety of one's world. Ultimately, people are working on matters of the heart—replete with all of the games, idiosyncrasies, and mood swings that have always existed in dating, romance, and love. Online dating offers a new medium with different norms, bringing new challenges and opportunities to an old and well-established game.

ACKNOWLEDGMENTS

Thank you to Lisa Moise, Alex Silverman, Ana Lomidze, and Matthew Berler for their execution of the online dating study and their work in developing the ideas shared in this chapter through extensive analysis of the focus groups. Thank you also to Vendela Parker for her valuable contributions and edits during the revision process.

Leora Trub is an associate professor of psychology in the school/ clinical-child PsyD program at Pace University, and a practicing psychologist based in New York City. She runs the Digital Media and Psychology lab, which explores how technologies affect our conceptions of ourselves and our relationships with others, as well as the underlying psychological and emotional needs they meet. Recent projects include a qualitative study of the perspectives and experiences of psychoanalytic clinicians on the impact of technology on psychotherapy practice, and the development of an app aimed at increasing mindfulness during text-based interactions.

REFERENCES

Anderson, M., Vogels, E., & Turner, E. (2020, February 6). The virtues and downsides of online dating. Pew Research Center. https://www.pewresearch.org/internet/2020/02/06/the-virtues-and-downsides-of-online-dating/

Balick, A. (2018). *The psychodynamics of social networking: Connected-up instantaneous culture and self.* Routledge.

Blackwell, C., Birnholtz, J., & Abbott, C. (2014). Seeing and being seen: Co-situation and impression formation using Grindr, a location-aware gay dating app. *New Media and Society, 17*(7), 1117–1136.

Brown, A. (2020). Nearly half of U.S. adults say dating has gotten harder for most people in the last 10 years. Pew Research Center. https://www.pewsocialtrends.org/2020/08/20/nearly-half-of-u-s-adults-say-dating-has-gotten-harder-for-most-people-in-the-last-10-years/

Brown, B. (2015). *Daring greatly: How the courage to be vulnerable transforms the way we live, love, parent, and lead.* Penguin.

Clement, J. (2020). Online dating in the United States—statistics and facts. Statista. https://www.statista.com/topics/2158/onlinedating/

Cody, M. J., Hall, J. A., Park, N., & Song, H. (2010). Strategic misrepresentation in online dating: The effects of gender, self-monitoring, and personality traits. *Journal of Social and Personal Relationships, 27*(1), 117–135.

Couch, D., & Liamputtong, P. (2008). Online dating and mating: The use of the internet to meet sexual partners. *Qualitative Health Research, 18*(2), 268–279.

Drouin, M., Miller, D., Wehle, S. M. J., & Hernandez, E. (2016). Why do people lie online? "Because everyone lies on the internet." *Computers in Human Behavior, 64,* 134–142.

Essig, T., Trub, L., & Magaldi, D. (2018). Technology, Intimacy and the Simulation of Intimacy. In G. Kanwal & S. Akhtar (Eds.), *Intimacy: Clinical, cultural, digital and developmental perspectives.* Routledge.

Gibbs, J. L., Ellison, N. B., & Lai, C. H. (2010). First comes love, then comes Google: An investigation of uncertainty reduction strategies and self-disclosure in online dating. *Communication Research, 38*(1), 70–100.

Hall, J. A., Park, N., Song, H., & Cody, M. J. (2010). Strategic misrepresentation in online dating: The effects of gender, self-monitoring, and personality traits. *Journal of Social and Personal Relationships, 27*(1), 117–135.

Heino, R. D., Ellison, N. B., & Gibbs, J. L. (2010). Relationshopping: Investigating the market metaphor in online dating. *Journal of Social and Personal Relationships, 27*(4), 427–447.

High, A. C., & Wotipka, C. D. (2016). An idealized self or the real me? Predicting attraction to online dating profiles using selective self-presentation and warranting. *Communication Monographs, 83*(3), 281–302.

Hobbs, M., Owen, S., & Gerber, L. (2016). Liquid love? Dating apps, sex, relationships and the digital transformation of intimacy. *Journal of Sociology, 53*(2), 271–284.

Leonhardt, D. (2006, March 28). The famous founder of Operation Match. *New York Times.* https://www.nytimes.com/2006/03/28/business/the-famous-founder-of-operation -match.html

Meisenzahl, M. (2020, August 5). These charts from Match Group show more people are turning to online dating during the pandemic. Business Insider. https:// www.businessinsider.com/tinder-hinge-match-group-dating-apps-more-users -coronavirus-2020-8

Orchard, T. (2020, February 11). Gen Z dating culture defined by sexual flexibility and complex struggles for intimacy. *Science X.* https://phys.org/news/2020 -02-gen-dating-culture-sexual-flexibility.html

Ramirez, A., Sumner, E. M. B., Fleuriet, C., & Cole, M. (2014). When online dating partners meet offline: The effect of modality switching on relational communication between online daters. *Journal of Computer-Mediated Communication, 20*(1), 99–114. doi:10.1111/jcc4.12101

Rosenfeld, M. J., Thomas, R. J., & Hausen, S. (2019). Disintermediating your friends: How online dating in the United States displaces other ways of meeting. *Proceedings of the National Academy of Sciences, 116*(36), 17753–17758.

Runions, K., & Bak, M. (2015). Online moral disengagement, cyberbullying, and cyber-aggression. *Cyberpsychology, Behavior, and Social Networking, 18*(7), 400–405.

Schneider, K. J. (2019). *The spirituality of awe: Challenges to the Robotic Revolution* (rev. ed.). University Professors Press.

Schwartz, B. (2004, January). *The paradox of choice: Why more is less.* Ecco.

Suler, J. (2004). The online disinhibition effect. *Cyberpsychology and Behavior, 7*(3), 321–326.

Trub, L., & Barbot, B. (2016). The paradox of phone attachment: Development and validation of the Young Adult Attachment to Phone Scale (YAPS). *Computers in Human Behavior, 64,* 663–672.

Trub, L., & Barbot, B. (2020). Great escape or path to self-expression? Development and validation of a scale of motivations for text messaging. *Measurement and Evaluation in Counseling and Development, 53*(1), 44–61.

Trub, L., Revenson, T., & Salbod, S. (2014). Getting close from far away: Mediators of the relation between adult attachment and blogging behavior. *Computers in Human Behavior, 41,* 245–252.

Turkle, S. (2011a). *Alone together: Why we expect more from technology and less from each other.* Basic Books.

Turkle, S. (2011b). *Evocative objects: Things we think with.* (Ed.). MIT Press.

Weigel, M. (2016). *Labor of love: The invention of dating.* Farrar, Straus and Giroux.

CHAPTER 12

Graduating Into a Pandemic

New Grads Navigating Work Life in 2020

ZACHARY GELLER

"**E**ven though I haven't started my new job yet, I'm nervous I'm going to mess up." It is mid-August, the season when college grads with new jobs would typically be getting ready to head off to new cities for their first experiences away from home, with schooling now behind them. But this year is different. Will is speaking to me from his childhood bedroom in his parents' suburban home. He won't be heading into an office any time soon; he will be starting this job remotely. And though he hasn't even started work yet, he's worried that he's already lost his spot.

"And what is going to happen if you mess up?" I ask. I sense the anxiety in Will's voice—the worry that things as they stand are tenuous. One mistake and he's out. As we get started in this first consultation, I hope to give him a chance to speak freely about his worries.

"I don't know. Maybe I'd mess something up, and my boss would get angry, and I'd get fired. . . . It's weird because I interned there last summer, and everything went fine. But this will be different—this is a real job, not an internship."

As I hear a bit more about the job and the internship, I am struck by how clearly this advertising firm wants Will, and how well he did in the internship. The full-time job has him working in the same industry and with the same client as during the internship; his boss has let him know how excited she is that he's returning; and he's been given a generous compensation package.

In addition to the truly global uncertainty in which we are all living, what is it about Will's life progression so far—which he shares with his contemporaries—that adds to this anxiety? As I get to know Will, I get more of the sense that there is almost no amount of reassurance that will let him feel comfortable with his current situation.

Lindsey is also a recent college graduate. Having just finished with an engineering degree, she—like others of her cohort—finds herself living back with her parents. Near her childhood home on Long Island, New York, she has found a job in a shipping fulfillment center. The work is satisfying and keeps her busy, which in itself is important. But Lindsey struggles aloud to know whether or not the work is sufficiently fulfilling to her—if it is setting her off on a path, not to mention her sense of knowing that she is not using her engineering degree in this first job.

I hear Lindsey's conflict about her current work situation as both developmentally appropriate and specifically impacted by the current acute global situation. In one sense, she is in the thick of Erikson's identity versus role confusion conflict, a strong resolution of which would result in a sense of fidelity to herself and her own developing sense of values and beliefs. In another sense, though, I hear her as in the throes of something more paralyzing and more specific to this moment in time: she is being pulled toward a more familiar, close-to-home situation, with the inertia of her childhood home being stronger than ever.

In what ways is her choice of work playing out in a way typically seen? Lindsey had an internship at an engineering firm after her junior year of college, and a subpar end-of-summer project submission seems to have knocked her out of the running for a full-time job offer. While previous to that Lindsey would tell me that she was excited about a full-time engineering position, after that blow, it all seemed up for debate. The idea of pursuing a full-time regular job became mired in her view of her parents' life of "just living to work," which meant no opportunity for recreation or passion—an empty existence. The failure to convert the internship into a job also seemed to up the ante in terms of taking the risk to shoot for a more competitive position: it might hurt to try and then not achieve the goal. When Lindsey started talking about taking a "more humble" job, I heard this as possibly an interest in a different sort of work, but more likely a signal that she was afraid to take a risk again.

But in what ways is her career situation also facilitated by the current context, and what might it mean for Lindsey and her cohort? What does the coronavirus pandemic, which in 2020 turned the world upside down, have to do with it? For one thing, in the fall of her senior year, in 2019, Lindsey thought about graduating and going on to live in a city with college friends, taking an apartment and beginning to step out on her own. Maybe she'd pick a city further from home. At that time, she looked forward to the period after graduation with an understandable mix of excitement and trepidation. While she'd be able to live freely, she'd also be responsible for herself. When she let herself think about this period of time, it made sense to me: it would be a fun period, a new period, but also a tough adjustment. She would have to take care of herself.

But only a few months later, the world changed. Lindsey's final semester at school was cut short, and she finished it from her parents' home. While some members of the class of 2020 were recruited to new jobs, the pandemic also gave many college graduates the opportunity to avert the task of confronting the difficulties of stepping out on one's own for the first time. While the economic crises of the past, such as 2008, created a tougher job market for many who otherwise would be able to secure a job, the pandemic of 2020 added on a new sort of crisis: the inability to move freely in the world. And while it would be possible for someone in Lindsey's shoes to move to a new city on her own, it would be very hard. New barriers abound. Not only is there inertia toward home, not only is it more comfortable, but it is also more realistic.

As Lindsey delved more into the difficulty of figuring out whether she should stay in her "more humble," satisfying, but in other ways not-challenging job, or pursue a line of work that might more fully engage her intellectual capacities, she got stuck on feeling like nothing was pushing her. "Maybe if I *had* to work," she said. "Maybe if I had to support myself. Really this job right now is just to keep me busy. But I wouldn't need to have it." For Lindsey, being at home takes away her opportunity to see this as a moment when something is actually at stake in terms of her own choices and desires. That is, while there is not a financial imperative, there is a more invisible developmental imperative for her to begin to consolidate one aspect of herself around work and the desire to support herself. And the need—or, perhaps, the option—to be at home in the pandemic situation allows for a way around that developmental imperative.

In more typical times, many young adults like Lindsey and Will would fulfill a particular cultural expectation of moving away; living at home might be seen only as a manifestation of conflicted feelings about leaving the family and going out on one's own. Depending on one's point of view, one could see a college graduate living at home as a financial reality, or perhaps a choice for the moment to push off to another day the need to leave the nest. In 2020, though, the real-life scenario has tilted the scales of our understanding of the situation much more strongly in the direction of necessity. That is to say, the need to stay home, the inability to mix socially with others, and the ripple effects of the economic constriction have meant that many 20-somethings all but *must* move back home. What does this mean for their individual development, over and above the ways that these conflicts might present themselves in more typical times?

For one, many 20-somethings today miss out on the opportunity to struggle through the small and big choices that make up in total what it means to carve out one's own new identity and choice of work. A first job, and the next few jobs that may quickly follow that one—which we know are more typical in the modern economy—are all opportunities to begin to create work that is meaningful to the individual. While the adolescent years are spent trying on different ways of being in the interpersonal world, the early work years are spent trying on different ways to make meaningful contributions to the world and to develop one's sense of self through work. A more challenging economy results for many in an inability to find that first job—which does not mean just financial stressors to the individual and the family, but also represents a loss of the chance to try on that first way of contributing. A first job and those that follow are all steps of establishing both identity and independence. Identity is demonstrated not just in one's values or beliefs, or the company one keeps, but how one chooses to spend time productively. It answers questions like, What matters to me? How can I contribute? What do I like to do with my time, and how much money do I need to have for my work? And so a loss of a first job opportunity, or a loss of a first job that is a match for an individual's capacities and interests, presents the potential loss of starting to wrestle with these questions. For many from backgrounds where it is even financially possible for the family, the response can be a retreat to being taken care of by parents. For others, the response must be to jump into any available way to earn money, at the expense of beginning to consolidate an identity around work.

Separation from parents is a lifelong process. In infancy and childhood, the child explores safe physical distances away from the parents; in adolescence, the teenager explores emotional distance and relationships outside the home; and in emerging adulthood, the young person explores independence in terms of intimate relationships, but also in terms of responsibility for one-self. The loss of this opportunity dovetails with the loss of the opportunity to explore first meaningful jobs. Even if a young 20-something stays close to home, in a typical time, she has the chance to begin to establish independent rhythms in her own new living situation out of the family home. She begins to take stock of her income and what she can afford; she begins to prioritize how to fit in tasks of daily living and managing a household. The loss of work and the increased likelihood of living at home trickle down to dilute these developmental tasks (Fry et al., 2020). While it may be nice to be taken care of, young adults at home today fall back into adolescent ways of being that pad the responsibilities that surround work. Instead of fitting in their tasks of daily living around the work day, they may take a break to eat a meal prepared by their parents.

For Rebecca, I see a different set of phenomena unfolding that I take to be manifestations of patterns of parenting and how they impact 20-somethings heading into the workforce today. Rebecca was referred to me because of struggles dealing with the isolation of the pandemic. I understood from the referral that she was completing her first year of law school and maybe was struggling to know whether or not this was the path for her. We started working over video together in the summer, with her living at home with her parents outside of New York City, before returning to law school on the West Coast.

As I listened, she told me about her total indifference in the face of choosing whether or not to pursue this career. She told me it seemed to make the most sense; she couldn't think of anything else to do; and the fact that her parents were lawyers had nothing to do with her choice to also be a lawyer. It was almost as though she had finished her last year of college—grade 16—and the big assignment for grade 17 was to do the things necessary to pursue the most sensible job. She told me about having volunteered at legal aid societies and not having been very moved by the experience, and that she was even doubtful that as a lawyer she could have much impact or satisfaction.

I thought I'd have an opportunity to slow us down and consider other lines of work. Perhaps the train had not totally left the station. Being not even halfway through the first year, surely she could cut some of her losses and have the time and space to think about what might hold more meaning for her if law seem to be all but meaningless. But I was stymied: this was the path she would stay on. Met with almost a foregone conclusion, I saw that this was the way things were going to go.

What felt generational to me here wasn't the choice of law or even the difficulty in broadening the choices but more the difficulty in seeing the possibility that work could be an expression of what Rebecca might want to do, or what she might find interesting. This fits into a broader narrative for 20-somethings of being raised by parents who were much more motivated than those before them to set their children up for success, which for many entering the workforce today was measured in grades, names of institutions, and prestige of jobs. These parents are often described as "helicopter" or even more recently as "snowplow" parents who variously hovered around their kids, ready to swoop in should anything go wrong, or in the latter case, to preemptively clear obstacles out of the way ahead of them.

The helicoptering around or snowplowing in front of 20-somethings entering the workforce today may have eased their difficult moments in childhood. Their parents, seeing any potential problems unfolding around them, were able to help them continue to move forward through their achievements. What's lost in that arrangement, though, is the notion that through confronting obstacles on their own, burgeoning adults might—in the act of confronting them—begin to build a sense not just of how to manage obstacles but how and why and which ones they might want to manage. From the bottom up, in taking on challenges, kids take practice steps toward building their own identities. When ease is privileged above opportunities to wrestle, the idea is reinforced that only progress matters. "Just get to the next step." And a sense of why things are even worked through is lost.

As I reflected on Rebecca's assessment of her situation, I felt like she had arrived exactly where she and her family would have hoped. And on the face of it, from one perspective, that would be OK. She was set up to finish her first year—about which she actually was not concerned—and proceed further into law. It would seem like a dream.

But developmentally, it seemed as though Rebecca might buzz right past the point at which she would get to stop and think about what would be meaningful for her to do and to contribute through, to see what would make up a major part of her life. It wasn't as though she said to me, "I just don't know what else I could do." The question wasn't available to her. My efforts to bring up even the possibility that other work exists—that she could do work that she might be drawn to—were fruitless, and it was clear that we would be left to do what we could where we were: on her path into law.

"I just want someone to tell me exactly what I need to do. If they can tell me what I need to do, I can do it." This statement to Rebecca made perfect sense: this would be grade 17 of being told what to do and having the task clearly teed up, and she could then hit the task head-on. Even in law—a highly regimented training progression—the tasks appeared too loosely formed for her. Who exactly should she ask for letters of recommendation? When she is assigned to a group project, who in the group should decide the meeting time? Why did it take so long for the instructor to release the answer key for a recent exam?

I came to see my task as trying to create a little space in which Rebecca might now and then be able to see an opportunity for agency as she goes along her path. Her training could proceed in a series of default choices: take the required courses, sign up for the required exams, attend office hours at an optimal frequency. But there are times when each step along the way is not just an obstacle to be cleared but, rather, an opportunity to see that there are options from which she can choose—which can start to seed her capacity to later take steps toward identity and independence through work. For instance, in an elective course, students watched prerecorded videos of lectures and then submitted responses to questions via message board. On the informal part of the message board, she saw other students talking about a live discussion section happening in a video conference, which she realized was an alternative to some of the prerecorded lectures. For weeks she had been telling me how isolated she felt, that she felt unable to connect with other students because of COVID-19. Despite this sense of isolation, she had no interest in joining the live video discussion group. The opportunity to join a discussion section was only seen as inefficient: a poor use of time and an impediment to getting through requirements on the way to the degree. I heard this perception as a product of a goal-oriented, progress-focused upbringing in the context of a generation of parents who in many cases wanted to clear the way for their kids. In Rebecca's case—illustrative of many others her age—she wasn't too used to stopping to smell the roses, even when they were exactly what she needed.

When Rebecca became slightly open to the possibility that a discussion section might help her meet classmates and ease her isolation, these positives came right up against the drive to proceed. And for the first time that I got to hear, she wrestled with a choice on her own terms. Could she enroll in a less efficient discussion section, giving herself a chance to meet people and hear others' perspectives, at the cost of watching prerecorded lectures at accelerated speed and cramming in the material at a faster pace? The emergence of this conflict was meaningful progress, as it had heretofore been out of the realm of possibility altogether.

There are a few themes I observe as characteristic of 20-somethings at work today that seem endemic to their generation and also embedded in the context of a pandemic. For one, they are getting off a high-pressured, success-focused track that they have been on for a long time. It's almost as if the tunnel vision goggles are coming off, and they may be able to look around and see how they feel about their choices, but it's more likely that they will have to build anew a sense of what matters to them and how they want to pursue that. It may be difficult for some of them to see the opportunity to make meaning through work that is separate from success. Second, the track of success may have been very well plowed ahead of them, and their first unaccompanied encounters with the ambiguities of independent life may be more painful than those of their parents' generation. And third, where perhaps the endemic features interact with the setting of the pandemic, I see 20-somethings heading to work today as stalled right before they have the chance to find and pursue work they care about, with something on the line practically and developmentally. That is, their grooming to succeed, the likelihood that their parents have cleared obstacles for them, and the increased chance that they may be living at home may all conspire to allow them to perhaps unwittingly abrogate their task of getting out there on their own, finding what they want to do, and making it all work.

My primary worry as I see these struggles is that some of these young people will get locked in to some kind of compromise wherein they feel both less responsible for themselves and less interested in making meaning during this period of time. And that the comfort of that compromise—despite the loss of opportunity—may be very tempting to stay in even once we have moved on from this pandemic, whatever that may mean. Will young adults live at home even longer? Will they settle for work that is less meaningful?

It would seem to me that on the other side of this compromise is tremendous opportunity for rejuvenated interest in independence and meaning. How will this be more likely to come about? It will certainly take some active intervening by both young adults and their parents to rouse everyone out of their unexpected new situation. While many young adults and their parents are experiencing the stresses of life together, they also experience its familiarity and ease. To be able to seize upon the developmental opportunity when the pandemic lifts will take a fight against inertia by everyone involved.

I imagine that many of us in the helping professions will continue to consult with young adults thrown for a loop by the interaction between their generational inheritance and the events of 2020. I see some of them as having been primed to stall at this moment of opportunity, and the coronavirus pandemic may have been just the right event to slow them down at this developmental milestone. For young people to release themselves from the compromised position in which many now find themselves, they'll have to find ways to see the opportunities for independence and meaning that await them.

Zachary Geller is a clinical psychologist in independent practice in Brooklyn, New York where he works with children, adolescents, and adults. He received his PhD from The City College of New York. Dr. Geller has taught undergraduate and graduate courses in psychotherapy, developmental and abnormal psychology, and the psychology of technology, and currently supervises clinical doctoral trainees from City College. He is also a psychoanalytic training candidate at the NYU Postdoctoral Program in Psychotherapy and Psychoanalysis. Prior to his training in this field, Dr. Geller worked in learning and development at Google in New York. He lives with his family in Brooklyn.

REFERENCE

Fry, R., Passel, J. S., & Cohn, D. (2020, September 4). A majority of young adults in the U.S. live with their parents for the first time since the Great Depression. Pew Research Center. https://www.pewresearch.org/fact-tank/2020/09/04/a-majority -of-young-adults-in-the-u-s-live-with-their-parents-for-the-first-time-since-the-great -depression/

CHAPTER 13

Treating Frontline Workers Analytically, Pandemic and All

DANIELLE LA ROCCO

On March 26, 2020, four days after Governor Cuomo's PAUSE order put New York City into suspended animation, my psychoanalytic institute exploded—or as much as it could over Zoom. In one of my courses, History of Drive Theory in Freud, a classmate announced that her analyst had written a letter to a professional society suggesting, essentially, that those of us continuing to practice psychoanalysis during the coronavirus pandemic, those of us who were keeping on keeping on, were kidding ourselves. What was left of analysis? What were we really offering to our patients, when the proverbial bombs were still falling from the sky? How could we be of any help? This classmate and myself, having heard this idea, were stricken. What did she mean, we didn't have analysis anymore? As we were digesting this, the instructor for the class took the side of the letter writer, arguing that we have to have some kind of freedom, some leisure, to have analysis, to let our minds wander, to let our unconsciouses speak and to have room for new ideas. We were swimming in time during lockdown, sure, but we had no leisure. Something had been lost, and we would do well to acknowledge that.

And, of course, something had been lost. The frontline workers I was treating in my practice needed no reminder of that. But I was hurt by the notion that I could not treat them analytically anymore. Why, though, was this such a painful idea? I had just learned that my own analyst had closed his Manhattan office permanently. I wondered if I had to hang on to the thought that what I had left—individual analysis over the phone, group therapy on a screen—was still analysis, because if it wasn't, what was I spending all this time even doing? Not to mention, what was I doing for my patients? And why had I pursued this extra training? Had my career as an analyst ended at the start?

I had graduated my fellowship in child and adolescent psychiatry the previous July, following four years of residency training in adult psychiatry. Much of that training is focused on symptom reduction, and often in the form of some kind of directive: Take this medication. Try this coping skill. See this specialist. Sometimes, people do follow through on those instructions, to great success. At others, though, the most motivated-seeming patients will stop taking their prescriptions, or won't try that mindfulness app, or give all kinds of reasons they can't go see that sleep medicine doctor, despite how distressed they were at their first appointment. This can ruffle some major feathers in the medical world—why won't this patient just do what I told them to, if they want to feel better?!

Some of the curriculum during training was focused on psychodynamic psychotherapy, which stands on the theory that we have an unconscious that might push us, out of our awareness, to do things that we do not (consciously) want to do. I took some additional courses in psychoanalysis (and got myself into analysis), and learned more about the reasons why people might reject the very help they say they want, sometimes more than once—the repetition is a memory, and symptoms have meaning. "The patient cannot remember the whole of what is repressed in him," describes Freud (1920/1955, p. 18) in "Beyond the Pleasure Principle." The patient is "obliged to *repeat* the repressed material as a contemporary experience instead of . . . *remembering* it as something belonging to the past." As an analyst, my role could be to help my patients find out what they are repeating and why, to help them bear whatever pain has been so destructive as to push them to act it out over and over again in a search for mastery. In other words, the patient may not be able to tell you what hurts, but they can show you.

I wanted more, and I was willing to commit for the long haul, so by January 2020, I had just opened my private practice as a full-time gig and started my first semester of formal analytic training. Then the pandemic hit, my analytic institute went online, and my practice filled immediately with young adult medical professionals looking for grounding and understanding in multiple areas of their lives, not only about the crisis. I loved working with this population, and in such an open-ended way. Being a new student, I had no illusions that I was offering my current patients a full-on analysis. That said, I was talking to my patients about their unconsciouses, and asking about transference, and doing a lot of listening, and thinking about resistance. If analysis were a full-option rental car, with a convertible roof and a GPS and heated seats, I at least thought I was offering more than the standard rental—a hybrid car with a moon roof, say? But now, should I be telling my patients there was no point in renting a car at all during this pandemic? I was dealing with frontline workers, after all. Who has time for all this slow listening, anyway? Why drive when a plane is faster?

At least one thing I could offer my patients during the pandemic, for sure, was privacy (at least from other humans—my cats love a video conference, so from them, not so much). To that end, the case that follows is fictional. However, the conflicts that arise in this story are real, and illustrate some of the reasons why, during a semester devoted to learning Freud's drive theory in the midst of a global crisis, I took the slow road with my patients.

CLARA, WHO SHOULD HAVE KNOWN

In April 2020, Clara was a third-year medical student in her mid-20s, rotating on a surgical unit. One morning, she had come into the hospital early to start her prerounding, which involves interviewing and examining patients before the rest of the team (the interns, residents, and attending physician) conducts formal rounds. She started with Tim, who had been admitted for an elective gallbladder removal. Practicing her thorough review of systems, Clara asked Tim about any symptoms he might be having. Neurological: Do you have a headache? Ear, nose, and throat: Runny nose? Respiratory: Sore throat, cough, shortness of breath? Gastrointestinal: Constipation? Abdominal pain? Apart from the expected right upper quadrant pain, he answered the rest of the questions "no." Dermatological: Any new rashes? When Tim indicated that, now that she mentioned it, his first toe on his right foot was itching, Clara took a quick look and saw a faint reddish lesion that looked like he'd been scratching it, but thought it could be from any number of common causes: a contact allergy from the detergent in the hospital-issued socks, or a minor abrasion from wearing uncomfortable ski boots on a recent trip. He wasn't sure when it had started. She noted it down, prerounded on her other patients, and in about an hour presented her findings during formal rounds to her team, none of whom were particularly alarmed. Tim was operated on and discharged the next day.

One week later, Tim returned to the emergency room, alarmed by the fact that the initial itching of his big toe had morphed into swelling and numbness, and now his other toes itched. An emergency room resident who had been following the latest COVID research had read case reports of patients presenting with "COVID toes" as a rare, but increasingly recognized presentation of COVID. He ordered a COVID test, which returned positive. Clara and her team were immediately notified of the possible exposure. During the time Tim was in Clara's team's care, they had been wearing adequate PPE in the form of simple surgical masks, but the hospital had advised them to save the now-infamous N95 masks for patients "under investigation" for COVID. Tim had had no respiratory symptoms or fever, and was not in any kind of isolation room during his first admission; Clara and her team had dutifully followed hospital policy, and were only wearing regular surgical masks. Her whole team was sent for COVID testing and asked to quarantine at least until their tests returned negative. Clara's was positive. While waiting out her isolation period, she and the chief of surgery went through all of her charts to find out who else she (and her entire team) may have exposed. This is how she learned about Anne. Clara had rounded on Anne after seeing Tim. She had been admitted for an appendectomy and was discharged shortly afterward, but, like Tim, had returned to the hospital COVID-positive, and was now intubated. Clara had a panic attack on the phone with the chief of surgery, who called her dean, who referred her to me.

In our first few sessions (over video), Clara talked about the anxiety she felt. "I took an oath to do no harm, and I did harm," she described tearfully, horrified by the idea that she, a medical student, in training to be a healer, may have given Anne a fatal illness. In an effort to help Clara see herself in a kinder light, I asked her, "How were you supposed to avoid this?" She and her team were adhering to hospital guidelines, trying to keep their colleagues and their patients safe by reserving the most protective PPE for the people most in need, and Tim had not presented with any symptoms suggesting that he needed that level of care. Was her other option to use an N95 with the knowledge that they were in short supply, and put a colleague—and thus that person's patients—at risk?

"I know, but I should have reviewed the literature," she went on, saying that in a once-in-a-generation medical event, the least she could have done was stay on top of the research. She was the first to know about Tim's skin lesion, and she should have investigated further. The medical student's role on the team, she would explain, is to pay attention to all of the details, to look up every little thing, to think of zebras when she hears hoofbeats. "I had enough time that morning. I could have stopped between patients and done a lit review. I could have known." We completed our three-session consultation, and I asked her if she'd like to continue seeing me. She thanked me for my time, saying that the sessions were helpful, but in the end, how could she justify taking up all this time with me when Anne's family needed more help than she did? I let her know that if at any time she wanted to come back, she was welcome to.

Ten days later, she called for an appointment. In our next session, Clara let me know that contact tracing on Anne found that it was much more likely she had gotten COVID at a house party the previous week. Anne had developed a cough the day after her discharge from the hospital, and within days had required intubation. The interval between Clara's contact with Tim and her contact with Anne was, now that she thought about it, too short for her to have been the vector. Nobody else on her surgical team tested positive, and Anne made a surprising and full recovery. Clara herself did not develop any symptoms and was soon to be cleared to return to work. Clara, it seemed, was off the hook.

Though it was a great relief to me, Clara did not gain any solace from this turn of events. In fact, she was having difficulty sleeping, finding herself lying in bed thinking the same thought over and over: "I should have known." We agreed to see each other weekly. Trying to sit equally between id, ego, super-ego, and reality, for the first few weeks, I kept trying to speak for the last of those, just because it seemed so clear: "But *how* were you supposed to know, Clara?" At the time she saw Tim, there were only a few case reports in Italy of COVID toes, and only in children. It was by the time Tim came back to the hospital thatprofessional organizations in the states had pieced together what was happening. "Yeah, but the news was out there. He *told* me on his review of systems, and I even *saw* the lesion." In another session, I tried humor, "Ah, so you were supposed to learn Italian on your surgical rotation, too?" "Not funny."

I wasn't getting anywhere. I changed up my approach, and took a page from modern analytical thought, joining her in her self-attack: "You got part of the story, and didn't try to get the rest." "Yeah, exactly!" she said between tissues. "I had the information nobody else had." "And that made you responsible to do something with it." "Precisely." Well, at least I was starting to form a rapport. As frightening as this experience was, her self-recrimination and expectations of herself didn't quite fit the situation. What from the past, I wondered, was repeating itself here? What else should she have known?

I kept an open ear. For one session, she logged on to my telemedicine site seven minutes late. "Sorry, I was talking to my dad." "What about?" "Oh nothing, I probably shouldn't have even picked up. He wanted to ask me how to log in to Instagram." "Ah, I see," I said, chuckling. It was the first time she was late, and for the moment, I took it at face value. For the next few sessions, though, while we would talk about how her anxiety symptoms were affecting her sleep, and we weighed the pros and cons of possibly starting an antidepressant to help, there would be some interruption related to her dad. He might text and she'd respond, or he'd call and she'd pick up, if just to say, "Can I call you back later?" This would be followed by her apologizing for the loss of time and talking about how annoyed she was that he called so frequently.

As the instructor for my class put it, "The conscious resists; the unconscious insists," and often in the form of some interruption (Hurst, 2014, p. 41). In his essay "The Repetition Compulsion; the Repetition Automatism; the Insistence of the Signifying Chain," Hurst relays a story Freud would tell lay audiences: imagine you are at a performance of a play. Some of the audience (let's put this in contemporary terms) refuses to turn off their cell phones, or unwraps their noisy candy packaging before the curtain comes up. Imagine, then, that these interruptions become so distracting as to lead the quieter audience members to kick the troublemakers out of the theater. This, points out Hurst, is repression. Ultimately, however, the outcast audience members start to bang on the doors and prevent the play from continuing. The interruptions become the main event, and the analyst's job is to hear them. "We have learned through our experience as analysts and analysands, to hear the interruptions, the intrusions—the background—as the insistence of the unconscious" (Hurst, 2014, p. 41).

Keeping this in mind, but exploring a bit of reality, I asked Clara, "Seems like it's bothering you to pick up. Do you have to answer right when he calls?" "I don't want to, but I feel bad." "Feel bad about what?" "Not answering." "Feel bad, like feel guilty?" "Yeah." "What's the crime?" "What do you mean?" "If you're feeling guilty, guilty of what crime?" "Oh, huh . . . I just always feel guilty not doing what my dad asks me to do." "Why? Is it your job to do everything he asks you to?" "Well . . . "

Over the next few sessions, out came the following story of her life. Clara had grown up with two parents and a younger brother, Paul. Her father, Steve, was a journalist, and her mother, Lucy, worked for a pharmaceutical company. She described the family as being close. As a little girl, she enjoyed cooking with her mother. Lucy was an excellent chef and taught Clara cooking skills that would later endlessly impress her friends: how to make the five French mother sauces, how to know when a roast chicken is ready without using a meat thermometer, how to hand-make noodles. Clara had a memory of being 11, making scones with her mom, and her mom forgetting the recipe, which she had never done.

"How many cups of flour is it, again, Clara?" Lucy asked, giggling, and then dropped the measuring cup. Clara remembered being a little nervous, but she was old enough to know that parents aren't perfect, and laughed it off. But little things would happen here and there: Lucy would forget she had put dinner in the oven already and go looking for it on the kitchen counter, or she would swap out key ingredients at the grocery store. Her dad and brother weren't interested in cooking (they were always on cleanup duty), and her mom was a good enough chef that she could rescue whatever they were cooking without the dish suffering, so Clara thought, "Well, what's the big deal?" Clara always felt older than her age, and in her preteen years, she remembered thinking that this is what maturity must feel like—you see your parents' imperfections in higher and higher relief.

One day, Lucy picked Paul up from soccer practice and got into a car accident—she turned right on red at a dangerous intersection where that was not allowed, despite the fact that she had driven this route numerous times. An oncoming car rear-ended them, and luckily, the driver was kind enough to stay and call an ambulance. When the EMTs arrived, they found that Lucy was explaining the series of events in a confusing manner—she could not seem to describe how or why she had gone through the light. Thinking she had suffered a concussion, the EMTs brought both Lucy and Paul (who had suffered some minor abrasions but was otherwise unhurt) to the hospital.

Clara remembers being 13 and going with her dad to the hospital to meet them. When she and her dad walked into Lucy's hospital room, she overheard the doctor say, "How many are you taking a day?" Steve asked, "How many what?" Lucy finally admitted that she had been taking samples of a sleep medication sold by her pharmaceutical company, in escalating doses, for years. It had started around the time that Clara saw her mom drop the measuring cup and forget the scone recipe. When Clara told her dad about what she had remembered, and all the other times her mom seemed off, her dad was furious. "Why didn't you tell me if you knew?" "I didn't know," insisted Clara. "I didn't know what was happening." Though Lucy achieved sobriety and Steve and Lucy went to couples therapy, nothing seemed to touch Steve's rage at being kept in the dark, and when Clara was 15, they divorced.

"I still feel guilty about not telling my dad what I saw. I thought something was different. I just didn't know what was wrong." "How could you have known?" "I was the one there who saw it happen, so many times. Imagine if I had said something earlier." "Ah, you had the information and—" "It was my responsibility to—oh. Wait."

Over the next several months, we began to unpack what Clara repeated during COVID-19: not only the horror of what had happened with her patients Tim and Anne, but the experience of feeling responsible for solving a problem when she had insufficient, preliminary information. Clara could see her overresponsibility popping up in other places, too, as when her friend got lost trying to meet her in Central Park, and Clara herself apologized. ("For what?" "For . . . picking a confusing meeting spot? I don't know!") And she began to understand, at least from a logical, conscious point of view, that both her father and the hospital had a responsibility to keep her safe, and both had failed, whether intentionally or just as a side effect of dealing with an enormous unknown threat. When I asked, "Your father was a journalist, right?," Clara followed up with, "Isn't that weird? His whole job is to investigate things that don't make sense." I let a long silence follow. I am hopeful that over time, she will come to see (in her own words) that her father projected onto her his own failure to see and report on what was going on, and that she took this to heart.

MOURNING TO MAKE ROOM FOR GROWTH

Why treat frontline workers psychoanalytically? Why take time and listen for interruptions? Because they are people, and not immune from repeating. And why do this work with young adults, who have a million other things to be doing? As the developmental psychologist Erik Erikson would say, emerging adults are navigating the central tension between intimacy and isolation; what could be more in tune with this developmental task of forming real intimacy with others than to offer to witness a pain that had heretofore gone unnamed and unseen? And why now? What is the point of psychoanalysis during such a time of crisis? Is it even psychoanalysis anymore? Why not give up, write some prescriptions, refer out, and binge-watch *Billions*?

In his essay "On Transience," Freud (1916) recounts a story of walking through a countryside with two friends, one of whom, a poet, is totally unable to enjoy the vista, citing its impermanence as the reason for his demeanor. This scene, Freud later reveals, took place one year before World War I, which did ultimately destroy the landscape they had traversed. Freud postulates that "what spoilt [his friend's] enjoyment of beauty must have been a revolt" in his mind "against mourning" (1916, pp. 306–307). He continues that mourning is the refusal to renounce loved objects, "even when a substitute lies ready to hand." This, I thought: this is why. Mourning is what we have to do.

At the time of this writing, the pandemic has claimed over 500,000 lives and counting (*New York Times*, 2021). Our job with our patients is to mourn with them, to be sad with them about losing the time we had before the pandemic, when we could see each other in person, hand off a three-dimensional box of tissues, and not even think to look for the Purell after the fact. As painful as it is, our job is not to revolt against this loss, not to refuse to engage in this new form of being with our patients because it is so very different from what we had before. That would be opting out of the whole procedure, being the poet, refusing to love the flowers in front of him because it will hurt him when they die. Mourning, points out Freud, is self-limiting. "When it has renounced everything that has been lost, then it has consumed itself, and our libido is once more free . . . to replace the lost objects by fresh ones equally or still more precious." If we can mourn what we no longer have, we will ultimately be freed up, with our patients, to love something new.

Danielle La Rocco, MD, is a psychiatrist in private practice in New York City, working with adults, children, and adolescents. After completing her residency and fellowship at NYU, she began training to become a psychoanalyst at the Center for Modern Psychoanalytic Studies. She has a specific interest in working with children and families with a history of foster care or adoption. She lives with her husband and two cats, all of whom edited her chapter.

REFERENCES

Freud, S. (1916). On transience. In J. Strachey (Ed. & Trans.), *The standard edition of the complete psychological works of Sigmund Freud*.

Freud, S. (1955). Beyond the pleasure principle (Part III). In J. Strachey (Ed. & Trans.), *The standard edition of the complete psychological works of Sigmund Freud* (Vol. 18, pp. 18–23). Hogarth. (Original work published 1920)

Hurst, W. (2014). The repetition compulsion, the repetition automatism; the insistence of the signifying chain. *Modern Psychoanalysis, 39*, 38–55.

New York Times. (2021, March 7). COVID in the US: Latest map and case count. https://www.nytimes.com/interactive/2020/us/coronavirus-us-cases.html

Section III

YOUNG ADULTS IN TREATMENT

CHAPTER 14

DBT-YA

DBT Adapted for Emerging Adults and Their Families

KRISTIN P. WYATT AND
COLLEEN M. COWPERTHWAIT

I t is well established that emerging adults (EA) with mental health needs have difficulty navigating and seeking care in the developmentally divided child-adult health care system (e.g., Singh, 2009; Skehan & Davis, 2017). Further, as early career psychologists working with EA and suicidality specifically, our journey to find our programmatic and professional home is much the same as EA trying to find developmentally appropriate treatment. Before meeting at Duke and collaborating on dialectical behavior therapy with young adults (DBT-YA), we each stumbled into this work in our own way.

For Colleen, it started at her college internship, entering self-report questionnaire data at a private practice. Upon finishing early one day, she was instructed by her psychologist supervisor to watch some therapy training tapes in order to fulfill her time requirement for the day. The tapes turned out to be the ever-charismatic Marsha Linehan teaching DBT skills, launching Colleen's interests in DBT and emotion dysregulation. This interest in emotion dysregulation led to a research job in a bipolar disorder lab, and then applying to graduate school to study the effectiveness of cognitive-behavioral therapy (CBT) and DBT for emotionally dysregulated adolescents.

In contrast to Colleen's decisiveness, Kristin's path to DBT-Adolescent was bit more winding. Less clear on her specific clinical path, she joined a child and family services clinic in her first year of graduate school, eager to work with adolescents. Not long after, she encountered her first clinical cases with suicidality—a middle schooler and a college student. Feeling underresourced to manage these cases, her lack of training and skill were further magnified when one of them stormed out of an early session threatening suicide, mid-risk assessment. The ensuing fear was undeniably activating, leading her to discover DBT and to scramble to obtain adequate training to apply it with these teenagers.

In parallel universes, Colleen in Atlanta and Kristin in New York, we came to find the interpersonal sass, sharp BS detectors, and palpable teen angst of emotionally dysregulated youth both endearing and captivating in their complexity. Coleading multifamily groups with our respective DBT-A expert mentors during practicum training was a spirited and colorful affair, with teens and their parents offering endless challenges, laughter, and heartwarming exchanges. We both were sold. We quickly learned this work played to our strengths.

In seeking predoctoral internship sites for adolescents and EA with aims to continue our beloved training in treating young people and families, we found that these programs didn't exist, especially for DBT. Internship sites were either oriented around children and adolescents, or oriented around adults or anyone over the age of 18.

We each matched to Duke's adult-focused CBT track internship, one year apart, choosing the program for its renowned full-model DBT training with DBT expert faculty, both choosing to sacrifice desired age range for quality of DBT training. In matching to a DBT-focused internship at a major medical center with high volumes of high-complexity adult outpatients, we found ourselves treating struggling EA and their families with a lot of needs, in a program without structures and supports to accommodate them. Once Colleen arrived at Duke and joined Kristin, a then-postdoc, we began sharing our experiences as family-trained DBT clinicians in a DBT program oriented around individual adults. When we couldn't find the program we wanted for us or our patients, we decided to create it: an outpatient DBT program for 18- to 25-year-olds and their families in an academic medical center clinic. Similar to our process, EA and their families who find our program tell us about their difficulty finding treatment that "meets them where they are" and express disbelief after years of being misunderstood by the health system.

For EA who struggle with the problems DBT treats (suicidality, multiple comorbidities, emotion dysregulation, and impulsivity), the combination of these problems and developmental challenges amplify their mismatch with much of the health system. Our EA patients report feeling infantilized in child clinic waiting rooms filled with toys and play tables, in a health system with dichotomized child and adult service divisions. When they're in our clinic's adult-only DBT groups with group members 30 or 40 years their senior, they report thinking that their problems that interfere with quality of life are very different than those of their fellow group members. Similarly, when they're in adolescent DBT groups, they report that both their problems and the potential solutions available to them don't match up with what high school students need and are experiencing. Consistent with the literature, they report ambivalence about parental involvement in treatment and with treatment more broadly, and feeling utterly confused about how to navigate insurance, health care systems, and coordinating care among their providers without parental help (Paul et al., 2015; Wilson et al., 2011).

Given that this age group is high risk for suicide relative to others (e.g., Kessler et al., 1999) and has developmental factors likely to contribute to emotion dysregulation, we've found that our developmentally tailored, family-inclusive DBT-YA program is a remedy for many. In this chapter, we provide an overview of our program for EA and families. The overview includes a description of DBT, its relevance to the arguably at-risk population of EA, our adaptation of DBT to EA and families, and clinical examples to support clinicians in their work with this population.

WHAT IS DBT?

Dialectical behavior therapy is a principle-based, comprehensive multimodal treatment. It was originally developed for the outpatient treatment of suicide and self-harm in adults (Linehan, 1993a), including those with borderline personality disorder (BPD). Since then, DBT has been extended to suicidal adolescents (Miller et al., 2007) and broader presentations of the core problem in BPD, pervasive emotional dysregulation (Linehan, 1993a; Yen et al., 2002), such as comorbid eating and substance use disorders (Courbasson et al., 2012), and depression and personality disorder (Lynch et al., 2007).

The DBT model blends behavior therapy, Zen Buddhism, and dialectical philosophy, resulting in a case formulation–driven treatment that integrates both acceptance and change-focused cognitive and behavioral strategies. The biosocial theory (see Linehan, 1993a; Crowell et al., 2009), upon which DBT is theoretically based, posits that biological predispositions to emotional sensitivity, reactivity, and delayed recovery transact with a chronically invalidating environment over time to yield pervasive emotional dysregulation. As a result of this transaction, individuals do not learn skills to express or modulate their emotions effectively. Instead, they engage in ineffective attempts to regulate high-intensity and long-lasting painful emotions through behavioral dysregulation (e.g., suicidal behaviors, substance use, disordered eating).

Linehan (1993a, 1993b) developed a treatment to address these problems, consisting of four modes (individual therapy, group skills training, phone coaching, and therapist consultation team) with the overarching goal of decreasing behavioral dyscontrol. Individual therapy occurs weekly and is oriented around a treatment hierarchy to prioritize the most critical targets: (1) life-threatening behaviors, (2) therapy-interfering behavior, (3) life-interfering behaviors, and (4) increasing behavioral skills. Intervention is guided by this target hierarchy to leverage traditional behavior therapy interventions (skills training, exposure, problem solving) and interventions from Zen (validation, mindfulness) together, with implementation of DBT stylistic strategies (reciprocal, irreverent, dialectical). Self-monitoring "diary cards" and behavioral analysis are used to guide behavioral skill–focused solutions.

The primary function of group DBT skills training is to increase behavioral skills. Skills groups meet weekly for two hours and last 12 months. Skills are taught in four modules: mindfulness, emotion regulation, distress tolerance, and interpersonal effectiveness, and in standard adult DBT each skill is taught twice in the treatment year (Linehan 1993a, 1993b, 2015a, 2015b). An additional skills module, Walking the Middle Path, is included for adolescents and families in family-based DBT (Miller et al., 2007; Rathus & Miller, 2015). Groups are structured, consisting of a brief mindfulness practice, review of home practice, teaching of a new skill, and assignment of home practice for the new skill. The interested reader may reference the DBT skills manual (Linehan, 2015b) for additional information, as well as additional resources on implementation (e.g., Cowperthwait et al., 2018).

Phone coaching functions primarily to promote generalization of skills from the treatment environment to the patient's natural environment. It is also used to increase and reinforce effective requests for help in context of crisis urges, as well as to maintain the therapeutic relationship. Between sessions, the patient may call their individual therapist requesting coaching around learning skills to use in the moment, practicing or generalizing skills, or repairing the therapy relationship. These calls are brief and targeted, emphasizing skills application over analyzing the crisis or problem solving.

The consultation team for DBT providers functions as therapy for the therapist, targeting therapist skill and motivation to ensure adherent treatment (see Sayrs & Linehan, 2019). In the DBT model, a community, or team, of DBT therapists work together to treat a community of DBT patients. The team meets weekly, and because DBT is a team-based intervention, therapists must be part of a consultation team in order to provide any mode of DBT. The consultation team uses DBT therapy principles to address therapist burnout and challenges arising in implementation of DBT for the patients and clinicians treated by the team.

EMPIRICAL SUPPORT FOR DBT

Dialectical behavior therapy has been rigorously tested and found to improve suicidal and self-harm behaviors in adults via randomized controlled trials (RCTs; e.g., Linehan et al., 1991, 1999, 2006; Clarkin et al., 2007; McMain et al., 2009; Carter et al., 2010; Verheul et al., 2003). Relative to comparison treatments, DBT has demonstrated significantly greater improvements in parasuicidal behavior (e.g., Linehan et al., 1991; Mehlum et al., 2014; Pistorello et al., 2012), suicidal behavior but not nonsuicidal self-injury (Linehan et al., 2006), and vice versa (Verheul et al., 2003; Linehan et al., 2015). Studies have also begun to examine the effects of DBT treatment and skills use on psychological processes common across disorders, and have found improvements in emotion dysregulation (e.g., Neacsiu et al., 2014). Of note, some studies have failed to find significant differences between DBT and comparison treatments (e.g., Linehan et al., 1999; McMain et al., 2009; Carter et al., 2010).

While this multimodal treatment has yielded significant improvements in adults with suicidal behavior and emotion dysregulation (see Rosenthal et al., 2020 for review), fewer rigorous studies have been conducted with younger populations. Given the developmental needs of younger populations, adaptations have been developed for suicidal adolescents (Miller et al., 2007) and children (Perepletchikova, 2018). Two RCTs demonstrate efficacy, with reductions in suicide-related behaviors in adolescents (McCauley et al., 2018; Mehlum et al., 2014, 2016) and one preliminary RCT demonstrates efficacy in children (Perepletchikova et al., 2017).

While EA appear to be particularly vulnerable to the very problems DBT treats, including high prevalence of suicidality, multiple mental health problems, and problems accessing and staying in treatment (e.g., Castellví et al., 2017; Skehan & Davis, 2017), when we started our program, we were unable to find any published adaptations or manuals for DBT for EA. However, outside of DBT treatment research, and in the context of growing advocacy for services attending to EA vulnerabilities (e.g., Iyer et al., 2015; Wilson et al., 2011), several empirical findings make a strong case for considering DBT for this age range. In the subsequent sections, we review data supporting our decision making in the presence of limited data to guide applying DBT to an emerging adult population.

EMERGING ADULTS: A COHORT AT RISK

In 2000, Arnett published a seminal article demarcating emerging adulthood as a separate developmental phase between adolescence and adulthood. Evidence suggests that EA have not yet completed parts of biological and task development, and experience prolonged exploration and frequent transitions (e.g., Chan et al., 2019; Roisman et al., 2004; Skehan & Davis, 2017). Further, authors have posited that developmental tasks and challenges navigating health care transitions exacerbate stress for this age range (e.g., Aro et al., 1993; Skehan & Davis, 2017), which may contribute to additional psychopathology and risk behaviors (Aro et al., 1993; Arpawong et al., 2015; Pelkonen & Marttunen, 2003; Zivin et al., 2009).

In 2018, the Centers for Disease Control reported that suicide was the second leading cause of death for three groups of young people in the United States: ages 10–14, 15–24, and 25–34 (Curtin & Heron, 2019; Hedegaard et al., 2019). Emerging adults demonstrate higher rates of suicidal ideation than adults (MacKinnon & Colman, 2016), as well as greater risk for suicidal thinking, planning, and attempts than older adults (Kessler et al., 1999). Among EA with histories of parasuicidal thoughts and behaviors, meta-analyses examining long-term associations between suicidal and self-injurious thoughts and actions found a higher risk of death by suicide than previously reported for adolescents and EA (Castellví et al., 2017) and that this age group is most vulnerable for future self-injurious thoughts and behaviors (Ribeiro et al., 2016). This risk is made even more concerning by two additional considerations: (1) the role of emotion dysregulation in suicide, and (2) treatment-seeking and access problems in this age range.

Emotion dysregulation has long been posited to have a role in suicidal behavior (Linehan, 1993a), and etiological models of suicide suggest that emotion regulation is an important factor in predicting suicidal ideation (Joiner, 2005; O'Conner et al., 2016; Swee et al., 2020). Additionally, emotional pain has been found to be a predictor of suicidal ideation (Klonsky & May, 2015; Swee et al., 2020). Taken together, EA experience developmentally normative stressors, are at increased risk for emotion dysregulation, and have not yet fully developed regulation capacities (e.g., Neece et al., 2013; Swee et al., 2020). This combination of emotion dysregulation and suicide risk factors for EA is concerning.

While treatment has been found to reduce suicide completion (Greenberg et al., 2001), several authors have noted that EA do not adequately connect with needed mental health care (Skehan & Davis, 2017; Wilson et al., 2011), in part due to the difficult-to-navigate transition to adult services from child services (see Paul et al., 2015). Emerging adults are also less likely to seek or connect with treatment than adults or adolescents (Chan et al., 2019), with MacKinnon and Colman (2016) observing this trend in suicidal EA specifically. Emotion regulation problems may exacerbate these treatment connection challenges (e.g., Ciarrochi & Deane, 2001; Vogel et al., 2008). Further, one study found that EA with emerging personality disorder characteristics and emotional disorders are even less likely to effectively transition from youth to adult services than others in their peer group, including those with a history of hospital admission, severe mental illness or psychiatric medications (Paul et al., 2015; Singh et al., 2009).

Taken together, emotionally dysregulated EA who struggle with suicidality and self-harm and difficulties connecting to treatment need a solution. Dialectical behavior therapy addresses problems experienced by EAs, including those that put them at greater risk or present a barrier to care: suicidal and self-harm behavior, emotion dysregulation, and personality disorder. And, in line with the target hierarchy, DBT prioritizes (1) life-threatening behavior and (2) treatment-interfering behavior. While DBT is not the only possible solution, we posit that DBT is an excellent fit for these problems and this developmental stage.

DBT: A SOLUTION FOR AT-RISK EMERGING ADULTS

Despite a dearth of strenuous studies applying DBT to EA, the studies of family-based DBT for adolescents and DBT for college students show promise for adaptation for this age range. This therapy has already been adapted to meet the needs of adolescents and their family members (DBT-A; Miller et al., 2007; Rathus & Miller, 2015), to intervene on both individual and environmental skills deficits that may contribute to emotional and behavioral dysregulation and family dysfunction (Fruzzetti et al., 2007; Woodberry et al., 2002).

The DBT-A model makes several adaptations from adult DBT, including: (1) shortening the length of treatment (one year to six months), (2) family inclusion in all modes of treatment, and (3) changes to the skills training curriculum, with the removal and simplification of some adult skills and the addition of a fifth skills module. This family-specific skills module, Walking the Middle Path, teaches dialectical thinking and perspective taking, validating one's own and others' emotional experiences, and principles of behavior change such as reinforcement of effective behaviors, shaping, and extinction of maladaptive behaviors (Miller et al., 1997, 2007; Rathus & Miller, 2000, 2002).

This model has been evaluated in both open trials and two RCTs with adolescents engaging in repetitive self-injurious and suicidal behavior (Mehlum et al., 2014, 2016; McCauley et al., 2018). DBT-A yielded significantly greater reductions in frequency of self-harm behavior, suicidal ideation severity, and depression symptoms than "enhanced usual care" (Mehlum et al., 2014). At the one-year follow-up, DBT-A retained superiority on frequency of self-harm behavior, but not other outcomes, largely due to improvement in the enhanced usual care group (Mehlum et al., 2016). McCauley et al. (2018) found that DBT-A outperformed comparison treatment individual/group supportive therapy (IGST) in reducing suicide attempts and nonsuicidal self-injury during treatment, though DBT did not retain superiority through follow-up. While differential treatment engagement across conditions was not found to impact suicide-related outcomes, DBT-A was found to have higher treatment completion rates, as well as greater numbers of individual and group session attendance for more weeks than IGST. When compared to other treatments for adolescent self-harm and suicide, DBT-A is the only intervention to demonstrate improvements in self-harm with RCT replication (Iyengar et al., 2018), making it a prime candidate for extension to EA. These findings are notable in context of both EA risk for suicide and difficulties engaging in treatment (Greenberg et al., 2001).

Investigations of DBT in emerging adulthood are limited. It has been adapted and applied to college students in open trials (see Chugani et al., 2020, for review) and one RCT. Pistorello and colleagues (2012) applied comprehensive DBT to college students ages 18–25 with current suicidality and BPD features, and compared DBT to optimized treatment as usual. The authors made four modifications to DBT for this population: (1) shortened the distress tolerance module and added validation skills, (2) increased flexibility of the four-consecutive-miss rule to accommodate school breaks, (3) shortened duration of skills training groups from two hours to 90 minutes to accommodate class schedules, and (4) aligned skills training modules with semesters, such that each content-specific skills module (distress tolerance, interpersonal effectiveness, emotion regulation) was taught once each year. Of note, the result of aligning skills training modules with semesters was a reduction in rate of skills training such that completers learned each skill once in a year, as compared to standard adult DBT in which each skill is taught twice per year. Students who completed DBT demonstrated significantly greater improvements in suicidality, depression, number of NSSI events, BPD criteria, psychotropic medication use, and social adjustment.

Beyond treatment studies demonstrating efficacy with young people, additional studies make a compelling argument for tailoring DBT for EA. One quasi-experimental study examined EA with BPD in two different year-long comprehensive DBT programs: mixed age (ages 18 and up) and EA only (ages 18–25; Lyng et al., 2019). Subjects in the EA-only condition demonstrated significantly greater reductions in BPD symptoms and general psychopathology than those in the mixed-age condition.

Linehan's (1993a) biosocial theory posits that difficulties regulating emotions stem from the transaction of chronic and pervasive invalidating interactions with caregivers and biological emotional vulnerabilities (with biology and environment influencing one another) over time. Thus, biosocial theory suggests that environmental intervention may be beneficial. Further, census data from 2015 shows more EA are living in their parents' homes, with EA child-parent cohabitation rates increasing 8.1% since 2005, such that as of 2015, 34.1% of 18- to 34-year-olds were living in their parents' homes (U.S. Bureau of the Census, 2015). Given this increased rate of cohabitation, family involvement could be even more important than in previous cohorts.

In a secondary analysis of McCauley et al. (2018), Adrian et al. (2019) identified family variables as important for determining who would benefit from DBT, as well as DBT versus comparison treatment IGST. Parental psychopathology, parental emotion dysregulation, and adolescent emotion dysregulation moderated treatment outcomes for self-harm and NSSI. That is, DBT yielded greater improvement in NSSI and self-harm than IGST among families demonstrating greater amounts of parent psychopathology and emotion dysregulation in adolescents and parents. Further, families who demonstrated greater conflict at pretreatment improved more by posttreatment than those with less conflict at pretreatment.

As we adapted full-model DBT, we considered shortening the commitment to treatment to six months, or one time through each set of skills in the skills training manual. This therapy is a time- and resource-intensive treatment, which can pose a barrier to its adoption in health care settings and access for patients (Swenson et al., 2002). In our clinical experience, the expectation of a one-year commitment also poses a barrier to willingness to participate in treatment, particularly among young people.

In community settings, DBT is often shortened or modified to fit existing clinic resources (Carmel et al., 2014) or patient presentations (Linehan, 2015b). Adults entering standard DBT in our clinic typically commit to one year of skills training group (Linehan, 2015b), or two rounds through each skills module. However, the standard commitment for DBT-A is six months (Rathus & Miller, 2015), or one round through each of the skills modules. Further, there is some evidence that briefer versions of full-model DBT may be effective. McMain et al. (2018) created a protocol to compare six versus 12 months of full-model DBT for chronically self-harming adults with BPD. Preliminary results suggest that there was no difference between conditions on frequency and severity of suicidal and self-harm behaviors or treatment dropout and, in fact, general psychiatric and BPD symptoms may improve faster in the six-month treatment condition (McMain et al., in preparation, as cited by Harned, 2019). Further, as noted above, EA who participated in a college-age DBT group demonstrated clinically significant improvements after completing only one round of each skills module (Pistorello et al., 2012). We used these data, as well as our adaptation of the DBT-A skills training manual (Rathus & Miller, 2015), to support our decision to set treatment commitment for DBT-YA at six months. This decision allowed us to review each skill module in group one time, use foot-in-the-door commitment strategies at the outset of treatment with ambivalent EA, and move families through the program quickly to maintain access to this treatment. Taken together, these studies make a convincing argument for applying DBT to emerging adulthood.

DBT-YA: PROGRAM DEVELOPMENT AND OUR ADAPTATIONS OF DBT FOR EMERGING ADULTS

In creating the DBT-YA program, we faced countless decisions. Chief among them: Who would this program be for? And how would we apply evidence-based DBT models with fidelity to meet the needs of this population? When we were creating our DBT-YA program, we did not find DBT-specific studies including families at the EA level. However, as we adapted DBT-A and standard adult DBT, we considered including families. This decision was based on (1) family inclusion in all modes of DBT-A (Miller et al., 2007; Rathus & Miller, 2015); (2) the aforementioned unique developmental needs, with incomplete biological and task development occurring in prolonged transitional contexts; (3) biosocial theory and relevant data; and (4) family-related outcomes in DBT-A (Adrian et al., 2019), as well as our own clinical observations of this population in our clinic's standard adult DBT program. For age, given that there is lack of empirical consensus on the age range beyond adolescence, we considered our options: DBT studies with college students, ages 18–22 (Chugani et al., 2020), evidence of ongoing brain development in the 20s to 30s (Taber-Thomas & Pérez-Edgar, 2015), a seminal article defining emerging adulthood as ages 18–25 (Arnett, 2000), and our clinical experience showing that many of our young patients are living with parents during and after college, which drops off after age 25. In true DBT fashion, we found synthesis: 18- to 25-year-olds who live with or have significant interaction with parents or caregivers could be eligible for a multifamily group. Those 18- to 25-year-olds without close caregiver relationships could do individual DBT with us or our trainees, and could do standard adult DBT skills group. For example, we enrolled a 24-year-old graduate student and his aunt in multifamily group because his aunt lived locally and was an emergency contact after the student's suicide attempt. However, we enrolled a 22-year-old college graduate in standard adult DBT skills group because, although her parents certainly contributed to her pervasive invalidating environment, they lived out of state and she had no local caregiving figures.

The DBT-YA model made adaptations from standard adult DBT to all four modes of DBT, using dialectics throughout to honor and synthesize the established manuals (Linehan, 1993a; Miller et al., 2007), limited empirical data, and observational clinical data. All adaptations were oriented around efficiently intervening on both individual and environmental factors that cause and maintain emotion dysregulation in EA. Dialectically, DBT-YA both treats the family system and prioritizes the EA as the identified patient. We've thus far been lucky to have limited experience with parents in our programs experiencing their own suicidal crises. In these cases, we've encouraged parents to seek their own individual therapy so that managing parents' risk behaviors doesn't interfere with therapy for the EA identified patient.

The individual therapy mode of treatment was modified to include weekly individual therapy for the EA as well as the expectation of at least monthly family therapy with caregivers. This monthly family therapy session may be in lieu of the young adult's individual therapy session that week, or in addition to the individual therapy session if appropriate. These family therapy sessions include direct intervention on ineffective processes within the family; double-chain analyses of both individual and environmental factors that precede, cause, exacerbate, or maintain target behaviors; improving family communication and reducing conflict; and increasing empathy, understanding, and validation among family members, consistent with DBT-A family sessions (Miller et al., 2007).

The standard sequence of modules taught in skills training (see Linehan, 2015b) was unchanged. However, content from the DBT-A skills training manual (Rathus & Miller, 2015) and standard adult DBT skills training manual (Linehan, 2015a) was combined, developmentally tailored, and modified. The primary source for skills training content was the DBT-A skills training manual, which includes the family-specific Walking the Middle Path module. This module was modified to include developmentally tailored teaching examples of topics and issues faced by EA and their families, psychoeducation about typical young adult development and developmental psychology, and instruction in behavioral parenting and contingency management in order to scaffold EA gaining autonomy and self-regulation. Homework sheets for this module were created specifically to facilitate between-session family discussion around identifying and problem solving in common areas of conflict, individual and family values clarification, and building menus of reinforcers and mutually agreed-upon contingencies for failing to meet family expectations.

Based on feedback received from EA and families in our skills training group, some of the standard adult skills training handouts and worksheets were incorporated when the content of the DBT-A skills handouts was overly simplistic. For example, we teach the standard adult Ways to Describe Emotions "emotion dictionary" because the EA in our group have enough life experience with varied prompting events and rich enough emotional vocabularies to benefit from the complexity and specificity of these handouts.

The coaching call mode of treatment was modified to provide coaching to parents or caregivers of EA engaged in full-model DBT-YA, consistent with DBT-A. These calls are provided by a therapist who is not the EA's individual therapist. The goals of phone coaching for parents is to promote the use of effective parenting strategies in the natural environment and help parents increase generalization of their own DBT skills. However, caregiver coaching calls are not intended to be focused on the parent or caregiver's experience of crisis urges.

Finally, a specialized DBT-YA consultation team was created, in addition to the standard DBT consultation team in our clinic. Consistent with the function of DBT consultation team as both therapy for the therapist and a forum to increase therapist skill and motivation, the DBT-YA team specifically attends to the unique and varied needs of our providers who treat EA and their families. The didactic focus in the DBT-YA team includes family- and systems-based interventions, developing family case formulations, and reviewing updated literature on best practices for family-based DBT. The DBT-YA team provides a space to practice specific family-based assessment and intervention skills, including role-plays around risk assessment and management, conducting double-chain analyses, and teaching skills in multifamily group. Time on the DBT-YA team has also been spent creating and sharing EA-specific resources with our employee health, college counseling center, and adolescent and EA psychiatry referral networks.

VIGNETTE

Derek is a 20-year-old, European American, heterosexual, cisgender man. His mother and father both have advanced graduate degrees and work in research at a private university in the area. His mother has her own history of generalized anxiety and recurrent major depression. His father has a history of alcohol abuse and is frequently emotionally distant and invalidating. He has a twin sister and a younger brother who both attend college and are on track to graduate within four years.

Derek took a medical withdrawal from college after making two suicide attempts (attempted hanging and intentional overdose on opioid pain medication) in the fall semester of his junior year. He was referred to our clinic through the employee assistance program at his parents' place of work after his mother pursued taking time off to coordinate Derek's care.

He presented to our clinic with historic diagnoses of panic disorder and ADHD. Derek had been seen by a variety of supportive and cognitive–behavioral therapists in the community since experiencing bullying and academic difficulties in early middle school. He did not find any of these therapists helpful for improving his mood, social anxiety, or academic functioning. At the time of the evaluation, he was prescribed a benzodiazepine for panic symptoms and agitation, a sedative-hypnotic for insomnia, and both short- and long-acting stimulants for ADHD.

During diagnostic evaluation, Derek endorsed depressed mood, anhedonia, low motivation, poor concentration, hypersomnia and daytime fatigue, weight gain, feelings of worthlessness, and recurrent suicidal ideation and intrusive images of his family members dying violently. He also endorsed fear of social situations, worries about negative evaluation by peers, avoidance of situations in which he might be exposed to scrutiny (e.g., participating in group projects in school), and freeze responses in social situations, including mumbling, poor eye contact, and failing to speak. Derek historically had often fallen behind on coursework and forgotten about deadlines and tests. He expressed ambivalence about completing college, due to both difficulty identifying career goals and hopelessness about his ability to get his academic life back on track. Derek reported engaging in significant daily alcohol and marijuana use, in part to manage high-intensity anxiety in social situations. However, substance use exacerbated depression and class attendance difficulties, and, since his return home, causes significant conflict with his parents. In addition to panic and ADHD, Derek was diagnosed with major depression, social anxiety, and substance use disorder. He identified treatment targets of improving mood, improving social and family relationships, getting a job, and moving out of his parents' house.

During a family orientation session for DBT-YA, Derek and his parents disagreed about the causes of his distress and the most effective path forward. When discussing the young adult and family dialectical dilemma around excessive leniency versus authoritarian control, Derek reported that his parents were overly rigid about academic expectations, while his parents believed that they didn't know how to set and enforce rules now that Derek was back home.

When discussing the dilemma of fostering dependence versus forcing autonomy, Derek's parents reported that they were taking too much care of Derek, for example, by dosing his medications daily, doing his laundry, changing his sheets, and adding money to his bank account. At the same time, they felt resentful that Derek has not taken steps toward self-regulation, getting a job, or moving out.

When discussing the dilemma of normalizing pathology versus pathologizing the norm, Derek and his parents disagreed about how Derek should be spending his time while on medical leave. Derek's parents reported that they "don't know how to motivate him anymore" and believed he should be "doing more by now than sleeping all day and getting high and playing video games all night." Derek reported that his parents were overly pathologizing his drug use and screen time, given that his level of use appeared to be typical of peers from college.

Finally, Derek's parents expressed frustration with his academic performance in college. They expressed that their family has high expectations for academic success, and his performance was not commensurate with his siblings' achievements and their perceptions of Derek's intelligence. The family decided that Derek would attend multifamily group with his mother. They identified family goals of increasing perspective taking, improving family communication patterns, using values and learning principles to facilitate behavior change, and gaining skills for managing crises.

The first few individual sessions with Derek focused on introducing the DBT model, identifying targets for the daily diary card, and behavioral chain analysis of each occurrence of suicidal ideation. Each chain helped Derek build insight into the interaction between emotional vulnerability, ineffective behavioral responses to emotional prompting events, and maintenance of depression and anxiety symptoms.

By the time Derek and his mother joined group, he had already experienced some reduction in hopelessness, and he appeared increasingly comfortable and behaviorally activated in individual therapy sessions (making small talk on the way into the therapy room, more collaborative in agenda setting). However, in the first several groups, Derek did not speak. Even during introductions and ice breaker games, he stared down at the table, and his legs shook for the duration of the group. None of the group members attempted to make conversation with him. After the fourth group, one of the EA muttered, "That new dude looks like a school shooter. The staring and shaking freak me out." Derek heard this comment, turned red, and left the room quickly. His mother expressed concern and hopelessness to the group leaders, and asked to remove Derek from group until he'd made more progress in individual therapy.

Derek's skills group leaders brought concerns about his presentation to his individual therapist in the next DBT-YA consultation team. The team recommended the therapist work with Derek to connect his group behavior to his treatment goals and behavior outside of session. The team also recommended having a family session to discuss changing family responses to Derek to block reinforcement of avoidance or accommodation of anxiety-driven behaviors. Derek, his mother and father, and the individual therapist met for a family session. The individual therapist coached Derek through how to use the skill of opposite action to anxiety in group. She coached Derek's parents to validate Derek's anxiety, hold firm on the expectation that he honor his commitment to treatment, and use praise and encouragement to reinforce his using emotion regulation and distress tolerance skills to approach social anxiety cues.

Three months into Derek's participation in DBT-YA, he made an impulsive suicide attempt by drinking and intentionally overdosing on his benzodiazepines. His mother took him to the emergency room as soon as she learned of the attempt, where he was evaluated but not hospitalized. In the next individual therapy session, Derek and his individual therapist conducted a behavioral chain analysis of the events leading up to the suicide attempt, including medication noncompliance over the previous week, binge drinking earlier in the evening, and several hours of rumination about his past social and academic failures. They discussed solution analysis, including consistently attending to self-care behaviors, distracting himself with other thoughts when he is ruminating, and to practice opposite action to anxiety and shame urges, to make a coaching call before attempting. They also discussed approach-oriented problem solving in order to repair trust with his parents.

Five months into treatment, Derek's parents requested another family session. They were planning to visit their younger son at his college to attend a football game, and they wanted Derek to go with them. Derek didn't want to go, due to his intense dislike of football and large crowds, as well as shame about not being enrolled in college. His parents expressed concern that Derek would make another suicide attempt if unsupervised at home. The therapist coached Derek through validating his parents' concerns, while at the same time practicing his interpersonal effectiveness skills to clearly communicate his desire to stay home. The therapist practiced problem solving with Derek's parents to establish appropriate limits and stimulus control measures, while at the same time scaffolding Derek's independence and self-regulation. Finally, the therapist coached Derek's parents through practicing their own distress tolerance skills to cope with their high-intensity anxiety about his safety.

As the family continued in multifamily group, Derek's depression and anxiety symptoms gradually improved. Five months into treatment, he began to ride his bike to individual therapy and group. He reported that this was fun and activating, which boosted his mood and helped him feel more independent than when his mother was driving him to appointments. Derek's mother reported that, much to her surprise, she found acceptance-oriented skills like validation, mindfulness, and radical acceptance to be most helpful. She found that validation of his emotions and acceptance of his "different path" helped improve her relationship with Derek. And she found that regular mindfulness practice helped decrease her own experience of anxiety and worry.

Beyond anecdotal reports from families like Derek's, we have objective evidence from our program to suggest that this developmentally tailored family-based model of DBT is effective. Over 60% of families who start DBT-YA multifamily skills group complete it (Schmeling et al., 2019). We also collect Beck Depression Inventory, 2nd edition (Beck et al., 1996), Beck Anxiety Inventory (Beck et al., 1988), McLean Screening Instrument for Borderline Personality Disorder (Zanarini et al., 2003), Difficulties in Emotion Regulation Scale (Gratz & Roemer, 2004), and DBT–Ways of Coping Checklist (DBT-WCCL; Neacsiu et al., 2010) every three months from EA, and the DBT-WCCL every three months from caregivers who participate in group as part of both routine outcome monitoring and quality improvement efforts in our clinic. Emerging adults who complete the program demonstrate significant reductions in anxiety, depression, and BPD symptoms and emotion dysregulation. Both EA and caregivers who complete the program demonstrate significant improvements in DBT skills use (Schmeling et al., 2019). These results suggest that integrating developmental adaptations and family-based intervention for multiproblem EA is both well tolerated and effective for EA and caregivers alike.

DBT-YA IN PRACTICE

In practice, DBT-YA is a constant challenge and joy to the writers. There were many administrative barriers to starting this program in an academic medical center. Prepandemic, we had a consistent flow of new families needing and wanting treatment throughout the year, with predictable surges after school starts in the fall and in the winter months after the holidays, and relative lulls during the summer. In this program, we've worked with high school students, college students, masters and doctoral students, individuals who never attended college, and young people pregnant with children of their own. We've engaged in family-based treatment with parents, grandparents, stepparents, and aunts and uncles. We've treated all classes of DBT life-threatening behaviors, and celebrated graduations, first jobs, and engagements. Given the ever-changing nature and transition of emerging adulthood, we are constantly faced with novel presentations to treat, flex our case formulation skills, practice dialectical synthesis, and apply DBT principles in new ways.

Multifamily skills group is high energy. It is filled with both predictable and unpredictable moments of delight, bids for improvisation, and flexibility. For the writers, the ongoing complexity and novelty of multifamily group are rewarding and full of adventure. For coleaders new to multifamily group, however, the learning curve can be steep. Coleading multifamily group requires mastery in standard DBT skills content, developmental and family skills content, and developmental behavioral processes and content. It also requires knowledge of interpersonal and family systems processes both within and across families, all in the context of emotion dysregulation and multiple clinical problems. The interaction of all these variables requires constant use of case formulation–driven choice of intervention, dialectics, and stylistic strategies. Coleaders must prioritize among many possible topics, choosing, for example, when to push group members in an effort to drag out effective behaviors versus when to drop the rope, or when to be the omnipotent expert in the room versus when to model vulnerability and uncertainty by saying, "I don't know!" Multifamily group also provides ample opportunity to practice the DBT principle of speed, movement, and flow to intentionally vary both nonverbal and verbal behavior to keep group members on their toes and engaged.

The reward of this all of this complexity is at least one endearing exchange between EA and caregivers per session and dozens of opportunities to witness longitudinal flourishing within families. Our preliminary data is promising, demonstrating improved family interactions, more confidence, less anxiety about life-threatening behaviors, and more skills. With outcomes like these, we're delighted to work with these families "in the gap" every day.

CONCLUSION

Emerging adulthood is a distinct developmental phase. It is characterized by frequent transitions, ongoing biological development and identity formation, incomplete development of emotion and behavioral regulation capacities, and tension between the continued involvement of the family environment and shifts toward increasing autonomy and independence. Emerging adulthood is also a period of increased risk for stress, psychopathology, and risk behaviors including suicide and self-harm. Neither clinical settings nor existing empirically supported treatments are well suited for treating these problems in a developmentally tailored way.

Dialectical behavior therapy is an empirically well-supported, principle-based treatment for pervasive emotion and behavioral dysregulation. It has been adapted for and demonstrated to be effective for populations from childhood through late adulthood, and can be helpful for a variety of emotions, behaviors, and problems for individuals and families. We relied on these existing adaptations, as well as research about emerging adulthood, to inform our clinical practice and decision making to create DBT-YA: a developmentally tailored, family-inclusive outpatient DBT program. Adaptations include limiting age of identified patients to 18 to 25 years, shortening treatment commitment to six months from one year in standard adult DBT, including parents or caregivers in all modes of treatment, providing skills coaching to parents or caregivers, and creating a weekly multifamily skills training group with skills curriculum adapted from both adolescent and adult skills training manuals.

This therapy has been well received by our patients and their families, as well as the health system in which we work, trainees we've taught, and community providers in our area. It works to reduce symptoms, decrease emotion dysregulation, and increase use of effective skills. Perhaps even more important than these outcomes is the process by which we got here: we followed the existing research, considered the context of patients in this developmental stage, leveraged our clinical interests and training, and collected our own evidence of effectiveness along the way.

Kristin Wyatt, PhD, is a licensed psychologist and cofounder of Arise Psychological Wellness and Consulting, PLLC, a private practice dedicated to trauma-informed care and empirically-supported practices. She has expertise in dialectical behavior therapy and contemporary cognitive and behavioral therapies, specializing in the treatment of young adults, adolescents, and their families, emotion dysregulation, family integration into evidence-based models, and exposure-based treatments. In her previous faculty role at Duke University Medical Center, she cofounded, codirected, and trained learners in DBT-YA services for young adults and their families. She is active in providing trainings for mental health providers and in scholarly writing on DBT-related topics.

Dr. Colleen Cowperthwait is a licensed clinical psychologist and assistant professor in the Department of Psychiatry and Behavioral Sciences at Duke University Medical Center. Dr. Cowperthwait codeveloped family-integrated DBT for Young Adults services. She provides individual and family-based cognitive behavioral interventions for adolescents, young adults, and adults with a variety of psychiatric and medical diagnoses, including personality pathology, chronic suicidality, non-suicidal self-injury, and trauma-related disorders. Dr. Cowperthwait also provides training, supervision, and education for graduate students, clinical psychology interns, and psychiatry residents. Her research has focused on adaptation and implementation of contemporary, family-based cognitive behavioral therapies and dialectical behavior therapy.

REFERENCES

Adrian, M., McCauley, E., Berk, M. S., Asarnow, J. R., Korslund, K., Avina, C., Gallop, R., & Linehan, M. M. (2019). Predictors and moderators of recurring self-harm in adolescents participating in a comparative treatment trial of psychological interventions. *Journal of Child Psychology and Psychiatry, and Allied Disciplines, 60*(10), 1123–1132. doi:10.1111/jcpp.13099

Arnett, J. J. (2000). Emerging adulthood: A theory of development from the late teens through the twenties. *American Psychologist, 55*(5), 469–480. doi:10.1037/0003-066X.55.5.469

Aro, H. M., Marttunen, M. J., & Lönnqvist, J. K. (1993). Adolescent development and youth suicide. *Suicide and Life-Threatening Behavior, 23*(4), 359–365.

Arpawong, T. E., Sussman, S., Milam, J. E., Unger, J. B., Land, H., Sun, P., & Rohrbach, L. A. (2015). Post-traumatic growth, stressful life events, and relationships with substance use behaviors among alternative high school students: A prospective study. *Psychology and Health, 30*(4), 475–494. doi:10.1080/08870446.2014.979171

Beck, A. T., Epstein, N., Brown, G., & Steer, R. A. (1988). An inventory for measuring clinical anxiety: Psychometric properties. *Journal of Consulting and Clinical Psychology, 56*(6), 893–897. doi:10.1037/0022-006X.56.6.893

Beck, A. T., Steer, R. A., & Brown, G. K. (1996). *Manual for the Beck Depression Inventory— II.* Psychological Corporation.

Carmel, A., Rose, M. L., & Fruzzetti, A. E. (2014). Barriers and solutions to implementing dialectical behavior therapy in a public behavioral health system. *Administration and Policy in Mental Health, 41*(5), 608–614. doi:10.1007/s10488-013-0504-6

Carter, G. L., Willcox, C. H., Lewin, T. J., Conrad, A. M., & Bendit, N. (2010). Hunter DBT Project: Randomized controlled trial of dialectical behaviour therapy in women with borderline personality disorder. *Australian and New Zealand Journal of Psychiatry, 44*(2), 162–173. doi:10.3109/00048670903393621

Castellví, P., Lucas-Romero, E., Miranda-Mendizábal, A., Parés-Badell, O., Almenara, J., Alonso, I., Blasco, M. J., Cebrià, A., Gabilondo, A., Gili, M., Lagares, C., Piqueras, J. A., Roca, M., Rodríguez-Marín, J., Rodríguez-Jimenez, T., Soto-Sanz, V., & Alonso, J. (2017). Longitudinal association between self-injurious thoughts and behaviors and suicidal behavior in adolescents and young adults: A systematic review with meta-analysis. *Journal of Affective Disorders, 215*, 37–48. doi:10.1016/j.jad.2017.03.035

Chan, V., Moore, J., Derenne, J., & Fuchs, D. C. (2019). Transitional age youth and college mental health. *Child and Adolescent Psychiatric Clinics of North America, 28*(3), 363–375. doi:10.1016/j.chc.2019.02.008

Chugani, C. D., Wyatt, K. P., & Richter, R. K. (2020). Dialectical behavior therapy in college counseling centers. In J. Bedics (Ed.), *The handbook of dialectical behavior therapy.* Academic Press.

Ciarrochi, J. V., & Deane, F. P. (2001). Emotional competence and willingness to seek help from professional and nonprofessional sources. *British Journal of Guidance and Counselling, 29*(2), 233–246. doi:10.1080/03069880020047157

Clarkin, J. F., Levy, K. N., Lenzenweger, M. F., & Kernberg, O. F. (2007). Evaluating three treatments for borderline personality disorder: A multiwave study. *American Journal of Psychiatry, 164*(6), 922–928. doi:10.1176/ajp.2007.164.6.922.

Courbasson, C., Nishikawa, Y., & Dixon, L. (2012). Outcome of dialectical behaviour therapy for concurrent eating and substance use disorders. *Clinical Psychology and Psychotherapy, 19*, 434–449. doi:10.1002/cpp.748

Cowperthwait, C. M., Wyatt, K. P., Fang, C. M., & Neacsiu, A. (2018). Skills training in DBT: Principles and practicalities. In M. Swales (Ed.), *Oxford handbook of dialectical behaviour therapy.* Oxford University Press.

Crowell, S. E., Beauchaine, T. P., & Linehan, M. M. (2009). A biosocial developmental model of borderline personality: Elaborating and extending Linehan's theory. *Psychological Bulletin, 135*(3), 495–510. doi:10.1037/a0015616

Curtin, S. C., & Heron, M. (2019). Death rates due to suicide and homicide among persons aged 10–24: United States, 2000–2017. *NCHS Data Brief*, no. 352. National Center for Health Statistics.

Fruzzetti, A. E., Santisteban, D. A., & Hoffman, P. D. (2007). Dialectical behavior therapy with families. In L. A. Dimeff & K. Koerner (Eds.), *Dialectical behavior therapy in clinical practice: Applications across disorders and settings* (pp. 222–244). Guilford.

Gratz, K. L., & Roemer, L. (2004). Multidimensional assessment of emotion regulation and dysregulation: Development, factor structure, and initial validation of the Difficulties in Emotion Regulation Scale. *Journal of Psychopathology and Behavioral Assessment, 26*(1), 41–54. doi:10.1023/B:JOBA.0000007455.08539.94

Greenberg, M. T., Domitrovich, C., & Bumbarger, B. (2001). The prevention of mental disorders in school-aged children: Current state of the field. *Prevention and Treatment, 4*(1), Article 1a. doi:10.1037/1522-3736.4.1.41a

Harned, M. (2019). *Annual update on DBT research.* Invited address presented at the 24th International Society for the Improvement and Teaching of Dialectical Behavior Therapy Conference, Atlanta, GA.

Hedegaard, H., Curtin, S. C., & Warner, M. (2018, November). Suicide mortality in the United States, 1999–2017. *NCHS Data Brief*, no. 330. National Center for Health Statistics.

Iyengar, U., Snowden, N., Asarnow, J. R., Moran, P., Tranah, T., & Ougrin, D. (2018). A further look at therapeutic interventions for suicide attempts and self-harm in adolescents: An updated systematic review of randomized controlled trials. *Frontiers in Psychiatry, 9,* 583. doi:10.3389/fpsyt.2018.00583

Iyer, S., Boksa, P., Lal, S., Shah, J., Marandola, G., Jordan, G., Doyle, M., Joober, R., & Malla, A. (2015). Transforming youth mental health: A Canadian perspective. *Irish Journal of Psychological Medicine, 32*(1), 51–60. doi:10.1017/ipm.2014.89

Joiner, T. (2005). *Why people die by suicide.* Harvard University Press.

Kessler, R. C., Borges, G., & Walters, E. E. (1999). Prevalence of and risk factors for lifetime suicide attempts in the National Comorbidity Survey. *Archives of General Psychiatry, 56,* 617–626. doi:10.1001/archpsyc.56.7.617

Klonsky, E. D., & May, A. M. (2015). The three-step theory (3ST): A new theory of suicide rooted in the "ideation-to-action" framework. *International Journal of Cognitive Therapy, 8*(2), 114–129. doi:10.1521/ijct.2015.8.2.114

Koerner, K. (2011). *Doing dialectical behavior therapy: A practical guide.* Guilford.

Linehan, M. M. (1993a). *Cognitive-behavioral treatment of borderline personality disorder.* Guilford.

Linehan, M. M. (1993b). *Skills training manual for treating borderline personality disorder.* Guilford.

Linehan, M. M. (2015a). *DBT skills training handouts and worksheets* (2nd ed.). Guilford.

Linehan, M. M. (2015b). *DBT skills training manual* (2nd ed.). Guilford.

Linehan, M. M., Armstrong, H. E., Suarez, A., Allmon, D., & Heard, H. L. (1991). Cognitive-behavioral treatment of chronically parasuicidal borderline patients. *Archives of General Psychiatry, 48*(12), 1060–1064. doi:10.1001/archpsyc.1991.01810360024003

Linehan, M. M., Comtois, K. A., Murray, A. M., Brown, M. Z., Gallop, R. J., Heard, H. L., Korslund, K. E., Tutek, D. A., Reynolds, S. K., & Lindenboim, N. (2006). Two-year randomized controlled trial and follow-up of dialectical behavior therapy vs therapy by experts for suicidal behaviors and borderline personality disorder. *Archives of General Psychiatry, 63*(7),757–766. doi:10.1001/archpsyc.63.7.757

Linehan, M. M., Korslund, K. E., Harned, M. S., Gallop, R. J., Lungu, A., Neacsiu, A. D.,

McDavid, J., Comtois, K. A., & Murray-Gregory, A. M. (2015). Dialectical behavior therapy for high suicide risk in individuals with borderline personality disorder: A randomized clinical trial and component analysis. *JAMA Psychiatry, 72*(5), 475–482. doi:10.1001/jamapsychiatry.2014.3039

Linehan, M. M., Schmidt, H., III, Dimeff, L. A., Craft, J. C., Kanter, J., & Comtois, K. A. (1999). Dialectical behavior therapy for patients with borderline personality disorder and drug-dependence. *American Journal on Addictions, 8,* 279–292. doi:10.1080/105504999305686

Lynch, T. R., Chapman, A. L., Rosenthal, M. Z., Kuo, J. R., & Linehan, M. M. (2006). Mechanisms of change in dialectical behavior therapy: Theoretical and empirical observations. *Journal of Clinical Psychology, 62*(4), 459–480. doi:10.1002/jclp.20243

Lynch, T. R., Cheavens, J. S., Cukrowicz, K. C., Thorp, S. R., Bronner, L., & Beyer, J. (2007). Treatment of older adults with co-morbid personality disorder and depression: A dialectical behavior therapy approach. *International Journal of Geriatric Psychiatry, 22*(2), 131–143. doi:10.1002/gps.1703

Lyng, J., Swales, M. A., Hastings, R. P., Millar, T., & Duffy, D. J. (2020). Outcomes for 18 to 25-year-olds with borderline personality disorder in a dedicated young adult only DBT programme compared to a general adult DBT programme for all ages 18. *Early Intervention in Psychiatry, 14*(1), 61–68. doi:10.1111/eip.12808

MacKinnon, N., & Colman, I. (2016). Factors associated with suicidal thought and help-seeking behaviour in transition-aged youth versus adults. *Canadian Journal of Psychiatry, 61*(12), 789–796. doi:10.1177/0706743716667417

McCauley, E., Berk, M. S., Asarnow, J. R., Adrian, M., Cohen, J., Korslund, K., Avina, C., Hughes, J., Harned, M., Gallop, R., & Linehan, M. M. (2018). Efficacy of dialectical behavior therapy for adolescents at high risk for suicide: A randomized clinical trial. *JAMA Psychiatry, 75*(8), 777–785. doi:10.1001/jamapsychiatry.2018.1109

McMain, S. F., Chapman, A. L., Kuo, J. R., Guimond, T., Streiner, D. L., Dixon-Gordon, K. L., Isaranuwatchai, W., & Hoch, J. S. (2018). The effectiveness of 6 versus 12-months of dialectical behaviour therapy for borderline personality disorder: The feasibility of a shorter treatment and evaluating responses (FASTER) trial protocol. *BMC Psychiatry, 18,* 230. doi:10.1186/s12888-018-1802-z

McMain, S. F., Links, P. S., Gnam, W. H., Guimond, T., Cardish, R. J., Korman, L., & Streiner, D. L. (2009). A randomized trial of dialectical behavior therapy versus general psychiatric management for borderline personality disorder. *American Journal of Psychiatry, 166*(12), 1365–1374. doi:10.1176/appi.ajp.2009.09010039

Mehlum, L., Ramberg, M., Tørmoen, A. J., Haga, E., Diep, L. M., Stanley, B. H., Miller, A. L., Sund, A. M., & Grøholt, B. (2016). Dialectical behavior therapy compared with enhanced usual care for adolescents with repeated suicidal and self-harming behavior: Outcomes over a one-year follow-up. *Journal of the American Academy of Child and Adolescent Psychiatry, 55,* 295–300.

Mehlum, L., Tørmoen, A. J., Ramberg, M., Haga, E., Diep, L. M., Laberg, S., Larsson, B. S., Stanley, B. H., Miller, A. L., Sund, A. M., & Grøholt, B. (2014). Dialectical behavior therapy for adolescents with repeated suicidal and self-harming behavior: A randomized trial. *Journal of the American Academy of Child and Adolescent Psychiatry, 53*(10), 1082–1091. doi:10.1016/j.jaac.2014.07.003

Miller, A. L., Rathus, J. H., Leigh, E., Landsman, M., & Linehan, M. M. (1997). Dialectical behavior therapy adapted for suicidal adolescents. *Journal of Practical Psychiatry and Behavioral Health, 3,* 78–86.

Miller, A. L., Rathus, J. H., & Linehan, M. M. (2007). *Dialectical behavior therapy with suicidal adolescents.* Guilford.

Neacsiu, A. D., Lungu, A., Harned, M. S., Rizvi, S. L., & Linehan, M. M. (2014). Impact of dialectical behavior therapy versus community treatment by experts on emotional experience, expression, and acceptance in borderline personality disorder. *Behaviour Research and Therapy, 53,* 47–54. doi:10.1016/j.brat.2013.12.004

Neacsiu, A. D., Rizvi, S. L., Vitaliano, P. P., Lynch, T. R., & Linehan, M. M. (2010). The Dialectical Behavior Therapy Ways of Coping Checklist: Development and psychometric properties. *Journal of Clinical Psychology, 66*(6), 1–20. doi:10.1002/jclp.20685

Neece, C. L., Berk, M. S., & Combs-Ronto, L. A. (2013). Dialectical behavior therapy and suicidal behavior in adolescence: Linking developmental theory and practice. *Professional Psychology: Research and Practice, 44*(4), 257–265. doi:10.1037/a0033396

O'Connor, R. C., Cleare, S., Eschle, S., Wetherall, K., & Kirtley, O. J. (2016). The integrated motivational-volitional model of suicidal behavior: An update. In R. C. O'Connor & J. Pirkis (Eds.), *The international handbook of suicide prevention* (2nd ed., pp. 220–240). Wiley. doi:10.1002/9781118903223.ch13

Paul, M., Street, C., Wheeler, N., & Singh, S. P. (2015). Transition to adult services for young people with mental health needs: A systematic review. *Clinical Child Psychology and Psychiatry, 20*(3), 436–457. doi:10.1177/1359104514526603

Pelkonen, M., & Marttunen, M. (2003). Child and adolescent suicide: Epidemiology, risk factors, and approaches to prevention. *Paediatric Drugs, 5*(4), 243–265. doi:10.2165/00128072-200305040-00004

Perepletchikova, F. (2018). Dialectical behavior therapy for pre-adolescent children. In M. Swales (Ed.), *Oxford handbook of dialectical behaviour therapy.* Oxford University Press.

Perepletchikova, F., Nathanson, D., Axelrod, S. R., Merrill, C., Walker, A., Grossman, M., Rebeta, J., Scahill, L., Kaufman, J., Flye, B., Mauer, E., & Walkup, J. (2017). Randomized clinical trial of dialectical behavior therapy for preadolescent children with disruptive mood dysregulation disorder: Feasibility and outcomes. *Journal of the American Academy of Child and Adolescent Psychiatry, 56*(10), 832–840. doi:10.1016/j.jaac.2017.07.789

Pistorello, J., Fruzzetti, A. E., MacLane, C., Gallop, R. G., & Iverson, K. M. (2012). Dialectical behavior therapy (DBT) applied to college students: A randomized clinical trial. *Journal of Consulting and Clinical Psychology, 80*(6), 982–994. doi:10.1037/a0029096

Rathus, J. H., & Miller, A. L. (2000). DBT for adolescents: Dialectical dilemmas and secondary treatment targets. *Cognitive and Behavioral Practice, 7*(4), 425–434. doi:10.1016/S1077-7229(00)80054-1

Rathus, J. H., & Miller, A. L. (2002). Dialectical behavior therapy adapted for suicidal adolescents. *Suicide and Life-Threatening Behavior, 32*(2), 146–157. doi:10.1521/suli.32.2.146.24399

Rathus, J. H., & Miller, A. L. (2015). *DBT skills manual for adolescents.* Guilford.

Ribeiro, J. D., Franklin, J. C., Fox, K. R., Bentley, K. H., Kleiman, E. M., Chang, B. P., & Nock, M. K. (2016). Self-injurious thoughts and behaviors as risk factors for future suicide ideation, attempts, and death: A meta-analysis of longitudinal studies. *Psychological Medicine, 46*(2), 225–236. doi:10.1017/S0033291715001804

Roisman, G. I., Masten, A. S., Coatsworth, J. D., & Tellegen, A. (2004). Salient and emerging developmental tasks in the transition to adulthood. *Child Development, 75*(1), 123–133. doi:10.1111/j.1467-8624.2004.00658.x

Rosenthal, M., Wyatt, K., & McMahon, K. (2020). Cognitive behavioral approaches. In C.

Lejuez & K. Gratz (Eds.), *The Cambridge handbook of personality disorders.* Cambridge University Press.

Sayrs, J. H. R., & Linehan, M. M. (2019). *DBT teams: Development and practice.* Guilford.

Schmeling, N. E., Wyatt, K. P., & Cowperthwait, C. M. (2019). *Effects of multifamily DBT skills training for emerging adults on anxiety and skills use.* Poster presented at the 24th International Society for the Improvement and Teaching of Dialectical Behavior Therapy Conference, Atlanta, GA.

Singh, S. P. (2009). Transition of care from child to adult mental health services: The great divide. *Current Opinion in Psychiatry, 22*(4), 386–390. doi:10.1097/YCO.0b 013e32832c9221

Skehan, B., & Davis, M. (2017). Aligning mental health treatments with the developmental stage and needs of late adolescents and young adults. *Child and Adolescent Psychiatric Clinics of North America, 26*(2), 177–190. doi:10.1016/j.chc.2016.12.003.

Swee, G., Shochet, I., Cockshaw, W., & Hides, L. (2020). Emotion regulation as a risk factor for suicide ideation among adolescents and young adults: The mediating role of belongingness. *Journal of Youth and Adolescence, 49*, 2265–2274. doi:10.1007 /s10964-020-01301-2

Swenson, C. R., Torrey, W. C., & Koerner, K. (2002). Implementing dialectical behavior therapy. *Psychiatric Services, 53*(2), 171–178. doi:10.1176/appi.ps.53.2.171

Taber-Thomas, B., & Pérez-Edgar, K. (2015). Emerging adulthood brain development. In J. J. Arnett (Ed.), *The Oxford handbook of emerging adulthood* (pp. 126–141). Oxford University Press.

U.S. Bureau of the Census. (2015). *Current population survey: Annual social and economic (ASEC) supplement survey, 2015.* Inter-university Consortium for Political and Social Research. doi:10.3886/ICPSR36525.v1

Verheul, R., Van Den Bosch, L., Koeter, M., De Ridder, M., Stijnen, T., & Van Den Brink, W. (2003). Dialectical behaviour therapy for women with borderline personality disorder: 12-month, randomised clinical trial in the Netherlands. *British Journal of Psychiatry, 182*(2), 135–140. doi:10.1192/bjp.182.2.135

Vogel, D. L., Wade, N. G., & Hackler, A. H. (2008). Emotional expression and the decision to seek therapy: The mediating roles of the anticipated benefits and risks. *Journal of Social and Clinical Psychology, 27*(3), 254–278. doi:10.1521/jscp.2008.27.3.254

Wilson, C., Rickwood, D., Bushnell, J., Caputi, P., & Thomas, S. (2011). The effects of need for autonomy and preference for seeking help from informal sources on emerging adults' intentions to access mental health services for common mental disorders and suicidal thoughts. *Advances in Mental Health, 10*, 29–38. doi:10.5172/jamh.2011.10.1.29

Woodberry, K. A., Miller, A. L., Glinski, J., Indik, J., & Mitchell, A. G. (2002). Family therapy and dialectical behavior therapy with adolescents: Part II: A theoretical review. *American Journal of Psychotherapy, 56*(4), 585–602.

Yen, S., Zlotnick, C., & Costello, E. (2002). Affect regulation in women with borderline personality disorder traits. *Journal of Nervous and Mental Disease, 190*(10), 693–696.

Zanarini, M. C., Vujanovic, A. A., Parachini, E. A., Boulanger, J. L., Frankenburg, F. R., & Hennen, J. (2003). A screening measure for BPD: The McLean Screening Instrument for Borderline Personality Disorder (MSI-BPD). *Journal of Personality Disorders, 17*(6), 568–573. doi:10.1521/pedi.17.6.568.25355

Zivin, K., Eisenberg, D., Gollust, S. E., & Golberstein, E. (2009). Persistence of mental health problems and needs in a college student population. *Journal of Affective Disorders, 117*(3), 180–185. doi:10.1016/j.jad.2009.01.001

CHAPTER 15

Queer Enough or Too Queer?

The Effectiveness of Group Therapy in the Facilitation of Queer Young Adult Identity Formation

KATERI BERASI

Data collected from multiple sources over the past 10 years indicates that an ever-increasing percentage of Americans do not identify as heterosexual and/or cisgender.* While research indicates an upward trend in these identifications, the percentages vary widely. For example, a Gallup poll taken in 2017 indicates that the percentage of American adults identifying as lesbian, gay, bisexual, or transgender (LGBT) is 4.5% of the general population, up from 3.5% when this measure was first taken in 2012 (Newport, 2018). However, according to polling by the J. Walter Thompson Innovation Group, more than half of Generation Z (ages 7–22) does not identify as strictly heterosexual, whereas for Millennials (ages 23–38) this figure is 35% (Moreno, 2019). Similarly, this research group found that 56% of Gen Z and 43% of Millennials report knowing someone who goes by gender-neutral pronouns and identifies as a gender other than cisgender (Moreno, 2019).

These discrepancies in percentages highlight two important points. First, regardless of the exact percentage of people who identify as nonheterosexual and/or noncisgender, this figure clearly has changed and is continuing to

---

* The first part of this chapter utilizes the terms "nonheterosexual and noncisgender" so as to be the most inclusive of generational differences in language regarding a person who might identify as LGBT, queer, or some other term. The latter portion, focused on clinical relevancy, utilizes the term "queer" to refer to this population as this is the term used by the majority of young adults generally and more specifically the young adults within my clinical practice.

increase with time. Second, language is important in understanding who is included and who is excluded in these polls when looking at nonheterosexual and/or noncisgender individuals; that is, a poll inquiring if a person identifies as lesbian, gay, bisexual, or transgender will produce different results than a poll inquiring if a person identifies in some way as nonheterosexual and/or noncisgender. Such differences in language matter greatly today as an increasing number of young people do not wish to subscribe to one particular set identity or group, but rather experience themselves as existing along a continuum of sexual orientation and gender that cannot be located so specifically.

HISTORICAL CONTEXT

The historical context of rights and protections offered to nonheterosexual and noncisgender individuals is important to note, as these have had an impact on the safety needed for these groups to be out versus remaining closeted. Examining the interplay of social justice movements and increases in freedoms over time helps to explain the widening gap between the Baby Boomer generation and younger generations for nonheterosexual and noncisgender people. Throughout history, the United States has been largely inhospitable to these groups through practices of cultural and legal exclusion as well as outright violence. Until recently, many of the legal protections afforded heterosexual and cisgender individuals were denied to people with different sexual orientation and gender identities. Positive political change is attributable to activism rallying for change; with such activism grows the collective consciousness surrounding discrimination toward nonheterosexual and noncisgender individuals and encourages further attempts to right these wrongs.

Stonewall Riots

The Stonewall Riots of 1969 ignited public attention to the discrimination toward nonheterosexual and noncisgender people. Briefly summarized, the Stonewall Riots began on June 28, 1969, when police raided the Stonewall Inn, a gay bar in New York City, igniting a riot among patrons and police. Six days of protests and violent clashes with neighborhood residents and police ensued, catalyzing the gay rights movement in the United States (Stein, 2019). While nonheterosexual and noncisgender individuals from all generations look to this historic period with reverence and gratitude for those that took action, the lived experience of being nonheterosexual or noncisgender in New York City today is quite different than it was in 1969: a person from Generation Z is often less capable of fully grappling with the lack of social visibility or acceptance that the Baby Boomer generation contended with at this time.

HIV/AIDS

Just as a dialogue about the rights of nonheterosexual and noncisgender individuals began to open up following the Stonewall Riots, the global HIV/AIDS epidemic ignited. Because HIV/AIDS was initially identified primarily within the gay male community, discrimination and violence toward this group as well as other nonheterosexual and noncisgender individuals increased, and along with it myths, misinformation, and fear. While there continues to be stigma regarding HIV/AIDS for nonheterosexual and noncisgender individuals, especially gay men, the trauma of this epidemic particularly impacted those in Generation X, born between 1965 and 1979, who were coming of age as the epidemic blossomed. Due to recent changes in public perception of HIV/AIDS largely attributable to public relations efforts as well as medical advances in treatment, younger generations, particularly Generation Z and younger, do not contend with the same level of stigma or fear regarding HIV/ AIDS. They are therefore less inhibited in exploring their sexual orientation and/or gender identity because the negative consequences that older generations experienced are less pronounced.

Recent Laws Affecting Nonheterosexual and Noncisgender People

The Defense of Marriage Act (DOMA) of 1996 defined marriage for federal purposes as the union between a man and a woman and allowed states to refuse to recognize same-sex marriages licensed under the laws of other states (Clinton, 2013). Although DOMA was repealed in 2015 through *Obergefell v. Hodges*, which legalized same-sex marriage in all 50 states and required states to honor out-of-state same-sex marriage licenses, there remain institutionalized discriminatory laws that negatively affect these populations (Denniston, 2015). For example, in 2018, only 19 states and the District of Columbia prohibited discrimination based on sexual orientation and gender identity in employment, housing, and public accommodations (Human Rights Watch, 2020). In fact, protections that have been instituted are also being repealed, such as a new regulation rewriting section 1557 of the Affordable Care Act, undoing protections for transgender patients against discrimination by doctors, hospitals, and health insurance companies (Stubbe, 2020). While LGBT individuals in the United States have a protected status through the Matthew Shepard and James Byrd, Jr. Hate Crimes Prevention Act of 2009, hate crimes against this population persist and have risen slightly (Human Rights Campaign, 2018).

Despite these facts and figures, it remains incontrovertible that more people are out today than at any point in the past. The highest concentrations of LGBT individuals are found in localities that are progressive and accordingly offer greater legal and social protections to these groups, often large metropolitan areas. Young generations now enter romantic relationships knowing that they can marry whomever they choose. The increased visibility and positive media portrayal of public figures who are out as nonheterosexual and noncisgender also serve to normalize diverse sexual orientation and gender identities for the general public.

While an ever-increasing number of people identify as nonheterosexual or noncisgender, what does this mean for this group as a whole? Does a queer identity still speak to those who identified as LGBT 5, 10, or 40 years ago, or has the identification of being queer become so expansive that the struggles and discrimination that marked the experiences of previous LGBT generations and gave shape to these identities become less relevant? For the purposes of our discussion, we will examine why these questions matter for clinical work with young adults.

THE IMPORTANCE OF LANGUAGE

An identifier adopted by many to signal the spectrum of sexuality and gender is the word "queer." According to the Lesbian, Gay, Bisexual, and Transgender Community Center in New York City, considered to be one of the preeminent resources for concerns related to being nonheterosexual or noncisgender, "queer" is "an adjective used by some people, particularly younger people, whose sexual orientation is not exclusively heterosexual. . . . Some people may use queer . . . to describe their gender identity and/or gender expression." The Center states that many individuals use the identifier "queer" instead of the terms lesbian, gay, or bisexual (LGB) because these are perceived as too limiting and/or fraught with cultural connotations they feel don't apply to them.

This difference in use of identifying language—LGB versus queer—is notable within different generations, with Millennials and Generation Z preferring queer and those of older generations identifying more readily as lesbian, gay, bisexual, and/or transgender. A cultural shift toward increased tolerance for diverse sexual orientations and gender expressions is underway, helping to explain why there is such a significant change between the Baby Boomer generation and Generation Z in those who openly identify as nonheterosexual and/or noncisgender. This increased societal tolerance has a pronounced impact on the life experiences of people identifying as nonheterosexual and/or noncisgender: while there continues to be a degree of overlap between nonheterosexual and noncisgender people from the Baby Boomer generation and from Generation Z, their in-group relatability is quickly decreasing as the forces of homophobia and transphobia become less pronounced on a societal level.

Of great significance regarding the interplay of language, identity, and generational differences is the use of personal pronouns. In English, the most commonly used pronouns are "he/him/his" for those who identify with a male gender, and "she/her/hers" for those who identify with a female gender. Although there are outliers, for much of history pronouns were limited to this binary, and people assigned male at birth were expected and assumed to use masculine pronouns and those assigned female at birth were expected and assumed to use female pronouns. However, such expectations and assumptions began to change in the new millennium as a result of people questioning and challenging the strictures of the gender binary. Different pronouns began to emerge, to the effect that by 2014 Facebook provided 50 different gender identity options for users to select from (Steinmetz, 2014). For people who don't identify along the gender binary, including but not limited to those who may identify as queer, gender nonconforming, nonbinary, and transgender, the use of different pronouns that are in alignment with their sense of self can be affirming. Pronouns most often used by those eschewing the binary include "they/them/theirs," while some individuals choose to use only their names, or any and all pronouns to refer to themselves.

CLINICAL IMPLICATIONS

Almost all of my patients who are queer report that they sought out my services specifically because I advertise that I specialize in working with queer
folks. Although it is not explicitly stated, the implication is that I am queer
(accurate), which is part of what makes my patients comfortable working with
me, trusting that I likely understand their experiences at least to some degree
from a personal identity and community-based level. Many of these patients
stated that they had seen a previous therapist who wasn't queer and that therapy wasn't as effective as they wished because their therapist couldn't empathize with the feelings related to being queer that they were trying to convey.
I have been told that quality session time was often spent trying to educate
a previous therapist on language specific to queer folks and cultural aspects
of being queer with which the therapist was unfamiliar. Several patients
have reported that their previous experience in therapy actually caused harm
because the therapist perpetuated negative stereotypes of queer people, causing the patient to experience a lack of emotional safety in a space that is supposed to produce the opposite function. Fatigue and resentment eventually
grew, motivating these patients to find a therapist with whom they would feel
better understood and less judged.

While there will always be those who seek therapists similar to themselves
on a specific identity level out of the desire to have a shared language and
mutual understanding, there is also much that therapists who aren't queer can
do to educate themselves to help their patients feel better understood, diminishing the capacity to do harm and increasing generative opportunities. Given
my experience working with queer young adults in a therapeutic context, I can
suggest several dynamics that are important to understand: Queerness is not a
monolith; one person's experience of queerness is likely different from another's. As previously expressed, the label "queer" is broad and quite limitless outside the bounds of strict heterosexual and cisgender identities. Generational
differences are real: A young adult identifying as queer has likely experienced
oppression differently than a nonheterosexual and/or noncisgender person of
an older generation. More often than not, queer young adults have grown up
with messages of inclusivity and greater protections from which older people did not benefit. Nonetheless, homophobia, transphobia, and systems of
oppression continue to persist and impact queer people of all ages.

Owing to the interplay of their generational and identity statuses, queer young adults can struggle to feel affirmed within themselves and to navigate a confusing world that is at once accepting and encouraging of their sexual and gender identities while also rejecting and potentially dangerous. While individual therapy can help patients work through this confusion, the group format is particularly ideal for addressing these concerns because it is a space in which queer young adults likely feel understood by their peers on an identity and generational level, thereby enabling them to support one another with the nuanced difficulties that arise in their lives that heterosexual and/or cisgender people and people of older generations may not understand.

According to Dr. Irvin D. Yalom (2008), a leading expert on group therapy, group is effective in promoting the following therapeutic benefits: the installation of hope, universality, the imparting of information, altruism, the corrective recapitulation of the primary family group, the development of socialization techniques, imitative behavior, interpersonal learning, group cohesiveness, catharsis, and existential factors. In group, members can give one another feedback, share information, offer support, express emotions, and hold space for one another. By fostering such opportunities, group therapy is particularly helpful for socially isolated queer young adults. While many people realize that they are queer at a young age, they often do not come out until adolescence or early adulthood, and can be at a developmental disadvantage as a result. For example, activities and rites of passage such as dating and sex that their heterosexual and/or cisgender peers often experience at younger ages may still be new and unfamiliar to queer young adults. Openness with one's family about one's queerness may be fraught. The ability to get a job as an openly queer person or a closeted, visibly queer person may also be challenging. Ideally, the holding environment of group provides a safe and supportive forum for such issues to be explored and worked through.

Two clinical vignettes follow to demonstrate how the group format provides opportunities for helping queer young adults navigate their identity.

CASE EXAMPLE: QUEER GROUP

I created the Queer Psychotherapy Group in January 2020 to establish a space for queer folks to be able to both give and receive support to each other and to process emotions related to their experiences, within a setting in which there is a shared language and some overlap in life experiences related to their identity as queer people. I invited the members to this group because they expressed feelings of isolation in their queerness by not having many queer friends or a sense of queer community. They felt alone in trying to navigate their queer identity in its formation and in its embodiment in their daily life. The group is composed of seven individuals in their 20s and early 30s. All of the members identify as nonheterosexual, and a multitude of gender identities are represented.

During the first session's introductions, patients shared names and preferred pronouns. The initial focus was on establishing norms, gaining comfort, and building trust with one another, and uniting over shared experiences related to queerness, such as the coming-out process and navigating difficult relationships with family members who are not affirming. Members soon realized that they each had experienced childhood trauma as a result of their queer identity and homophobia/transphobia, whether this was sexual abuse, physical abuse, bullying, or being deeply shamed for being different than their peers and family. While the exact nature of their trauma was different, upon sharing their stories with others who could empathize, members attested to feeling seen and less alone or stigmatized.

Given that a spirit of understanding and safety had been established based on expressed similarities, it was alarming to group members when, after seven months of being together, one patient, John, misgendered another patient, Taylor, several times over the course of speaking in a group session, calling Taylor "she" rather than "they," their preferred pronoun. John is a gay, cisgender male, and Taylor is a queer, AFAB (assigned female at birth), nonbinary person. As this was occurring, many of the other group members balked at the error: "How could John misgender Taylor after group had been meeting for so long?" Of all spaces, Queer Group is supposed to be a place where group members experience affirmation and allyship in their queer identities, rather than engagement in a manner that perpetuates their negative experiences with society at large. After John finished speaking, I brought attention to his misgendering of Taylor, and John was quite upset that he had unconsciously been in error and potentially hurt Taylor's feelings. One of the primary reasons John joined Queer Group is because the majority of his friends were heterosexual and cisgender and he wanted to experience a feeling of belonging with other people whom he could relate to in ways that he could not with his friends. Being one of the two gay cisgender males in group, John voiced doubt about whether he even belonged in group, questioning if he was "queer enough" to be in that space. John stated that he was afraid that he would now be viewed by group as perpetuating a white, gay, cisgender male stereotype in not acknowledging his various privileges that separated him from other members of group, particularly the trans members.

Taylor replied that they were not upset with John for misgendering them in that they believed it was in error and was unintentional. Taylor also stated that they have even misgendered themselves and other trans people accidentally in the past. For Taylor, what mattered was that John wanted to gender them according to their preferred pronouns and in making this effort, demonstrated that he valued and cared for Taylor as a person. None of Taylor's family members correctly gendered them most of the time, and many of them never made an effort to do so. Taylor was also often misgendered at work. Taylor had had top surgery and expressed frustration that despite this as well as other physical markers they had altered so as not to appear stereotypically feminine, they felt stuck as they were often read as female by society. Other group members chimed in to support Taylor, either by sharing their own experiences of being misgendered or similar experiences of not being read and treated by society in an affirming manner. Although John was terrified of being canceled by group and made to feel he did not belong in that space, the group rallied behind him, encouraging him not to hold back from participating in the future out of fear of "getting something wrong," but to persevere with openness and vulnerability so that he and the group could continue to grow. Group members stated that John's efforts mattered and that they knew through all of the previous group sessions that his intentions were in the right place. John in turn stated that he would continue to try to educate himself about queerness, including pronouns and different gender expressions. The group related that they would be happy to help him navigate this.

As this interaction demonstrates, just because a person identifies as queer does not mean that they are immersed in queer culture; they may be the only queer person they know. Therefore, while often there is shared experience related to queerness that group members can relate to, there will be differences and areas in which misunderstandings are prevalent. As with any group, it is important that the facilitator recognizes and highlights such moments instead of potentially allowing them to be brushed aside as they might be in everyday life. Calling attention to Taylor being misgendered created the opportunity for John to verbalize his fears of not belonging and to work through his mistake with Taylor. It also presented Taylor with the ability to process being misgendered and to work through this in the here and now under safe conditions. Knowing what it feels like to be othered, it was important to the group to rally around both John and Taylor. In doing so, the entire group was able to have what I hope was a corrective emotional experience. By ensuring that both John and Taylor felt like they belonged and mattered, the group affirmed that there was space for all forms of queerness, and the concern that one wouldn't be "queer enough" to maintain membership in group was worked through.

CASE EXAMPLE: WOMXN'S GROUP

The creation of the Womxn's Psychotherapy Group was inspired by my observation that many of my female-identified patients expressed difficulties navigating boundaries in relationships, whether familial, professional, friendship, or romantic. While this concern is not exclusive to women, many of my female-identified patients voiced that these boundary difficulties are at least partially related to their gender because women tend to be encouraged by society to disavow their needs in the service of others. Grounded with this understanding, I created Womxn's Group in February 2020 for patients who are female-identified to provide a space to explore and practice boundary setting as well as to give and receive support to one another within a framework of the lived experience of being a woman.

Womxn's Group consists of eight members, all of whom identified as cisgender females at the time they joined. The age range is mid-20s to late 30s; five identify their sexual orientation as queer and three as heterosexual. Two of the five queer members came out as queer approximately four months into group, both within the same session, and received positive affirmation by all. Previous to the latter two patients coming out, sexual orientation was discussed minimally, always within the context of whom one was dating, never directly about the experience of being queer. Gender identity was always discussed through the lens of being cisgender female.

Members explored what the two individuals coming out meant for the group dynamic, as it appeared to shift from majority heterosexual to majority queer. There was a notable shift in focus and relatability as the queer members began to talk directly about their experience of queerness, including what this identity meant to them and how they embodied this identity in the world and in group. All the members of group expressed positive sentiments that the two members felt safe and comfortable enough to come out and discuss this process with the group. There was also discussion about what it meant for all the group members to hold space for one another. Group was described as a place where all could feel a sense of belonging, despite any differences related to sexual orientation.

A notable change occurred after one of the members, Tanya, opened up to the group that they had been thinking about their gender identity, concluding that they were nonbinary and preferred "they/them" pronouns. The response of the group was notably different than when the two members came out as having queer sexual orientations a month earlier—two of the heterosexual members and two of the queer members were largely silent for the remainder of group and did not respond to Tanya coming out, while the other three members of group were verbally affirming. A discussion of gender ensued, with the affirming group members discussing and exploring their relationship to their gender as females. In an effort to be inclusive and make Tanya feel welcome, they relayed that they were not always gender conforming. When asked about their reticence to engage more fully in the conversation, the other group members reported that they needed more time to process this change as they were surprised. The following week Tanya decided not to return to group, telling me that they no longer felt that group could hold space for them since they now identified as nonbinary rather than female. Tanya reported that they felt alone and isolated in their identity and that being in the group magnified these feelings. When I informed the group of this news, members were disappointed and wished Tanya had remained. The group stated that although Tanya no longer identified as female, they still felt comfortable with them in the group space and welcomed any group member sharing their authentic self with group, whatever form that might take.

While Womxn's Group originally felt supportive and welcoming to Tanya when they came out as having a queer sexual orientation, they ultimately felt that they no longer belonged due to differences in gender identity. Tanya was unable to tolerate having what they perceived as incomplete support from the group and was unable to process their disappointment, hurt, and anger because they terminated participation so abruptly. Had they remained, they would have been able to work through these feelings with the group, to eventually discover that they are not in fact too queer for this space. Instead, what occurred re-created Tanya's experience of feeling different and ostracized in their everyday life.

Of note is that the continued discussion about gender that ensued following Tanya's departure, whereupon members examined their own gender identities and attitudes toward diverse genders, did encourage another member to eventually come out as genderqueer and remain as a vital member of group. Given these events, I have since modified my consent form to specifically state that upon joining group all members identify as female as it is explicitly a space for female-identified individuals; however, if one's gender identity changes over the course of their participation, this does not serve as a disqualifier but instead something to be processed and explored with the group.

CONCLUSION

So, not queer enough for one space, too queer for another—how is this negotiated? As society's definition of and engagement with queerness continue to evolve, people, particularly young adults in the process of identity formation, continue to try to figure out who they are, what queerness means to them, and how, as queer people, they relate to others. Some queer young adults are lucky: they have supportive family, friends, and partners, do not struggle to be hired and employed, and have a source of community. They may have learned about the Stonewall Riots in their high school history class, but this historic period is as foreign to them as any other chapter in their textbook. Their dreams can include marriage if they so choose. And they have a panoply of personal pronouns they may assume.

Nevertheless, while an increasing number of people identify as queer, creating a society that is now more familiar with and accepting of queerness than ever before, many queer people continue to experience isolation and shame related to their queer identity. Group provides an ideal setting in which to work through such struggles and receive support, thereby helping the individual establish a more secure queer identity and an integrated sense of self. And yet, as in the real world, group members do not always respond in the way a patient may wish, and the pain, shame, and feelings of differentness that are experienced in their everyday lives can arise within group. Given time and attention, such feelings can be worked through in the group context, providing a corrective emotional experience and motivating the patient to navigate such challenges in their everyday life.

There is no right or wrong answer as to whether a queer young adult patient would be better served by a queer-specific group or a more general psychotherapy group, as both have their merits. One aspect to consider is where the patient resides regarding their identity as a queer person. Questions to consider include: Are they recently out or still closeted and want to gain more comfort with their identity? Do they lack community with other queer people and would benefit from more contact with them? However, as we have seen, just because a queer person is in a queer group does not automatically mean that they will feel secure in their queer identity in that therapy space. Ultimately, the ability to work through feelings of differentness toward self-acceptance can be a meaningful and healing experience regardless of the particular group setting. For young adults coming into their queerness, group therapy can provide a transformative space to do this.

Dr. Kateri Berasi is a licensed clinical psychologist and the founder of Transcendent Self, a psychotherapy private practice in Brooklyn, New York. She specializes in working with queer folks and people working in the creative industries. Dr. Berasi utilizes a person-centered, humanistic model of therapy and encourages all forms of self-expression in her work with patients. She has written and lectured on best practices for working with LGBTQ individuals in psychotherapy, and has created a novel form of treatment, "costume therapy," as a means of furthering self-expression, exploration, and healing.

REFERENCES

Clinton, B. (2013, March 7). It's time to overturn DOMA. *Washington Post.* https://www.washingtonpost.com/opinions/bill-clinton-its-time-to-overturn-doma/2013/03/07/fc184408-8747-11e2-98a3-b3db6b9ac586_story.html

Denniston, L. (2015, June 26). Opinion analysis: Marriage now open to same-sex couples. *SCOTUSblog.* https://www.scotusblog.com/2015/06/opinion-analysis-marriage-now-open-to-same-sex-couples/

Human Rights Campaign. (2018, November 13). New FBI statistics show alarming increase in number of reported hate crimes. https://www.hrc.org/news/new-fbi-statistics-show-alarming-increase-in-number-of-reported-hate-crimes

Human Rights Watch. (2020, June). Human Rights Watch country profiles: Sexual orientation and gender identity. https://www.hrw.org/world-report/2020/country-chapters/united-states#3802c6

Moreno, L. (2019, July 25). This is why the future will be queer. Metrosource. https://metrosource.com/this-is-why-the-future-will-be-queer/

Newport, F. (2018, May 22). In U.S., estimate of LGBT population rises to 4.5%. Gallup. https://news.gallup.com/poll/234863/estimate-lgbt-population-rises.aspx

Stein, M. (2019, June 3). Queer rage: Police violence and the Stonewall Rebellion of 1969. *Process: A Blog for American History.* https://www.processhistory.org/stein-stonewall/

Steinmetz, K. (2014, February 14). A comprehensive guide to Facebook's new options for gender identity: An expert walks through what they mean, from transgender to pangender. Time. https://techland.time.com/2014/02/14/a-comprehensive-guide-to -facebooks-new-options-for-gender-identity/

Stubbe, D. E. (2020). Practicing cultural competence and cultural humility in the care of diverse patients. *FOCUS: The Journal of Lifelong Learning in Psychiatry, 18,* 49–51.

Yalom, I. D. (2008). *The theory and practice of group psychotherapy.* Basic Books.

CHAPTER 16

The College Counseling Center

A Developmental Playground for Emerging Adults

SHERINA PERSAUD

A dolescence is a critical time in terms of the salience of identity formation and development (Erikson, 1959). Throughout early to late adolescence, children are negotiating an individuation process from their parents, which ultimately results in a separation from them in terms of their identity (Collins & Laursen, 2004; Collins & Steinberg, 2005). This separation enables the formation of a unique identity, a goal of adolescence, which often leads to normative conflict in relationships with parents or caregivers (Smetana et al., 2006). Identity exploration in adolescence is characterized by the consideration of alternatives in personal values and beliefs, and this exploration is integral to identity development (Matteson, 1977). Adolescent identity exploration flourishes in relationships: interactions between family members, friends, lovers, and other important people during this time of life often spurs young people's identity construction (Grotevant & Cooper, 1985). Individuation can be understood as consisting of individuality and connectedness: individuality, in that one is gaining a sense of separateness and asserting one's self as unique; and connectedness, in that the young person is more aware of mutuality and the permeability of others' views (Grotevant & Cooper, 1985). Having both individuality to communicate personal beliefs and connectedness to respect others' views while also maintaining boundaries provides the necessary context for adolescent identity exploration (Grotevant & Cooper, 1985).

A DEVELOPMENTAL CONTEXT FOR COLLEGE MENTAL HEALTH

Attending college, and residing on a college campus in particular, can provide a distinctive opportunity to explore one's growing agency and autonomy while simultaneously deepening interpersonal relationships as the young adult transitions from family life to the "real world." At college, each young person comes in with their own cultural background, their own different values placed on family, individualism, and community. At the same time, each college student is engaging with the important process of defining personal goals and learning how to relate to others and adapt to their new environment. Blos (1967) described adolescence as a second individuation process after toddlerhood, in which the adolescent disengages from early object relations to achieve autonomy and a newfound sense of self. Autonomy at this stage can be multidimensional and can vary across situations: main facets include emotional autonomy from parents, feeling self-reliant, and resisting peer pressure (Steinberg & Silverberg, 1986). Burgeoning autonomy leads to an important maturational stage in personality organization, ideally resulting in the adolescent developing into an adult member of society (Blos, 1967). In order to achieve this, the focus shifts from internalized objects to externalized ones in the form of other relationships that facilitate independence from parental figures (Blos, 1967). This disengagement causes a renewal of the infantile ego and drive positions and a reorganization of the superego to manage fantasies of being unique. The adolescent thus seeks relationships with people outside of the family as a means of developing an idiosyncratic self.

The importance of peer groups generally shifts from early to late adolescence, with a higher emphasis on the peer group in early adolescence, increased tolerance of individuality and nonconformity in middle adolescence, and emphasis on intense dyadic relationships that are more intimate in late adolescence (Erikson, 1959; Balassone, 1991). Social groups across these stages of adolescence can facilitate exploration of identity, along with a commitment to understanding oneself and one's role in society. A sense of one's historical narrative as way of making meaning of identity is essential to creating a cohesive story of the self. The university setting offers the possibility of exploring various peer groups and, with this, exposure to new kinds of people. As such, at college, young people often meet people with beliefs, values, and cultural norms different from their own. Psychotherapy during this time can be particularly useful in helping young adults put words to these experiences and their life story, as well as providing a space to work through the developmental challenges related to the conflicting desires of both separation and closeness.

Under the best of circumstances, a university setting can provide students with important opportunities to "try on for size" different potential selves in an environment that permits independence from their caregivers. Ideally, university life is a space to safely explore, among other things, aspects of sexual and gender identity, personal values and opinions, and relationships, as well as likes and dislikes, within a context that does not have the same restrictions and consequences as life in full-on adulthood. This exploration period is an important developmental milestone in emerging adulthood, without which young people are at risk of facing lasting existential crises of identity. Limitations in exploration during this time can possibly lead to following the status quo or stereotyped expectations from caregivers or society as a model of how to behave in the absence of having the emotional and physical space to find one's own footing. R. J. Eichler, executive director of the Columbia Counseling Center, describes this "psychosocial moratorium" (Erikson, 1956) as an essential complement to the psychotherapy setting on college campuses. He writes that "the dialogue, be it in word or deed, between students trying to work out relationships with important others invites a loose comparison to the mutual effort made by analyst and patient, emphasized by the intersubjective turn in psychoanalytic discourse, to achieve new relational positions and to overcome that which threatens, rather than enriches, connections" (Eichler, 2011, p. 303). The college counseling therapist can thus serve as a close relationship through which to understand the student's place in other relationships, and they can experiment with this in the office, out on campus, and beyond.

LIFE AS A COLLEGE COUNSELING PSYCHOLOGIST

There are often misconceptions about what the work of a psychologist at a college counseling center entails. Coming from a background working with people with severe mental health disorders in hospitals and inpatient psychiatric units, I imagined working with college students to be primarily assisting students with managing stressors related to classes and their social lives. I was immediately surprised when I met with my first patient in this setting, who had a severe dissociative episode in my office, and I had to make a quick decision about how to keep her safe enough to determine whether she should return to her dorm or receive a higher level of care. Perhaps surprisingly, but throughout my work with college students, I have encountered the kind of severe psychopathology that I had seen in hospital settings. My work involves understanding developmental concerns with young adults as well as managing crises, making appropriate referrals, collaborating with various entities within the university, and providing rapid triage while experiencing what seems to be an increasing number of students with complex needs. Part of the job involves helping students successfully get through college, while at other times it is to help them manage when it is not feasible for them to do so—whether that is through determining if a medical leave of absence is appropriate or if maybe they should drop out altogether. Students often come in with a sense of urgency and acuity in their symptoms, perhaps about an upcoming exam, a relationship issue, questioning their gender or sexual identity, or having experienced a recent sexual assault. This is reflected in the frequency of students using drop-in type sessions on college campuses. This type of therapy requires a different way of working with college students at the counseling center than one might do in a private practice setting in terms of flexibility of the treatment (Eichler, 2006). Many students will come and go, or will come for a few sessions after a crisis and never return. It is therefore especially important to establish as much of a sense of rapport, safety, and relationship as possible in the initial session.

The number of students utilizing mental health services on campuses appears to be rising, and many counseling centers have struggled to find ways to manage the increasing demand. According to the 2019 Association for University and College Counseling Center Directors Annual Survey, 90% of the 562 counseling centers represented in the survey noted a significant increase in demand in their services on campus from the previous year. This increase is likely explained by a combination of factors, including reduced mental health stigma and increased use of psychopharmacology, among other treatments, to treat more severe psychopathology, which permits students to enter college who may not have done so before (Ketchen Lipson et al., 2019). For many students, the college counseling center provides their first access to mental health services that were not available to them before. An online survey of over 150,000 students from nearly 200 college campuses across the United States examining 10 years of data, 2007–2017, concluded that there was a significant increase in the utilization of college counseling services and diagnoses of depression and anxiety, as well as suicidal ideation (Ketchen Lipson et al., 2019). In many cases, psychopathology on campus can be viewed as an attempt by a student to communicate their needs, albeit in a maladaptive, painful, or sometimes dangerous way. Grayson (2006) aptly notes how this can be a way for college students to work out parts of their identity and to increase their sense of belonging: "scratch the surface of a bulimic or binge drinker or suicidal student—or any student—and the same gnawing insecurities tend to appear: 'Am I good enough?' 'Am I loveable?' 'Am I normal?' 'Where do I belong?'" (p. 3). It is often the goal of the college counseling therapist to help students grapple with these important developmental questions in a way that does not involve acting them out in a harmful manner.

DEVELOPMENTAL CONSIDERATIONS IN THE THERAPEUTIC ENCOUNTER

For many students, my role as a therapist can feel akin to being a parental figure. There is a process of attachment and connection, followed by an appropriate separation as many students come and go at the college counseling center. The seemingly conflicting desire for closeness and need to separate is often reflected in the ways in which students engage in therapy. I find this can be expressed in the ways in which the students I meet with both challenge and align with me as they work out this dynamic. My therapeutic approach tends to be more active as we navigate the understandable feelings of loss and excitement that come with establishing personal values of their own that they realize may be different from what they were taught growing up. In many cases, the nature of working in college mental health setting necessitates a more active approach—the traditional psychoanalytic style with limited disclosure can be viewed as withholding to students who are in need of validation of their thoughts and feelings as they play with new ideas and ways of being. Moreover, many counseling centers limit how many therapy sessions a student can have in an academic year, which can also impact the therapeutic style given the knowledge that treatment is not open ended.

I have met with many students flexibly throughout their years of pursuing an undergraduate degree. One student described me as their "point person" during their college career—someone they could rely on for support and validation, whom they could check in with as their life unfolded. This works well within a short-term therapy model adopted by most college counseling centers in that treatment does not often take place in a traditional weekly, consistent manner. This seems developmentally appropriate as students balance a need for independence with the need for a close relationship, guidance, and support from an adult figure.

A student I met with on and off during his four years in college exemplifies this phenomenon. Henry, a cisgender, straight, young Black man, was an international student from a low-income family. He had never been to therapy prior to coming to the college counseling center during his freshman year, mostly because his culture and community at home stigmatize mental health care and value working through issues independently. Henry first came to meet me at the recommendation of a professor who was concerned about his mental health, as evidenced by his recent absences and poor performance in his coursework. When he entered my office, Henry was silent, arms crossed, keeping his eyes down and looking away from me. He quickly uttered, "I don't think I need to be here, but my professor thinks I should, and I need you to write him a note." I obliged; it was clear to me in my initial assessment that Henry was severely depressed, as evidenced by his flat affect, psychomotor retardation, passive suicidal ideation, and sense of hopelessness about the future. He also had an extensive trauma history that made asking for help very challenging. It became evident that an off-campus referral for long-term therapy would be useful for Henry as he could benefit from more in-depth treatment. However, given the fact that he could not afford it and how prone to feeling rejected he was, we decided to continue meeting with each other. He came consistently, though he was usually quite guarded and sometimes arrived with only a few minutes left in our session. We later discussed how he was "testing [me] out" in these early sessions. Toward the end of our treatment, he reflected that in our initial sessions he felt a deep longing to connect with me while also being very afraid of this intimacy. Given his history of betrayal and abandonment from those who were meant to care for him, it was hard for him to believe that I would have his best interests in mind.

Henry described college as like deep sea diving: you can swim and explore for a while, but you're expected to, and need to, go down into more dangerous and pressure-filled ocean depths as you progress. He seemed to have this sense of impending doom awaiting him after graduation, in part because of the very real pressures he felt to provide financially for himself and his family. He recounted several instances of sexual, emotional, and physical abuse growing up in a matter-of-fact tone and would look up at me after sharing something particularly painful as if to scan me for a reaction. If I expressed empathy or reflected how difficult it must have been for him, he would sometimes look down with a slight smile that quickly vanished. If I expressed what he later told me was "too much" in the form of sentence-long statements of validation and support, he would disappear from treatment and return on his own terms weeks or months later.

Henry was as hungry for love and affection as he was starved of it throughout his life; he also had, however, a strong need for independence. He felt he could only rely on himself, which had been quite adaptive for him growing up, yet simultaneously he seemed to be afraid of just how much he would need me if he allowed himself to take in the reparative aspects of our relationship. He would often appear in my schedule after making an appointment with the front desk. Each time he came back reinforced for him that I was not going anywhere, no matter how many times he tested this theory. He began to experiment with different ways of relating to me—sometimes more closed off, sometimes more open, sometimes humorous or sarcastic. I viewed this as an important part of him discovering his identity and who he wanted to be in relation to the world.

The way in which Henry would look up at me as he described his various goals, aspirations, longings, and fears reminded me of some of the research I had done in my graduate training on attachment in which toddlers were observed playing with a new toy for the first time. I remember watching toddlers pick up a toy, lifting it up to show it to their parent as if to say, "Is this safe?" Then a simple nod or smile from their parent would suffice as the happy babies continued to play. My (attempted) consistent validation, especially after several months of separation, seemed to provide Henry with a sense of security that promoted exploration. He began to play out this exploration in his relationships with his peers, and eventually entered a romantic relationship. One session, after not having met with me for two months, Henry came in to let me know that he and his girlfriend had broken up. He repeated a variation of something I had said to him before: "It hurts a lot. But I took the risk to be vulnerable with her and that gave me something. Maybe next time I'll get even closer to someone." I listened and provided support, encouraged him to mourn the loss and keep up his relationships. By the end of our treatment, around the time of his graduation, he came in to update me on his job prospects, potential living situation, and fears about leaving college. His academic performance dropped a bit in his last semester, which is something I often observe in students who have anxiety around graduation. In that session, Henry questioned what his identity was outside of being a college student, while also questioning his ability to continue to develop outside the bounds of the university. Anxious about leaving the security of college, Henry was failing so as to avoid separation. In our work, we discussed the importance of processing the fear and loss that came with graduation so that he did not act this out in the form of failing his classes to prolong graduation and the anxieties it brings. Up until this point, Henry had known he could return to see me as needed, but with graduation coming up, this would no longer be an option. There was so much to both mourn and celebrate in this, and we worked to hold both of these sentiments simultaneously.

This was a reality that was important to accept and highlighted the very real limitation that exists in the college counseling relationship; like life, some-times relationships end, and there are boundaries in our relationships. We returned to his simile of college as like deep diving into the ocean. It was true that graduation marked the end of a time for exploration and play with minimal consequences, a developmental milestone necessary for emerging into adult-hood. However, he now described life after graduation with an addendum: being able to put on and take off his oxygen tank as needed, to go above and below the surface more flexibly. I interpreted this as a shift in responding to the world and relationships in terms of his parental attachments, which were fraught with fear and the need to prepare himself for the worst, to a freer and more flexible way of being. Working through his past trauma, while simulta-neously engaging in the various developmental challenges he faced through-out college within the safety of our therapeutic space, had given Henry the opportunity to graduate in a much different psychological place than when he started. Henry later emailed me a picture of himself in his cap and gown, with a smile on his face, and wrote that he felt an appropriate mixture of fear and excitement as he began his new job and met with a new therapist off campus.

THE THERAPIST ROLE ON AN INTERCONNECTED COLLEGE CAMPUS

The interconnectedness of many resources and services on the modern uni-versity campus can provide an important transitional space for many students going from the care received at home to being in the "real world." It is a unique experience to provide psychological services within the context of a college counseling center, because in this role, the therapist can easily communicate with other people involved in the student's life on campus. A multidisciplinary approach is truly possible, with access to advising deans, professors, disability services, medical services, and other supportive offices. In any setting, the relationship with the therapist can provide safety, validation, and support in ways that patients perhaps have not received throughout their lives. However, it is not sufficient for this to occur only within the therapeutic relationship, and I believe that part of the work of psychotherapy can be to encourage these experiences outside of the psychotherapy office. The college counseling therapist can use the interconnected system available on campus to their advantage by encouraging and/or actively enlisting supportive and validating relationships that are inherently valuable and supplement the work done in therapy. There is no one correct way to heal and work through psychological conditions—I have found that referrals to the chaplain's office, movement and somatic interventions such as trauma-informed yoga or acupuncture, student groups for those with similar interests such as singing, dancing, or creating art, or finding purpose in a student-run government position, and so on, to be incredibly useful in many students' journeys.

Students have varying abilities to advocate for their needs prior to starting college. At times it can be developmentally appropriate to model how to navigate asserting their needs, desires, and boundaries. I recall a student I worked with, Terry, who had been feeling triggered by a past traumatic event and as a result had been struggling to maintain his academic performance. Terry had learned from an early age that adults are not reliable, and he therefore must manage by himself; however, he had entered a depressive episode that made this very challenging. During one of our psychotherapy sessions, I asked Terry about how he was doing in his classes, and it became clear he needed some extra time to complete an essay. He noted feeling he did not have a choice but to "push on," even if this was at the expense of his mental health. We challenged this thought together, discussed how it may once have been adaptive for him to ignore cues of needing assistance from others, and noted that ultimately this was no longer helpful for him. Terry sent an email to his professor during our session, and his professor followed up with me to verify his psychological condition. Terry later expressed gratitude for my suggestion that he reach out to his professor, and for providing him the space to do so during our session. This encounter appeared to give Terry confidence that he could manage difficult situations by being able both to advocate for his needs and to rely on others. With Terry's consent, I maintained contact with his professor throughout the semester. Our collaboration gave us the opportunity to care for the student in a way that would not have been possible outside of the counseling center. Of course, this intervention is not appropriate for every student, particularly as it has the potential to be infantilizing or to create an unhelpful dependency on the therapist. For this student, however, it seemed to provide a corrective emotional experience. The student later told me that he felt that the professor and I were like the parental figures he never had. He said that because both of us watched out for him, while simultaneously holding him accountable for what he could do to take better care of himself, he grew more confident and capable of taking care of himself.

The transitory state between late adolescence and early adulthood has unique challenges in the therapeutic space. As previously mentioned, as a therapist in a counseling center, I often see students experience a parental transference, and I often have a similar countertransferential experience. However, I recognize the importance of balancing these transferential paradigms with the student's developmental need to separate and explore. It is important to observe the tendency that my colleagues and I often feel to do too much for our students, in much the same way we might for our own younger children. There have been a few instances, particularly shortly after I became a licensed psychologist, when I have entered a problematic dynamic with a student. I recall one of my first cases with a college freshman, Jules, just weeks into the fall semester—they had immense fear of asking for help and the accommodations they needed, and I felt compelled to advocate for them. This started with writing a letter to disability services requesting extended time on examinations, but soon developed into Jules asking me to write on their behalf to professors with great frequency. Perhaps I felt particularly inclined to be so active in this student's life as there was a parallel process of the both of us just beginning something—Jules in their college career and me in my early career as a therapist at a college counseling center. I brought this up in a session after I had reflected on some of the frustration I felt after a series of such requests. We discussed that while their fear of reaching out was valid, I was doing a disservice to them by communicating on their behalf. Much like Jules's parents did in their early life, I was preventing Jules from developing a sense of autonomy by managing conflicts with their professors for them, which exacerbated their sense of shame and doubt about their own abilities to do so (Erikson, 1959). As with any new skill, there needs to be space to fumble and figure things out through trial and error. What they needed from me was a supportive space to talk about the barriers to doing this on their own and for me to do less.

In most outpatient treatment settings, few options are available when there is concern about a patient's well-being other than to consider breaking confidentiality to speak to a close friend or family member, ask the patient to go to the nearest emergency room, or to send a mobile crisis unit or the police to the patient's residence. These interventions can often be experienced as traumatic for the patient, and can cause a rupture in the therapeutic relationship. This dynamic highlights a larger concern within the mental health field about the lack of crisis intervention services performed by those trained in psychological first aid. Within the university setting, however, it is possible to enlist residence hall directors to check in on a student of concern as a means of avoiding a more potentially traumatic intervention. Of course, even with this option, potentially traumatic interventions may be unavoidable. While staffing an evening drop-in service on a university campus, I met with a student who was clearly at risk of harming herself and determined that she needed to be taken to the psychiatric emergency room for further evaluation. She had been making threats of suicide to her roommates, who were very upset, and who had accompanied her to the drop-in appointment. It became clear that my responsibility was not only to keep this student safe, but also for the well-being of her roommates and others in the campus community who may have been in distress. As per protocol, the campus security team was called to enlist a security guard to escort the student to the emergency room. Given that the student was a Black woman with a history of sexual trauma and who had understandable difficulty trusting male figures of authority and the police, I requested to walk with her and to have the security guard walk two paces behind us. Once we arrived at the emergency room, I waited with her until she was admitted to the psychiatric unit. She later recalled to me that this was very traumatizing to her, and though she was angry that it happened, she was ultimately grateful that I made sure she was safe. We both regretted that this was the only available way to keep her safe.

WORKING WITH STUDENTS WHO ARE TRAUMA SURVIVORS

Sometimes the academic environment reinforces and rewards ways of being that originate from traumatic circumstances in a student's life. Our autonomic nervous system is wired to protect us and to scan the environment for signs of threat or safety. We may fluctuate between states of hyperarousal, when our sympathetic nervous system is activated for fight or flight, and hypoarousal, when our parasympathetic nervous system is activated for freeze or shutdown responses (Ogden et al., 2006). Psychoeducation about these responses can be particularly useful with college students, who often see the counseling center therapist as an extension of the university as a whole. Many students have commented to me that they feel incentivized to maintain a hyperaroused state in order to complete their coursework. They tend to think that relief from anxiety would result in letting go of something necessary to prevent them from "falling apart" or failing altogether. Other students may become depressed and remain in hypoaroused states when they feel incapable of meeting the expectations they perceive.

When a student has experienced trauma in their life that has necessitated adapting to protect themselves, it can be difficult to change the thoughts and behaviors associated with this protection; it can feel akin to taking off a piece of their suit of armor in battle. Part of the therapeutic work involves helping students to compassionately acknowledge the origins of the suit of armor, recognize how to put it on and take it off more flexibly according to what is happening in the present moment, and expand their window of tolerance (Siegel, 2010) and capacity to self-regulate enough to reach a sense of safety and connection so that they can engage with their surroundings in a healthier way. Sometimes a student will require university accommodations related to their trauma history and its impact on their mental health, such as housing accommodations for the student who feels triggered living in a building where they were sexually assaulted, or extra time on tests for the student who experiences decreased attention and concentration as a result of trauma-related symptoms. Ironically, it is often students who are most in need who can be the most hesitant to ask for accommodations—some feel that they do not need them, and some are concerned about appearing to take advantage of the university. Disability and critical race theory scholars at the National Center for Institutional Diversity write,

Recently expressed suspicions that disability accommodations are simply mechanisms for students to secure learning advantages in higher education are not only unfounded, but also ignore and obscure the ethno-racial, ableist, and sanist assumptions of learning, behavior, and engagement woven into the structures of postsecondary institutions. It assumes that college classrooms are neutral environments for learning and that campus arrangements are racially, physically, emotionally, and psycho-socially equitable. (Taylor et al., 2020)

By encouraging those who need it most to pursue necessary accommodations, the college counseling therapist can take some part in challenging this assumption and help to create a more equitable classroom.

At times there can be pressure from other departments on campus to evaluate a student's ability to perform and succeed in their academic work. The college counseling therapist, though ostensibly holding a neutral position, can at times be perceived by students, parents, and administrators as part of the university, like a dean or professor. This involves managing calls from concerned parents, friends, or roommates, conducting outreach to students across campus during major political and world events, and making difficult assessments about a student in crisis. Taking on such work changes the traditional frame in therapy and the role of the therapist—it requires a much more active intervention that often involves collaborating and communicating with multiple others. I recall a student with an extensive trauma history with whom I had met a handful of times after she had been discharged from a psychiatric inpatient unit following a suicide attempt. Jeanie described herself as a high-achieving student who, with ease, had always done quite well throughout high school; this had become a large part of her identity: "I am the smart one." Being the "smart one" was reinforced by her parents, who praised her only for her achievements in school. Jeanie felt as if she were only lovable to them if she continued on the path of high academic achievement. She often described feeling "disconnected" and unsure of herself, which she felt stifled her ability to discover important aspects of herself. She struggled to label her affect or to know what her needs and desires were.

When she began her college coursework, she soon realized that it was much harder for her to perform at the same level she had before. This was a remarkable injury to Jeanie's sense of self and felt intolerable to her. Rather than perceiving this shift as a challenge she could overcome by altering her pattern of study or enlisting the help of others in the form of tutoring or accommodations, Jeanie felt hopeless. Her grades dropped and she became depressed as she questioned her worthiness. This was a familiar pattern for her: Both her parents were physically and emotionally abusive to her, and to cope with this she would often shut herself in her room, where she felt she could more freely express her "dark feelings" of depression and worthlessness. This would often lead to a period of anxiety that "rescued" her from her depression as she turned her focus to obsessive studying and perfecting her schoolwork. She made multiple suicide attempts in college, which we soon came to understand as a way for her to communicate to her parents her anger, her desire for them to see her more fully, and how much she was struggling. Though she could understand this intellectually, Jeanie continued to struggle with suicidality, and in turn had failed a couple courses.

Ultimately, I suggested she take a medical leave of absence. It was clear that Jeanie needed comprehensive treatment to feel better and to be well enough to perform in school, yet a leave of absence necessitated her moving back to her parents' home—an environment that did not feel supportive and made her feel like a failure for not "pushing through." In the end, the decision would be made for her, with an academic suspension for multiple failed courses. I collaborated with her parents to enroll her in a partial hospitalization program, and a year later she had not yet returned to school. This highlights the profound importance of adolescence as a time that can foster either identity development or fragility: Jeanie did not feel safe enough to explore during her adolescence, which ultimately resulted in a very fragile sense of self.

THE EFFECT OF THE PANDEMIC ON DEVELOPMENT

It is difficult to determine the lasting effects of the novel coronavirus (COVID-19) pandemic on mental health. As noted earlier, the demand for services at college and university counseling centers across the country has been rising for decades. This was true before the COVID-19 pandemic, and many students have experienced trauma and loss associated with the pandemic, including contracting COVID-19 or experiencing the death of a loved one. For many students, COVID has greatly altered their college experience. I have heard many students ask, "Is college worth it?" as they struggle with the realities of taking care of themselves and family members. Other students have described feeling guilty for being in college during a time when they perceive "bigger things" happening in the world. While young people appear to be the least affected by COVID-19 in terms of physical health, those ages 18–24, as well as Black and Latinx people across all ages, are reporting the worst mental health outcomes (Czeisler et al., 2020). This is not surprising given the political unrest, police brutality, and murders of Black people that have recently received more media attention and public outcry. Coping with these stressful situations is challenging at any time, but is particularly so now with physical distancing, lack of social supports, and increased time on screens and decreased time outdoors. Young people are at a time in their lives when they are meant to explore and discover alternative ways of being separate from their caregivers, and to begin the process of developing their career choices. To do so, there needs to be social interaction and some sense of safety, a secure base from which to explore (Siegel, 1999). This sense of safety has been called into question for many of the young adults I work with, who have reported feeling in denial, anxious, depressed, hopeless, suicidal, with increasing engagement in risky behaviors and substance abuse, having exacerbated trauma-related symptoms, and so on. This has been a tough time for people's mental health. With the major life-altering restrictions that have been in place since the pandemic began, young people have been experiencing many existential questions about their life goals, identity, and hope (or lack thereof) for the future. It may be that having less life experience can make tolerating the current uncertainty of our world particularly challenging. My colleagues and I have had many questions about this: How will living in a virtual world affect the college experience? What is learning without the social context? How does this differ for students according to their experiences prior to college?

In a virtual world, it is very challenging to activate our social engagement system, the crux of what allows young people to establish a sense of safety and connection (Porges, 2011). Without the social context, it will be particularly challenging for young people to explore various parts of their identity necessary for development into adulthood. College often represents an important milestone for students who may be leaving their homes to live on their own for the first time, with responsibilities of caring for themselves in ways they have not had to before. Transitioning to college can help build skills that promote independence and provide the space necessary for play and exploration outside of one's own family. A concern about virtual learning is that this may lead young people to struggle with their sense of self and follow along more stereotyped versions of their perceptions of adulthood in the absence of being able to explore on their own. While online interactions can provide some sense of connection, staying online can also feel alienating and reinforce social avoidance. It can also be much easier to perform a version of oneself online that limits vulnerability and genuine relationship building. It is in our face-to-face interactions that we establish intimacy as we notice changes in body language, facial expressions, and physiologically coregulate one another (Porges, 2011).

On the other hand, I have also noticed a remarkable resilience and creativity in young people during these times. Since March 2020, we have offered many services virtually through telehealth, including individual therapy, psychiatric medication evaluation and management, and group support spaces. Many students have joined virtual group offerings at the college counseling center that they may not have felt comfortable joining in person. Socially anxious students have utilized the chat functions of online platforms to express themselves in ways that were not possible in person. Others maintain a social connection through online parties or live streaming movies and games together. As the COVID-19 pandemic continues, I imagine there will be more creative ways of connecting that attempt to mimic as much of the college experience as is possible at a distance. Of course, the virtual realm does lead to many losses of the college experience. An incoming college freshman noted to me feeling disappointed that they would not be able to reside on the university campus where they hoped to explore aspects of their sexuality that they did not feel comfortable exploring within their conservative family and community at home. Others have similarly expressed disappointment about not coming in for classes in person and missing out on the parties, student-led activity groups, late-night discussions with peers, and so on that they imagined as integral to their college experience.

One point of major concern is for those students who are in abusive environments at home who were relying on residing on campus for safety. Worries about privacy and limited access to technology and a stable internet connection have made it particularly challenging for some students to engage with the telehealth and virtual psychological services available through the university. University counseling centers across the country are grappling with how to reach the students who need their services most, particularly as many students will continue virtual classes, or some hybrid model, for the foreseeable future. The disparities among students who are most marginal-ized are augmented as these students struggle to keep up with classes and manage the various life stressors they experience at home. One student I have met with virtually exemplifies this: they are living with multiple family members in a one-bedroom apartment, with limited access to the internet, and are worried about their family's finances as their single parent has been out of work for the past several months. We have talked about how it feels impossible to perform well in their classes under these circumstances, but if they take a leave of absence they will lose access to many benefits of being a student, including access to the affordable mental health care they need. They expressed a sense of hopelessness as they reflected that college and living on campus have been such a necessary reprieve for them from being parentified at home, and wondered what the upcoming semesters will be like if they cannot live on campus.

Ultimately, whether virtually or in person, the university context ideally creates a developmental space that provides some of the ingredients necessary for emerging into adulthood. The college counseling therapist is tasked with an ethical responsibility to develop more creative ways to engage with students during the COVID-19 pandemic when mental health care is needed the most. The development of robust virtual individual and group therapy, workshops, chat spaces, and other outreach programs have been especially important. That said, it can be challenging to build rapport, establish trust, and manage moments of silence within the virtual therapeutic space. As we all navigate the collective trauma of these times, an increase in therapist self-disclosure during sessions can help connect with the humanity in all of us. For many therapists, online therapy has invited patients into their homes and vice versa. There are certainly cases in which this does not feel helpful or appropriate, although it can also establish some intimacy that is not present within an office setting. Students may inquire more about the therapist's well-being or learn information they otherwise would not by the nature of practicing within a home office. There may be lasting changes to the way mental health services are offered in colleges and universities as a result of the pandemic, which will require flexibility and commitment to understanding the changing needs as they evolve.

Sherina Persaud, PhD (she/her/hers), is a licensed clinical psychologist in New York City specializing in the treatment of trauma in young adults. She works in independent practice and provides individual and group psychotherapy to students at Columbia University's Counseling & Psychological Services. She has clinical and research interests in somatic-based interventions, attachment theory, and trauma and affective physiology. She strives to incorporate these interests with an understanding of our multiple identities within institutional and societal structures and systems.

REFERENCES

Balassone, M. L. (1991). A social learning model of adolescent contraceptive behavior. *Journal of Youth and Adolescence, 20,* 593–616.

Blos, P. (1967). The second individuation process of adolescence. *Psychoanalytic Study of the Child, 22,* 162–186.

Collins, W. A., & Laursen, B. (2004). Parent-adolescent relationships and influences. In R. M. Lerner & L. Steinberg (Eds.), *Handbook of adolescent pyschology* (2nd ed., pp. 331–361). Wiley.

Collins, W. A., & Steinberg, L. (2005). Adolescent development in interpersonal context. In W. Damon & N. Eisenberg (Eds.), *Handbook of child psychology* (Vol. 4, pp. 1003–1076). Wiley.

Czeisler, M. E., Lane, R. I., Petrosky, E., Wiley, J. F., Christensen, A., Njai, R., Weaver, M. D., Robbins, R., Facer-Childs, E. R., Barger, L. K., Czeisler, C. A., Howard, M. E., & Rajaratnam, S. M. W. (2020). Mental health, substance use, and suicidal ideation during the COVID-19 pandemic—United States, June 24–30, 2020. Centers for Disease Control and Prevention. *Morbidity and Mortality Weekly Report, 69*(32), 1049–1057.

Eichler, R. J. (2006). Developmental considerations. In P. Grayson & P. W. Meilman (Eds.), *College mental health practice* (pp. 21–41). Routledge.

Eichler, R. J. (2011). The university as a (potentially) facilitating environment. *Contemporary Psychoanalysis, 40,* 289–316.

Erikson, E. H. (1956). The problem of ego identity. *Journal of the American Psychoanalytic Association, 4,* 56–121.

Erikson, E. (1959). Identity and the life cycle. *Psychological Issues,* Monograph 1.

Fischer, J. (2017). *Healing the fragmented selves of trauma survivors: Overcoming internal self-alienation.* Routledge.

Grayson, P. (2006). Overview. In P. Grayson & P. W. Meilman (Eds.), *College mental health practice* (pp. 1–21). Routledge.

Grotevant, H. D., & Cooper, C. R. (1985). Patterns of interaction in family relationship and the development of identity exploration in adolescence. *Child Development, 56,* 415–428.

Ketchen Lipson, S., Lattie, E. G., & Eisenberg, D. (2019). Increased rate of mental health service utilization by U.S. college students: 10-year population-level trends (2007–2017). *Psychiatric Services, 70*(1), 60–63.

Matteson, D. R. (1977). Exploration and commitment: Sex differences and methodological problems in the use of identity status categories. *Journal of Youth and Adolescence,* 6, 349–370.

Ogden, P., Minton, K., & Pain, C. (2006). *Trauma and the body: A sensorimotor approach to psychotherapy.* Norton.

Porges, S. (2011). *The polyvagal theory: Neurophysiological foundations of emotions, attachment, communication, and self-regulation.* Norton.

Siegel, D. J. (1999). *The developing mind: How relationships and the brain interact to shape who we are.* Guilford.

Siegel, D. J. (2010). *Mindsight: The new science of personal transformation.* Bantam.

Smetana, J. G., Campione-Barr, N., & Metzger, A. (2006). Adolescent development in interpersonal and societal contexts. *Annual Review of Psychology, 57,* 255–284.

Steinberg, L., & Silverberg, S. B. (1986). The vicissitudes of autonomy in early adolescence. *Child Development, 57*(4), 841–851.

Taylor, A., Smith, M., & Shallish, L. (2020). (Re)Producing white privilege through disability accommodations. National Center for Institutional Diversity. https://medium .com/national-center-for-institutional-diversity/re-producing-white-privilege -through-disability-accommodations-4c16a746c0dc

Index